Frontiers in South and Southeast Asian Development Research

This book series publishes monographs and edited volumes devoted to studies on various aspects of development and policies in South and Southeast Asia. The books cover in-depth analyses of individual countries, regions, sectors, and comparative cross-country studies. They include both a specific and a general focus on the latest advances of the various aspects of development. In cross-country studies, the geographical scope will be inclusive to the developed Asian economies when it comes to issues like security, economic cooperation, energy, finances, trade, environment, and technology transfer. The books in this series are expected to go beyond the traditional concepts of inequality, poverty, growth, and development and offer a broad, in-depth analysis and inclusive view on sustainable development and well-being. The series provides a platform for researchers to carry out rigorous analyses, to promote, share, and discuss issues, findings, and perspectives in various areas. The topics may include, but not limited to agriculture, industry, services, business, governance, institutions, politics, security, globalization, international relations, gender, culture, religion and society, economics, and social development strategies of South and Southeast Asia. Not only that, given the current pandemic and its multifaceted impacts on trade, production, supply chain and organization of economic activities, this series also purports to highlight changes in research on development economics in the post-pandemic timeframe. Frontiers in South and Southeast Asian Development Research allows for a deeper appreciation of the various issues around Asian development with high quality and peer reviewed contributions. Volumes published in the series are important reading offering original research supported empirically which can serve as reference sources for researchers, educators, and graduate students, as well as consultants, business professionals, and policy makers, interested in the private and public sectors development of the Asian continent and its challenges and strategies for sustainable development.

Pham Khanh Nam · Almas Heshmati
Editors

Recent Trends in Vietnam's Rapid Economic Development

1990–2023

Springer

Editors
Pham Khanh Nam
Vietnam - the Netherlands Programme
University of Economics Ho Chi Minh City
Ho Chi Minh City, Vietnam

Almas Heshmati
Research Fellow at University
of Economics Ho Chi Minh city
Ho Chi Minh City, Vietnam

ISSN 2948-1279 ISSN 2948-1287 (electronic)
Frontiers in South and Southeast Asian Development Research
ISBN 978-981-97-6078-7 ISBN 978-981-97-6079-4 (eBook)
https://doi.org/10.1007/978-981-97-6079-4

This Springer imprint is published by the registered company Springer Nature Singapore Pte Ltd.
The registered company address is: 152 Beach Road, #21-01/04 Gateway East, Singapore 189721, Singapore

Contents

Contributors

Ung Trieu Gia Bao Vietnam - the Netherlands Programme, University of Economic Ho Chi Minh City, Ho Chi Minh City, Vietnam;
Erasmus University Rotterdam, Rotterdam, The Netherlands

Nhu Nam Do Vietnam – the Netherlands Programme, University of Economics Ho Chi Minh City, Ho Chi Minh City, Vietnam

Lam Nguyen Do Khoa Vietnam - the Netherlands Programme, University of Economics Ho Chi Minh city, Ho Chi Minh City, Vietnam

Thanh Thien Trang Duong The Economy and Environment Partnership for Southeast Asia (EEPSEA), Ho Chi Minh City, Vietnam

Almas Heshmati Jönköping University, Jönköping, Sweden

Huy Thanh Huynh Vietnam - the Netherlands Programme, University of Economics Ho Chi Minh City, Ho Chi Minh City, Vietnam;
International Institute of Social Studies (ISS), Erasmus University Rotterdam, Rotterdam,
The Netherlands

Dương Duy Lâm Vietnam - the Netherlands Programme, University of Economics Ho Chi Minh city, Ho Chi Minh City, Vietnam

Anh Ngoc Le University of Economics Ho Chi Minh City, Ho Chi Minh City, Vietnam;
Erasmus University Rotterdam, Rotterdam, The Netherlands

Quang Dong Quan Le Vietnam - the Netherlands Programme, University of Economics Ho Chi Minh City, Ho Chi Minh City, Vietnam

Pham Khanh Nam University of Economics Ho Chi Minh City, Ho Chi Minh City, Vietnam

Nguyen Viet Ngan University of Economics Ho Chi Minh city, Ho Chi Minh City, Vietnam

Duc Duy Ngo Vietnam - the Netherlands Programme, Ho Chi Minh city, Vietnam

Hieu Minh Ngo The Economy and Environment Partnership for Southeast Asia (EEPSEA), Ho Chi Minh City, Vietnam

Anh Ngoc Hai Nguyen Vietnam - the Netherlands Programme, University of Economics Ho Chi Minh City, Ho Chi Minh City, Vietnam

Hoang Huy Nguyen Vietnam - the Netherlands Programme, University of Economics Ho Chi Minh City, Ho Chi Minh City, Vietnam

Doan Trong Nhan University of Economics Ho Chi Minh city, Ho Chi Minh City, Vietnam

Nguyen Thi Kieu Nhung University of Economics Ho Chi Minh City, Ho Chi Minh City, Vietnam

Ngoc-Thanh Pham Vietnam - the Netherlands Programme, University of Economics Ho Chi Minh City, Ho Chi Minh City, Vietnam

Uyen Phuong Dang Pham University of Economics Ho Chi Minh City, Ho Chi Minh City, Vietnam;
Erasmus University Rotterdam, Rotterdam, The Netherlands

Pham Quoc Tien Vietnam - the Netherlands Programme, University of Economics Ho Chi Minh City, Ho Chi Minh City, Vietnam

Long Hoang Vo Vietnam - the Netherlands Programme, University of Economics Ho Chi Minh City, Ho Chi Minh City, Vietnam

Tung Lam Ha University of Economics Ho Chi Minh City, Ho Chi Minh City, Vietnam;
Vietnam - the Netherlands Programme, University of Economics Ho Chi Minh City, Ho Chi Minh City, Vietnam

Võ Ngọc Tường Vy Vietnam - the Netherlands Programme, University of Economics Ho Chi Minh City, Ho Chi Minh City, Vietnam

List of Figures

Chapter 6

Chapter 7

Chapter 8

Chapter 13

Chapter 15

List of Tables

Chapter 10

Chapter 11

Chapter 12

Chapter 13

Chapter 15

Chapter 1
Introduction, Summary, and Policy Recommendations

Pham Khanh Nam and Almas Heshmati

Abstract This chapter introduces the book on Vietnam's economic development from 1990 to 2023. It provides an overview of how Vietnam has grown into a strong economy in Southeast Asia through investments in education, health, and infrastructure. The chapter summarizes the main points from the other chapters in the book, which discuss various topics like agriculture, energy, finance, industry, economic development, and productivity. It highlights key findings and challenges, such as dealing with climate change, reducing income inequality, and promoting sustainable development. The chapter ends with policy recommendations based on these findings that offer strategies for boosting economic growth, encouraging innovation, developing human capital, and improving governance and infrastructure. These recommendations aim to help Vietnam continue its economic progress and adapt to changing conditions.

Keywords Vietnam economic development · Foreign direct investment · Sustainable agriculture · Circular economy · Renewable energy · Human capital · Urbanization · Income inequality · Economic policy · Southeast Asia

1 Introduction and Summary

This book offers an up-to-date picture of the Vietnamese economy—the fast-growing economy in Southeast Asia. The country has invested heavily in education, health, and development infrastructure across the country. Progress in recent decades has

P. K. Nam (✉)
University of Economics Ho Chi Minh City, Ho Chi Minh City, Vietnam
e-mail: khanhnam@ueh.edu.vn

A. Heshmati
Jönköping University, Jönköping, Sweden
e-mail: almas.heshmati@ju.se

P. K. Nam and A. Heshmati (eds.), *Recent Trends in Vietnam's Rapid Economic Development*, Frontiers in South and Southeast Asian Development Research,
https://doi.org/10.1007/978-981-97-6079-4_1

been strong and the country has built up local production capacity, attracted significant relocation and outsourcing of production from Organization of Economic Cooperation and Development (OECD) countries. The economy recovered quickly from the COVID-19 negative growth effects. In recent years much of withdrawn foreign direct investment from China is channeled to Vietnam indicating its strong comparative cost advantage. The development-oriented economic policy has created optimal conditions for further expansion of production, supply chain, education, and finances. Investment in education, health, infrastructure, administration, and regulations is facilitating investment inflows, technology transfer and spillover to the growing national companies. The educated young population, disciplined labor force, and a government willing to invest in infrastructure and implement necessary reforms and protect intellectual property rights have provided a strong basis for the growth in the economy. The high level of productivity, improved quality of products, low and competitive cost of production, and more than 100 million population provide a strong base for a continuous economic growth.

This edited volume is written by the professional, young, educated, and active entrepreneurial generation with good insights into the features of the economy and its development potential. They provide an up-to-date view and empirical research-based picture of the recent trends in Vietnam's economic development. The target audience are educators, undergraduate and graduate students, domestic and foreign investors, government agencies, provincial and industrial sector decision-makers, trade partners, libraries, individual researchers, and professional and practitioners. This book helps to fill the gap in knowledge and inform planners and investors about different sectors of the Vietnamese economy and its development potential.

This book consists of 15 chapters including an introduction and summary chapter. The period 1990–2023 refers to collection of time periods by pooling cross sections, time series, and panel data used in different chapters at firm, farm, province, sector, region, and national levels. The contributed chapters are divided into 6 research areas: (i) agriculture, (ii) environment and energy, (iii) bank, finance, and development, (iv) manufacturing and service industries, (v) economic development and welfare, and (vi) productivity growth. They are written by Vietnamese researchers and cover different sectors of the fast-growing economy which is characterized a new Southeast Asian tiger economy. The different parts of the book and contributions are summarized below. The final section, based on the different chapters, provides summary, conclusion, and policy recommendations.

1.1 Part One: Agriculture

This part consists of three chapters on the impact of climate change on agriculture, discussion of factors influencing productivity in farming, and in particular efficiency and productivity in rice farming.

Vietnam, located in Southeast Asia, is currently facing challenges due to growing and dense population and climate change with impact on economy and society. The country is heavily dependent on the agriculture sector and rural areas for tourism, export of goods, employment creation, and food security. Le Ngoc Anh and Pham Dang Phuong Uyen in the second chapter entitled "*The effects of climate change on Vietnamese* agriculture" provide a thorough analysis of Vietnam's historical and current climate change trends and offer predictions for the future development of the sector. In the empirical part, the authors utilize data from Food and Agriculture Organization of the United Nations (FAO) to emphasize the significant connection between Vietnam's agricultural sector, a vital component of the nation's economy, and climate change. Over the past thirty years, these environmental challenges with increasing frequency of disrupted farming, have resulted in lower productivity, decreased product quality, and reduced farm incomes. This study analyzes issues faced by rural communities, including CO_2 emissions, temperature changes, precipitation and ecosystem damages, utilization of agricultural land area, application of fertilizer, and rural population and labor force increases. This research underscores the significance of implementation of effective national policies, and the receipt of international support to tackle the challenges and bolster Vietnam's capacity to both adapt to and mitigate the effects of climate change particularly the effects of various indicators on agricultural sector.

Vietnam is an agricultural country, and rice production has been a cornerstone of the economy for a long time. As a result, it is important to have a deep understanding of the factors that affect rice production. The third chapter is written by Nguyen Thi Kieu Nhung. In "*Factors affecting rice farm productivity in Vietnam*," the author identifies the determinants of rice farms productivity. Based on the results analyzed, policymakers and agricultural stakeholders are encouraged to design effective policies to boost the development of agriculture in Vietnam. To implement the above goals, this study conducts analyses of the relationship between rice yield and several key determinants for Vietnam's agriculture. These include rice cultivation area, rice export, gross domestic product (GDP) growth, and employment and fertilizer consumption in agriculture and horticulture. The empirical findings from the conducted analysis form the basis for the proposed policies in the final section of the study. Regarding determinants or rice production productivity, throughout the essay, the author explores how fluctuations in rice cultivation areas influence the rice output, shedding light on the importance of land allocation in rice farming. The role of international trade in the rice sector is also investigated to examine how rice export affects the overall domestic production. Furthermore, the effects of macroeconomic indicators, such as GDP growth on rice yield are examined, emphasizing their influence on food security and agricultural sectors stability. Employment in agriculture and its relationship with rice output are also scrutinized, elucidating the socioeconomic implications of fluctuations in the rice industry. Finally, fertilizer consumption is another critical factor under investigation, as it plays a pivotal role in enhancing crop yields and land and labor productivities. Thus, this study particularly explores the intricate relationship between fertilizer usage and rice production in Vietnam.

Rice is a staple food which supports over half of the global population. The world is facing increasing challenges due to population growth, rising hunger levels, exacerbated by factors such as the COVID-19 pandemic, climate change, natural catastrophes, geopolitical conflicts, and export bans from countries like India. Vietnam is a significant rice exporter which must navigate these challenges while seizing general economic and export opportunities. However, Vietnam's rice agriculture has faced transformations and sustainability issues over the past two decades, including land fragmentation and climate change vulnerabilities. The fourth chapter is by Doan Trong Nhan, "*Strategy of productivity and sustainability of rice farms in Vietnam*," where the author addresses the abovementioned challenges and contributes to global food security. Vietnam's rice sector strategy emphasizes mechanization, awareness, and collaboration, along with land consolidation, as cost-effective solutions to boost productivity, reduce poverty, and mitigate climate change impacts.

1.2 Part Two: Environment and Energy

This part covering environment and energy sectors consists of two contributions related to implementation of circular economy and sustainable development and use of renewable energy and its impacts on economic welfare in Vietnam.

The literature on circular economy and sustainable development and their implementations is growing fast. It is a result of availability of data, development of methods, and consideration about the nexus of environment, health, and well-being. The fifth chapter is provided by Ngo Minh Hieu and Duong Thien Trang Thanh. In their study, "*Implementation of circular economy and sustainable development in Vietnam*," they employ the Sankey diagram and material taxonomy of the European Union (EU) to construct a representative material flow database for Vietnam. Within the scope of this study, the authors exclusively focus on two pivotal indicators, namely Domestic Material Consumption (DMC) and Resource Productivity, for their material flow analysis. Accordingly, they have endeavored to gather data that elucidate the flow of selective key materials, including wood (representing biomass), iron and steel (representing metallic minerals), coal and crude oil (symbolizing fossil energy), and cement clinker (representing non-metallic minerals). The result and findings delineate an upward trend in the DMC index for all flows of materials from 2016 to 2022. The development shows a diminishing trend observed in the Resource Productivity index over the study period. This result can be interpreted as evidence indicating that Vietnam has ineffectively implemented the circular economy model. Nevertheless, there is a positive signal in the development process suggesting the commencement of Vietnam's initial strides toward a circular economy. The development is found positive notably following the enactment of Decision 687 and the revision of the Law on Environmental Protection (LEP) by the Vietnamese government in 2022.

Renewable energy is a crucial component of moving toward sustainable development in Vietnam. It has a significant impact on the economic welfare of the dense and large population in Vietnam. The sixth chapter is authored by Huynh Thanh Huy and Nguyen Huy Hoang, "*Renewable energy consumption impacts on economic welfare in Vietnam.*" This research evaluates the effects of renewable energy on economic welfare measured in several ways such as total GDP, GDP per capita, and rural and urban household incomes both measured in per capita. To estimate the effects of renewable energy consumption on economic welfare, several factors are considered, including consumption of renewable energy, share of renewable energy consumption, gross capital formation, and total number of employees. This research uses regression analysis to estimate the effects of renewable energy consumption on welfare conditional on controlling for heterogeneity and multicollinearity in the data. The statistical data are extracted from World Development Indicators (WDI), International Monetary Fund (IMF), Our World in Data (OWD), and General Statistics Office of Vietnam (GSO) covering period from 2002 to 2022. The findings are expected to contribute to understanding of the economic effects of renewable energy consumption on welfare and environment in Vietnam, and it offers valuable insights for policymakers, energy sector, and social planners. This aids the development of evidence-based strategies for a cleaner and more prosperous future.

1.3 Part Three: Banks, Finance and Development

This part on banks, finance, and development in Vietnam consists of three studies shedding lights on the topics studied. They cover issues of bank equity as a predictor of economic growth, measurement of technological progress and productivity in the banking industry, and comparative analysis of remittance impacts on Vietnamese economy.

The equity market is often regarded as a thermometer of the economy due to its unique ability to not only accurately reflect on the current conditions, but also provide valuable insights about future trends in the economy. The predictive power stems from the foundation that the equity market is significantly influenced by a wide range of macroeconomic variables. Vietnam, despite its relatively low level of development but with a developmental state, the country has witnessed its financial market growth rapidly surrounding three key pillars including bank credit and equity and bond markets. The seventh chapter authored by Pham Quoc Tien, "*Bank equity as a predictor of economic growth: evidence from Vietnam,*" aims to inspect such predictability by examining the correlation between the economic crisis and the underperformance of banking equity. This research is conducted as a replication of previous research on banking crises without panic but focuses mainly on the context of Vietnam. The research methodology employed is primarily based on the local projection specification, with slight modifications to align it with the specific context of the research. Despite the absence of statistically significant results in the analysis, several noteworthy and useful conclusions can still be drawn. These findings are anticipated to carry significant implications for decisions by policymakers, financial investors, and other relevant stakeholders who seek to enhance their understanding and in forecasting economic development. Notably, the government should prioritize the development of the equity market, not only as a supplementary funding channel to the banking sector but also as a dynamic platform that effectively represents market expectations.

The interaction between the banking system and other entities in society constitutes a force that influences the entire national economy and the path of economic development. This relationship has progressively been strengthened over the past few decades. The eighth chapter authored by Ung Trieu Gia Bao, "*Measuring technological progress and productivity growth in Vietnam's banking industry*," evaluates the banking system's performance at the individual banks level. It is crucial for providing an overview of their market position and can provide valuable insights for practitioners. This study assesses performance of 17 commercial banks in Vietnam observed from 2017 to 2022 and employs the Malmquist productivity index and data envelopment analysis (DEA) methods. The assessment covers seven dimensions of bank performance, including operating expenses, assets, liabilities, and deposits as inputs, and it considers loans, bad debt, and profit before tax as outputs. The banks' total productivity index is decomposed into technological and technical evolutions. According to the results, most banks experienced a decline in productivity from 2017 to 2022, showing reductions in both technical and technological indexes. The managerial implication of this research is providing a comprehensive insight into the performance of Vietnamese commercial banks and provides strategic advice for managerial level aiming at sustainable development in the banking sector.

Vietnam is attracting significant FDI rechanneled from mainland China following USA trade policy changes and comparative production cost alterations. Yet in recent years, labor export in Vietnam has evolved from its traditional role to alleviate poverty and generate employment for the growing population. The trend is increasingly viewed as a source of rising remittances. According to the recent data, Vietnam dispatches approximately 100,000 workers abroad annually, resulting in remittances exceeding 3 billion USD each year and significant transfer of knowledge. This substantial influx significantly has contributed to the country's GDP and its development capacity. The ninth chapter is by Ngo Duc Duy, "*Comparative analysis of the impact of remittances on Vietnam's economy*." The objective is to gain a more precise and comprehensive understanding of how remittances have impacted Vietnam's economic development over the past two decades and beyond. This research employs an autoregressive distributed lag (ARDL) model with bounds testing approach for co-integration and error correction. The framework, which is frequently employed by time series researchers, facilitates an analysis of both the long-term trends and short-term dynamics among the studied variables. The findings based on dataset collected from 2000 to 2022 enrich the existing body of literature on the relationship between remittances and economic growth in context of Vietnam. It offers more up-to-date empirical evidence concerning whether remittances and financial development are substitutes or complements in driving the relatively high GDP growth.

1.4 Part Four: Manufacturing and Service Industries

Part four on industry consists of one study. It examines the relationship between innovation activities and their effects on performance of firms in both services and manufacturing industries.

National innovation system, innovation investment, and innovation activities are widely considered key drivers for economic growth and progress. Innovation at the firm level influences a firm's productivity, profitability, competitiveness, survival, and market share. While not a new concept, innovation has become an essential element for obtaining competitiveness in the ever-changing environment and speeding up the economy's development. The tenth chapter is prepared by Ngoc-Thanh Pham, "*Relationships between innovation and firm performance in Vietnam's manufacturing and services industries.*" The objective of this research is to examine the relationships between innovation and firm performance in Vietnam. It considers the four innovation types (product, process, organizational, and marketing) acknowledged by the Oslo Manual, across two main industries (manufacturing and services). To achieve this, a sample of 965 firms was taken, comprising 666 manufacturing firms and 299 services firms. The data was obtained through a survey conducted in Vietnam between November 2014 and April 2016, as part of the Enterprise Survey project initiated by the World Bank. The data allows for specification and estimation of a knowledge production function. It will shed light on the innovation behavior of firms and its impacts on their performance, growth, and survival. The results will have implications for public policies supporting innovation and performance of manufacturing and services firms.

1.5 Part Five: Economic Development and Welfare

Part 5 of this edited volume consists of 3 studies examining the effects of governance quality and development infrastructure on income inequality among provinces, the role of human capital dynamics and health status on economic growth, and population growth and urbanization in Vietnam.

There is a large variation in level of development and productivity per capita among Vietnamese provinces and regions. Most part of the variations are attributed to differences in geographic conditions for industrial development and service sector expansion, as well as development infrastructure and provincial policies. The eleventh chapter is authored by Duong Duy Lam and Vo Ngoc Tuong Vy, "*Governance quality, infrastructure development, and income inequality in Vietnam's provinces.*" This study examines the possible effects of investment in development infrastructure on reducing income inequality in the provinces/districts of Vietnam. Panel data from population of 63 provinces in Vietnam over a 3-year period (2018–2020) is collected. The Gini index serves as the proxy for income inequality among provinces. The study utilizes the fixed effects regression estimator with robust standard errors to investigate the relationship between investment in development infrastructure, governance effectiveness, institutional quality, and income inequality. The findings support the hypotheses that governance quality and infrastructure development are negatively correlated with income inequality. By employing robust statistical techniques, the study further enhances the validity and reliability of the findings, thereby providing valuable insights for policymakers in their attempts to achieve inter-provincial equality in productivity and welfare. The study highlights the need to redirect investment away from industrial development and toward other infrastructure projects to effectively close the income gap and improve living standards of the population across provinces and regions. However, the study acknowledges limitations in data availability, suggesting the need for further research to explore specific income segments and causality relationships. It will allow to inform more targeted redistribution of resources to more equal development and policy implications for local governance in Vietnam.

Education, health, information technology, and infrastructure represent essential pillars that serve as fundamental objectives and vital components of development and economic growth. They are integral to enhancing human capacity, which lies at the heart of a nation's productivity, progress, and growth. Thus, several empirical studies have focused on the relationship between human capital and economic growth, particularly emphasizing education, and health as crucial determinants of growth. However, most existing studies have mainly explored the one-way interrelation or causality between these factors and economic growth. The twelfth chapter is authored by Nguyen Viet Ngan and Lam Nguyen Do Khoa, "*The roles of human capital dynamics and health status in Vietnam's economic growth.*" This study examines the bidirectional correlation relationship between human capital, specifically regarding health and education and economic growth in Vietnam. The results are based on employment of the 2SLS estimation method and panel data covering years from 2020 to 2022. The result highlights the significance of both measures of human capital. Specifically, education and health positively affect Vietnam's GDP growth. Empirical result reported in the chapter reveal that the contribution of health to economic growth is substantially more extensive than education in sub-Saharan African countries. This finding is new to Vietnam and highlights the partial substitution of each variable when measuring human capital and its quality dimensions. The result is more likely to contribute toward existing literature and emphasize the importance of considering these variables when assessing human capital's growth impact. Accordingly, local researchers and policymakers can utilize this finding to develop better policies striving for Vietnam's prosperity in the future.

Population growth and urbanization are two important factors for industrialization, development, and economic growth in Vietnam or any other emerging economies. The thirteenth study is conducted by Nhu Nam Do and Dong Quan Le Quang, "*Population growth and urbanization in Vietnam.*" This study provides an in-depth analysis of the established trends in population growth and urbanization in Vietnam. It aims to offer insights into underlying implications of Vietnam's changing demographic landscape and its correlation with urbanization and sustainable development.

The research demonstrates that while the country's population has been growing at a slower pace, Vietnam's urbanization rate has been increasing rapidly. The stylized facts of urbanization's drivers include natural population growth, inter-provincial migration owing to heterogeneity in industrialization, socioeconomic and geopolitical factors, as well as statistical effects derived from Vietnam government's administrative urban planning policies. The authors analyze the correlation between urbanization and economic growth in the country. By adopting a panel-regression approach, their analysis substantiates the correlation between urbanization and economic development in Vietnam's 63 provinces. However, rapid urbanization and slowing population growth pose several development policy implications for the country, including aging population, urban labor market quality and supply-demand imbalance, as well as navigating urban-rural socioeconomic welfare and infrastructure development. These include migrating women empowerment, delayed marriage age and low fertility rate, unemployment in urban areas, high dependency ratio, and concentration of low-skill employment in rural areas.

1.6 Part Six: Productivity Growth

This last part of the edited volume covers two chapters' contributions. The first chapter examines the relationship between intellectual property rights protection and economic growth and the second is an analysis of the impacts of trade and FDI inflows on total factor productivity and its decomposition in Vietnam.

Land-use rights in Vietnam are of utmost importance for individuals and businesses entering the market, particularly due to the country's historical reliance on agriculture. There is a growing alarm regarding the potential loss of highly skilled individuals, such as intellectuals, scientists, researchers, and creative professionals like musicians. This event happened due to their works and creations have not been protected enough by law, specifically intellectual property rights laws. Currently, protection of intellectual property rights in Vietnam is relatively loose and it lacks effective enforcement measures, leading to low protection of these rights. The fourteenth chapter is authored by Lam Ha Tung, "*The relationship between intellectual property rights protection and economic development in Vietnam.*" It examines the relationship between intellectual property rights and economic development in Vietnam. Through Doi-Moi reform period, which is from mid to late 1980, Vietnam has made significant strides in transforming its economy to the adoption of free market principles. The reforms implemented aimed to establish property rights protection, recognize private ownership, and provide a legal framework to protect these rights. Intellectual property rights laws reform is also one of the 3 focus areas of the 2023 Vietnam government considering reform of different laws. Therefore, as discussion and analysis of historical and future relationship between property rights and economic development in Vietnam, this study focuses on these two rights development based on main events and release of new laws.

Study of total factor productivity (TFP) growth and identifying its drivers has always been crucial for Vietnam's economic development. Given Vietnam's extensive process of economic integration and high level of openness, international trade, and inward foreign direct investment (FDI) are recognized as having significant impacts on the country's productivity growth. The final fifteenth chapter is written by Nguyen Ngoc Hai Anh and Long Hoang Vo, "*The impacts of trade and FDI on total factor productivity growth in Vietnam.*" This study examines the effects of trade and FDI on productivity growth across 24 Vietnamese provinces in the four key economic zones from 2015 to 2021. Using the Malmquist productivity index, the study decomposes TFP growth into two main components of efficiency change and technological change. The aim is to provide a comprehensive evaluation of the conditions of TFP growth in Vietnam. Additionally, the study employs a generalized method of moments (GMM) technique to jointly examine the impacts of international trade and FDI on TFP growth. The results show that the FDI-induced spillover is revealed to have a negative impact on Vietnam's TFP growth, whereas international trade seems to be a significant driver of TFP growth in Vietnam, regardless of the difficulties arising from external shocks such as the COVID-19 pandemic. These results highlight the importance of effective management of FDI spillovers and leveraging trade to ensure sustainable productivity growth in Vietnam.

2 Policy Recommendations

2.1 Agriculture

The first part of this book discussed the critical aspects of agriculture in Vietnam, focusing on the challenges posed by climate change, factors influencing productivity in rice farming, and the efficiency and productivity of rice farms. The first chapter provides a comprehensive analysis of the impact of climate change on agriculture in Vietnam. It highlights the historical trends, current challenges, and future predictions regarding climate change's effects on the agricultural sector. The second chapter explores the factors affecting rice farm productivity in Vietnam. The study identifies key determinants such as rice cultivation area, rice export, GDP growth, employment, and fertilizer consumption, shedding light on their intricate relationships with rice production. The third chapter focuses on the efficiency and productivity of rice farms in Vietnam. The chapter addresses sustainability issues and outlines strategies to enhance productivity, reduce poverty, and mitigate climate change impacts in the rice sector. Mechanization, collaboration, and land consolidation emerge as key solutions to bolster productivity and contribute to global food security.

From the three chapters, we can see (1) the urgent need for effective national policies and international support to address these challenges and enhance Vietnam's capacity to adapt to and mitigate the impacts of climate change; (2) the importance of designing tailored policies to boost agricultural development and ensure food security in Vietnam; and (3) the necessity of a robust national policies aimed at enhancing the resilience of the agricultural sector to climate change impacts that may include promoting climate-smart agricultural practices, investing in resilient infrastructure, and facilitating technology transfer and adaptation measures. In particular, the government may consider the following strategies.

- Enhance climate resilience: While the government already developed and implemented national policies aimed at enhancing the resilience of the agricultural sector to climate change impacts, the policies should focus on promoting climate-smart agricultural practices, investing in resilient infrastructure, and facilitating technology transfer and adaptation measures.
- Promote sustainable agriculture: The government should continue its policies on adoption of sustainable farming practices, including efficient use of fertilizers and water resources, integrated pest management, and diversified cropping systems. Sustainable agriculture not only enhances productivity but also contributes to environmental conservation and resilience.
- Encourage collaboration: Policies should foster stronger cooperation among farmers to establish effective cooperatives, facilitating collective decision-making and resource-sharing for enhanced productivity and market access. Simultaneously, policies should promote collaborative efforts among farmers, government agencies, businesses, and academic institutions to leverage diverse expertise and resources. This cross-sector collaboration can drive innovation, knowledge exchange, and sustainable agricultural practices, fostering holistic development across the agricultural sector.

2.2 Environment and Energy

This part examines the critical domains of environment and energy sectors in Vietnam, with a focus on the implementation of circular economy principles and sustainable development practices, as well as the impact of renewable energy consumption on economic welfare. The findings of the two chapters contribute to a deeper understanding of the economic implications of renewable energy consumption on welfare and environment as well as circular economy policy development, offering valuable insights for policymakers, the energy sector, and social planners to formulate evidence-based strategies for a cleaner and more sustainable future of Vietnam. Specifically, the following policy recommendations can be of consideration.

- Strengthen circular economy initiatives: The government should implement targeted policies and regulatory frameworks to enhance the adoption of circular economy principles across industries. This includes incentivizing resource efficiency, promoting recycling and reuse practices, and fostering innovation in eco-friendly technologies.
- Promote renewable energy adoption: As evidence produced by the chapter, the government should develop comprehensive policies to accelerate the transition

toward renewable energy sources, including solar, wind, and hydropower. Provide incentives for investment in renewable energy infrastructure and research and streamline regulatory processes to facilitate market entry and expansion.
- Promote Sustainable Development Goals (SDGs): Energy and environmental policies should be aligned with the SDGs to achieve a balance between economic growth, social development, and environmental protection.

2.3 Bank, Finance, and Development

Part three of this edited volume discusses the complex linkages of banks, finance, and development in Vietnam, comprising three studies that examine relevant issues within these domains such as the predictive power of bank equity on economic growth, the measurement of technological progress and productivity in the banking industry, and remittance impacts on the Vietnamese economy. The three papers in this part provide the following policy recommendations.

- Enhance equity market development: The government should prioritize initiatives to foster the development of the equity market, recognizing its significance as a predictor of economic trends and a dynamic platform for representing market expectations. Specifically, the government may implement regulatory reforms and incentives to attract investment and enhance market liquidity.
- Promote banking sector sustainability: The government should provide strategic advice and support to commercial banks to enhance their productivity and ensure sustainable development. In the Vietnamese contexts, policies may focus on encouraging technological innovation, efficiency improvements, and risk management practices to bolster the resilience of the banking sector.
- Maximize benefits of remittances: The government should develop policies and programs to maximize the positive impacts of remittances on economic development. The policies may include facilitation of financial inclusion, entrepreneurship, and investment opportunities for remittance recipients to harness the potential of remittances as a driver of economic growth and poverty reduction.

2.4 Industry and Services

This part of the edited volume investigates the industrial sector, including one study that explore the dynamics of innovation and entrepreneurship in Vietnam's manufacturing and services sectors. This study examines the relationships between innovation activities and firm performance. The findings from this study suggest the following policy recommendations.

- Foster innovation ecosystem: The Vietnamese government should develop policies and initiatives to foster a conducive environment for innovation in both manufacturing and services industries. Specifically, the policies may support research and development efforts, provide incentives for innovation activities, and facilitate collaboration between firms, research institutions, and government agencies. The policies, such as targeted support and provision of incentives for firms, should aim at encouraging firms to prioritize innovation activities to enhance their performance, productivity, and competitiveness in the market.

- Promote FDI impact and labor mobility: The government should strengthen state oversight and management of FDI to maximize its positive impact on economic development while mitigating associated risks and challenges. Policies should be designed to ensure that FDI inflows contribute to sustainable development, job creation, and technology transfer, while safeguarding the interests of local communities and businesses. Moreover, given the study finds that labor migration contributes to economic growth, poverty reduction, and social inclusion, the government should develop policies to facilitate internal and external labor mobility. The policies should provide support and resources for skills development, job training, and reintegration programs to maximize the benefits of labor migration for both individuals and communities.

2.5 Economic Development and Welfare

In this book, we explore the different dimensions of economic development and welfare in Vietnam, including three studies that examine the dynamics of governance quality, infrastructure development, human capital, health, income inequality, population growth, and urbanization. Specifically, the eleventh chapter investigates the relationship between governance quality, infrastructure development, and income inequality among Vietnam's provinces. The next chapter investigates the bidirectional correlation between human capital, specifically education and health, and economic growth in Vietnam. From the angle of population growth and urbanization in Vietnam, the thirteenth chapter highlights the implications of rapid urbanization and slowing population growth for development policies, emphasizing the need for addressing challenges such as aging population, urban labor market dynamics, and socioeconomic welfare imbalances between urban and rural areas. Overall, these studies underscore the importance of investment in development infrastructure and governance effectiveness in reducing income inequality; the significant positive impact of education and health on GDP growth, emphasizing the importance of considering these variables when formulating policies for Vietnam's future prosperity; and the impact of income inequality on growth through various channels, suggesting policy measures to narrow the gap between the rich and poor and ensure a fairer distribution of economic resources and opportunities. These findings suggest several policy recommendations as follows.

- Enhance infrastructure investment: The government should prioritize investment in development infrastructure, including transportation, communication, and utilities, to reduce income inequality and promote balanced economic development across provinces and regions. It should be noted that there have been policy debates on the efficiency versus the equity of infrastructure investment. Our research shows that a balanced point of view should be the policy direction in this case.

- Invest in human capital: The findings suggest that the government should allocate more resources to improve education and healthcare systems, ensuring access to quality and matched education and healthcare services for all citizens.
- Implement poverty alleviation measures: The government should continue its targeted poverty alleviation measures to address multidimensional poverty and reduce income inequality. Specifically, the policies should focus on improving access to education and health care for underdeveloped areas, social protection programs, and rural development initiatives to uplift marginalized communities and enhance their active labor market participation and socioeconomic well-being.
- Manage urbanization challenges: The government should develop comprehensive urbanization policies to address challenges associated with rapid urbanization, including aging population, urban labor market dynamics, and socioeconomic welfare imbalances. Policies on infrastructure development, affordable housing, and inclusive economic opportunities in urban areas should be prioritized.

2.6 Productivity Growth

The book has two chapters focusing on aspects crucial for productivity growth in Vietnam. The first one investigates the relationship between intellectual property rights (IPR) protection and economic development, highlighting the significance of robust IPR laws in fostering innovation and creativity. The second chapter explores the impacts of trade and foreign direct investment (FDI) on total factor productivity (TFP) growth, shedding light on the role of international trade and FDI in shaping Vietnam's productivity landscape. The findings from these two studies suggest several policy implications on the productivity development for Vietnam as follows.

- Strengthen intellectual property rights protection, innovation, and technology transfer: In general, the government should build a legal framework that enhance intellectual property rights laws and enforcement mechanisms to safeguard the rights of creators and innovators. The government should implement measures to deter intellectual property noncompliance and promote a culture of innovation and creativity. Moreover, policies should foster an environment conducive to innovation by incentivizing research and development activities. Technology transfer through partnerships between academia, industry, and government agencies should be facilitated to accelerate technological advancements and enhance productivity.
- Enhance trade integration: The government should continue its policies that deepen integration into regional and global markets and leverage international trade agreements to promote trade liberalization and FDI inflows and facilitate the flow of goods and services. Specifically, the policies should prioritize trade policies that support export-oriented industries and encourage diversification of

exports to enhance competitiveness and productivity. Moreover, the government should implement policies to maximize the benefits of foreign direct investment while mitigating potential negative impacts such as FDI-induced spillovers and fostering linkages between foreign and domestic firms to facilitate knowledge transfer, skill development, and technology diffusion.

Acknowledgements The editors are grateful to an anonymous reviewer, Gouranga Das and Mantu Kumar Mahalik for their comments and suggestions on an earlier version of the book manuscript, and William Achauer, Anushangi Weerakoon, and Tăng Thị Xuân Hồng for their support during the preparation of the manuscript. The editors thank the contributing authors for their invaluable and diverse contributions to this volume.

Pham Khanh Nam is Associate Professor of Economics at University of Economics Ho Chi Minh city. He is Rector of the College of Economics, Law and Government, and Director of the Vietnam—the Netherlands Program (VNP), University of Economics Ho Chi Minh city. He received his Ph.D. in Economics from the University of Gothenburg, Sweden. His areas of research interest are environmental and natural resources economics, climate change, and experimental economics. Currently, his research focuses on forest devolution policy, marine plastic pollution, and renewable energy in Vietnam. He has published in a number of peer-reviewed journals, including Journal of Human Resources, Journal of Public Economics, Journal of Economic Behavior and Organization, Journal of Economic Psychology, Oxford Economic Paper, Land Use Policy, Journal of Cleaner Production, and Journal of Development Studies. He has consulted the World Bank, Asian Development Bank, IUCN, and Vietnam Environment Administration, among others.

Almas Heshmati is Professor of Economics at Jönköping University, Sweden, and Research Fellow at the University of Economics Ho Chi Minh city. He held similar positions at the Sogang University, Korea University, Seoul National University, University of Kurdistan Hawler, and the MTT Agrifood Research (Finland). He was Research Fellow at the World Institute for Development Economics Research (WIDER), The United Nations University during 2001–2004. From 1998 until 2001, he was Associate Professor of Economics at the Stockholm School of Economics. He has a Ph.D. degree from the University of Gothenburg (1994), where he held Senior Researcher position until 1998. His research interests include applied microeconomics, globalization, development economics, efficiency, productivity, and growth with application to agriculture, manufacturing and services, environmental economics, energy economics, and well-being. In addition to many scientific journal articles, he has published books on EU Lisbon Process, Global Inequality, East Asian Manufacturing, Chinese Economy, Technology Transfer, Information Technology, Water Resources, Landmines, Power Generation, Renewable Energy, Development Economics, World Values, Poverty, Well-being, and Economic Growth.

Part I
Agriculture

Chapter 2
The Effects of Climate Change on Vietnamese Agriculture

Anh Ngoc Le and Uyen Phuong Dang Pham

Abstract Vietnam, located in Southeast Asia, is currently facing challenges due to climate change with impact on economy and society. This study provides a thorough analysis of Vietnam's historical, current climate trends and offers predictions for the future. In this paper, the authors utilize data from FAO to emphasize the significant connection between Vietnam's agricultural sector, a vital component of the nation's economy, and climate change. Over the past thirty-one years, these environmental challenges have disrupted farming, resulting in lower productivity, decreased product quality, and reduced farm incomes. This study analyses issues faced by rural communities, including CO_2 emissions, temperature, precipitation and ecosystem damage, agricultural land area, fertilizer consumption, and labour force increases in agricultural sector. This research underscores the significance of implementation of effective policies, and the receipt of international support to tackle the challenges and bolster Vietnam's capacity to both adapt to and mitigate the potential impacts of changing climate.

Keywords Vietnam · Climate change · Agricultural sector · Agricultural factors

1 Introduction

Climate change has had a significant impact on agriculture and food security, affecting both developing and developed countries (Wiebe et al., 2019). Agriculture, susceptible to factors like temperature fluctuations, unpredictable rainfall level, and heightened flood occurrences, and periods of drought, tends to face greater challenges in

---

A. N. Le (✉) · U. P. D. Pham
University of Economics Ho Chi Minh City, Ho Chi Minh City, Vietnam
e-mail: anh.ln@vnp.edu.vn

Erasmus University Rotterdam, Rotterdam, The Netherlands

U. P. D. Pham
e-mail: uyen.pdp@vnp.edu.vn

P. K. Nam and A. Heshmati (eds.), *Recent Trends in Vietnam's Rapid Economic Development*, Frontiers in South and Southeast Asian Development Research,
https://doi.org/10.1007/978-981-97-6079-4_2

comparison to other industries (Ahsan et al., 2020a). The consequences of climate change, such as extreme weather events, pose a threat to food security globally, with the Asia Pacific region experiencing substantial losses in agricultural production and socio-economic devastation (Chandio et al., 2020).

Developing countries, such as Vietnam, are especially vulnerable to disasters and the effects of climate change. This vulnerability is attributed to their dependence on the agricultural industry, the constraints in resources, the instability within institutional frameworks, and the inadequacies in infrastructure. Given its sprawling coastline, heavy reliance on agriculture and natural resources, Vietnam is widely recognized as one of the countries that faces most profound effects by climate change. According to the Climatology report of World Bank (2022), during the period of 31 years, Vietnam witnessed an average annual temperature increase of 0.89 °C. This temperature rise was not consistent and varied across regions and seasons. Consequently, there has been a noticeable rise in the number of hot and scorching days, along with a decrease in the occurrence of cold days. Moreover, although annual rainfall across the country marginally increased by 5.5% during this period, regional disparities were evident. Vietnam is currently grappling with the ongoing challenges posed by climate change. Fluctuations in rainfall patterns, temperature spikes, and evolving precipitation trends have presented significant obstacles for agriculture. In some regions, there has been a decrease in rainfall, while others have witnessed an increase. These conditions highlight Vietnam's ongoing struggle with climate change and the occurrence of extreme conditions like storms, droughts, or floods.

In the context of the economic challenges brought on by the COVID-19 pandemic, agriculture stood out as a robust and fundamental cornerstone within Vietnam's economic framework (GSO, 2023). By engaging roughly half of the country's labour force, agriculture emerged conspicuously as a sector ensuring national food security and contributing significantly to global food supplies via the exportation of goods, such as rice, seafood, and coffee (Asian Development Bank, 2022). However, Vietnam's agricultural sector also faces a substantial risk from the challenges posed by climate change, inducing instability in food supply, a concern shared with other Southeast Asian nations (Lin et al., 2022; Xiang & Solaymani, 2022).

While a large body of literature have explored the undeniable effects of climate change on specific aspects of agriculture in the Vietnam context, such as rice production, crops, farm revenue, agricultural output, and GDP, a comprehensive macroeconomic assessment is lacking. Existing studies often centre on particular crops or regional contexts, and its data sets are rarely updated frequently, making it challenging to draw key conclusions about the relationship between the overall agricultural sector's performance and various factors of production and climate change. Given the rapidly changing weather conditions, updated research is essential to inform policymakers and develop effective strategies to mitigate the adverse effects of climate change on agriculture.

The objective of this research is to address this gap in the literature by utilizing rigorous econometrics techniques, such as the Granger causality test proposed by Toda and Yamamoto (1995), as well as the Autoregressive Distributed Lag model, with data spanning from the period 1990 to 2021. This study aims to investigate the climate change's impact, including changes in CO_2 emissions, rainfall patterns, and temperature on agricultural production in both short and long term, measured by the agricultural gross production index (AGRI). Factors such as land use, the labour used in agriculture, and the usage of fertilizer are considered in assessing their impact on AGRI. The study not only aims to provide a comprehensive perspective on the impact of climate change on agriculture in Vietnam, but also offers insights to aid policymakers in formulating effective strategies for sustainable development and poverty alleviation in Vietnam.

The subsequent sections of this paper include a literature review in Sect. 2, and data and methodology in Sect. 3, the empirical results in Sect. 4, the detailed discussion of the results with conclusions in Sect. 5 and the policy implications of the results in Sect. 6.

2 Literature Review

Climate change is a global phenomenon with far-reaching consequences for agriculture, affecting food security, economic performance, and rural populations' livelihoods. In Vietnam, the agricultural sector plays a vital role; hence, understanding the consequences of climate change is significant. This literature review consolidates essential discoveries from previous research, shedding light on the implications of climate change on agriculture in the context of Vietnam, emphasizing critical insights into the intricate connection between climatic factors and agricultural results. The review is classified into varieties of production and climate factors.

2.1 Climate Change and Agricultural Vulnerabilities

Vietnam's diverse geographical and climatic conditions make it particularly vulnerable to climate change. Rising temperatures, erratic precipitation patterns, and weather events have been identified as key challenges affecting agriculture. Recent studies have highlighted the importance of implementing adaptive strategies to mitigate the adverse effects of climate change on Vietnam's agricultural sector. Additionally, various literature has also uncovered intricate relationships between carbon emissions and the Index of Agricultural Gross Production (AGRI). This complexity highlights the need for tailored adaptive measures that consider these intricate relationships (García, 2013).

2.2 Climate Factors

Climate change is a significant driver of agricultural challenges, other factors, including technology adoption, market dynamics, and government policies, also play substantial roles in shaping agricultural systems. Recent research underscores the intertwined relationship between technological advancements, market forces, and agricultural dependence, particularly.

This literature review provides an overview of the current research related to the relationship between climate change and Vietnam's agricultural factors, as well as presents some specific aspects of this complex issue and proposes strategies for enhancing climate resilience in Vietnamese agriculture.

2.3 Agricultural Challenges in a Changing Climate

The agriculture sector, which has seen significant growth over the past two decades, plays a pivotal role in the country's economic development and improving citizens' lives in Vietnam. However, this sector is increasingly vulnerable to the powerful effects of climate change and societal pressures.

2.4 Indicators Impacted by Climate Change

In their study, World Bank (2022) discusses a metric: Agricultural Gross Production Index (AGRI)—an index that measures the total value of agricultural production in a country. AGRI is affected by many different factors, including climate change. Climate change can cause droughts, erratic rainfall, and unstable weather patterns, leading to reduced agricultural productivity and lower AGRI. According to a World Bank study (2022), climate change could reduce Vietnam's AGRI by 6–20% by 2050 compared to the case without climate change. This could have serious consequences for food security, farmers' income, and economic development of Vietnam. Therefore, it is necessary and urgent to research the causes and apply adaptation measures to mitigate climate change in agriculture.

2.5 *Direct and Indirect Factors Influencing Vietnamese Agriculture*

CO_2 Emissions: The substantial increase in CO_2 emissions in Vietnam is a critical climate change issue. According to data from Vietnam's General Statistics Office, the country's total CO_2 emissions from sources like agriculture, industry, and transportation doubled between 1994 and 2017. In 1994, Vietnam released around 35 million tons of CO_2 into the atmosphere, but by 2017, this number had surged to over 70 million tons. (Thomas et al., 2021). Increased CO_2 emissions led to global warming, which changes weather patterns and makes it harder for farmers to decide which crops to grow and when to plant them.

Temperature: Over the past decade, climate change has had a significant impact on temperatures in Vietnam, particularly in tropical and subtropical regions. Rising temperatures have made growing conditions more challenging for crops (Moore et al., 2021). Higher temperatures lead to rapid water loss in plants and soil. Moreover, excessive heat can stunt crop growth, reducing agricultural productivity and product quality. For example, during scorching summers, extreme temperatures can cause early crop stress for crops like rice, pepper, and fruit trees (Verma et al., 2020). These higher temperatures create favourable conditions for the proliferation of harmful pests, increasing the risk of agricultural diseases.

Precipitation: Climate change has significantly affected rainfall patterns in Vietnam, introducing many challenges and instabilities to agriculture. Shorter and reduced rainy seasons have led to water scarcity in the soil, posing risks for crop cultivation during the dry season. Research spanning from 2000 to 2020 reveals a considerable decrease in annual rainfall in Northern Vietnam, an area heavily reliant on rainfall for agriculture. Conversely, during the rainy season, some regions in Central and Southern Vietnam have experienced intense, concentrated rainfall over short periods, leading to issues like flooding and land erosion. For instance, in October 2020 and 2021, Central Vietnam witnessed severe floods, causing substantial damage to agriculture and communities. The severe floods lead to inundation, land destruction, crop loss, and disruption of seasonal production.

Agricultural Land Area Degradation and Loss: Like many other countries, Vietnam has faced an increase in the use of agricultural land to meet the needs of its growing population. This can lead to issues such as land degradation and nutrient depletion, especially in delta and coastal regions. Some studies indicate that from 1990 to 2015 (Pham Thi et al., 2021), the agricultural land area in Vietnam significantly decreased. The growth in population and economic development exerted substantial pressure to expand agricultural land. This often resulted in the conversion of agricultural land into urban or industrial areas (Tuyen et al., 2013).

Fertilizer Consumption: Vietnam has seen a substantial rise in fertilizer consumption over the past decade. From 2011 to 2020, total fertilizer consumption nearly doubled, increasing from around 1.5 million tons in 2011 to approximately 2.8 million tons in 2020 (Van Toan et al., 2019) It may result in environmental pollution due to fertilizers containing chemical compounds that can contaminate water sources and soil. Additionally, imbalanced fertilizer use can disrupt soil nutrient equilibrium, affecting soil quality and crop yields.

Labour Force: The number of people working in agriculture in Vietnam has gone through significant changes. Data from the General Statistics Office of Vietnam reveals that between 2009 and 2019, the agricultural workforce decreased from about 24.7 million to 22.6 million (Agricultural Restructure Policy/WB: Transforming Vietnamese Agriculture: Gaining More from Less). When rainy seasons become longer or shorter than usual, farmers must change how they work and when they plant crops, which adds uncertainty to farming. This shift in the agricultural workforce can have several negative effects. A big drop in the number of people working in agriculture may mean Vietnam has to rely more on imported food and could lead to unstable food supplies. It also brings challenges to rural communities and makes traditional farming less attractive, which contributes to more people moving to cities.

Other Factors: Climate change creates favourable conditions for the proliferation of certain harmful pests and diseases that affect crops and livestock. Water supply for agriculture becomes scarce, especially during dry seasons, impacting irrigation and livestock. Rising temperatures can induce heat stress in livestock, resulting in decreased meat, milk, and egg production. Based on data and research, it is evident that crop productivity in Vietnam is affected by climate factors as well as non-climate factors. The results indicate that crop yields are expected to decrease in the near future (Nocita, 2019). This decline is driven not only by the influence of temperature and rainfall but also by factors such as fertilizer usage, agricultural land area, and changes in the agricultural workforce.

3 Methodology and Data

The methodology used should encompass climate-resilient agricultural practices, sustainable land management, responsible fertilizer utilization, and support for the agricultural workforce. It underscores the crucial role of government policies, regulations, and international collaboration in mitigating climate change's impact on Vietnamese agriculture and rural communities.

In this research, data in 31 observations from 1990 to 2021 between dependent variables (AGRI) and independence variables will be analysed to demonstrate the impact of climate change on agriculture in Vietnam. Data will be used by applying logarithm transformation to the variables, facilitating data handling and analysis. Subsequently, will perform statistical analyses to examine the averages, variations, and distributions of each variable. This step aims to provide a better grasp of the data's characteristics and variability. Compute a correlation matrix to analyse the interrelationships among variables and gauge their degree of interaction. Additionally, will perform stability tests, such as unit root tests, to confirm the statistical robustness of the subsequent model.

For the estimation, employs the autoregressive distributed lag (ARDL) model to investigate how independent variables influence the dependent variable, considering their effects over both the short and long terms. Subsequently, will conduct cointegration tests to assess the long-term relationships among these variables.

3.1 ARDL Model

To measure the impact of climate change factors on agriculture in Vietnam, develop the suitable model according to the conceptual framework. We estimate the regression model of the agricultural production value on other factors that may affect it by ARDL method. The empirical model is studied as follows:

$$\text{AGRI} = f(\text{FCON}, \text{COEM}, \text{MRAI}, \text{EMPA}, \text{ALAN}, \text{MTEM}),$$

where AGRI denotes the Index of Agricultural Gross Production. We manually collect yearly time series data for these factors in the 1990–2020 period. The variables are defined in Table 1.

Table 1 Summary of the variables, their definitions, and sources

Variable	Describe variable	Unit	Data source
AGRI	Agricultural gross production index, (2014–2016 = 100)	Index	FAOSTAT
COEM	CO_2 emission on agricultural land. When the climate changes, can increase CO_2 emission to environment. Increased atmospheric CO_2 concentrations can affect the growth rate of crop plants and weeds directly (Mohammad et al., 2023)	Kt	FAOSTAT
MTEM	Mean temperature annual	Celsius degree	WORLD BANK
MRAI	Mean annual precipitation	Mm	WORLD BANK
ALAN	Agricultural land	1000 ha	FAOSTAT
EMPA	Employment in agriculture (% of total employment)	%	WORLD BANK
FCON	Fertilizer consumption, measured in kilograms per hectare of arable land	kg per ha	WORLD BANK

Source Authors' collection

Due to the values of the dependent and independent variables, the variables are transformed into natural logarithmic form (except to labour variables because of its unit is percent and less changes, so don't transform it to the logarithmic form) to analyse, so the model is reformed as follows:

$$\ln \text{AGRI}_t = \alpha_0 + \alpha_1 \text{COEM}_t + \alpha_2 \ln \text{MARI}_t + \alpha_3 \ln \text{MTEM}_t + \alpha_4 \text{EMPA}_t + \alpha_5 \ln \text{FCON}_t + \alpha_6 \ln \text{ALAN}_t + \varepsilon_t.$$

In order to estimate and analyse this model clearly, apply the ARDL method to assess the short-run and long-run relationships between these factors and Vietnam's agricultural production. ARDL technique was developed by Charemza and Dorr (1997) and then is further improved in the research of Pesaran et al. (2001) and Pesaran and Shin (1995).

There are several reasons that we choose to estimate an ARDL model. Generally, the ARDL model is the best model used to estimate long-run and short-run relationships between time series in a single equation. In the traditional method, one must use the Ordinary Least Squares (OLS) method to estimate long-run equilibrium, and then estimate error correction model (ECM) for the short-run relationships; this method is more complicated than the one-step ARDL method. According to the results of articles of Min B. Shrestha and Bhatta (2018), Makuyana and Odhiambo (2019), one of the most advantages of ARDL method is that it is more robust and performs better for small sample size of data. This norm is very suitable for this research with the small size of the data set with only 31 observations to estimate the ARDL model.

Some traditional cointegration techniques require all variables to be non-stationary or unit root at level I(0), but stationary in any similar order. This challenge can be effectively tackled using advanced cointegration methodologies, exemplified by the ARDL model, which enables us to estimate when the series exhibit a mixture of I(0) and I(1) with possible cointegration between I(1) series. The result showed that when estimating the ARDL model, the variables in the model can be endogenous and correlated with each other (based on the study of Pesaran et al., 2001).

Using ARDL method can optimize the lag length based on the Akaike information criterion (AIC) value. Moreover, employing lagged fit and simultaneously estimating the ARDL model in both short-term and long-term phases serves as the method to mitigate issues related to both endogeneity and serial correlation. These estimable properties substantiate the reliability of the ARDL technique for achieving accurate estimation results.

To assess the climate-agriculture relationship, we begin by testing the variables for unit roots and stationarity. Then, we use the ARDL method and Granger causality for estimation. Begin test variables for unit roots and stationarity then use ARDL method and Granger causality for estimation. To observe the short-run influence in this study, we will utilize the ARDL method and apply the ARDL unrestricted ECM to investigate the effects in the long run.

3.2 ARDL Model for Long-Term Effects

According to La et al. (2021), the relative income (or distance income) is the difference between the average income of the area that the household currently lives in and the total income of this household. La et al. (2021) used the Vietnam Access to Resources Household Survey (VARHS) to calculate this variable in the original paper. Motivating by this approach, but with changes in calculating the average income of all household members at the district level, we construct the household relative income (HRI) variable with the VHLSS data as equation (3) below:

$$\begin{aligned}\Delta \mathrm{LNAGRI}_i = {} & a_0 + a_1\mathrm{LNAGRI}_{i-1} + a_2\mathrm{LNCOEM}_{i-1} + a_3\mathrm{LNMTEM}_{i-1} \\ & + a_4\mathrm{LNMRAI}_{i-1} + a_5\mathrm{LNALAN}_{i-1} + a_6\mathrm{LNEMPA}_{i-1} \\ & + a_7\mathrm{LNFCON}_{i-1} + \sum_{i=1}^{P} \Delta a_{8i}\Delta\mathrm{LNAGRI}_{i-1} + \sum_{i=0}^{q} \Delta a_{9\mathrm{i}}\Delta\mathrm{LNCOEM}_{i-1} \\ & + \sum_{i=0}^{r} \Delta a_{10i}\Delta\mathrm{LNMTEM}_{i-1} + \sum_{i=0}^{s} \Delta a_{11i}\Delta\mathrm{LNMRAI}_{i-1} \\ & + \sum_{i=0}^{u} \Delta a_{12i}\Delta\mathrm{LNALAN}_{i-1} \sum_{i=0}^{v} \Delta a_{13i}\Delta\mathrm{LNEMPA}_{i-1} \\ & + \sum_{i=0}^{w} \Delta a_{14i}\Delta\mathrm{LNFCON}_{i-1} + \varepsilon_i,\end{aligned}$$

where LNAGRI denotes the natural logarithm term; Delta (Δ) denotes the first difference; epsilon (ε) denotes the white noise; and α denotes the intercept. The optimal lags for the variables are represented by the letters p, q, r, s, u, v, and w, respectively. For Eq. (3), the joint F-statistic (the ARDL bounds test is employed to examine the presence of cointegrations in the long-term relationship among the variables).

The null hypothesis is

$$\mathrm{H}_0\text{: } \alpha_1 = \alpha_2 = \alpha_3 = \alpha_4 = \alpha_5 = \alpha_6 = \alpha_7 = 0 \quad \text{(no cointegration)},$$

while the alternative hypothesis will be

$$\mathrm{H}_1\text{: } \alpha_1 \neq \alpha 2 \neq \alpha_3 \neq \alpha_4 \neq \alpha_5 \neq \alpha_6 \neq \alpha_7 \neq 0 \quad \text{(Possible cointegration)}.$$

If the p-value is small or the F-test statistic surpasses the upper bound of I(0), the null hypothesis (H_0) is rejected, showing the evidence of a possible relationship between changing climate and agricultural factors in the long run. Conversely, when the F-test results lies below the lower bound, it indicates a failure to reject the null hypothesis. However, if the F-test statistic results lies within the bounds, suggesting the absence of cointegration, the hypothesis remains inconclusive. To provide further clarity on cointegration consistency, researchers often utilize the cumulative sum recursive residuals method (i.e. CUSUM) or the cumulative of square recursive residuals method (i.e. CUSUMSQ) for verification.

3.3 ARDL Model for Short-Term Effect

Using ARDL error correction regression to estimate the short-term impact of climate change on Vietnam's agricultural production, Eq. (4) is specified as follows:

$$\begin{aligned}\Delta \mathrm{LNAGRI_t} = \alpha_{15} &+ \sum_{i=1}^{P} \Delta a_{16i} \Delta \mathrm{LNAGRI}_{t-i} + \sum_{i=0}^{q} \Delta a_{17i} \Delta \mathrm{LNCOEM}_{t-i} \\ &+ \sum_{i=0}^{r} \Delta a_{18i} \Delta \mathrm{LNMTEM}_{t-i} + \sum_{i=0}^{s} \Delta a_{19i} \Delta \mathrm{LNMRAI}_{t-i} \\ &+ \sum_{i=0}^{u} \Delta a_{20i} \Delta \mathrm{LNALAN}_{t-i} \sum_{i=0}^{v} \Delta a_{21i} \Delta \mathrm{LNEMPA}_{t-i} \\ &+ \sum_{i=0}^{w} \Delta a_{22i} \Delta \mathrm{LNFCON}_{t-i} + \varepsilon_i,\end{aligned}$$

where in the context of error correction modelling, λ denotes the coefficient for the error correction term, which captures the adjustment process towards equilibrium in long-term after short-term disturbances. This coefficient λ reflects the rate at which adjustments occur towards the long-term equilibrium after a short-term shock. We also employ the F-bounds test at this step. In case the null hypothesis (H_0) of this test is rejected, we can confirm the presence of cointegration, and λ should be significantly negative. At this juncture, it is imperative to employ the causality method proposed by Toda and Yamamoto (1995) to validate the presence of Granger causality directions. This step is crucial as the correlations among variables may be spurious and insufficient to offer a completed comprehension of the correlations among variables in our time series model. This method is particularly suitable for this research due to the integration orders of variables being mixed (I(0) and I(1)), irrespective of the cointegration condition of the variables.

Table 2 Description of non-logarithmic variables in the empirical model

	AGRI	COEM	MTEM	MRAI	ALAN	EMPA	FCON
vars	1	2	3	4	5	6	7
n	31	31	31	31	31	31	31
mean	70.18	6601.38	24.78	1769.82	9645.35	0.54	330.91
Std dev	25.29	1973.14	0.31	105.51	1856.43	0.13	103.68
median	69.78	5677.00	24.79	1762.60	10,054.10	0.52	342.97
trimmed	70.27	6298.58	24.78	1767.93	9663.35	0.55	338.72
mad	35.18	875.71	0.30	143.12	2433.09	0.17	110.40
min	32.09	4670.27	24.13	1622.83	6726.00	0.29	104.94
max	107.48	11,282.00	25.42	1946.59	12,388.00	0.75	483.86
range	75.39	6611.73	1.29	323.76	5662.00	0.46	378.92
skew	− 0.01	1.12	0.09	0.07	− 0.12	− 0.07	− 0.62
kurtosis	− 1.47	− 0.16	− 0.23	− 1.43	− 1.29	− 1.19	− 0.59
Std error	4.54	354.39	0.06	18.95	333.42	0.02	18.62

4 Empirical Results

4.1 Descriptive Statistics

In this section, the empirical analysis will utilize time series data describing the statistics of the ARDL model variables. Descriptive statistics for the variables included in the analysis are presented in Tables 2 and 3.

To check for multicollinearity issues, we calculate the pairwise correlations of the variables. Table 3 shows that no correlation coefficient is above 0.80, so multicollinearity is not a major problem. The analysis also shows positive relationships between climate factors (CO_2, temperature, precipitation, land, fertilizers) and agriculture production index. Labour has unexpectedly negative correlations with agriculture measures (Table 4).

4.2 Estimation Results

4.2.1 Unit Root Test

Before estimating the long-run impact of climate change factors on agriculture gross production index (AGRI), it is important to test stationary of the series. In this model, we have to test unit roots by Augmented Dickey–Fuller (ADF) test and verify these results by Phillips-Perron (PP) test.

Table 3 Description of logarithm variables in the empirical model

	lnAGRI	lnCOEM	lnMTEM	lnMRAI	lnALAN	EMPA	lnFCON
vars	1	2	3	4	5	6	7
n	31	31	31	31	31	31	31
mean	4.18	8.76	3.21	7.48	9.16	0.54	5.74
Std dev	0.40	0.27	0.01	0.06	0.20	0.13	0.40
median	4.25	8.64	3.21	7.47	9.22	0.52	5.84
trimmed	4.20	8.73	3.21	7.48	9.16	0.55	5.80
mad	0.51	0.16	0.01	0.08	0.26	0.17	0.29
min	3.47	8.45	3.18	7.39	8.81	0.29	4.65
max	4.68	9.33	3.24	7.57	9.42	0.75	6.18
range	1.21	0.88	0.05	0.18	0.61	0.46	1.53
skew	− 0.37	0.88	0.05	0.02	− 0.34	− 0.07	− 1.25
kurtosis	− 1.28	− 0.67	− 0.23	− 1.44	− 1.25	− 1.19	0.61
Std error	0.07	0.05	0.00	0.01	0.04	0.02	0.07

Notes The table shows the summary statistics of AGRI and other factors over 31 years. AGRI index increased from 70.18 to 107.48, with a low level of 32.09. According to the Vietnam's Climatology report of World Bank (2022) the Global temperature rose, affecting Vietnam's climate zones, monsoon and it was impacted by the El Niño Southern Oscillation (ENSO). Vietnam's temperature was 24.78 °C, and precipitation was 1769.82 mm. Land area and fertilizer use increased from 67.26 to 123.6 million ha and from 1049.41 to 4676.56 kg/ha. Labour share in agriculture decreased during the period from 75.04 to 29.04%. Labour and land productivity improved over time

Table 4 Correlation matrix

	lnAGRI	lnCOEM	lnMTEM	lnMRAI	lnALAN	EMPA	lnFCON
lnAGRI	1.000						
lnCOEM	0.780	1.000					
lnMTEM	0.294	0.355	1.000				
lnMRAI	0.000	0.011	− 0.313	1.000			
lnALAN	0.989	0.752	0.334	− 0.008	1.000		
EMPA	− 0.970	− 0.770	− 0.353	0.056	− 0.970	1.000	
lnFCON	0.893	0.633	0.244	0.016	0.871	− 0.828	1.000

Table 5 shows unit roots test results for variables at 1st difference level. For ADF test, null hypothesis is H_0: series has unit root and is non-stationary. At I(0), *p*-values of lnCOEM, lnMTEM, lnMRAI, lnFCON are below 10%, so H0 is rejected. It means series are stationary at I(0). At I(1), *p*-values of lnAGRI, lnALAN, EMPA are below 10%, so H_0 is rejected. It means series are stationary at I(1). Consequently, it is advisable to employ the ARDL cointegration method in investigating the influence of changing climate on the agricultural factors of Vietnam throughout the period from 1990 to 2021.

Table 5 Unit roots testing

Variable	ADF test I(0)		PP test I(0)	
	Intercept	*P*-value	Intercept	*P*-value
lnAGRI	0.577	0.990	1.178	0.990
lnCOEM	– 3.514	0.059	– 3.220	0.089
lnMTEM	– 1.878	0.025	– 4.978	0.010
lnMRAI	– 4.296	0.011	– 5.246	0.010
lnALAN	– 1.180	0.888	– 1.640	0.711
EMPA	– 2.463	0.394	– 1.737	0.673
lnFCON	– 4.549	0.010	– 3.325	0.086
1st different level I(1)				
Variable	ADF test I(1)		PP test I(1)	
	Intercept	*P*-value	Intercept	*P*-value
lnAGRI	– 3.900	0.027	– 9.136	0.010
lnCOEM	–	–	–	–
lnMTEM	–	–	–	–
lnMRAI	–	–	–	–
lnALAN	– 5.368	0.010	– 6.085	0.010
EMPA	– 2.039	0.071	– 3.298	0.080
lnFCON	–	–	–	–

4.3 ARDL Estimation Results

To estimate long-run and short-run effect between the climate change and other variables by ARDL method, one must determine the optimal lag length by AIC index. Table 6 shows the result of numerous selection criteria, that is the top orders of lag length. The smallest AIC is the best order, lag length will be optimized. In this result, choose order (1,2,1,0,2,1,1) with smallest AIC = – 15,120.

To check whether the model, ARDL (1,2,1,0,2,1,1) model, has long-run relationships between dependent and independent variables or not and then use the Bounds F-test to check the existence of cointegration as the result in Table 7.

The null hypothesis of the bounds *F*-test: H_0: the model has no cointegration and alternative hypothesis: H_1: Possible cointegration. With significant level at 5%, *p*-value = 0.001436; $F = 5.4017$ is larger than upper bound I(1) = 3.2247. The null hypothesis is rejected, there has been cointegration in this model. It means that there are long-run relationships between dependent and independent variables in the ARDL (1,2,1,0,2,1,1) model.

In the ARDL bounds test results, Table 7 illustrates the enduring impacts of changing climate on agricultural outputs and related variables. Notably, CO_2 emissions demonstrate a statistically significant relationship with AGRI. This implies that over the long term, every one percent rise in CO_2 emissions responds to a 0.12%

Table 6 Top orders of ARDL

lnAGRI	lnCO_2	LNMTEM	lnRAIN	lnLAND	LABOR	lnFERTL	AIC
1	2	1	0	2	1	1	− 15.120
1	2	0	0	2	1	1	− 15.074
1	2	0	0	2	0	1	− 15.055
1	2	0	0	2	1	2	− 14.974
1	2	1	0	2	1	2	− 14.948
1	2	1	0	2	2	1	− 14.944
1	2	0	0	1	1	1	− 14.830
1	2	0	1	1	1	1	− 14.706
2	2	2	2	2	2	2	− 14.695
1	2	1	1	1	1	1	− 14.528
1	1	1	1	1	1	1	− 14.402

Table 7 ARDL bounds test results

Bounds *F*-test (Wald) for no cointegration				
Estimate model	*F*-stat	*p*-value	Critical value	
			Lower bound I(0)	Upper bound I(1)
ARDL1210211	5.401	0.001	2.136	3.224

growth in agricultural outputs. This finding is consistent with studies by Chandio et al. (2020) and Xiang et al. (2021), which also reported related results in their studies on the possible effects of CO_2 emissions on the crop outputs. These results suggest that CO_2 emissions contribute to the enhancement of crop photosynthesis.

Temperature and precipitation negatively affect agricultural outputs. A 1% increase in temperature and rainfall corresponds to a reduction in production by 1.54% and 0.02% at the 10% significance level, respectively. Similar results are found by Korres et al. (2017) and Chandio et al. (2020) for rice and agriculture, and by Janjua et al. (2014) for wheat and rainfall. This evidence supports our findings of climate change's detrimental effect on Vietnam's agriculture in the period studied.

Regarding agricultural inputs factors, at Table 7, variables lnALAN, EMPA, lnFCON are significant at 1, 5, 10% levels. In the long term, variables such as lnALAN and lnFCON exhibit positive effects on the agricultural outputs, while the variable labour has a negative effect. The efficiency of Vietnam's rural workers and the cereal crops land size emerge as crucial factors for agricultural outputs growth, particularly in the long-term period, with a 1% increase in agricultural land resulting in a 1.24% boost in outputs.

The analysis also highlights the critical role of fertilizers in easing potential adverse impacts on agricultural outputs in the long term. A 1% increase in fertilizer consumption corresponds to a 0.14% increase in agricultural production. Hence, appropriate fertilizer application emerges as a strategy to enhance soil health and fertility. Among all the factors investigated, CO_2 emissions hold the most significant positive sway over agricultural output, while global warming manifests as the most substantial negative influence on long-term agricultural production in Vietnam's agricultural context.

Table 9 shows how climate and non-climate factors affect the output of agriculture in the short run. The observed effects align with those identified in the long run, except for rainfall, which has little or no impact. The coefficients are smaller compared to the long-term scenario. Specifically, a 1% increment in temperature reduces output by 0.77%. For a 1% increase in CO_2 emissions, land area, fertilizer use, and labour force increase output by 0.04%, 0.25%, 0.013%, and 0.49%, respectively.

4.4 Marginal Effects Analysis of Key Determinants

Table 8 reveals a significantly negative coefficient for ECM (− 1) at the 1% significance level, suggesting the presence of cointegration among the variables. The ECM coefficient, valued at 0.36 and significant at the 1% level, represents the adjusted period that the long-term equilibrium adjusts to potential shocks in short term. In particular, the deviation from the short-run balance between agricultural outputs and other factors can be rectified and restored at a speed of nearly 0.4% per annum in the long run. These findings offer evidence supporting a long-term relationship among the related factors of changing climate and other employed explanatory variables.

To assess the consistency of the ARDL models, diagnostic tests were employed. The results from the diagnostic tests presented in Table 9 demonstrate the absence of issues related to normality, heteroscedasticity, autocorrelation, and misspecification issues in this ARDL model (Table 10).

To assess the coefficients' constancy in both short-run and long-run perspectives, (CUSUM) and (CUSUMSQ) tests were employed, considering that structural changes among variables may arise because of possible structure's breaks (can be either multiple or single way). The cumulative of (square) recursive residuals method

Table 8 ARDL analysis results for the long-term effects

Variable	Coefficient	*t* value	Pr(>|*t*|)
(Intercept)	− 3.679	− 1.130	0.269
lnCOEM	0.120*	2.429	0.023
lnMTEM	− 1.544*	− 2.088	0.047
lnMRAI	− 0.017*	− 0.114	0.05
lnALAN	1.243***	6.256	0.000
EMPA	− 0.583*	− 2.105	0.046
lnFCON	0.143***	3.348	0.002

Notes *t* statistics in parentheses
* $p < 0.05$, ** $p < 0.01$, *** $p < 0.001$

Table 9 ARDL model for short-term impacts of climate change on agriculture production

Variable	Coefficient	*t* value	Pr(>|*t*|)
(Intercept)	0.161***	9.569	6.60E−09
d(lnCOEM)	0.040*	2.676	0.014
d(L(lnCOEM,1))	− 0.014	− 0.917	0.369
d(LNMTEM)	− 0.771***	− 5.066	5.91E−05
d(lnALAN)	0.129	1.424	0.170
d(L(lnALAN,1))	0.245*	− 2.663	0.014
d(EMPA)	0.494*	2.561	0.018
d(lnFCON)	0.013	0.914	0.371
ECM (− 1)	− 0.361***	− 7.350	4.21E−07

Notes t statistics in parentheses
* $p < 0.05$, ** $p < 0.01$, *** $p < 0.001$

Table 10 Diagnostic tests for ARDL model

Diagnostic post-tests for ARDL models		
Breusch-Godfrey (BG) test for serial correlation	*F*-statistic	5.246
	p-value	0.337
Breusch-Pagan (BP) test for heteroskedasticity	*F*-statistic	18.986
	p-value	0.165
Jarque-Bera two-side test for normality	*F*-statistic	0.905
	p-value	0.637
Ramsey test for detecting omitted variables	*F*-statistic	0.430
	p-value	0.660

lines for agricultural outputs, as depicted in Figs. 1 and 2, remain within the 5% significance level's boundaries, affirming the stability of the ARDL model.

Finally, the Granger causality test was employed to examine causality among the variables. Table 11 indicates significant relationships between factors of climate change (rainfall, carbon emissions, and temperature) and fertilizer use. This means crops need more fertilizer under climate change conditions. Land area also relates to fertilizer use. The test shows significant directions of Granger causality in the tested models and confirms cointegration among variables.

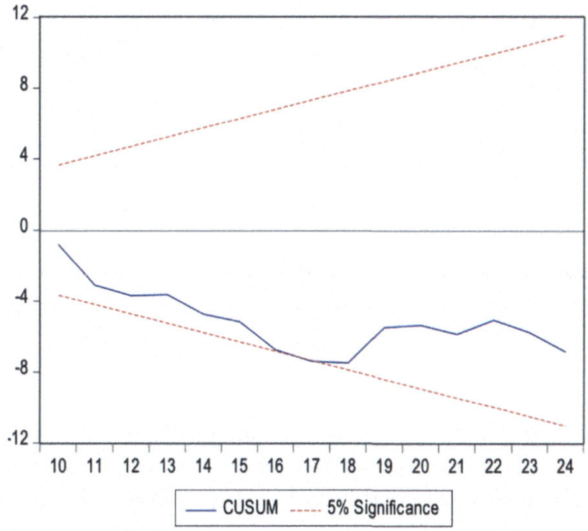

Fig. 1 CUSUM plot to assess the coefficients stability in the ARDL model for the period 1990–2021

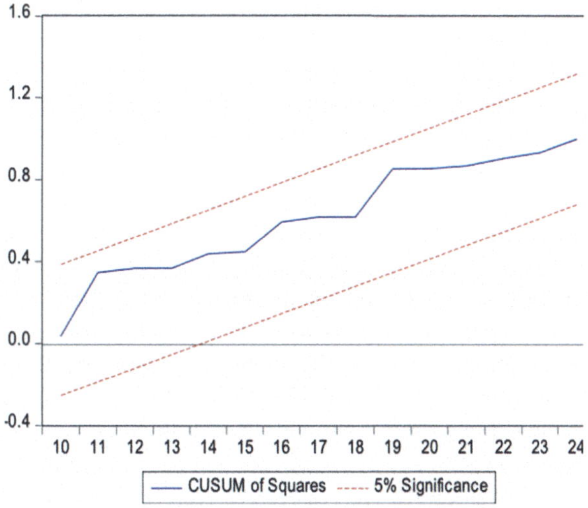

Fig. 2 CUSUMSQ plot to the coefficient's stability in the ARDL model for the period 1990–2021

5 Discussion and Conclusion

The significance of the agricultural sector in ensuring food security and driving economic growth in Vietnam cannot be overstated. Gaining insights into the climate change's impact and the diverse factors influencing agriculture is essential for Vietnamese officials and farmers. This study examines how climate changing issues can affect agricultural outputs, agricultural-related variables, as well as economic output from short-term and long-term perspectives in the Vietnam's context.

Table 11 Granger causality test for ARDL model

Responding variable	lnAGRI	lnCOEM	lnMTEM	lnMRAI	EMPA	lnALAN	lnFCON
lnAGRI	–	0.056	0.069	1.043	2.059	0.721	14.113***
lnCOEM	0.994	–	0.571	0.838	0.446	0.044	12.471***
LNMTEM	4.465	0.335	–	1.192	0.301	0.590	8.752**
lnMRAI	0.931	0.568	0.272	–	0.601	3.671	10.237***
EMPA	1.097	2.936	3.337	0.824	–	0.954	3.449
lnALAN	3.021	0.373	0.818	1.134	0.091	–	11.837***
lnFCON	1.221	0.039	0.909	0.671	1.495	2.262	–

In the context of the agricultural production index, denoted as AGRI in this paper, factors associated with CO_2 emissions show a notably positive correlation with AGRI in both short run and long run. This finding aligns with the conclusions drawn by Ahsan et al. (2020b), who also observed a positive link among similar variables in the context of another country. Notably, the influence of carbon emissions on the outputs of agriculture is more pronounced in the long run (0.12) compared to the short term (0.04).

In the case of temperature, it is evident that this variable consistently exerts a negative impact on AGRI not only in the short term but also in long term. These results corroborate the conclusions drawn by Nguyen and Scrimgeour (2022) regarding the adverse consequences of rising temperatures on agricultural productivity in Vietnam. Furthermore, our results are consistent with a body of literature including studies by Baxtiyar and Abdimalik (2021), Ul-Haq et al. (2022), Ben Zaied and Ben Cheikh (2015), and Anh et al. (2023), which collectively suggest the crucial effects of temperature on agricultural outputs across diverse regions and climate conditions.

In terms of the long-term effects of labour, the negative impact on agriculture indicates inefficiency among Vietnam's rural workers. World Bank (2016) highlights the labour-intensive and manual nature of Vietnam's agriculture, with workers lacking training, possessing low skills, and limited access to technology, resulting in low productivity.

In investigating the short- and long-term impacts of fertilizer and land on the outputs of agriculture in Vietnam, our analysis positively reveals associations at the 1% level. Xiang and Solaymani (2022) similarly conclude that there is a positive relationship between agricultural land and production. The strong relationship between fertilizer and agricultural outputs is tightly aligned with previous studies, such as Chandio et al.'s (2020) research, which emphasize the role of fertilizer in enhancing soil quality and benefiting cultivation.

In conclusion, climate change is likely to harm the economy by affecting agricultural production and rural livelihood and incomes. To counteract these impacts, we need to thoroughly study how climate change affects farming. Our study used data from 1990 to 2020 to see how climate change affects agriculture in Vietnam. We found that climate change, including factors like CO_2 emissions and temperature, has a lasting impact on farming. More CO_2 and energy use help agriculture, while higher temperatures and altered rainfall hurt it. Non-climate factors like the amount of land used for crops and fertilizer application also boost agricultural productivity. Additionally, we checked the stability of these factors using statistical tests like the CUSUM and CUSUMSQ tests.

6 Policy Implications

Vietnam has policies to address effects of climate change on agriculture. Current policies, like the National Strategy and the National Action Plan, promote climate-smart farming practices, such as drought-resistant crops and application of precise techniques. These policies increase resilience and reduce emissions. The National Target Programme builds the capacity of vulnerable areas and communities, with focus on human capital through training and provision of extension services.

In response to the changing climate landscape, Vietnam has introduced new policies that further strengthen its commitment to sustainable agriculture and green growth. The National Policy on Low-Emission Development in Agriculture sets specific targets and mechanisms to control greenhouse gas emissions, promoting low-emission farming practices. The National Policy on Climate Risk Management in Agriculture establishes a robust framework for assessing and managing climate risks, enhancing the sector's adaptive capacity. Furthermore, the National Policy on Sustainable Land Use Planning in Agriculture defines criteria for land resource allocation, aligning land use decisions with sustainability goals and promoting sustainable land management practices.

To facilitate the implementation of these policies and ensure effective outcomes, Vietnam has also focused on improving its institutional structure and framework. The establishment of the Inter-ministerial Coordinating Board for VGGS under the National Committee on Climate Change facilitates coordinated efforts, ensuring that policies related to climate resilience and green growth are effectively implemented and monitored. Moreover, efforts to complete the institutional framework for economic restructuring aim to enhance coordination among various agencies, supporting sustainable agriculture and green growth. These policies foster transparency, accountability, incentives, community involvement, and global participation.

Data and Material Availability Declaration The data sets we used to analyse in this research is accessible upon reasonable request from the corresponding author. This ensures transparency, and we are willing to assist anyone who wants to check or replicate our research.

Competing Interest Declaration We declare that we do not have any known financial conflicts of interest or personal relationships that could have influenced our research findings or its status. We make this statement to ensure the integrity and independence of our research and to avoid any potential conflicts of interest.

References

Ahsan, F. M., Sinha, A., & Srinivasan, R. (2020a). Exploring firm-level antecedents that drive motives of internationalization: A study of knowledge intensive Indian firms. *Management and Organization Review, 16*(4), 867–906.

Ahsan, F., Chandio, A. A. A., & FangFang, W. (2020b). Climate change impacts on cereal crops production in Pakistan. *International Journal of Climate Change Strategies and Management, 12*(2), 257–269.

Anh, D. L. T., Anh, N. T., & Chandio, A. A. (2023). Climate change and its impacts on Vietnam agriculture: A macroeconomic perspective. *Ecological Informatics, 74*, 101960.

Asian Development Bank. (2022). *Agriculture, Natural Resources and Rural Development Sector Assessment, Strategy and Road Map—Viet Nam 2021–2025*. Asian Development Bank.

Baxtiyar, P., & Abdimalik, P. (2021). Efficient organization of harvesting and processing of cotton seeds. *Universum: технические науки*, (3–4(84)), 77–79.

Ben Zaied, Y., & Ben Cheikh, N. (2015). Long-run versus short-run analysis of climate change impacts on agricultural crops. *Environmental Modeling & Assessment, 20*, 259–271.

Chandio, A. A., Jiang, Y., Rehman, A., & Rauf, A. (2020). Short and long-run impacts of climate change on agriculture: An empirical evidence from China. *International Journal of Climate Change Strategies and Management, 12*(2), 201–221.

Charemza, W., & Dorr, D. (1992). *New directions in econometric practice: General to specific modelling, cointegration and vector autoregression*. Edward Elgar.

García, M. D. M. H. (2013). The impact of climate change on food security. *Cuadernos De Estrategia, 161*, 62–80.

General Statistics Office of Vietnam. (2023, January). *Socio-economic Situation in the Fourth Quarter and 2022*. Retrieved October 03, 2023, from https://www.gso.gov.vn/en/data-and-statistics/2023/01/socio-economic-situation-in-the-fourth-quarter-and-2022/

Janjua, P. Z., Samad, G., & Khan, N. (2014). Climate change and wheat production in Pakistan: An autoregressive distributed lag approach. *NJAS-Wageningen Journal of Life Sciences, 68*, 13–19.

Korres, N. E., Norsworthy, J. K., Burgos, N. R., & Oosterhuis, D. M. (2017). Temperature and drought impacts on rice production: An agronomic perspective regarding short-and long-term adaptation measures. *Water Resources and Rural Development, 9*, 12–27.

La, B. T., Lim, S., Cameron, M. P., Tran, T. Q., & Nguyen, M. T. (2021). Absolute income, comparison income and subjective well-being in a transitional country: Panel evidence from Vietnamese household surveys. *Economic Analysis and Policy, 72*, 368–385.

Lin, H. I., Yu, Y. Y., Wen, F. I., & Liu, P. T. (2022). Status of food security in East and Southeast Asia and challenges of climate change. *Climate, 10*(3), 40, 1–35.

Makuyana, G., & M Odhiambo, N. (2019). Public and private investment and economic growth in Malawi: An ARDLbounds testing approach. *Economic research-Ekonomska istraživanja, 32*(1), 673–689.

Mohammed Idris, F., Seraj, M., & Özdeşer, H. (2023). Renewable energy consumption, CO_2 emissions and trade balance nexus in OECD countries: Evidence from ARDL bounds approach. *International Journal of Energy Sector Management, 17*(4), 645–660.

Moore, C. E., Meacham-Hensold, K., Lemonnier, P., Slattery, R. A., Benjamin, C., Bernacchi, C. J., Lawson, T., & Cavanagh, A. P. (2021). The effect of increasing temperature on crop photosynthesis: From enzymes to ecosystems. *Journal of Experimental Botany, 72*(8), 2822–2844.

Nguyen, C. T., & Scrimgeour, F. (2022). Measuring the impact of climate change on agriculture in Vietnam: A panel Ricardian analysis. *Agricultural Economics, 53*(1), 37–51.

Nocita, N. (2019, October 28). *The Vietnamese struggle with climate change*. Harvard International Review. https://hir.harvard.edu/the-vietnamese-struggle-with-climate-change/

Pesaran, M. H., & Shin, Y. (1995). *An autoregressive distributed lag modelling approach to cointegration analysis* (Vol. 9514). Department of Applied Economics, University of Cambridge.

Pesaran, M. H., Shin, Y., & Smith, R. J. (2001). Bounds testing approaches to the analysis of level relationships. *Journal of Applied Econometrics, 16*(3), 289–326.

Pham Thi, N., Kappas, M., & Faust, H. (2021). Impacts of agricultural land acquisition for urbanization on agricultural activities of affected households: A case study in Huong Thuy Town, Thua Thien Hue Province, Vietnam. *Sustainability, 13*(15), 8559.

Shrestha, M. B., & Bhatta, G. R. (2018). Selecting appropriate methodological framework for time series data analysis. *The Journal of Finance and Data Science, 4*(2), 71–89.

Thomas, F., Culas, C., Đức, L. V., & Pannier, E. (2021). Climate change and adaptation in Viet Nam: Contributions from Environmental History. HAL Open Science. https://hal.archives-ouvertes.fr/hal-03508872

Toda, H. Y., & Yamamoto, T. (1995). Statistical inference in vector autoregressions with possibly integrated processes. *Journal of Econometrics, 66*(1–2), 225–250.

Tuyen, T. Q. (2013). Livelihood strategies for coping with land loss among households in Vietnam's sub-urban areas.

Ul-Haq, Z., Mehmood, U., Tariq, S., Qayyum, F., Azhar, A., & Nawaz, H. (2022). Analyzing the role of meteorological parameters and CO_2 emissions towards crop production: Empirical evidence from South Asian countries. *Environmental Science and Pollution Research, 29*(29), 44199–44206.

Van Toan, P., Minh, N. D., & Van Thong, D. (2019). Organic fertilizer production and application in Vietnam. In *Organic fertilizers-history, production and applications*. IntechOpen.

Verma, S., Kumar, N., Verma, A., Singh, H., Siddique, K. H., & Singh, N. P. (2020). Novel approaches to mitigate heat stress impacts on crop growth and development. *Plant Physiology Reports, 25*, 627–644.

Wiebe, K. S., Harsdorff, M., Montt, G., Simas, M. S., & Wood, R. (2019). Global circular economy scenario in a multiregional input–output framework. *Environmental Science & Technology, 53*(11), 6362–6373.

World Bank. (2016). *Transforming Vietnamese agriculture: Gaining more from less*. Vietnam Development Report. World Bank. Retrieved April 22, 2021, from https://openknowledge.worldbank.org/handle/10986/24375

World Bank. (2022). For Mekong Delta farmers, diversification is the key to climate resilience. (2022, March 15). World Bank. https://www.worldbank.org/en/news/feature/2021/10/21/for-mekong-delta-farmers-diversification-is-the-key-to-climate-resilience

Xiang, H., Ch, P., Nawaz, M. A., Chupradit, S., Fatima, A., & Sadiq, M. (2021). Integration and economic viability of fueling the future with green hydrogen: An integration of its determinants from renewable economics. *International Journal of Hydrogen Energy, 46*(77), 38145–38162.

Xiang, X., & Solaymani, S. (2022). Change in cereal production caused by climate change in Malaysia. *Ecological Informatics, 70*, 101741.

Anh Ngoc Le is a current postgraduate student enrolled in the Vietnam—the Netherlands programme, a collaborative master's programme jointly offered by the Ho Chi Minh City University of Economics and Erasmus University Rotterdam. She is a Junior Market Researcher and Business Development Associate, with a background in international economics.

Uyen Phuong Dang Pham with a background as an auditor, having worked in various roles across diverse companies. Currently, she is a postgraduate student majoring in Applied Economics as part of the collaborative programme between Vietnam and the Netherlands, a joint effort between the Ho Chi Minh City University of Economics and Erasmus University Rotterdam. She has a particular interest in agricultural issues and has dedicated her studies to exploring this field.

Chapter 3
Determinants of Rice Farm Productivity in Vietnam

Nguyen Thi Kieu Nhung

Abstract Vietnam is an agricultural country, and rice production has been a cornerstone of the economy for a long time. It is important to understand the determinants of rice production and productivity. This research aims at identifying factors important to rice farm productivity in Vietnam. It analyzes the relationship between rice yield and several key factors: rice cultivation area, rice export, Gross Domestic Production (GDP) growth, employment in agriculture, and fertilizer consumption. The study explores how fluctuations in rice cultivation areas influence rice output, highlighting the importance of land allocation in rice farming. It also investigates the role of international trade, particularly how rice export affects domestic production. The analysis also considers the effects of macroeconomic indicator, GDP growth on rice yield, emphasizing their influence on agricultural stability. The relationship between employment in agriculture and rice output are also scrutinized to understand the socioeconomic implications of the rice industry. Finally, the study examines the fertilizer consumption, a critical factor in enhancing crop yields, and its relationship with rice production.

Keywords Agriculture · Rice output · Fertilizer consumption · GDP growth · Rice export

1 Research Background

Many previous studies are researching the relationship between rice output and determinants to figure out depending on geographic conditions the best ways to promote the agriculture industry of a country. This literature review part explores key research findings on these relationships before going further to analyze the Vietnam's rice market.

N. T. K. Nhung (✉)
University of Economics Ho Chi Minh City, Ho Chi Minh City, Vietnam
e-mail: nhung.ntk@vnp.edu.vn

P. K. Nam and A. Heshmati (eds.), *Recent Trends in Vietnam's Rapid Economic Development*, Frontiers in South and Southeast Asian Development Research,
https://doi.org/10.1007/978-981-97-6079-4_3

Rice Cultivation Area

Numerous studies have highlighted the direct correlation between rice cultivation area and rice production output. In a study about resource-use efficiency of rice production in Kura Local Government area of Kano State, Nigeria, Nkwi et al. (2022) demonstrated that odd farm size has a beneficial and statistically significant impact on rice output at the 1% level of significance. These findings suggest that a unit increase in farm size will result in a 0.63 unit increase in rice yield.

In another study, using an ARDL model for South Korea, Nasrullah et al. (2021) show that the land (or harvested area) elasticity of rice output is + 1.65 in the long run, which is significant at the 1% level. When other factors remain constant, it means that this relationship is elastic, meaning that a 1% increase in the harvested area is associated with a 1.65% rise in rice yield. In the short run, if the harvested area increases by 1%, the production of rice increases by 1.31%, while other things being held constant.

Rice Export

Rice exporting is one of the motivations to increase demand for rice, as the result, it leads to a pressure to increase in rice production. It seems there is a positive relationship between these two variables and there is no research before doing studies about whether this relationship is statistically significant or not. Because in some countries, there are many determinants that have crucial affect to rice production than exporting. In this study, I will explore this correlation and fill this gap in the Vietnam's rice market.

Macro Variables: GDP Growth and Employment in Agriculture

Higher GDP growth rates are often associated with increased demand for rice products, leading to greater production and economic growth. This can also enhance investment in agricultural infrastructure and advanced technology, further boosting rice output.

Similarly, to employment in agriculture, because humans are the main resources for agriculture, when employment in agriculture increases, motivation to increase output will rise too.

Rice production affects the economy. Dey (2020) in research in Bangladesh demonstrates that rice production and Bangladesh's gross domestic product (GDP) have a substantial and positive link. Furthermore, his study suggests that a 1% increase in rice production resulted in a 1.89% increase in GDP. In researching agriculture sector workers and rice production in Riau (2020), Yolla Yulianda and Rika Harini indicate that the effect of labor on rice production varies considerably each year. Generally, regencies classified as high in human resources (labor) produce rice production. Regencies that are classified as high in the number of workers, but rice production is still relatively low due to not optimal productivity. Absorption of workers in the agricultural sector generally decreases due to reduced employment.

This research examines the relationship in Vietnam rice market to know whether GDP growth, employment in agriculture have affected on rice production and whether these relationships are statistically significant.

Fertilizer Consumption

Fertilizer consumption has a complex relationship with rice yield. Proper nutrient management can substantially increase rice productivity. However, excessive, or improper fertilizer use can have negative environmental consequences. Nasrullah et al. (2021) indicate that rice production's fertilizer elasticity is less than 0.05, which is not statistically significant. It also demonstrates that this variable's effect on rice production is inelastic.

In conclusion, the relationship between rice output and inputs and socioeconomic factors is intricate and context specific. Comprehensive and sustainable strategies for rice production must consider these multifaceted interactions, incorporating measures that promote land use efficiency, trade balance, economic growth, and environmental sustainability. Future research in this field should continue to explore these relationships within the framework of both national and global food security and climate change mitigation.

2 Vietnam's Agricultural Sector

According to the General Statistics Office, as of mid-March 2023, the whole country planted 2922.3 thousand hectares of winter-spring rice fields, equal to 98.7% of the same period last year. In which, the Mekong River Delta reached 1478.7 thousand hectares, equaling 98.1% and harvested 792.4 thousand hectares, accounting for 53.6% of the cultivated area and equaling 101.9% of the same period the year before. Previously, the yield reached 71.2 tons/ha, an increase of 0.4 tons/ha; output is estimated at 10.5 million tons, down from 145.4 thousand tons due to a decrease in planted area of 28.1 thousand ha.

According to data from the General Department of Customs, Vietnam's rice exports in March 2023 reached a record of 961,608 tons, worth nearly 509 million USD, an increase of 80% in volume and 78% in value compared to the previous month, and at the same time increased 81% in volume and 93.5% in value compared to the same period but the year before. With this result, rice exports reversed from negative growth in the first two months of the year to growth rate of 23.4% in volume and 34.3% in value in the first quarter of 2023, reaching 1.85 million tons with a value of up to 981.4 million USD. This is the highest export volume in the first quarter in the past 12 years and the highest turnover in the first quarter ever observed.

Faced with the increasing demand for rice, it is necessary to consider and evaluate factors influencing rice productivity and have more appropriate policies in the next period, which is an urgent requirement not only in Vietnam but also very important for food security in many other countries that are facing the risk of shortages of food necessary for daily life.

3 Data and Methodology

3.1 Data Collection

For this analysis, data were collected over a 21-year period from 2000 to 2020, including rice output as the dependent variable and various inputs and socioeconomic factors as independent variables. These factors include rice cultivation area, rice export, GDP growth, employment in agriculture, and fertilizer consumption. The dataset comprises historical records from Vietnam General Statistics Office (GSO), Vietnam Food Association and the World Bank.

3.2 Methodology

When undertaking a comprehensive study to explore the relationship between rice output and a myriad of inputs and socioeconomic factors, selecting the appropriate statistical method is of paramount importance. In this research endeavor, the decision to employ Ordinary Least Squares (OLS) regression analysis as the method of choice is rooted in its robustness, interpretability, and applicability to the task at hand.

Because there are some issues that can affect to the reliability of the regression, before implementing modeling, it is essential to test two basic issues:

Multicollinearity: One of the assumptions of the classical linear regression model is that there is no perfect linear relationship among the regressors. The consequences of multicollinearity will be several. The OLS estimators are still BLUE, but one or more regression coefficients have large standard errors relative to the values of the coefficients, thereby making the *t*-ratios small. Even though some regression coefficients are statistically insignificant, the $R2$ value may be very high. Therefore, one may conclude (misleadingly) that the true values of these coefficients are not different from zero. Also, the regression coefficients may be very sensitive to small changes in the data, especially if the sample is relatively small. Additionally, in some cases, wrong expected signs of estimated coefficients are observed. The method used to detect multicollinearity include variance inflation factor (VIF) and correlation matrix. If VIF < 10: there is no sign of multicollinearity. If the correlation coefficient between the two variables is between $\pm$ 0.8: this shows low correlation and results from the model are reliable.

Heteroskedasticity: One of the assumptions of the classical linear regression (CLRM) is that the variance of u (the error term) is constant, or homoskedastic. The consequence of heteroskedasticity will be: The OLS estimators are still unbiased and consistent, yet the estimators are less efficient (i.e., the estimated standard errors may be unreliable). Thus, estimators are not the best linear unbiased estimators (BLUE); they are simply linear unbiased estimators. In the presence of heteroskedasticity, we need alternative methods to obtain the BLUE estimators. In short, the estimated standard errors are unreliable in the presence of heteroskedasticity.

A common method used to detect heteroskedasticity is Breusch-Pagan (BP) test. Estimate the OLS regression and obtain the squared OLS residuals from this regression. Regress the square residuals on the k regressors included in the model. The null hypothesis here is that the error variance is homoskedastic—that is, all the slope coefficients are simultaneously equal to zero. Use the F-test to test this hypothesis. If the null hypothesis is rejected, we can reject the hypothesis of homoskedasticity.

3.3 Model Specification

This study examines the complexity of rice production within Vietnamese economy by employing a regression model that captures the complex relationships between key economic variables and annual rice output. This model considers factors such as rice cultivation area, export dynamics, GDP growth, employment trends, and fertilizer consumption as determinants of rice productivity.

In the analysis of 21 annual observations on rice output alongside various explanatory factors, this study chosen Ordinary Least Squares (OLS) regression that is particularly well-suited for this time-series dataset due to its interpretability and efficiency in handling relatively small sample sizes. Despite the simplicity of OLS, its flexibility and robustness make it a suitable choice for analyzing the changes in agricultural output within our dataset. The OLS regression model was formulated as follows:

$$\begin{aligned}\text{Rice Output}_i = \beta 0 + \beta 1 \times \text{Rice Cultivation Area}_i + \beta 2 \times \text{Rice Export}_i \\ + \beta 3 \times \text{GDP Growth}_i + \beta 4 \times \text{Employment}_i + \beta 5 \\ \times \text{Fertilizer Consumption}_i + \varepsilon_i,\end{aligned}$$

where $\beta 0$, $\beta 1$, $\beta 2$, $\beta 3$, $\beta 4$, $\beta 5$ are unknown regression coefficients to be estimated. ε_i is the random error term, representing unexplained variability in rice output. The variables used in the model specification, their level, unit of measurement and sources are explained in Table 1.

The study follows several steps, including a description of the data, testing for multicollinearity and heteroskedasticity issues, and estimating and discussing the results. This will involve identifying the independent variables that affect rice output and determining whether these relationships are positive or negative.

Table 1 Variable description

Variables	Definition	Measurement units	Data source
Rice output	The annual rice production	Thousand tons	GSO
Rice cultivation area	The total area under rice cultivation	Hectares	GSO
Rice export	The volume of rice exports	Thousand tons	Vietnam Food Association
GDP growth	The annual change in gross domestic product (GDP)	Percentage	World Bank
Employment	Employment in agriculture (% of total employment)	Percentage	World Bank
Fertilizer consumption	Fertilizer consumption	Kilograms per hectare of arable land	World Bank

3.4 *Results and Discussion*

3.4.1 Data Analysis

The descriptive statistics of the distribution of dependent and independent factors of production is provided in Table 2.

Figure 1 shows the development of rice production in Vietnam. Rice output changed 31.38% from 32.5 thousand tons in 2000 to 42.7 thousand tons in 2020.

Figure 2 shows the development of development of rice cultivation area in Vietnam. The figure shows that the total area under rice cultivation fluctuated so much and tend to decrease.

Table 2 Descriptive analysis

Variables	Mean	Std dev	MIN	Max	Range	se
Rice_output	39,595.65	4379.99	32,108.40	45,091.00	12,982.60	955.79
Rice_cultivation_area	7546.40	195.24	7207.40	7902.50	695.10	42.61
Rice_export	5.42	1.32	3.25	7.72	4.47	0.29
GDP_growth	6.43	1.05	2.87	7.55	4.68	0.23
Fertilizer_consumption	385.54	57.75	286.73	483.86	197.12	12.60
Employment	49.03	9.10	32.61	65.26	32.64	1.99

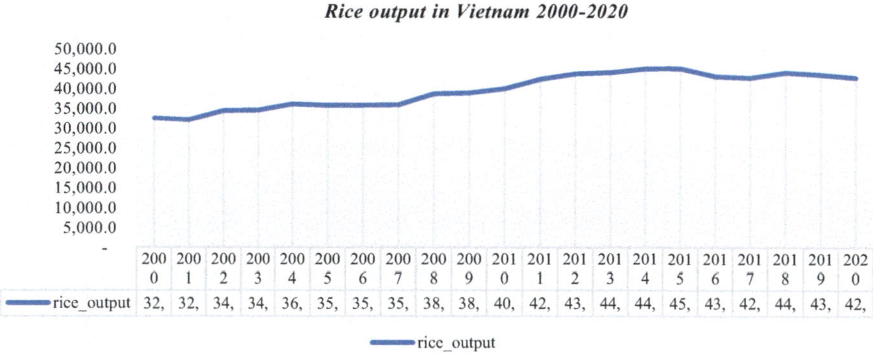

Fig. 1 Rice output in Vietnam 2000–2020

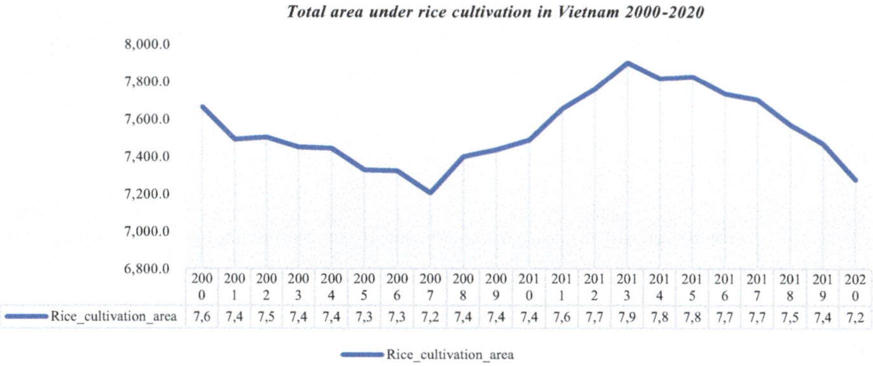

Fig. 2 Total area under rice cultivation in Vietnam 2000–2020

Figure 3 shows the development of rice export from Vietnam over time. The figure shows that the volume of rice exports in Vietnam fluctuated through 2000–2020, but the general trend is increasing.

Figure 4 illustrates the development of GDP growth in Vietnam for period 2000–2020. The figure shows that GDP growth in Vietnam maintained a high level at 6.5% on average per year. Although in 2020, Vietnam and global faced to Covid-19, which led to a big plummet in GDP, the GDP growth of Vietnam was still positive.

Figure 5 shows trend in employment in agriculture in Vietnam. The figure shows a clearly decreasing trend in relative to employment in agriculture (% of total employment) in Vietnam 2000–2020. It is easy to explain as industrialization and modernization gradually become popular in Vietnam. The farmers' participation in and migration to urban industrial zones is increasing, leading to a reduction in the labor force in the agricultural sector.

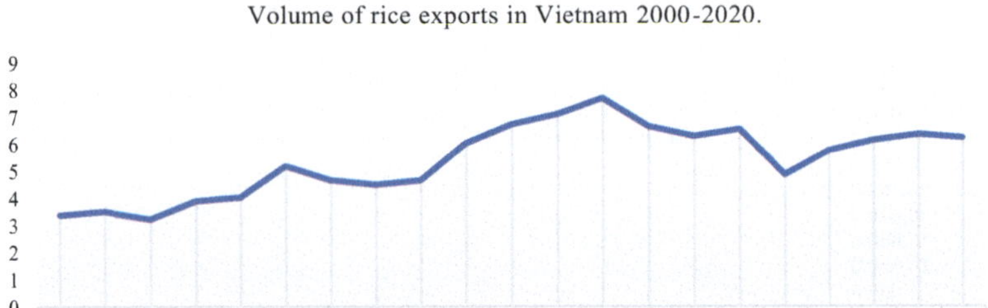

	2000	2001	2002	2003	2004	2005	2006	2007	2008	2009	2010	2011	2012	2013	2014	2015	2016	2017	2018	2019	2020
Rice_export	3.39	3.53	3.25	3.92	4.06	5.21	4.69	4.53	4.68	6.05	6.75	7.13	7.72	6.68	6.32	6.57	4.89	5.77	6.15	6.37	6.25

Fig. 3 Volume of rice exports in Vietnam 2000–2020

	2000	2001	2002	2003	2004	2005	2006	2007	2008	2009	2010	2011	2012	2013	2014	2015	2016	2017	2018	2019	2020
GDP_growth	6.7	6.1	6.3	6.9	7.5	7.5	6.9	7.1	5.6	5.4	6.4	6.4	5.5	5.5	6.4	6.9	6.6	6.9	7.4	7.3	2.8

Fig. 4 GDP growth in Vietnam 2000–2020

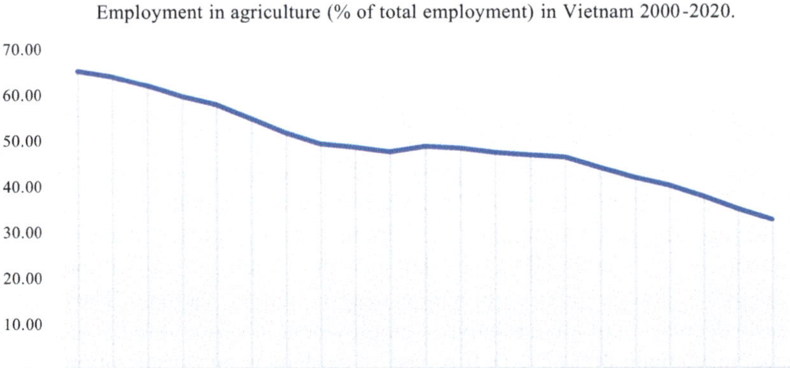

	2000	2001	2002	2003	2004	2005	2006	2007	2008	2009	2010	2011	2012	2013	2014	2015	2016	2017	2018	2019	2020
Employment	65.	63.	62.	59.	57.	54.	51.	49.	48.	47.	48.	48.	47.	46.	46.	44.	41.	40.	37.	34.	32.

Fig. 5 Employment in agriculture (% of total employment) in Vietnam 2000–2020

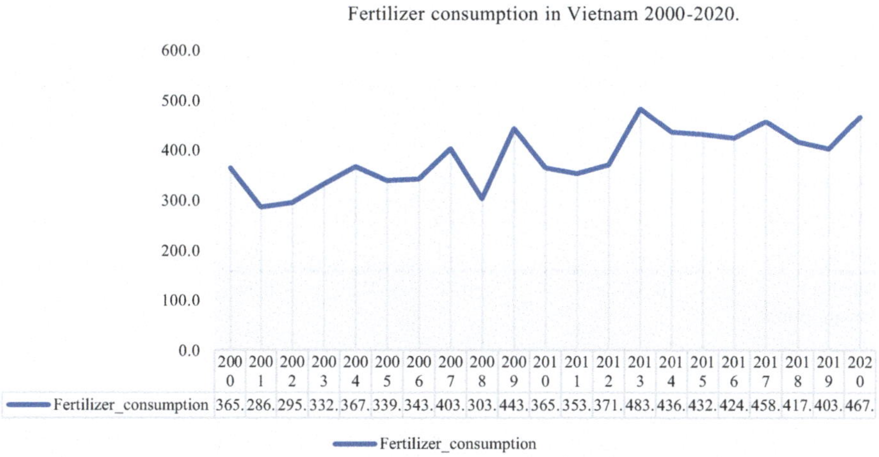

Fig. 6 Fertilizer consumption in Vietnam 2000–2020

Figure 6 shows that, similar to export volume, fertilizer consumption in Vietnam 2000–2020 fluctuated but the overall trend is increasing. Use of fertilizer is a key determinant of higher productivity and competitiveness of the farmers.

3.4.2 Multicollinearity Testing

Variance inflating factor is used to test for prevalence of multicollinearity. The results for different factors of rice production and export are presented in Table 3.

Table 3 shows that all coefficients are below 10. It illustrates that there is no multicollinearity or there is no perfect linear relationship among regression and thereby no evidence of confounded effects.

Table 4 reports the correlation coefficients of the rice production factors. As mentioned previously a coefficient below 0.80 indicated no serious correlation relationship between pairs of the production factors.

Hence, all correlation coefficients are between ± 0.8 show low correlation coefficients suggesting no prevalence of serious collinearity.

Table 3 Testing for multicollinearity

Rice-cultivation_area	Rice_export	GDP_growth	Employment	Fertilizer_consumption
1.65	2.72	1.15	3.68	2.62

Table 4 Correlation coefficients matrix

Variables	Rice-cultivation_ area	Rice_ export	GDP_ growth	Employment	Fertilizer_ consumption
Rice-cultivation_ area	1.00				
Rice_export	0.40	1.00			
GDP_growth	0.05	– 0.26	1.00		
Employment	– 0.11	– 0.71	0.27	1.00	
Fertilizer_ consumption	0.37	0.56	– 0.26	– 0.71	1.00

Table 5 Testing for heteroskedasticity

Variables	Estimate	Std. error	*t* value	Pr(>|*t*|)
(Intercept)	– 10,183,897.88	6,296,548.85	– 1.62	0.13
Rice_cultivation_ area	1250.74	1017.76	1.23	0.24
Rice_export	– 243,053.10	192,803.39	– 1.26	0.23
GDP_growth	70,860.31	157,378.04	0.45	0.66
Employment	16,207.24	32,572.19	0.50	0.63
Fertilizer_ consumption	3455.76	4335.08	0.80	0.44

3.4.3 Heteroskedasticity Testing

BP test is conducted to test for heteroskedasticity. The results are reported in Table 5. The null hypothesis (H_0): the error variance is homoskedastic—that is, all residuals are distributed with equal variance at each level of the predictor variable.

The residual standard error: 691,100 on 15 degrees of freedom. The multiple regression *R*-squared is 0.3114, and the adjusted *R*-squared is 0.08186. The *F*-statistic is estimated 1.357 on 5 and 15 DF, *p*-value: 0.2948. The test result suggests that it does not reject H_0. That means there is no heteroskedasticity.

Based on the results presented above, it is concluded that after checking for multicollinearity and heteroskedasticity, the results show that variables used in the model specification are suitable and reliable.

3.4.4 OLS Regression Results

Table 6 presents the OLS regression results from estimation of the rice output model. Tests of performance of the model are provided below the table.

Table 6 OLS regression results

Variables	Coefficient	t value	Pr(>|t|)
(Intercept)	– 16,435.67*	– 2.12	0.05
Rice_cultivation_area	9.19***	7.32	0.00
Rice_export	807.00***	3.39	0.00
GDP_growth	48.52	0.25	0.80
Employment	– 328.39***	– 8.17	0.00
Fertilizer_consumption	– 4.87	– 0.91	0.37

Significance codes: 0 '***' 0.001 '**' 0.01 '*' 0.05 '.' 0.1 '.'
Residual standard error: 852.4 on 15 degrees of freedom
Multiple R-squared: 0.9716, Adjusted R-squared: 0.9621
F-statistic: 102.6 on 5 and 15 DF, p-value: 4.712e−11

3.4.5 Results Explanation and Discussion

The estimation results in Table 6 show that rice_cultivation_area: $\beta 1 = 9.19$ and statistically significant. A 01 ha increase in the rice_cultivation_area on average will lead to 9.19 ton increase in rice output. The reported increase of 9.19 tons in rice output pertains to a yearly timeframe. Given that Vietnam typically cultivates two rice crops annually, it follows that each additional hectare of rice farming results in approximately a 4.5-ton increase in rice output per hectare for each crop cycle. The positive relationship between rice output and rice_cultivation_area aligns with findings from previous studies, as shown by Nasrullah et al. (2021) and Nkwi et al. (2022).

As industrialization increases and climate change makes farming more difficult, the vast majority of Vietnamese people have shifted location to big cities such as Hanoi and Ho Chi Minh City. By the end of 2022, Ho Chi Minh City's population density is estimated to be 14.73 times higher than the average for the country (if calculated on average 297 people/km^2). As for Hanoi, it is the second most populous city in the country (after Ho Chi Minh City) with a population of more than 8 million and 400 thousand people. Hanoi's average population density is about 2398 people/km^2, 8.2 times higher than the average population density of the country.

The changes and rapid flow of population to major cities lead to more and more land in the countryside being abandoned and depleted of nutrients. Faced with this problem, to ensure current and future food sources, the state needs to have specific policies to encourage the agricultural sector to create more favorable conditions for farmers in farming as well as ensure output for agricultural products. In addition, the government ought to have measures to help improve soil and increase rice productivity to ensure food supply security.

In the long term, the state needs to have policies to encourage and attract investment in opening production and business companies in rural areas instead of urban areas. This policy will create jobs for rural people, helping them to feel secure to stay in their hometown while working in the fields and working in factories instead of now having to leave their homes, fields, and family to set up a career in the cities.

In cities the living area is in serious shortage, and they cannot guarantee a stable and comfortable life for the people.

Rice export, with a coefficient of 807, is statistically significant. A 1% increase in rice exports corresponds to an 807 (thousands)-ton increase in rice output. This finding supports the idea of a positive correlation between rice export and rice production. In 1989, Vietnam exported rice for the first time, ending the rice shortage period and shifting to export orientation. After more than 30 years of exporting rice, up to now, Vietnamese rice is present in more than 150 countries and territories.

In the first 6 months of 2023, rice export turnover reached 4.24 million tons of rice with a value of 2.26 billion USD, an increase of 21.3% in volume and an increase of 32.2% in turnover compared to the same period in 2022 (Vietnam National Trade Repository, 2023). The average export price reached 533 USD/ton, up 9% compared to the average level in the same period in 2022.

The Asian market is the largest export region in the first 6 months of 2023, reaching nearly 3.3 million tons, accounting for 77.7% of total exports, up 35.8% over the same period in 2022; Next is the European market area, accounting for a small proportion (about 2%) of Vietnam's total exports, reaching 84.5 thousand tons, growing more than 28% over the same period in 2022. The African market grows, rice exports reach more than 631 thousand tons, accounting for 15% of total rice exports, up nearly 5% over the same period in 2022.

Specifically, the Philippines—Vietnam's largest rice import market—accounts for nearly 40.1% of total exports in the first 6 months of 2023 (equivalent to exports of nearly 1.7 million tons), an increase of 7% compared to compared to the same period in 2022. Ranked 2nd is China, accounting for over 16% of total exports (equivalent to 677.4 thousand tons), an increase of 60.7% over the same period in 2022. Indonesia ranks 3rd, accounting for 11.6% of the country's total rice exports (equivalent to 492.8 thousand tons), an increase of 15 times in volume and turnover compared to the same period in 2022.

Regarding the type structure, the regular white rice category continues to account for the largest proportion, reaching 55.5% of the total export volume (equivalent to about 2.35 million tons); followed by fragrant rice of all kinds, accounting for 24.2% of the total export volume (about 1 million tons); sticky rice category ranks third, accounting for about 8.5% of total export volume (volume reaching about 358.5 thousand tons); broken rice accounts for 7.6% of total exports (volume is about 324.1 thousand tons).

However, in the face of a food shortage in the world, Vietnam needs to take measures to increase export output, contributing to bringing Vietnamese rice to the world to partially solve the global food shortage and demand.

To accomplish this, the government needs to have specific policies to create conditions for rice export. Encourage export for private enterprises, and at the same time, the government needs to have programs to improve understanding of international trade and export standards to help people improve production efficiency and rice quality to meet the high requirements of export goods.

This study finds that GDP growth is not statistically significant in explaining rice output level and variations. Conversely, employment, with a coefficient of – 328.39, emerges as statistically significant. This means that a 1% increase in employment in agriculture results in a decrease of 328.39 tons in rice output. This trend can be seen in Figs. 1 and 5, where despite a decrease in agricultural employment throughout the year, rice output continues to rise. This outcome underscores the impact of technological advancements in agricultural practices, which speed up processes, enhance yield, and improve harvest quality, thereby increasing productivity while requiring less labor. In the context of fertilizer consumption, it is noteworthy that it is not statistically significant in explaining rice output.

Under pressure from the reduction of labor resources in agriculture in Vietnam, technology emerges as a potential solution to this challenge. The government should implement policies to incentivize farmers to adopt technology and boost productivity. This can be achieved through specific instructions outlining the benefits and usage of modern machinery and equipment in various stages of production, harvesting, and storage. Moreover, encouraging and supporting businesses to offer agricultural machinery at affordable prices, along with clear user instructions and assistance for maintenance, repair, and warranty services, is essential.

Additionally, the government should incentivize the import of machinery and advanced technology to meet the growing domestic demand. By facilitating access to advanced equipment, the agricultural sector can modernize and mitigate the impact of labor shortages.

4 Conclusion and Recommendations

In conclusion, the study considered five factors affecting rice output in Vietnam: total area under rice cultivation, volume of rice exports, annual GDP growth, employment in agriculture, and fertilizer consumption. Only three of these factors impact rice output. The total area under rice cultivation and the volume of rice exports positively affect rice output. However, employment in agriculture negatively impacts rice output due to the labor-intensive nature of rice farming. GDP growth and fertilizer consumption were not statistically significant in explaining changes in rice yield. Vietnam is renowned for its wet rice agriculture. As the cultivated area fluctuates, the number of workers decreases because of urbanization, but annual output still increases due to specific agricultural extension policies from the government to create the most favorable conditions for farmers. Cultivation activities such as testing new rice varieties and introducing new fertilizers into cultivation both bring high productivity and protect the environment to reduce the increase in climate change. In addition, the government also builds infrastructure smoothly in the countryside, creating conditions for people to combine working in urban areas and farm and harvest rice. With the contribution of science and technology, Vietnamese agriculture is poised to transition into a modernized sector, fostering prosperity for its people and nation, while also supporting global food security.

References

Beaman, L., Karlan, D., Thuysbaert, B., & Udry, C. (2013). Profitability of fertilizer: Experimental evidence from female rice farmers in Mali. *American Economic Review, 103*(3), 381–386.

Bustos, P., Caprettini, B., & Ponticelli, J. (2016). Agricultural productivity and structural transformation: Evidence from Brazil. *American Economic Review, 106*(6), 1320–1365.

Chandio, A. A., Nasereldin, Y. A., Anh, D. L. T., Tang, Y., Sargani, G. R., & Zhang, H. (2022). The impact of technological progress and climate change on food crop production: Evidence from Sichuan—China. *International Journal of Environmental Research and Public Health, 19*(16), 9863.

Dey, S. (2020). Relationship between rice production, fisheries production and gross domestic product (GDP) in Bangladesh: Co integrating regression analysis (1971–2017). *International Journal of Economics and Financial Issues, 1*(4), 201–216.

Fiszbein, M. (2022). Agricultural diversity, structural change, and long-run development: Evidence from the United States. *American Economic Journal: Macroeconomics, 14*(2), 1–43.

Le, T. T. H. (2016). Effects of climate change on rice yield and rice market in Vietnam. Published online by Cambridge University Press, November 21, 2016.

Nasrullah, M., Rizwanullah, M., Yu, X., Jo, H., Sohail, M. T., & Liang, L. (2021). Autoregressive distributed lag (ARDL) approach to study the impact of climate change and other factors on rice production in South Korea. *Journal of Water and Climate Change, 12*(6), 2256–2270.

Nguyen, T.- T., Nguyen, T. T., & Grote, U. (2023). Credit, shocks and production efficiency of rice farmers in Vietnam. *Economic Analysis and Policy, 77*, 780–791.

Nkwi, G. E., Mukhtar, U., & Fani, D. C. R. (2022). Resource-use efficiency of rice production in Kura Local Government Area of Kano State, Nigeria. *FUDMA Journal of Agriculture and Agricultural Technology, 8*(1), 131–141.

Vietnam National Trade Repository. (2023, October 30). Rice exports set record in just 10 months of 2023. https://vntr.moit.gov.vn/news/rice-exports-set-record-in-just-10-months-of-2023.

Yulianda, Y., & Harini, R. (2020). Agriculture sector workers and rice production in Riau Province in 2010–2018. In *E3S Web of Conferences* (Vol. 200, p. 04001). EDP Sciences.

Nguyen Thi Kieu Nhung is a postgraduate student majoring in Applied Economics in the Vietnam – the Netherlands Programme. She is currently working in the agricultural sector, where Vietnam has developed numerous factories and farms specializing in crops such as corn, cassava, and rice. Her work involves an R&D team specializing in developing machines and software in high-tech agriculture such as self-charging drones for crop protection, irrigation, and fertilization as well as high-capacity dryers.

Chapter 4
Strategy of Productivity and Sustainability of Rice Farms in Vietnam

Doan Trong Nhan

Abstract Rice, a staple food supporting over half of the global population, faces increasing challenges due to climate change, rising hunger levels, exacerbated by factors such as the COVID-19 pandemic, geopolitical conflicts, and export bans like India's. Vietnam, a significant rice exporter, must navigate these challenges while seizing economic and development opportunities. However, its rice agriculture has faced transformations and sustainability issues over the past two decades, including land fragmentation and climate change vulnerabilities. To address these challenges and contribute to the global food security, Vietnam's current strategy emphasizes mechanization, environmental awareness, adaptation, and collaboration, along with land consolidation, as cost-effective solutions to boost productivity, reduce poverty, and to mitigate climate change impacts.

Keywords Efficiency and productivity · Rice farms · Land consolidation · Agricultural transformation · Vietnam

1 Challenges of Hunger and Food Insecurity

Rice is grown in more than 100 countries with 90% of total global production coming from Asian countries. Rice is the staple food of more than half of the world's population, providing more than 20% of calories consumed worldwide, especially in East and South Asia, the Middle East, the West Indies and Latin America. Fukagawa and Ziska (2019, 2019b). FAO estimated that between 691 and 783 million people faced hunger in 2022, increasing by 122 million people compared to year 2019 (FAO, 2023). Although there were improvements in addressing hunger in Asia and Latin America, the prevalence of hunger continued to increase in Western Asia, the Caribbean, and all regions within Africa (FAO, 2023). Africa has a significantly higher hunger rate

D. T. Nhan (✉)
University of Economics Ho Chi Minh City, Ho Chi Minh City, Vietnam
e-mail: nhan.dt@vnp.edu.vn

P. K. Nam and A. Heshmati (eds.), *Recent Trends in Vietnam's Rapid Economic Development*, Frontiers in South and Southeast Asian Development Research,
https://doi.org/10.1007/978-981-97-6079-4_4

within its population compared to other world regions, with nearly 20% experiencing hunger, whereas the hunger figures are 8.5% for Asia, 6.5% for Latin America and the Caribbean, and 7.0% for Oceania (FAO, 2023).

The UN's goal of ending hunger by 2030 is facing a huge setback due to recent events such as the impact of the COVID-19 pandemic, the Russia–Ukraine war and most recently the impact of the El Nino phenomenon that has caused India to ban rice export. The COVID-19 pandemic, through measures like lockdowns and trade restrictions, has exacerbated hunger, particularly in low- and middle-income countries, by disrupting agricultural production and raising concerns about food access for millions of people globally (Aborode et al., 2021). As FAO informed, the number of undernourished had significantly increased from 701 to 743 million people in the year 2020 and it continued to reach peak 797 million in a year later (Appendix 1). Furthermore, India, the world's leading rice exporter (40% of global market share), recently imposed a ban on rice exports due to its severe weather conditions. India plays a substantial role in supplying rice to crucial markets in Asia and sub-Saharan Africa, thus leaving these regions susceptible to disruptions in the rice market (Appendix 2).

Food and Agriculture Organization of United Nations (FAO) estimated that around 600 million people may suffer chronic malnutrition in 2030. This presents a significant obstacle for leading rice-exporting nations like Vietnam as they strive to achieve the UN's goal of ending hunger, but it also represents an economic development opportunity for Vietnam's rice industry. Enhancing rice production and productivity, leveraging the advantages of rice cultivation, not only contributes to global food security but also offers substantial economic development prospects for Vietnam.

Rest of this paper is organized as follows. In Sect. 2, the challenges in rice production sustainability in Vietnam are discussed. Strategies for Agricultural Development and Climate Resilience in Vietnam are outlined in Sect. 3. The final Sect. 4 provides conclusion and recommendations.

2 Challenges to Sustainable Rice Production in Vietnam

Over the past two decades, Vietnam's wet rice agriculture industry has undergone significant transformations. In 2000, rice cultivation occupied a substantial 66.4% of the total cultivated area for all crops. 10 years later, this figure had declined to 53.3%, marking a notable drop of 13.1 percentage points compared to 2000. In 2020, this trend continued, with the rice cultivation area decreasing to 50.3%, representing a further reduction of 16.1 percentage points. Despite the shrinking rice cultivation area, there has been a shift toward the use of certified rice varieties and diverse cultivation methods, tailored to local weather conditions. These changes have led to consistently high yields and an increased proportion of high-quality rice with significant export value. In 2020, approximately 40% of the export turnover was attributed to high-quality and fragrant rice varieties (GSO, 2022).

However, over the analyzed period from 2000 to 2022, distinct trends emerged in rice cultivation area and production volume. The data reveals a consistent decrease in total rice cultivation area, notably commencing after its peak in 2010 at 7,489,000 ha (Appendix 3). In contrast, total rice production volume displayed an upward trajectory from 2000 to 2015, culminating in a zenith of 45,091,000 tons in 2015. However, subsequent years witnessed a decline in production, marked by intermittent fluctuations. Notably, a noteworthy inverse relationship between cultivation area and production volume emerged; as the area under rice cultivation diminished, production volume generally increased until 2015, potentially reflecting advancements in productivity and rice yield. Yet, in recent years (2016–2022), both cultivation area and production volume have shown a declining pattern, raising concerns about the sustainability and challenges of maintaining rice production levels.

One of the inherent causes that inhibit rice production productivity is land fragmentation. Land fragmentation, as defined by King and Burton (1982), refers to the situation where landholders' plots are dispersed and intermixed with the land of other farmers. One of the well-documented drawbacks associated with land fragmentation, as evidenced by Tran and Van Vu (2019), is the escalation of production costs, which ultimately hampers farming efficiency. Moreover, this fragmentation has an adverse effect on the adoption of farm mechanization, as highlighted by Nguyen and Warr (2020). One of the key drivers behind land fragmentation was initiated by redistribution of land occurring during the government's decollectivization process in the late 1980s. In this period, each household was allocated land based on factors such as the number of household members and specific geographical locations. This allocation aimed to ensure a fair distribution of land area and soil quality among households (Do et al., 2023). Furthermore, land fragmentation condition was worsened due to the custom of dividing land among descendants.

Besides that, the deficiency in mechanization within the agricultural sector is undeniably at the core of the shortage of production productivity. Although Vietnam's agriculture had addressed a remarkable change in mechanization in the period 2011–2021 (Chu Khoi, 2022), a significant portion, approximately 70%, of the agricultural tasks still rely on manual labor, with mechanization primarily employed in activities like tree felling and transportation, leaving crucial stages such as planting, maintenance, and firefighting largely untouched. Mechanization in the industry is slow, contributing to substantial post-harvest losses, with the current loss rate in the country at 13–16%, in contrast to Thailand's 7–10% (Do, 2021). Additionally, this is exacerbated by inadequate infrastructure and technology for preserving and processing agricultural products, ultimately hindering value addition and deep processing of rice products. Furthermore, the efficiency of transportation, loading, and unloading processes remains relatively low, ranging from 2 to 5%. Domestically manufactured mechanical equipment only fulfills around 33% of the market demand, and there is a shortage of skilled labor in the mechanical manufacturing sector (Chu Khoi, 2022). The absence of structured development, limited information exchange between technology suppliers and consumers, inadequate state support, complex technical processes related to mechanization, and a lack of incentive policies for advancing science, technology, and infrastructure training all contribute to these challenges of the sector.

Labor productivity stagnates in rice farming despite great geographical and soil advantages. In rural regions, agricultural land parcels are typically small and fragmented, making it challenging to implement modern technologies such as mechanization for land preparation and other farming tasks. The average agricultural land size per household is 0.94 ha in the Mekong Delta, 1.83 ha in the Central Highlands, and 0.85 ha nationwide. As a result, agricultural operations predominantly rely on labor-intensive and traditional low productive methods. The absence of mechanisms to facilitate land consolidation means that labor-intensive agricultural practices persist despite a diminishing rural workforce, thus impeding labor productivity in rural areas. With a slowdown in labor growth, reduced migration from rural to urban areas, and limited available arable land to absorb surplus labor, there is an immediate need to enhance labor productivity, especially in the agricultural sector. Additionally, the farming population's skill levels are relatively low as land is typically passed down from one generation to the next, and higher education appears to have limited relevance for those continuing to work on family farms. This farming low skill level further hinders the adoption of new technologies when opportunities arise.

The irrigation system is not effective, causing water waste and increasing production costs. The changing demographics, evolving dietary preferences, and the emergence of new value chains in food and crop production have led to a rising demand for irrigated agriculture in Vietnam. However, many irrigation projects are hindered by incomplete structures and operational water losses, causing them to function at only 60–70% of their efficient capacity (Asian Development Bank, 2022). Vietnam's agricultural water productivity lags behind that of other Asian countries, with a water productivity of 0.03 USD/m^3 for rice, which is half that of China and three times lower than that of India (Appendix 4). This low water productivity is a concern, especially in the context of climate change and growing competition for water resources. Additionally, water demand is projected to increase by 32% by 2030 during the dry season (World Bank Group, 2019), with agriculture accounting for the majority of this demand.

Climate change, particularly the rising sea levels, has begun to impact rice production in the Mekong Delta region of Vietnam. In 2019, water with a salinity level of 4‰ infiltrated inland to varying distances, reaching approximately 100 km along the Hau River, 75 km along the Ham Luong River, 70 km along the Co Chien River, and nearly 60 km along the Cua Tieu River, the Cua Dai River, and the Cai Long River (Lavane, et al., 2023). Additionally, Lavane et al. (2023) also concluded that rice productivity was negatively affected not only by drought but also by elevated humidity levels. The combined effects of drought and saltwater intrusion have led to a reduction in the rice cultivation area and a deterioration in land quality. World Bank Group & Asian Development Bank (2021) shows that Vietnam is one of the five nations most impacted by climate change because of its extensive coastline, large population of economically active people in coastal areas and high dependency on agriculture, natural resources, and forestry. Recently, Vietnam has experienced many extreme weather events, such as floods, storms, and droughts, that harm the agricultural sector and the nation's food security.

3 Strategies for Agricultural Development and Climate Resilience in Vietnam

In Decision No. 858/QD-TTg, The Prime Minister of Vietnam set goals of ensuring productivity, quality, economic and social efficiency and agricultural environmental protection in concentrated mechanized agricultural production areas. Developing modern, effective and sustainable agricultural product processing, etc., striving to turn Vietnam into an agricultural product processing center.

Enhancing agricultural mechanization documentally is mentioned in the Prime Minister's approvals. The outline of a strategy is aimed at achieving a 70% level of agricultural mechanization and agricultural processing by 2030. It is initial to boost awareness and adoption of mechanization within the agricultural sector, several significant measures have been proposed. Primarily, there is a focus on raising awareness about the role of mechanization in sustainable agricultural development among farmers and communities. Leveraging various media channels such as television, radio, social networks, and websites is identified as a potent means to disseminate information on mechanization to a wide audience. Notably, United Nations International Children's Emergency Fund (UNICEF) data indicates a high level of media accessibility in the Mekong Delta region, with 87% having access to television, 97% owning mobile phones, and 72% having internet access (UNICEF, 2021). Additionally, the creation of multimedia content centered around mechanization is recommended to augment comprehension and acceptance of this technology within the agricultural community. Concurrently, it is crucial to establish an enabling environment that allows individuals and agricultural scientists to access financial support packages, which are vital for the application of science and technology in production advancement. Collaboration with educational institutions and training centers plays a pivotal role in imparting mechanization knowledge to the younger generation of farmers. This approach aims to foster community networks where farmers and experts can engage in knowledge exchange, share experiences, and offer mutual support.

Land consolidation is an effective solution to increase farming efficiency. This does yield favorable outcomes by lowering particular expenses tied to land preparation and harvesting for rice farmers (Do et al., 2023). The study's results reveals that households engaged in land consolidation experience reduced land preparation costs, amounting to approximately purchase chasing power (PPP) $24.35 per ha, and diminished harvesting expenses, with savings of about PPP $41.82 per ha in comparison to those not participating in consolidation efforts.

Furthermore, when evaluating the potential impact on poverty reduction, the analysis underscores that land consolidation carries a notable positive effect. This effect becomes evident when measuring poverty at varying income thresholds, such as PPP $2.05 (Vietnam's poverty line) and PPP $3.20 (the World Bank's poverty line) per capita per day. In essence, this implies that land consolidation has the potential to contribute significantly to poverty alleviation among rice farming households, particularly when considering specific income levels (Do et al., 2023).

Besides the mechanism, adapting new innovation to rice production processes is highly effective. The International Rice research Institute (IRRI) is deploying its sustainable intensification program by working with partners to develop practices to help reduce greenhouse gas emissions from the rice farming landscapes through the promotion of water-saving technologies such as alternate wetting and drying (AWD). AWD is one of the effective technologies for conserving water resources, and reducing greenhouse gas (GHG) emissions without yield penalty (IRRI, 2023). In this irrigation method, water is applied a few days after the ponded water has drained or disappeared from the fields. Consequently, the fields undergo a cycle of being alternately flooded and then allowed to dry. The duration of time that the soil remains unflooded between successive waterings can vary, ranging from short period as 1 day to more than 10 days. The specific length of this period depends on various factors, including the type of soil, prevailing weather conditions, and the growth stage of the crop being cultivated.

In a study conducted in An Giang province of Vietnam, Leon and Izumi (2022) demonstrated that AWD not only contributes to water conservation but also exhibits significant enhancements in the availability of seed resources by 5.1%. Furthermore, it results in noteworthy reductions in fuel and electricity consumption ranging from 11 to 26%, and a decrease in fertilizer usage (specifically N and P_2O_5) by 8.9% to 10.8%, respectively. Remarkably, these improvements in resource utilization are achieved while maintaining a consistent yield productivity of 6.2 tons per ha. Moreover, AWD implementation leads to a substantial reduction in emissions to the atmosphere, encompassing methane (CH_4) emissions, burning-related emissions, greenhouse gas (GHG) emissions, and overall life cycle GHG indicators.

Climate change makes rice crops globally vulnerable. Greenhouse gases such as carbon dioxide (CO_2), nitrous oxide (N_2O), and methane (CH_4) are primary contributors to global warming, alongside human activities like fossil fuel burning and changes in solar irradiance (Hussain et al., 2020). Various approaches have been proposed to mitigate and adapt to climate change. Enhancing crop performance is a highly effective solution to alleviate impacts such as heat, chilling, and drought. Developing a climate-resilient rice system is essential to address the growing risks of climate change. Traditional breeding methods, molecular techniques, genome editing, and speed breeding tools can significantly help develop rice varieties that withstand climate change challenges.

4 Conclusion

Rice is a vital global food staple, primarily grown in Asia and supporting over half the world's population. However, global hunger is increasing, particularly in regions like Western Asia, the Caribbean, and Africa. The United Nations' goal of eradicating hunger by 2030 faces significant challenges, including the COVID-19 pandemic, the Russia–Ukraine conflict, and India's ban on rice exports. India, as the world's top rice exporter with a 40% global market share, through its restrictive policies can have a significant impact on crucial markets in Asia and Africa. For rice-exporting nations like Vietnam, this presents both challenges and economic opportunities. Increasing rice production is essential for global food security and economic development.

Vietnam's wet rice agriculture has transformed over the past two decades. Rice cultivation area has decreased, and production volumes have fluctuated. Initially, production increased until 2015, reflecting improved productivity. However, subsequent years saw declines in both area and production, driven by issues like land fragmentation, high production costs, limited mechanization, and post-harvest losses. Despite increased productivity of land, it is difficult for agriculture to compete with manufacturing in hiring labor and sub-urban property development. Inadequate irrigation infrastructure and low water productivity worsen concerns, especially given climate change and rising water demand. Mechanization, although growing, still relies heavily on manual labor. Climate change, particularly rising sea levels, threatens rice production in the Mekong Delta. These challenges underscore Vietnam's vulnerability to climate change due to its extensive coastline and reliance on agriculture. Addressing these issues requires comprehensive national strategies to boost productivity, mechanization, and climate resilience of the sector.

Efforts to enhance production efficiency are crucial for Vietnam to contribute significantly to the UN's goal of eradicating hunger while establishing itself as a global rice producer and warehouse. Emphasizing mechanization, awareness, and collaboration to enhance productivity and sustainability are keys for achieving goals of ensuring Vietnam's rice productivity, besides land consolidation. Identified as a cost-effective solution, land consolidation contributes to poverty reduction, while innovative techniques like alternate wetting and drying (AWD) and climate-resilient rice farming systems are crucial for mitigating climate change impacts and improving resource utilization in the agricultural sector and its inter- and intra-national competitiveness.

Appendices

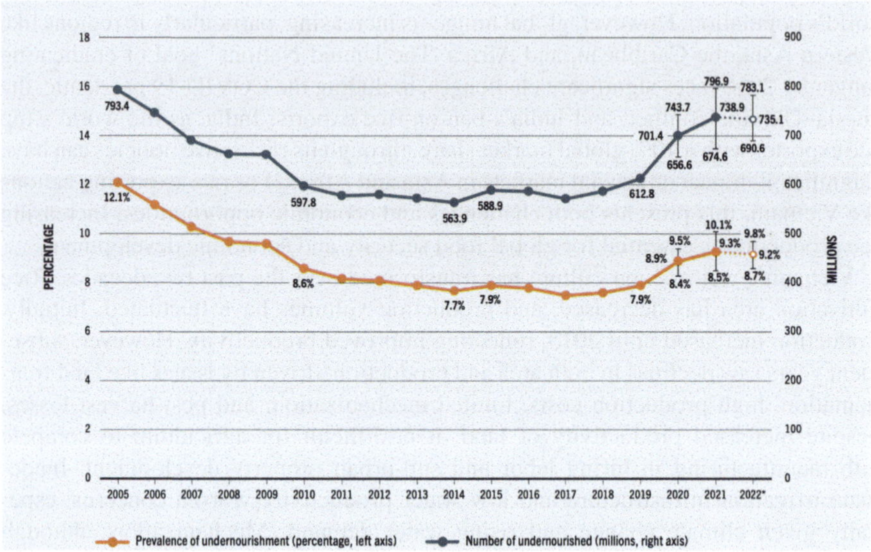

Appendix 1 Prevalence of global undernourishment, 2005–2022 (in million)

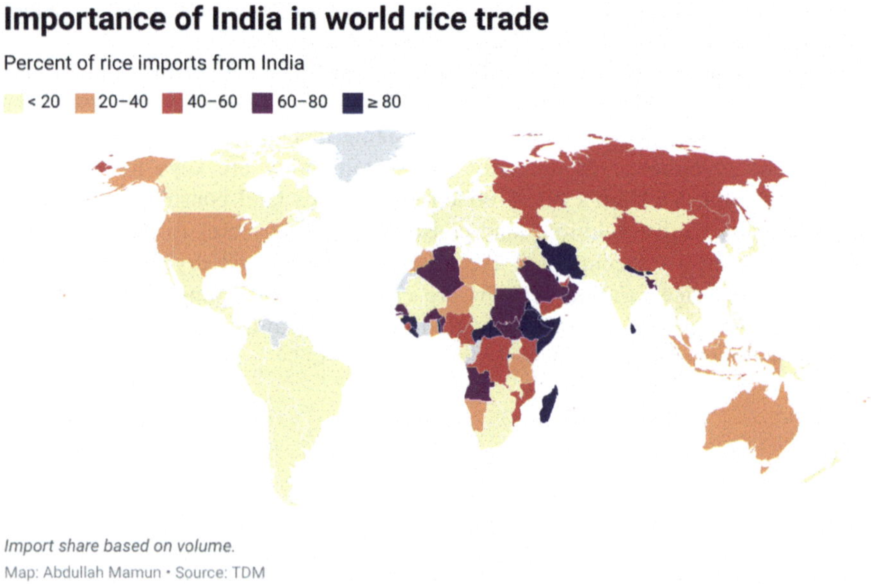

Appendix 2 Importance of India in the world rice trade

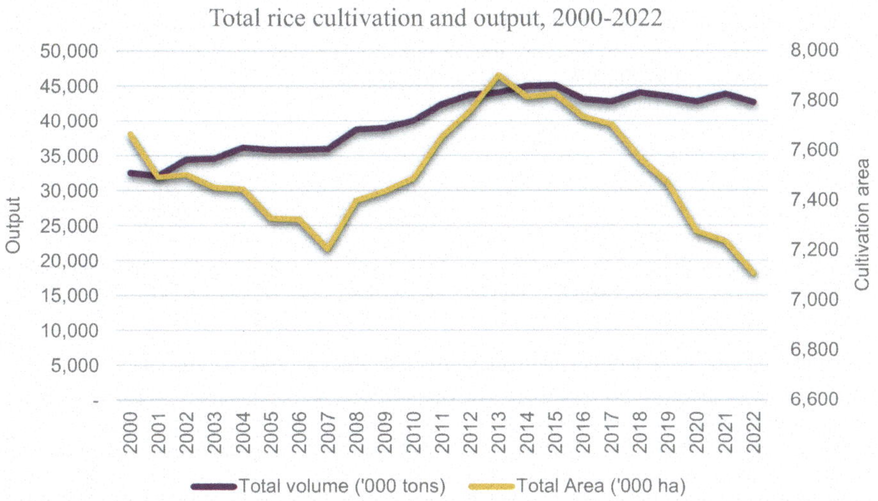

Appendix 3 Total rice cultivation and output in Vietnam, 2000–2022. *Source* General Statistics Office of Vietnam

Appendix 4 Water productivity in rice production

Country	Output per unit of (US$/Ha)	Irrigation water (US$/m^3)
Vietnam	654	0.03
China	1541	0.06
India	988	0.09

References

Aborode, A. T., Ogunsola, S. O., & Adeyemo, A. O. (2021). A crisis within a crisis: COVID-19 and hunger in African children. *The American Journal of Tropical Medicine and Hygiene, 104*(1), 30–31.

Asian Development Bank. (2022). *Agriculture, natural resources and rural development sector assessment, strategy and road Map—Viet Nam 2021–2025*. Manila, Philippines: Asian Development Bank.

Do., M. H., Nguyen, T. T., & Grote, U. (2023). Land consolidation, rice production, and agricultural transformation: Evidence from household panel data for Vietnam. *Economic Analysis and Policy, 77*, 157–173. ISSN 0313-5926.https://doi.org/10.1016/j.eap.2022.11.010

Do, T. B. T. (2021). *Vietnam institute of strategy and policy doe industry and trade: Vietnam's rice exports: Opportunities and challenges*. Retrieved from https://vioit.org.vn/en/strategy-policy/vietnam-s-riceexports--opportunities-and-challenges-4404.4144.html#:~:text=Besides%20opportunities%2C%20Vietnam%27s%20rice%20export,is%20a%20sensitive%20commodity%2C%20many

FAO, Ifad, UNICEF, WFP and WHO. (2023). The state of food security and nutrition in the world. Urbanization, agrifood systems transformation and healthy diets across the rural–urban continuum. *Rome, FAO*. https://doi.org/10.4060/cc3017en

Fukagawa, N. K., & Ziska, L. H. (2019). Rice: importance for global nutrition. *Journal of Nutition Science Vitaminol (Tokyo), 65*(Supplement), S2–S3. Retrived from: https://doi.org/10.3177/jnsv.65.S2. PMID: 31619630.

Glauber. J., & Abdullah, M. (2023). *International Food Policy Research Institute: India's new ban on rice exports: Potential threats to global supply, prices, and food security*. Retrieved from https://www.ifpri.org/blog/indias-new-ban-rice-exports-potential-threats-global-supplyprices-andfoodsecurity#:~:text=Blog%20%3A%20Issue%20Post-,India%27s%20new%20ban%20on%20rice%20exports%3A%20Potential%20threats%20to,supply%2C%20prices%2C%20and%20food%20security&text=On%20July%2020%2C%20India%20announced,October%202022%20(Figure%201)

GSO. (2022). TỔNG CỤC THỐNG KÊ*: Phát Triển Lúa Gạo Theo Hướng Hiệu Quả, Bền Vững*. (2022). Retrieved from https://www.gso.gov.vn/du-lieu-va-so-lieu-thongke/2022/05/phat-trien-lua-gao-theo-huong-hieu-qua-ben-vung/

Hussain, S., et al. (2020). Rice production under climate change: Adaptations and mitigating strategies. In S. Fahad et al. (Eds.), *Environment, climate, plant and vegetation growth*. Springer. Retrieved from: https://www.researchgate.net/publication/342150703_Rice_Production_Under_Climate_Change_Adaptations_and_Mitigating_Strategies#:~:text=Therefore%2C%20mitigating%20and%20adaptation%20strategies,organic%20fertilizers%2C%20and%20by%20developing

IRRI. (2023). *International rice research institute: IRRI holds training on revolutionary water saving technology for sustainable rice production*. Retrieved from https://www.irri.org/news-and-events/news/irri-holds-training-revolutionary-water-savingtechnology-sustainable-rice

Khoi, C. (2022). *VnEconomy: Agricultural mechanization still struggling*. Retrieved from https://en.vneconomy.vn/agricultural-mechanization-still-struggling.htm

King, R., & Burton, S. (1982). Land fragmentation: Notes on a fundamental rural spatial problem. *Progress in Human Geography, 6*(4), 475–494. https://doi.org/10.1177/030913258200600401

Lampayan, R. M., Yadav, S., & Humphreys, E. (2023). *IRRI rice knowledge bank: Saving water with alternate wetting drying (AWD)*. Retrieved from: http://www.knowledgebank.irri.org/training/fact-sheets/water-management/saving-wateralternate-wetting-drying-awd

Lavane, K., Kumar, P., Meraj, G., Han, T. G., Ngan, L. H. B., Lien, B. T. B., Van Ty, T., Thanh, N. T., Downes, N. K., Nam, N. D. G., et al. (2023). Assessing the effects of drought on rice yields in the Mekong Delta. *Climate, 11*(1), 13. https://doi.org/10.3390/cli11010013

Leon, A., & Izumi, T. (2022). Impacts of alternate wetting and drying on rice farmers' profits and life cycle greenhouse gas emissions in An Giang Province in Vietnam. *Journal of Cleaner Production, 354*, 131621, ISSN 0959-6526. Retrived from: https://doi.org/10.1016/j.jclepro.2022.131621

Nguyen, H. Q., & Warr, P. (2020). Land consolidation as technical change: Economic impacts in rural Vietnam. *World Development, 127*, 104750. ISSN 0305-750X. https://doi.org/10.1016/j.worlddev.2019.104750

Tran, T. Q., & Vu, H. V. (2019). Land fragmentation and household income: First evidence from rural Vietnam. *Land Use Policy, 89*, 104247, ISSN 0264-8377.https://doi.org/10.1016/j.landusepol.2019.104247

UNICEF. (2021). *Điều tra SDGCW Việt Nam 2020–2021*. Retrieved from https://www.unicef.org/vietnam/media/8771/file/Truyền%20thông,%20CNTT%20và%20internet.pdf

World Bank Group. (2019). *Vietnam: Toward a safe, clean, and resilient water system*. © World Bank, Washington, DC.

World Bank Group & Asian Development Bank. (2021). *Climate risk country profile: Vietnam*. World Bank.

Part II
Environment and Energy

Chapter 5
Implementation of Circular Economy and Sustainable Development in Vietnam

Hieu Minh Ngo and Thanh Thien Trang Duong

Abstract This paper contributes to the growing literature on implementation of circular economy and sustainable development in Vietnam. The research employs the Sankey diagram and material taxonomy of the European Union to construct a representative material flow database for Vietnam. Within the scope of this study, we exclusively focus on two pivotal indicators, namely Domestic Material Consumption (DMC) and Resource Productivity, for our material flow analysis. Accordingly, we have endeavored to gather data that elucidate the flow of selective key materials, including wood (representing biomass), iron and steel (representing metallic minerals), coal and crude oil (symbolizing fossil energy), and cement clinker (representing non-metallic minerals). Our results delineate an upward trend in the DMC index for all flow of materials from 2016 to 2022, concurrently with a diminishing trend observed in the Resource Productivity index over the same duration. This serves as evidence indicating that Vietnam has ineffectively implemented the circular economy model. Nevertheless, there is a positive signal suggesting the commencement of Vietnam's initial strides toward a circular economy, notably following the enactment of Decision 687 and the revision of the Law on Environmental Protection (LEP) by the Vietnamese government in 2022.

Keywords Circular economy · Sustainable development · Domestic material consumption · Resource productivity · Material flow analysis

H. M. Ngo (✉) · T. T. T. Duong
The Economy and Environment Partnership for Southeast Asia (EEPSEA), Ho Chi Minh City, Vietnam
e-mail: hieu.nm@vnp.edu.vn

T. T. T. Duong
e-mail: thanh.dtt@vnp.edu.vn

P. K. Nam and A. Heshmati (eds.), *Recent Trends in Vietnam's Rapid Economic Development*, Frontiers in South and Southeast Asian Development Research,
https://doi.org/10.1007/978-981-97-6079-4_5

1 Introduction

Vietnam is experiencing rapid economic growth, which has adversely impacted ever-increasing resource consumption and waste generation. Therefore, implementing the circular economy (CE) is considered as an effective and timely solution to address environmental issues and promote sustainable development during the rapid economic development period in Vietnam.

Realizing economic development and environment protection being treated separately in Vietnam, the government issued Decision 687 on circular economy development which was followed earlier by the revised Law on Environmental Protection (LEP) in June 2022. However, the term "circular economy" remains a relatively new concept in Vietnam, presenting numerous challenges that require resolution for its effective implementation. One of the most significant challenges pertains to the scarcity of data and information on the CE within the Vietnamese context. It is for this reason that we have undertaken this research endeavor, aiming to bridge the existing data gap, subsequently assessing the current state of CE implementation in Vietnam, and proposing viable solutions to promote CE practices.

The primary objective of this study is to investigate implementation of circular economy and sustainable development in Vietnam during the 2016–2022 period. This overarching objective is further delineated into the following specific aims. Firstly, we evaluate the current state of circular economy practices and their sustainability for Vietnamese primary materials using the "Three-circles" model, which encompasses the corporate (micro) level, inter-firm (meso) level, and societal (macro) level. The second objective is to identify the latent issues and challenges associated with the implementation of the CE across various material flows, including biomass, metallic, non-metallic minerals, and fossil energies, at different levels. Lastly, we demonstrate how to assess data availability and construct a structured material flow database for the evaluation of circular economy initiatives in Vietnam and elsewhere. For this step, the Sankey diagram and material taxonomy of the European Union is employed to construct a representative material flow database for Vietnam.

The remainder of this paper is organized as follows. Section 2 provides an overview of the literature review. Section 3 outlines the data collection process and its limitations. Section 4 presents the current implementation of CE in Vietnam. Lastly, in Sect. 5, we provide the conclusions and policy recommendations.

2 Literature Review

The term CE was initially introduced by Pearce and Turner (1990). This concept represented a novel economic model based on the fundamental principle that everything served as input for something else. Consequently, the CE model created a closed loop of resource utilization and waste minimization. At this point, when analyzing the circular economy, we could only consider these relationships allowing us to return to the initial starting point. Heshmati (2017) and Heshmati and Khezri (2023) provide comprehensive reviews of circular economy and its implementations.

Compared to CE, a linear economic system extracted natural resources to turn into basic materials or final products that were subsequently disposed of at the end of their cycle life, which led to inevitable consequences of resource scarcity and excessive waste generation. Hence, raised from an idea that waste was viewed as a resource, the key objective of CE was to maintain the life cycle of products, materials, and resources as long as possible so that nations and businesses could minimize waste generation, optimize material input, and benefit the environment (Fellner et al., 2017).

Undoubtedly, recycling has been a fundamental component of circular economy concepts and CE has been gradually built on three R's principles. For instance, the Japanese Government introduced its "3R Initiative" (reduce, reuse, recycle) in 2004 (Ekins et al., 2020). Meanwhile, the European Union's waste hierarchy included four Rs (reduce, reuse, recycle, recover) in its 2008 Waste Framework Directive (Ekins et al., 2020). Besides the 3R principle, the term "scarce resources" broadly covered four dimensions: material, land, water, and energy. In China, the concept of CE encompassed all critical resources to Chinese economic growth, such as water, land, energy, materials, and corresponding waste (Dajian, 2013; Su et al., 2013).

Furthermore, the CE has emerged as a significant area of academic research, with a substantial rise in the number of articles and journals over the past decade (Geissdoerfer et al., 2017). Corporations are increasingly growing more aware of the potential advantages of CE and starting to acknowledge its value for both their internal operations and relations with their stakeholders. For instance, Ellen MacArthur Foundation (EMF) founded in 2010 partnered with tremendous companies and the McKinsey consultancy to produce three publications 'Toward the Circular Economy' in 2013 (Ekins et al., 2020).

As a matter of fact, the CE literature lacked unambiguous definitions (García-Barragán et al., 2019). This became evident that there were at least 114 definitions of CE (Kirchherr et al., 2017). Therefore, translating concepts into metric is vital to nations and enterprises to monitor CE performance. In practice, both the Sankey diagram and circularity rate forms part of the EU monitoring framework for the CE.

From the Sankey diagram mentioned above, the European Union measures CE based on a wide range of aspects: production and consumption, waste management, secondary raw material, competitiveness and innovation, and global sustainability and resilience. Regarding production and consumption, key metrics monitored material footprint including Direct Material Input (DMI), Domestic Material Consumption (DMC), Resource Productivity, and Circularity Rate (CMU).

Further, the role of stakeholder engagement was of great importance to CE development and sustainability. Chinese CE comprised various spatial scales including individual enterprises, industrial parks, and entire regions (Dajian, 2013; Su et al., 2013). Narrowly speaking, according to Geng and Doberstein (2008), the first circle "micro" considered sustainable initiatives at corporate level such as eco-design of manufacturing plants, waste reduction, cleaner production, and environmental management systems (EMS). At meso level, eco-industrial parks (EIPs) have been designed to optimize the exchange of eco-products between industries such as heat energy, wastewater, and manufacturing wastes. The third circle "macro" was raised from an idea of eco-cities and eco-provinces.

3 Data Collection and Limitations

As mentioned above, the EU monitoring framework delivered a comprehensive material flow analysis to systematically record the inputs of material to European economies. Further, to identify the relative significance of various materials and their potential recycling, Eurostat classified materials into four main categories: biomass, metal ores, non-metallic minerals, and fossil energies. Thus, in line with the Eurostat material category, in our scope of research, we attempted to collect secondary data for some primary materials in Vietnam including wood, iron and steel, cement clinker, coal and crude oil. Due to timeline constraints and challenge of data collection, we did not cover all materials in the Vietnamese economy and our period was relatively short, from 2016 to 2022. Regarding review of CE implementation in Vietnam, we conducted desk research through the "Three circle" model including: micro (corporate and consumers), meso (eco-industrial parks), and macro (countries, provinces, large cities) levels.

Regarding indicators, although we were aware of the great importance of the circularity rate providing us further overview of national circularity progress, this indicator required us to collect secondary material input and waste management, which was a limited data source in Vietnam. Hence, we merely demonstrated two key indicators: domestic material consumption (DMC) and resource productivity for our material flow analysis. Resource productivity provided a measure of the relationship between economic activity and utilization of natural resources (EuroStat, 2023). It evaluated whether economic growth is linked to increased resource consumption or whether a decoupling effect existed. Resource productivity was defined as GDP divided by domestic material consumption (DMC) which can be broken down into domestic extraction and physical trade balance. Additionally, DMC was identified as a combination of domestic extraction and physical trade balance (imports minus exports) (EuroStat, 2023).

We faced three key challenges during data collection and analysis. First, our dataset was collected from two main sources, including the General Statistics Office of Vietnam (GSO) and the World Bank. However, some data might not be publicly available or accessible to the GSO, thus we had to combine it with data from the World Bank and other sources (Ministry of Industry and Trade). Data source dispersion could lead to inconsistency and tremendous challenges to analyze and interpret results. Second, trade data for our major materials in Vietnam might be unavailable or incomplete in our time interest. Therefore, we implemented multiple estimation techniques for missing years, which could increase additional uncertainty about our results. Third, for the wood material flow, we encountered difficulties in converting units, such as from cubic meters to tons. It was possible to contain estimation errors as the conversion factors might not be accurate or consistent.

Overall, these challenges could limit the accuracy and reliability of our findings. However, we believe that this research contributes to a better understanding of the major material flows in Vietnam at different level, primarily at a general meso-level.

4 Current Implementation of CE in Vietnam

4.1 The Concept of Circular Economy in Vietnam

A concept of circular economy has existed under various forms in Vietnam for 20 years. In the 1980s, some business models toward a sustainable economy were commonly known as the VAC model ("Vườn—Ao—Chuồng" as Garden—Pond—Livestock). Despite an incomplete system and small scale of households or cooperatives, this model initially showed resource efficiency and reduction of environmental impact from livestock waste. In the Socio-Economic Development Strategy for the period 1991–2000, approved at the 7th Party Congress, Vietnamese Communist Party advocated that "Economic growth must go hand-in-hand with progress and social justice, cultural development, and environmental protection".

A perspective of sustainable development was continuously affirmed in the resolutions of the subsequent Party congresses. Evidently, in 2004—a period of accelerating industrialization and modernization, the Politburo issued Resolution No. 41-NQ/TW on environmental protection to emphasize economical use of natural resources, energy, products, and environmental-friendly product packaging. In 2005, the Vietnamese government issued the first law on Environmental Protection, which introduced a concept of clean, eco-friendly, and efficient production and environmental conservation. To continue efforts to prevent environmental degradation, authorities formulated a relevant policy about a green industry in 2008.

The 11th Party Central Committee of Vietnam issued Resolution No. 24-NQ/TW in 2018 to take proactive measures in response to climate change, enhance the management of natural resources and environmental protection, and facilitate the shift of the growth model. This transformation was closely tied to economic restructuring, emphasizing green growth, and fostering sustainable development. In addition, the term CE was firstly mentioned in the draft Resolution of the 13th Party Congress with specific objectives "building a Green Economy, Circular Economy, Eco-friendly Economy" or "encouraging the development of a circular economy model for integrated and efficient use of the output of the production process". Notably, in 2022, the government issued Decision 687 on circular economy development which was followed earlier by the revised Law on Environmental Protection (LEP). The revised 2020 LEP highlighted extended producer responsibility (ERP) to emphasize responsibility of corporates and foreign investors to integrate the circular economy into their plans and strategies to prevent further environmental deterioration (Nguyen, 2022).

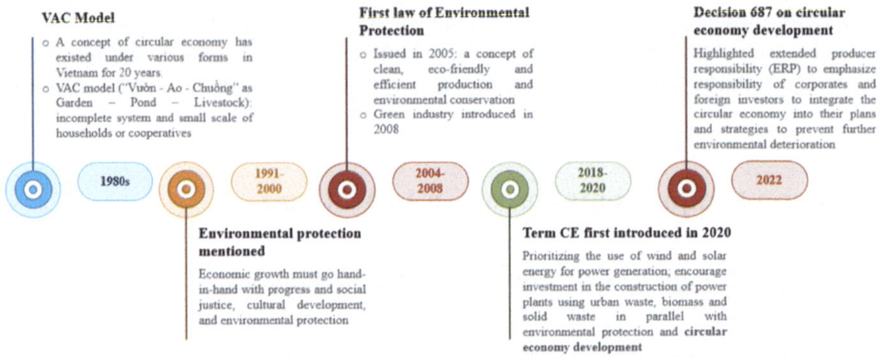

Fig. 1 Concept of circular economy in Vietnam

Overall, the concept of CE seems novel and sophisticated to Vietnam. Although CE contents had existed quite early, including the goal of environmental protection, proper exploitation and efficient resource utilization, the concept of CE has been merely understood and mentioned in recent Party documents (Fig. 1).

4.2 Current Implementation of Circular Economy by Materials

4.2.1 Agriculture and Biomass

Vietnam's agricultural sector has experienced rapid growth in recent years, contributing to national food security and rural livelihood improvement. In 2022, Vietnam produced 42.66 million tons of rice, 1896.8 thousand tons of coffee, and 1291.5 thousand tons of rubber (Duong, 2022). In addition, Vietnam is among the leading nations in terms of the value of wood exports and imports globally. Figure 2 shows the continuous growth of domestic extraction and physical trade of wood from 2016 to 2022. Notably, the growth rate of imports of wood and its products has increased dramatically since 2018, likely due to a surge in domestic and international demand, particularly from Vietnam's primary export markets such as the United States, Japan, China, the European Union, and South Korea.

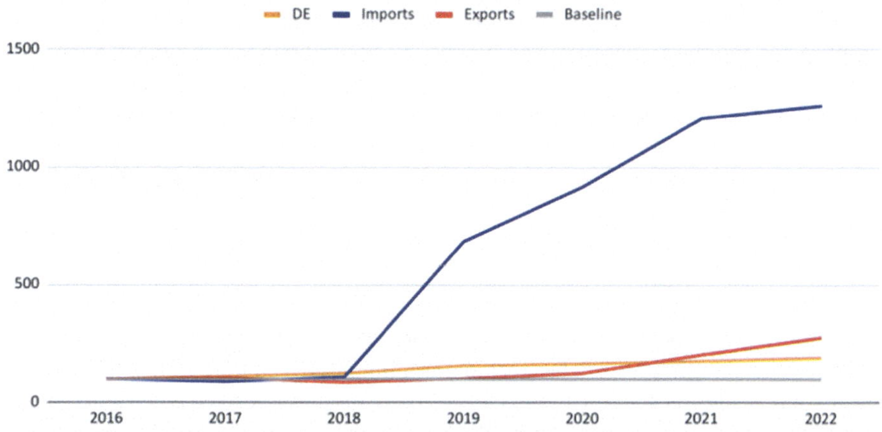

Fig. 2 Development of domestic extraction and physical trade—wood in Vietnam, 2016–2022 (year 2016 = 100)

Furthermore, the US–China trade war that began in early 2018 facilitated the importation of large quantities of wood and wood products from China into Vietnam. These goods are then processed, assembled, and the final products are labeled as products from Vietnam before being exported to the United States (Cao et al., 2021). This is one of the main reasons for the sudden increase in the number of imported woods in Vietnam since 2018. To limit extreme values, we only selected the 2019–2022 period to illustrate the development of resource productivity for wood in comparison with GDP and DMC in Vietnam, as shown in Fig. 3. The figure shows that the resource productivity for wood has notably declined in recent years.

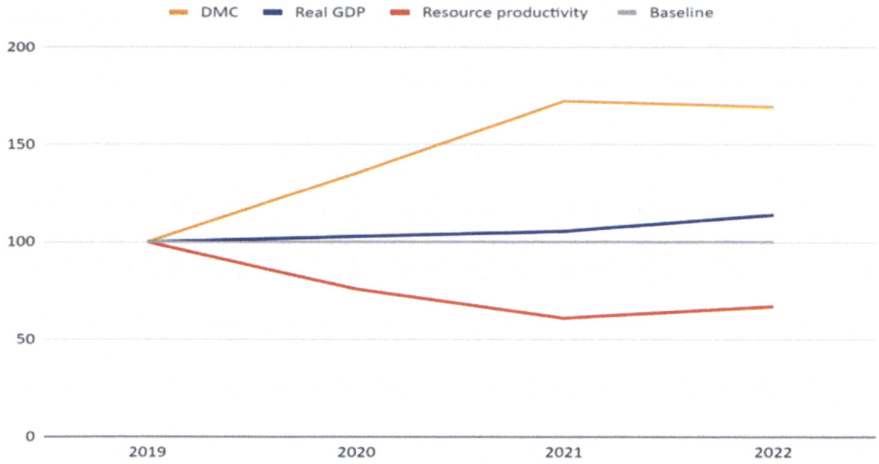

Fig. 3 Development of resource productivity in comparison with GDP and DMC—wood, Vietnam, 2019–2022 (year 2019 = 100)

Vietnam's long-standing agricultural tradition has endowed it with a significant potential for biomass energy development, given its abundant biomass resources from post-harvesting and post-processing agro-forest residues and waste. In addition, biomass energy has been applied in various sectors in Vietnam, with different levels of adoption. These sectors include biogas projects (mainly in rural areas), electricity generation and electricity-based production technology, and liquid fuels (bio-gasoline) (Ag-green energy, 2021).

Macro Level

At the macro level, Vietnam's government has introduced policies like the Vietnam Renewable Energy Development Strategy (VREDS) and Resolution No. 55-NQ/TW to boost biomass utilization. These strategies emphasize the importance of biomass power sources and set specific targets for utilizing biomass-derived electricity generation. Initiatives such as the "Climate Protection through Sustainable Bioenergy Markets in Vietnam (BEM)" project aims to promote sustainable biomass use such as rice husks. Furthermore, the government has revised the feed-in tariff (FIT) for biomass-based electricity projects to encourage the development of biomass-based electricity projects (Decision No. 08/2020/QĐ-TTg).

Meso Level

Currently, several biomass power plant projects have been officially put into operation. For instance, Doosan Group (South Korea) has invested in the construction and completion of a biomass thermal power plant in Minh Hung Industrial Park, Vietnam with a capacity of 19 MW, providing 70 m^3/h of steam. In addition, a biomass power plant, which burns rice husks, has been completed and put into operation by Dinh Hai Thermal Power Joint Stock Company in Tra Noc 2 Industrial Park with a capacity of 20 tons of steam per hour (Petro Times, 2020). In 2022, some of the projects that have been initiated and completed investment procedures, including Hau Giang 20 MW biomass power plant, Tra Vinh 25 MW biomass power plant, and a series of other biomass power projects proposed to be built in Quang Binh, Yen Bai, Dak Lak, and Thanh Hoa (Nguyen, 2023).

Micro Level

At the micro level, most rural households in Vietnam utilize biomass fuels such as wood, rice husks, sugarcane bagasse, and animal manure for heating, cooking, and lighting purposes (EVN, 2013; MOIT, 2021). In addition, some small and medium enterprises also use biomass briquettes or pellets made from agricultural residues as a substitute for charcoal.

Challenges

Although the potential and prospects for the development of biomass energy are enormous, Vietnam has not yet fully exploited this renewable energy source. Primary difficulties and obstacles can be mentioned as fluctuating fuel prices according to crop seasons, unstable and unsustainable fuel supply; high initial investment capital; unattractive electricity purchase pricing mechanisms for investors; and lack of experience in education and training skilled engineers and laborers for biomass fuel projects (MOIT, 2021).

4.2.2 Metals

Vietnam's mining industry has played a vital role in the national economy for decades, driving employment and income growth in impoverished regions (Nguyen et al., 2020). The country's mineral resources are diverse and abundant, with over 5000 ore occurrences representing 70 different types of minerals (Nguyen et al., 2020). Preliminary explorations and assessments have identified several metal minerals with industrial value and significant anticipated reserves, including iron (2 billion tons), copper (1 million tons of metal), titanium (600 million tons), bauxite (10 billion tons), lead, zinc, tin, and apatite (2 billion tons) (MiningVietnam, 2021).

Figure 4 presents the evolution of domestic iron and steel extraction and physical trade in metals in Vietnam from 2016 to 2022. The figure reveals a significant increase in domestic extraction during this period, with an average annual growth rate of approximately 38%. This can be attributed to rising domestic demand for iron and steel, driven by the expansion of industries such as shipbuilding and construction.

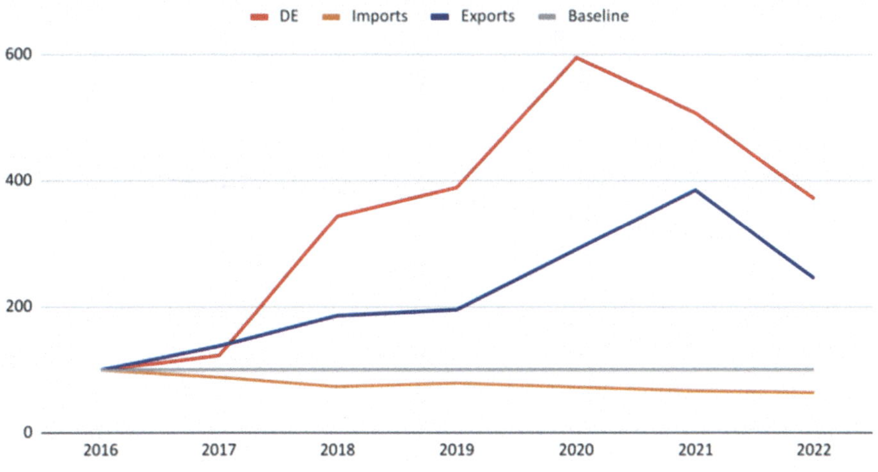

Fig. 4 Development of domestic extraction and physical trade—iron and steel, Vietnam, 2016–2022 (year 2016 = 100)

The increase in domestic extraction is also a key factor in the advancement of the Vietnamese iron and steel industry, as it reduces Vietnam's reliance on imported raw materials, reduces production costs for related industries, and enhances competitiveness in the global market dominated by the leading steel producers such as China and India. Consequently, physical imports of iron and steel in Vietnam have declined continuously, averaging approximately 7% annually during the period from 2016 to 2022.

In parallel with rising domestic extraction of metals, physical exports of iron and steel also experienced a remarkable increase in volume and value during the period 2016–2021, before declining slightly in 2022 due to the impacts of the COVID-19 pandemic and political instability around the world.

Figure 5 illustrates a significant increase in Vietnam's domestic material consumption (DMC) of iron and steel from 2016 to 2022, with an average annual growth rate of approximately 5.2%. The same period saw sustained growth in Vietnam's real GDP of approximately 5.9% per year, despite unforeseen volatility caused by factors such as global trade conflicts, the COVID-19 pandemic, and political instability.

In contrast, Vietnam's iron and steel resource productivity experienced a steady decline from 2017 to 2020, followed by a rebound from 2020 to 2022. This indicates that Vietnam was unable to efficiently utilize iron and steel resources to produce real GDP during the period 2017–2020. However, Vietnam has further improved its iron and steel resource productivity in recent years. This can be attributed to the acquisition and adoption of advanced technologies, high automation, and clean steel production by Vietnamese steel mills, which now comply with the rigorous standards of national and the global market (Ngan, 2021).

Steel production ranks among the key contributors to greenhouse gas emissions in industries (James & Eric, 2021). Consequently, Vietnam's steel industry is estimated

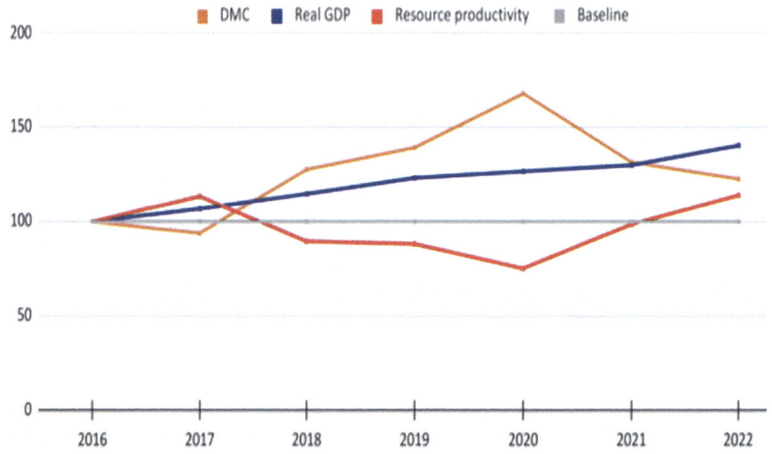

Fig. 5 Development of resource productivity in comparison with GDP and DMC—Iron and Steel, Vietnam, 2016–2022 (year 2016 = 100)

to emit around 38–40 million tons of CO_2 based on its 2022 production output (VSA, 2023). Moreover, the presence of small-scale, outdated, and energy-intensive factories in Vietnam raises environmental concerns (Duc, 2022). To mitigate these adverse impacts, Vietnam has implemented specific measures at different levels to address these issues.

Macro Level

Decision 866/QD-TTg, signed by Deputy Prime Minister Tran Hong Ha, approved the plan for exploration, exploitation, processing, and use of mineral resources for period 2021–2030, with a focus on vision of 2050. The plan emphasizes strict management of mineral resources, cost-effective exploitation and processing, environmental safeguarding, climate change adaptation, and carbon neutrality. It aims to phase out fragmented, small-scale mining in Vietnam while meeting market demands. Furthermore, the government encourages the firm's continual innovation and adoption of advanced clean technologies to efficiently process and recycle residues and waste from this industry, such as red mud.

Meso Level

Recent advancements in the Vietnamese mineral processing industry have significantly reduced environmental pollution through the implementation of modern technologies and investments in environmental treatment facilities. Two notable examples of this progress are the Dung Quat Steel Integrated Complex and the Hai Duong Steel Integrated Complex, both under the ownership of Hoa Phat Group. These complexes have embraced a circular economy approach by integrating blast furnace technologies, enabling streamlined production from iron ore to be finished steel, known as upstream steel production in Vietnam.

This approach facilitates the efficient recovery and reuse of CO_2 emissions, iron-based dust, residual heat, and solid waste as fuel, additives, or new products for the construction industry. Consequently, substantial cost savings amounting to billions of Vietnamese dongs have been achieved, adding value to the steel production chain (SCP, 2021). Furthermore, a distinctive characteristic of these complexes is that all production water is used in a closed-loop system, with no discharge to the environment (Hoaphat, 2023). This is pivotal as wastewater from steel production often contains harmful substances, like heavy metals and chemicals, which if untreated, can lead to severe environmental contamination.

Micro Level

Metal recycling villages play an important role in closing the life cycle of a product. In general, metal recycling villages in Vietnam are small in scale, operating mainly at the household or small enterprise level concentrated mainly in the Northern provinces, such as Bac Ninh, Nam Dinh, and Hanoi. The raw materials for these villages are scrap metal collected from various sources, including scrap metal, scrap yards, or imported sources. The recycled products of these villages include steel, crafts, household appliances, etc. These recycled products are sold on the market at low prices, contributing to resource conservation, waste and import reductions (Chi, 2022).

Challenges

Firstly, the legal metal policies are incomplete and inconsistent. Currently, Vietnam has some regulations on the exploitation of metal ores and the management and treatment of metal waste. However, there are still many shortcomings and inconsistencies. Secondly, metal recycling villages in Vietnam are often small-scale and operate mainly at the household or small business level. As a result, they often lack investment capital, use outdated technology for processing metal waste, and recycled products that have not been widely accepted by the market due to not meeting quality standards. The basic characteristics of metal recycling villages in Vietnam are manual production technology, raw materials that are mostly uncleaned scrap, and most production facilities do not have measures to control pollution, treat waste, and provide necessary labor standard and protection (Chi, 2022). Therefore, these recycling villages can cause more serious environmental problems.

4.2.3 Non-metallic Minerals

Vietnam is viewed as a significant cement producer, boasting a capacity of over 100 million tons annually during the last five years, according to Long Luong, Deputy President of the Vietnam National Cement Association (Vietnam Plus, 2022b). Vietnam Cement Industry Corporation (Vicem), a state-owned enterprise, is the leading producer of cement with a 34% share of the domestic market in Vietnam.

Figure 6 shows the development between 2016 and 2022 in the extraction of cement within the Vietnamese economy (domestic extraction), as well as physical imports and exports. Both Vietnamese domestic extraction and exports increased from 2016 to 2021, with an overall annual growth rate of 7%. However, in 2022, exports experienced a sudden drop as under pressure from rising input fuel prices and difficulties in product consumption, cement manufacturing enterprises were forced to adjust their production plans. Further, it could be partly explained by domestic overproduction and demand reduction from Chinese importers in 2022 (during the zero COVID policy) and the first quarter of 2023 (Global Cement, 2022). In contrast, imports decreased almost annually.

In the first seven months of 2023, cement excess supply has been still on the matter which resulted from weakening demand in both domestic and export markets due to a stagnant construction market, slow public disbursement, and slump in the real estate market.

From Fig. 7, resource productivity decreased slightly during the period 2017–2019 as environmental impact (DMC) was continuously growing at a higher rate than the economy. During 2019–2021, resource productivity remained stable as GDP and DMC grew almost in parallel. However, since 2021, decoupling occurred when the growth rate of cement DMC was likely to be less than that of its economic driving force GDP, so the economy witnessed a surge in resource productivity.

However, the ever-increasing growth of the cement industry caused severe air pollution in Vietnam. The World Bank indicated that "Cement plants have the

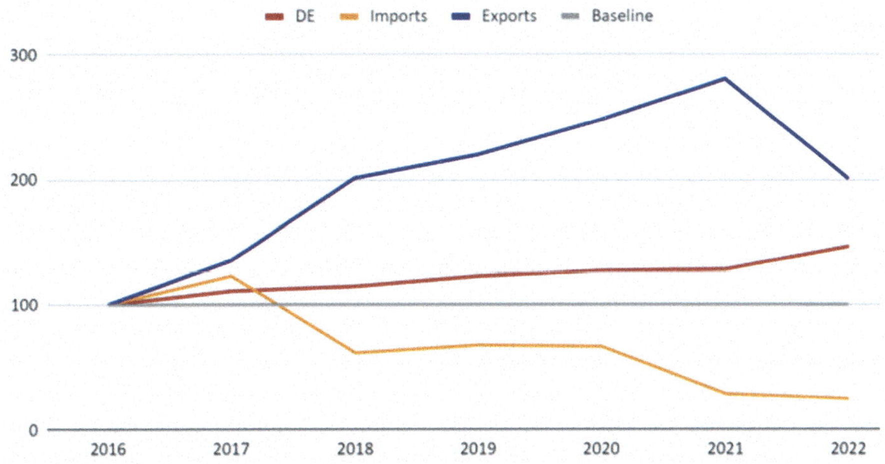

Fig. 6 Development of domestic extraction and physical trade—cement, Vietnam, 2016–2022 (year 2016 = 100)

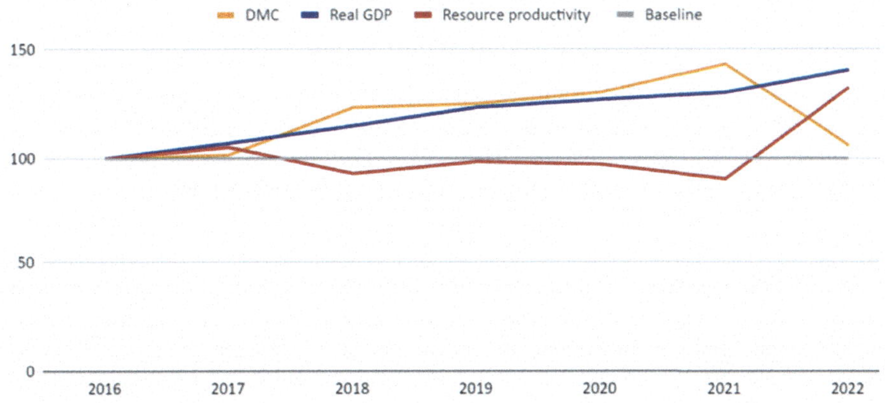

Fig. 7 Development of resource productivity in comparison with GDP and DMC—cement, Vietnam, 2016–2022 (year 2016 = 100)

highest hazardous content in their pollution to air than any other industry sector". The primary cause of air pollution was the increasing number of demolitions of the existing building and the cement powder used for constructing the new building, which generated substantial amounts of dust and particulate matter. Plus, the escalating extraction of raw materials for cement production contributes to the depletion of non-renewable resources, notably limestone and coal. Vietnam presently operates 82 clinker kilns, collectively consuming over 10 million tons of anthracite coal annually (Vietnam Plus, 2022b). Although the Vietnamese government has issued policies to increase the use of alternative fuels in the cement industry by 15% by 2030 and 30% thereafter, the current adoption rate remains low.

Macro Level

The government and Ministry of Construction (MoC) developed Vietnamese construction materials development strategy in the 2021–2030 periods to demonstrate two pivotal dimensions including production efficiency and proper waste management with orientations to 2050 to commit to the sustainable cement sector. Particularly, the government has encouraged cutting-edge technologies application to the production to create high-economic value of construction materials and improve market competitiveness of the sector. The plants have also seriously demonstrated waste treatment by saving mineral resources and energy, reducing greenhouse gas, combining materials production with recycling, and utilizing industrial and agricultural wastes (Dinh & Anh, 2020).

With aim at encouraging investment in emissions mitigation technologies, Vietnam's Ministry of Finance (MoF) has initiated a public consultation on a proposed environmental protection fee to require emitters of dust, NOx, sulfur oxides, and carbon monoxide to pay a base fee of US$127 per year and additional variable rates ranging from US$0.02 to US$0.03 per ton for emissions of each of these pollutants (Tien, 2023). Should this regulation come into effect, cement plants would need to submit quarterly fee declarations to the government.

Meso Level

Data from the Vietnam Environment Administration agency reveals that Vietnam has granted licenses for waste co-processing to four cement manufacturers, namely Holcim Hon Chong Cement Factory, Thanh Cong Group Joint Stock Company, Nghi Son Cement Company, and VICEM Ha Tien Cement Joint Stock Company.

Micro Level

Decarbonization seems a primary development trend to cement enterprises to gain competitive advantage while adhering to legal requirements. In the upcoming years, two critical technologies for emission control are Waste Heat Recovery (WHR) and Co-processing. WHR stands out as one of the most widely adopted, viable, and rapidly growing decarbonization technologies. In Vietnam, approximately one-third of cement plants have WHR systems in place owned by local private manufacturers (Khieu, 2023). Regarding co-processing, there has been a 2% reduction in conventional fuel consumption across the industry. Notably, industrial waste materials such as tires, rags, and sawdust are currently the top choices for co-processing practices (Khieu, 2023).

However, several cement companies have possessed existing plants with outdated technology and equipment, which led to low capacity and high consumption of raw materials, fuels, and energy. Realizing most plants' status quo, the government induced investment in a new cement clinker factory with a capacity of at least 5000 tons per day to meet a full range of technology to improve productivity and product quality, energy saving, and environmental protection (Dinh & Anh, 2020).

Challenges

In respect with policy making, there are insufficient current provisions about allocation of expenses for waste treatment during the cement production process, nor are there supportive mechanisms and policies in place for entities engaged in managing and treating ash, slag, synthetic gypsum, waste materials, and sludge. In technology and processing terms, currently waste materials are not being sorted, collected, and pre-processed by dedicated entities to meet the necessary criteria for supplying and co-processing in cement kilns, which leads to inconsistent quality and limited supply capacity.

4.2.4 Fossil Energy

Vietnam, traditionally known for exporting its indigenous coal, natural gas, and oil, presently relies heavily on fossil fuels, which constitute approximately 80% of its primary energy mix and nearly 50% of coal as dominant source (Domouchtsidis, 2022). Most of the country's coal is mined in the Northern regions, with the state-owned enterprise Vietnam National Coal-Mineral Industries Corp., commonly known as Vinacomin, is responsible for approximately 90% of Vietnam's coal production.

Figures 8 and 9 illustrate the development of domestic extraction and physical trade of coal and crude oil, respectively. In Fig. 8, there was a significant increase in imports during the period 2018–2020. Especially, in 2020, the imported coal increased dramatically, reaching 54,873 thousand tons (nearly 4 times higher than in 2016), with mainly serving thermal power plants due to unstable domestic production (Vietnam Energy, 2023). As a result, Vietnam has become a net importer of coal, with the top three markets for coal imports into Vietnam including Australia, Indonesia, and Russia. Figure 9 shows that, since 2016, crude oil import has experienced a surge during the period 2017–2019, which could be explained by expansion of Nghi Son Refinery and Petrochemical Plant in 2018.

Regarding resource productivity, based on Figs. 10 and 11, both coal and crude oil tend to follow the same pattern with positive correlation between GDP and DMC. Particularly, the DMC of the coal industry started to rise significantly in 2018 and reached a peak in 2020, thereafter experiencing a sudden drop in 2020 while GDP steadily rose, which led to relative decoupling between GDP and DMC from 2020 to 2021. Since 2021, however, both indicators seem to be re-coupling.

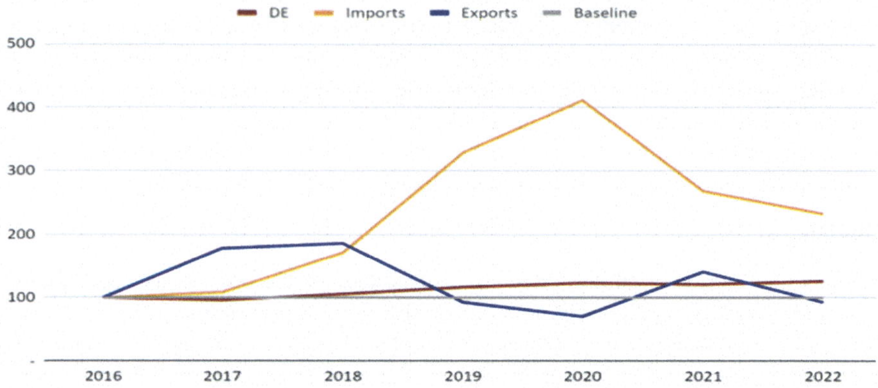

Fig. 8 Development of domestic extraction and physical trade—coal (pure), Vietnam, 2016–2022 (year 2016 = 100)

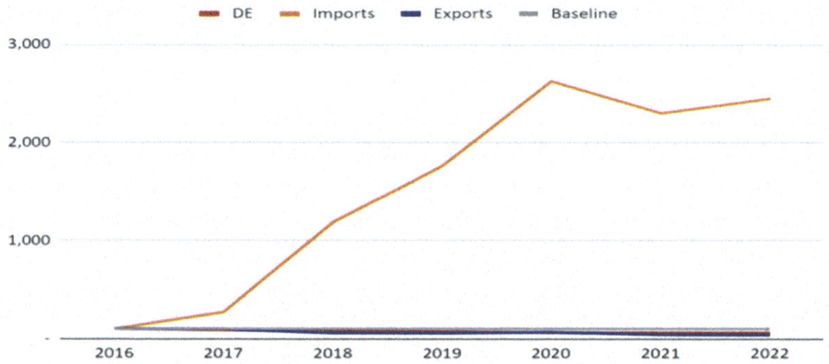

Fig. 9 Development of domestic extraction and physical trade—crude oil, Vietnam, 2016–2022 (year 2016 = 100

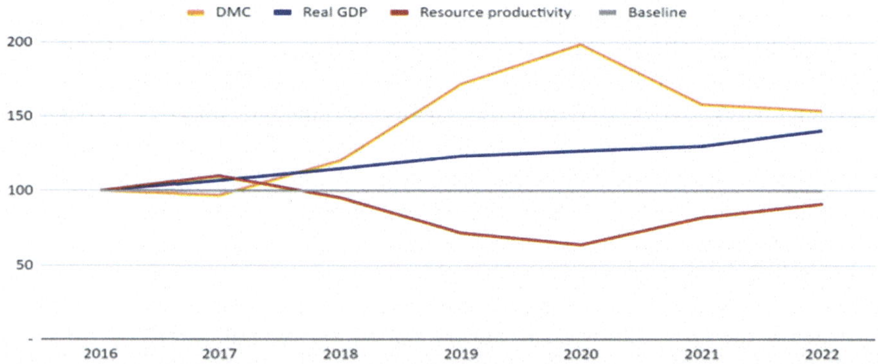

Fig. 10 Development of resource productivity in comparison with GDP and DMC—coal, Vietnam, 2016–022 (year 2016 = 100)

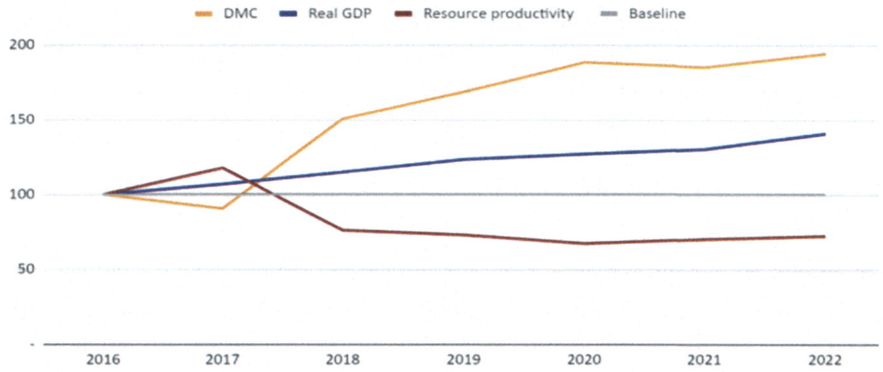

Fig. 11 Development of resource productivity in comparison with GDP and DMC—crude oil, Vietnam, 2016–2022 (year 2016 = 100)

In terms of crude oil illustrated by Fig. 11, GDP and DMC have exhibited a robust simultaneous growth trend since 2017, with both indicators gradually increasing over time. Crude oil resource productivity achieved 21,295 USD per thousand tons of crude oil domestic consumption in 2022. Hence, it seems there is no decoupling between real GDP and DMC in the crude oil industry during the period 2016–2022.

From the overview of the market landscape, it is no doubt that the Vietnamese economy has relied heavily on fossil fuel extraction and consumption, which has led to energy scarcity and adverse effects on the environment. It is an urgent call for gas and oil reserves in Vietnam as crude oil extraction became more challenging and Vietnam experienced a significant drop in oil and gas exports. Particularly, from 2011 to 2015, there were 21 new oil and gas contracts signed, but in the 2016–2020 period, the number of signed contracts dropped to only 3 new ones (Bang, 2022). This indicates reduced self-sufficiency in meeting the growing energy demand.

Regarding environmental issues, Vietnam experienced the second-highest levels of air pollution in Southeast Asia in 2019, primarily due to its swift economic growth and increased non-clean energy usage (Vietnam Asia Forum, 2020). Industrialization has boosted economic growth through increased fossil fuel use but has also negatively impacted the environment by contributing to pollution and climate change (Ali et al., 2021). The generation of electricity from coal-fired power plants was considered as a significant source of air pollution, accounting for a quarter of the nation's electricity production. Another evidence from the International Monetary Fund (IMF, 2018) ranked Vietnam as one of the top ten countries affected by air pollution with estimated double and triple greenhouse gas emissions between 2010 and 2020 and continuously by 2030, respectively.

Hence, the national challenge is to shift away from fossil fuel-based energy production and adopt low-carbon and renewable energy options, all the while guaranteeing fair and balanced economic growth across different regions.

Macro Level

In response to environmental pollution concerns, at the 26th Conference of the Parties (COP 26), the Vietnamese government committed to phasing out unabated coal power by the 2040s with a willingness to expedite this transition if economically and technologically feasible.

To concretize its commitments, Vietnam's long-awaited Power Development Plan 8 (PDP-8) received approval in May 2023, marking a significant step toward the transition from coal to natural gas and non-hydro renewable energy as the primary energy source by 2030. The plan calls for the complete decommissioning or conversion of all coal plants to utilize either biomass energy or ammonia as alternative sources (Barnes, 2023). By 2050, most of the country's gas power plants are anticipated to shift to hydrogen-based generation, with only 11,042 MW of power being produced from traditional gas sources (Barnes, 2023).

PDP-8 also demonstrates potential development of green energy, especially solar and wind power. Additionally, it outlines a goal that half of all buildings would rely on rooftop solar power, although it offers limited details on how this objective will be implemented (PWC, 2023). Regarding wind power, Vietnam targets to produce onshore power and offshore power with expected capacity of 21,880 Megawatts (MW) and 6000 MW, respectively by 2030.

Meso Level

The People's Committee of Quang Ninh Province has asked the coal mining sector to lower the height of coal dumps, plant trees to cover the dumps and monitor environmental depletion. In specific, Vinacomin and Dong Bac Corporation under the Ministry of Defense jointly collaborated to propose potential solutions including avoiding landslides and rocks floating; dredging and improving water drainage systems; relocating inhabitants out of risky areas; treating wastewater and surface water, toxic waste and solid waste; reducing level of dust, noise and emissions; and recovering environment of 190 ha of land with dumps at primary areas (Chinh Bac, Nui Beo, Dong Cao Son and Ha Rang) (Viet Nam News, 2017).

To ensure the successful implementation of the proposals, the Quảng Ninh Province's People's Committee has requested the two corporations to collaborate on the conveyor belt system to minimize waste and decrease dust emissions by misting systems. Additionally, companies were encouraged to initiate projects for river and stream dredging and establish automatic environmental monitoring stations that adhere to set standards (Viet Nam News, 2017).

In wind power terms, the PDP-8 also addresses the establishment of two interregional renewable energy service centers, which are expected to promote renewable energy generation, manufacturing of equipment, and the provision of related services.

Micro Level

TKV, a subsidiary of Vinacomin, has embarked on an eco-friendly approach to construction at the Suoi Lai mine in Quang Ninh province. From 2021 to 2025, the demand for leveling materials to support the development of land resources for registered projects in the local area is estimated to be around 640 million cubic meters (Vietnam Plus, 2022a, 2022b). With 2030 objectives, the demand for leveling materials for these registered projects is projected to increase to approximately 1.02 billion cubic meters (Vietnam Plus, 2022a, 2022b). Realizing potential economic value, the company has been utilizing mine waste, consisting of soil and rock, to level terrain for civil and industrial projects. This transformation aligns with Quang Ninh province's economic shift from a brown to a green model, emphasizing sustainable development in line with the principles of a circular economy.

Challenges

However, the renewable energy transition in Vietnam is facing a significant number of challenges from land scarcity and timely policymaking. Firstly, there is very little demand in areas with abundant solar resources, while in big consumption hubs such as HCMC or Hanoi, land scarcity becomes a main issue for solar development. Solar requires more land, which helps to build strong network congestion and a reduction of the hosting capacity of the grid.

Secondly, national power has heavily relied on state-owned enterprises to carry out numerous projects under PDP-8, where the government should seek out and encourage all economic players to participate in the plan. However, the PDP-8 Plan is encountering insufficient mechanisms to attract private sectors including green financing from foreign financing institutions to accelerate progress (Vietnam news, 2023). Consequently, a huge number of projects faced prolonged delays during the investment phase, or some approved projects were progressing slowly due to inadequate investment capital. Besides, the plan of renewable energy establishment provides insufficient information on the specific locations or strategies for setting up (PWC, 2023) (Tables 1, 2, 3, 4, 5 and 6).

5 Conclusion and Recommendations

From our research findings, it is evident that Vietnam relies significantly on agriculture and heavy industries (coal mining and metal ores), leading to consequent challenges of land and water resource scarcity and environmental pollution. Nevertheless, there is a promising shift in Vietnam toward embracing the early phases of a circular economy. This is apparent in the incorporation of CE concept and development strategies within state policies and ministry directives. Leading industries have exhibited heightened awareness and responsibility toward sustainable production, waste management, and resource recovery.

Table 1 The wood and wood products trade situation in Vietnam, 2016–2022

Exports									Source
Products	HS codes	2022	2021	2020	2019	2018	2017	2016	
		Unit: in tonnes	Unit: in tonnes	Unit: in tonnes	Unit: in tonnes	Unit: in tonnes	Unit: in tonnes	Unit: in tonnes	
Wood pellets	4401	4,882,000	3,503,698	3,207,472	3,076,680	3,022,645	2,019,680	1,746,192	GDVC
Wood chips, sawdust	440,122	15,814,911	13,609,338	11,607,583	12,021,921	10,375,720	8,201,298 1	7,221,613 9	GDVC
Charcoal	4402	4,882,470	3,503,698	3,207,472	2,791,391	88	104,709,000	78,683,100	GDVC
Wood wool and wood flour	4405	212,958	234,225	347,062	374,240	331,607	379,087	403,093	WB
Sawnwood	4407	36,271	48,287	44,595	94,736	106,400	228,114	269,800	WB
Veneer sheets	4408	46,066,287	33,739,474	14,835,693	11,008,331	7,867,781	9,152,805	9,674,174	WB
Flooring	4409	5,932	6,813	7,118	7,498	8,242	9,828	14,062	WB
Particle board	4410	15,621,583	14,185,020	9,901,331	15,992,138	10,517,918	12,593,419	11,459,675	WB
Fiberboard	4411	71,247,840	62,152,370	36,851,290	39,605,399	38,676,185	44,372,540	36,400,056	WB
Plywood	4412	960,568	813,023	500,438	1,363,365	1,267,601	804,303	636,248	WB
Densified wood, in blocks, plates, strips, or profile shapes	4413	10,082	4,086	4,612	9,394	3,230	403	11,863	WB
Seats	9401	185,762,454	118,567,534	25,281,985	254,927,573	235,121,257	254,175,275	245,493,934	WB
Furniture and parts of furniture	9403	1,569,370,114	1,153,730,648	761,430,328	365,755,487	297,189,899	304,768,421	305,250,227	WB

(continued)

Table 1 (continued)

Exports									Source
Products	HS codes	2022	2021	2020	2019	2018	2017	2016	
		Unit: in tonnes	Unit: in tonnes	Unit: in tonnes	Unit: in tonnes	Unit: in tonnes	Unit: in tonnes	Unit: in tonnes	
Total (Unit: in tonnes)		1,914,961,705	1,404,189,063	867,310,958	707,042,436	604,561,845	733,304,762	690,094,679	
Total (Unit: in thousand tonnes)		1,914,962	1,404,189	867,311	707,042	604,562	733,305	690,095	

Source Compiled by the authoring team from General Department of Vietnam Customs (GDVC) and World Bank (WB)
Note Data on wood and wood products were largely unavailable for 2022, so we used the average growth rate of the period 2016–2021 to forecast 2022 data. Additionally, we used conversion factors from two sources, "goviet.org.vn" (the official news agency of the Vietnam Timber and Forest Product Association) and "forestresearch.gov.uk" (Great Britain's principal organization for forestry and tree-related research), to convert units from cubic meters or items (such as seats and furniture) to tons of wood

Table 2 Wood material flow, Vietnam, 2016–2022

	Source	2022	2021	2020	2019	2018	2017	2016
Imports	General Department of Vietnam Customs, World bank	9,047,415	8,658,252	6,560,192	4,908,153	781,406	649,228	717,034
Domestic extraction/ production (DE)	General Department of Vietnam Customs, World bank	17,392	15,977	14,929	14,185	11,317	10,113	8,994
Direct material input (DMI)		9,064,807	8,674,229	6,575,121	4,922,338	792,723	659,341	726,028
Exports	General Department of Vietnam Customs, World bank	1,914,962	1,404,189	867,311	707,042	604,562	733,305	690,095
Domestic material consumption (DMC)		7,149,845	7,270,040	5,707,810	4,215,296	188,161	-73,964	35,933
Real GDP (in thousand USD, constant 2015)	World bank	358,918,000	332,271,000	323,972,000	314,948,000	293,359,000	272,981,000	255,265,000
Resource productivity		50.20	45.70	56.76	74.72	1,559.09	(3,690.73)	7,103.92

Unit: in thousand tonnes

Table 3 Iron and steel material flow, Vietnam, 2016–2022

	Source	2022	2021	2020	2019	2018	2017	2016
Imports	GSO	11,832	12,315	13,368	14,563	13,553	16,288	18,428
Iron and steel scrap—import	World Bank	6872	6225	6241	5542	5784	4727	3894
Domestic extraction/ production	GSO	19,167	26,154	30,673	20,066	17,723	6368	5154
Direct material input (DMI)		37,870	44,694	50,281	40,170	37,061	27,382	27,476
Exports	GSO	8278	13,000	9815	6598	6282	4665	3376
Iron and steel scrap—export	World Bank	29	29	25	25	24	110	71
Domestic material consumption (DMC)		29,563	31,665	40,442	33,547	30,755	22,608	24,029
Real GDP (in thousand USD, constant 2015)	World Bank	358,918,000	332,271,000	323,972,000	314,948,000	293,359,000	272,981,000	255,265,000
Resource productivity		12,141	10,493	8011	9388	9539	12,075	10,623

Unit: in thousand tonnes

Table 4 Cement clinker material flow, Vietnam, 2016–2022

	Source	2022	2021	2020	2019	2018	2017	2016
Imports	World Bank	133	154	355	361	328	654	532
Domestic extraction/production (DE)	GSO	115,472	101,219	100,115	96,540	90,247	87,400	78,700
Direct material input (DMI)		115,605	101,373	100,471	96,902	90,576	88,054	79,232
Exports	GSO	31,105	43,526	38,416	34,090	31,200	21,000	15,500
Domestic material consumption (DMC)		84,500	57,847	62,055	62,812	59,376	67,054	63,732
Real GDP (in thousand USD, constant 2015)	World Bank	358,918,000	332,271,000	323,972,000	314,948,000	293,359,000	272,981,000	255,265,000
Resource productivity		4248	5744	5221	5014	4941	4071	4005

Unit: in thousand tonnes

Table 5 Coal (pure) material flow, Vietnam, 2016–2022

	Source	2022	2021	2020	2019	2018	2017	2016
Imports	GSO	30,997	35,782	54,873	43,850	22,856	14,500	13,327
Domestic extraction/ production (DE)	GSO	49,771	47,845	48,617	46,137	41,782	37,999	39,599
Direct material input (DMI)		80,768	83,627	103,490	89,987	64,638	52,499	52,926
Exports	GSO	1200	1818	910	1199	2398	2297	1292
Domestic material consumption (DMC)		79,568	81,809	102,580	88,789	62,240	50,202	51,634
Real GDP (in thousand USD, constant 2015)	World Bank	358,918,000	332,271,000	323,972,000	314,948,000	293,359,000	272,981,000	255,265,000
Resource productivity		4511	4062	3158	3547	4713	5438	4944

Unit: in thousand tonnes

Table 7 The wood and wood products trade situation in Vietnam, 2016–2022

Imports									
Products	HS Codes	2022	2021	2020	2019	2018	2017	2016	Source
		Unit: in tonnes	Unit: in tonnes	Unit: in tonnes	Unit: in tonnes	Unit: in tonnes	Unit: in tonnes	Unit: in tonnes	
Roundwood	4403	1,889,486	1,440,596	1,507,390	1,732,960	1,702,585	1,673,407	1,408,881	GDVC
Wood wool and wood flour	4405	365.27	376.51	1,053.60	1,108.94	665.24	559.46	814.13	WB
Sawnwood	4407	1,645,710	1,706,753	1,559,245	1,580,959	1,478,656	1,337,259	1,131,486	GDVC
Veneer sheets	4408	182,481	230,195	207,503	163,026	124,417	92,358	94,441	GDVC
Flooring	4409	6,983	5,091	6,700	4,624	3,659	2,084	1,278	WB
Particle board	4410	191,656	234,925	282,285	244,182	209,466	171,590	121,217	GDVC
Fiberboard	4411	329,621	493,884	446,710	414,427	323,629	391,070	356,216	GDVC
Plywood	4412	232,575	356,286	392,392	336,855	293,758	247,127	209,585	GDVC
Densified wood, in blocks, plates, strips, or profile shapes	4413	2,648	2,408	3,469	1,764	2,509	2,991	2,310	WB
Wooden frame, cases, boxes, etc.	442,190	8,765,788,852	8,329,539,020	6,230,595,268	4,677,109,641	672,560,353	547,947,777	634,435,894	GDVC
Seats	9401	77,020,824	115,226,951	93,232,535	72,653,617	42,876,991	18,435,263	16,049,122	GDVC
Furniture and parts of furniture	9403	200,099,226	208,999,293	231,943,869	153,902,638	61,824,725	78,923,833	63,221,003	GDVC

(continued)

Table 7 (continued)

Imports									
Products	HS Codes	2022	2021	2020	2019	2018	2017	2016	Source
		Unit: in tonnes	Unit: in tonnes	Unit: in tonnes	Unit: in tonnes	Unit: in tonnes	Unit: in tonnes	Unit: in tonnes	
Total (unit: in tonnes)		9,047,415,206	8,658,251,635	6,560,192,287	4,908,152,944	781,406,280	649,228,235	717,034,080	
Total (unit: in thousand tonnes)		9,047,415	8,658,252	6,560,192	4,908,153	781,406	649,228	717,034	

Source Compiled by the authoring team from General Department of Vietnam Customs (GDVC) and World Bank (WB)

References

Ag-green energy. (2021, December 9). *Biomass energy in Vietnam—Current status and prospects*. AG Green Energy. Retrieved September 8, 2023, from https://ag-greenenergy.com/tin-chuyen-nganh/nang-luong-sinh-khoi-o-viet-nam-hien-trang-va-trien-vong-82

Ali, K., Bakhsh, S., Ullah, S., Ullah, A., & Ullah, S. (2021). Industrial growth and CO_2 emissions in Vietnam: The key role of financial development and fossil fuel consumption. *Environmental Science and Pollution Research, 28*(6), 7515–7527. https://link.springer.com/article/10.1007/s11356-020-10996-6

Barnes, M. (2023, May 17). *Vietnam's Power development plan 8: What you should know*. Vietnam Briefing. Retrieved September 2, 2023, from https://www.vietnam-briefing.com/news/vietnam-power-development-plan-approved.html/

Cao, C. T., To, P. X., & Tran, H. L. (2021, May 7). *VIỆT NAM*. Tạp chí Gỗ Việt. Retrieved September 10, 2023, from https://goviet.org.vn/upload/aceweb/content/Bao%20cao%20Viet%20Nam%20Xuat%20Nhap%20khau%20go%20nam%202021.pdf

Chi. (2022, January 11). *Làng nghề tái chế v ́ơi chính sách trách nhiệm mở rộng của nhà sản xuất: Điều hư ́ơng làng nghề tái chế theo hư ́ơng bền v ̃ưng*. Báo Tài nguyên và Môi trư ̀ơng. Retrieved September 8, 2023, from https://baotainguyenmoitruong.vn/lang-nghe-tai-che-voi-chinh-sach-trach-nhiem-mo-rong-cua-nha-san-xuat-dieu-huong-lang-nghe-tai-che-theo-huong-ben-vung-335844.html

Dajian, Z. (2013). Background, pattern and policy of China for developing circular economy. *Chinese Journal of Population Resources and Environment, 6*(4), 3–8. https://doi.org/10.1080/10042857.2008.10684889

Dinh, T., & Anh, M. (2020, July 21). *Workshop on sustainable development of Vietnam's cement industry*. Ministry of Construction. Retrieved August 29, 2023, from https://moc.gov.vn/en/news/63546/workshop-on-sustainable-development-of-vietnam-s-cement-industry.aspx

Domouchtsidis, G. (2022). *Vietnam—An energy snapshot*. Asia Natural Gas & Energy Association. Retrieved August 29, 2023, from https://angeassociation.com/vietnam-gas-policy-brief/

Duc. (2022, May 10). *Bộ Công Thương đề xuất xây dựng "Chiến lược phát triển ngành thép" để giảm nhập khẩu*. VnEconomy. Retrieved September 8, 2023, from https://vneconomy.vn/bo-cong-thuong-de-xuat-xay-dung-chien-luoc-phat-trien-nganh-thep-de-giam-nhap-khau.htm

Dương, H. M. (2022, December 29). *Nh ̃ưng điểm sáng nổi bật của ngành Nông nghiệp Việt Nam năm 2022*. Tạp chí Con số & Sự kiện. Retrieved September 8, 2023, from https://consosukien.vn/nhung-diem-sang-noi-bat-cua-nganh-nong-nghiep-viet-nam-nam-2022.htm

Ekins, P., Domenech, T., Drummond, P., Bleischwitz, R., Hughes, N., & Lotti, L. (2020). *The circular economy: What, why, how and where*. The OECD Centre for Entrepreneurship: Paris, France. https://discovery.ucl.ac.uk/id/eprint/10093965/

EuroStat. (2023, August 10). *Material flow accounts and resource productivity—Statistics explained*. European Commission. Retrieved September 17, 2023, from https://ec.europa.eu/eurostat/statistics-explained/index.php?title=Material_flow_accounts_and_resource_productivity

EVN. (2013, March 11). *Biomass electricity—A useful renewable energy source*. EVN. Retrieved September 8, 2023, from https://www.evn.com.vn/d6/news/Dien-sinh-khoi-nguon-nang-luong-tai-tao-huu-ich-141-17-6947.aspx

Fellner, J., Lederer, J., Scharff, C., & Laner, D. (2017). Present potentials and limitations of a circular economy with respect to primary raw material demand. *Journal of Industrial Ecology, 21*(3), 494–496. https://doi.org/10.1111/jiec.12582

García-Barragán, J. F., Eyckmans, J., & Rousseau, S. (2019). Defining and measuring the circular economy: A mathematical approach. *Ecological Economics, 157*, 369–372. https://doi.org/10.1016/j.ecolecon.2018.12.003

Geissdoerfer, M., Savaget, P., Bocken, N. M. P., & Hultink, E. J. (2017). The circular economy—A new sustainability paradigm? *Journal of Cleaner Production, 143*, 757–768. https://doi.org/10.1016/j.jclepro.2016.12.048

Geng, Y., & Doberstein, B. (2008). Developing the circular economy in China: Challenges and opportunities for achieving leapfrog development. *The International Journal of Sustainable Development & World Ecology, 15*(3), 231–239. https://doi.org/10.3843/SusDev.15.3:6

Global Cement. (2022, September 12). *Vietnam's cement and clinker export tariff to rise from 1 January 2023*. Global Cement. Retrieved August 28, 2023, from https://www.globalcement.com/news/item/14623-vietnam-s-cement-and-clinker-export-tariff-to-rise-from-1-january-2023

Heshmati, A. (2017). A review of the circular economy and its implementation. *International Journal of Green Economics, 11*(3/4), 251–288.

Heshmati, A., & Khezri, M. (2023). The circular economy. *Handbook of Labor, Human Resources and Population*, pp. 1–15.

Hoaphat. (2023). *Gi ́ơi thiệu – Công ty CP Thép Hòa Phát Dung Quất. Thép Hòa Phát Dung Quất.* Retrieved September 9, 2023, from https://hoaphatdungquat.vn/gioi-thieu/

IMF. (2018, January 9). *For Vietnam, greener growth can reduce climate change risks. International monetary fund*. Retrieved September 2, 2023, from https://www.imf.org/en/News/Articles/2018/01/09/NA010918-For-Vietnam-greener-growth-can-reduce-climate-change-risks

James, P., & Eric, H. (2021, April 15). *How the circular economy can help heavy industry reduce emissions*. The World Economic Forum. Retrieved September 8, 2023, from https://www.weforum.org/agenda/2021/04/4-ways-circular-economy-help-heavy-industry-reduce-emissions-wcef/

Khieu, H. (2023, August 22). *FiinGroup's expert analysis on Vietnam cement market outlook: Challenges and key development trends*. FiinResearch. Retrieved August 29, 2023, from https://fiinresearch.vn/NewsInsights/NewsDetail/10660279

Kirchherr, J., Reike, D., & Hekkert, M. (2017). Conceptualizing the circular economy: An analysis of 114 definitions. *Resources, Conservation and Recycling, 127*, 221–232. https://doi.org/10.1016/j.resconrec.2017.09.005

Luong Bang. (2022, November 7). Crude oil nearly exhausted, finding new mines difficult. VietNamNet. Retrieved August 30, 2023, from https://vietnamnet.vn/en/crude-oil-nearly-exhausted-finding-new-mines-difficult-2076874.html

MiningVietnam. (2021, May 16). *Định hư ́ơng khai thác khoáng sản Việt Nam. Mining Vietnam*. Retrieved September 9, 2023, from https://miningvietnam.com/2021/05/16/dinh-huong-khai-thac-khoang-san-viet-nam/

MOIT. (2021, December 13). *"Awakening" of biomass electricity—Energy development*. Ministry of Industry and Trade. Retrieved September 8, 2023, from https://moit.gov.vn/tin-tuc/phat-trien-nang-luong/-danh-thuc-dien-sinh-khoi.html

Ngan. (2021, September 16). *Cách mạng công nghiệp 4.0 đã mở ra hư ́ơng phát triển cho ngành sản xuất sản phẩm t ̀ư s ́ăt thép*. Bộ Công thương. Retrieved September 9, 2023, from https://moit.gov.vn/tin-tuc/phat-trien-cong-nghiep/cach-mang-cong-nghiep-4.0-da-mo-ra-huong-phat-trien-cho-nganh-san-xuat-san-pham-tu-sat-thep.html

Nguyen, C. (2022, July 15). *Vietnam's circular economy: Decision 687 development plan ratified*. Vietnam Briefing. Retrieved August 27, 2023, from https://www.vietnam-briefing.com/news/vietnams-circular-economy-decision-687-development-plan-ratified.html/

Nguyen, H. P., Hoang, A. T., Le, A. T., Pham, V. V., & Tran, V. N. (2020). Learned experiences from the policy and roadmap of advanced countries for the strategic orientation to electric vehicles: A case study in Vietnam. *Energy Sources, Part A: Recovery, Utilization, and Environmental Effects*, pp. 1–10.https://doi.org/10.1080/15567036.2020.1811432

Nguyen, N. B., Boruff, B., & Tonts, M. (2017). Mining, development and well-being in Vietnam: A comparative analysis. *The Extractive Industries and Society, 4*(3), 564–575. https://doi.org/10.1016/j.exis.2017.05.009

Nguyen, T. A. (2023, January 15). *Vietnam renewable energy in 2022: Events, achievements and identifying challenges*. Năng lượng Việt Nam Online. Retrieved September 8, 2023, from https://nangluongvietnam.vn/nang-luong-tai-tao-viet-nam-nam-2022-cac-su-kien-thanh-tuu-va-nhan-dien-thach-thuc-30046.html

Pearce, D. W., & Turner, R. K. (1990). *Economics of natural resources and the environment*. Johns Hopkins University Press.
PetroTimes. (2020, April 21). *Unlocking investments in Vietnamese biomass power*. PetroTimes. Retrieved September 8, 2023, from https://petrotimes.vn/khoi-thong-dau-tu-dien-sinh-khoi-viet-nam-569839.html
PWC. (2023, August). *Vietnam's eighth national power development plan (PDP VIII): Insights and key considerations for investors*. PwC. Retrieved September 2, 2023, from https://www.pwc.com/vn/en/publications/vietnam-publications/pdp8-insights.html
SCP. (2021, September 20). *Thép Hoà Phát ´ưng dụng kinh tế tuần hoàn tiết kiệm chi phí*. Văn phòng sản xuất và tiêu dùng bền v˜ưng. Retrieved September 8, 2023, from https://scp.gov.vn/tin-tuc/t12335/thep-hoa-phat-ung-dung-kinh-te-tuan-hoan-tiet-kiem-chi-phi.html
Su, B., Heshmati, A., Geng, Y., & Yu, X. (2013). A review of the circular economy in China: Moving from rhetoric to implementation. *Journal of Cleaner Production, 42*, 215–227.
Tien, L. (2023, August 15). *Vietnam to introduce new environmental fee for emissions*. Vietnam Investment Review. Retrieved September 3, 2023, from https://vir.com.vn/vietnam-to-introduce-new-environmental-fee-for-emissions-104364.html
Viet Nam News. (2017, June 26). *Quang Ninh coal mining sector to protect environment. vietnamnews.vn*. Retrieved September 2, 2023, from https://vietnamnews.vn/environment/379009/quang-ninh-coal-mining-sector-to-protect-environment.html
Vietnam Asia Forum. (2020, November 19). *Vietnam pioneer's post-pandemic carbon pricing*. East Asia Forum. Retrieved September 10, 2023, from https://www.eastasiaforum.org/2020/11/19/vietnam-pioneers-post-pandemic-carbon-pricing/
Vietnam Energy. (2023, March 31). *The deadlock of Vietnamese enterprises in importing and investing in coal mining abroad*. Vietnam Energy Online. Retrieved September 10, 2023, from https://vietnamenergy.vn/the-deadlock-of-vietnamese-enterprises-in-importing-and-investing-in-coal-mining-abroad-30499.html
Vietnam news. (2023, August 16). *VN's power plan lacks mechanisms to attract private investors*. vietnamnews.vn. Retrieved September 17, 2023, from https://vietnamnews.vn/economy/1582495/vn-s-power-plan-lacks-mechanisms-to-attract-private-investors.html
Vietnam Plus. (2022a, December 2). *Quang Ninh uses mine waste for construction to save the planet | Business | Vietnam + (VietnamPlus)*. Vietnam Plus. Retrieved September 3, 2023, from https://en.vietnamplus.vn/quang-ninh-uses-mine-waste-for-construction-to-save-the-planet/244885.vnp
Vietnam Plus. (2022b, September 30). *Vietnam has huge potential for co-processing of waste in cement industry | Environment | Vietnam + (VietnamPlus)*. Vietnam Plus. Retrieved August 28, 2023, from https://link.gov.vn/WPKCSzRe
VSA. (2023, April 14). *Tổng Quan Ngành Thép Việt Nam Trong Xu Hư´ơng Trung Hoà Cacbon*. Trung tâm WTO. Retrieved September 8, 2023, from https://trungtamwto.vn/file/22342/02_theptong-quan-nganh-thep-va-xu-huong_vsa-14.04.2023.pdf

Hieu Minh Ngo and Thanh Thien Trang Duong are pursuing their master's degrees in applied economics at the University of Economics Ho Chi Minh City (UEH)—The Vietnam – the Netherlands Programme (VNP). Hieu graduated with a Bachelor of Finance and Banking from UEH, while Thanh received her Bachelor of Business Administration at UEH—International School of Business (ISB). Their academic focus centers on socio-economic issues. Further, Hieu engages in researching environmental issues and shadow economies, while Thanh is interested in tackling environmental challenges and poverty alleviation.

Chapter 6
Impact of Renewable Energy Consumption on Economic Welfare in Vietnam

Huy Thanh Huynh and Hoang Huy Nguyen

Abstract In Vietnam, integrating renewable energy is vital for advancing toward sustainable development. It has a significant impact on the economic welfare of the large population. This research will evaluate the effects of renewable energy on economic welfare, measured by total GDP, GDP per capita, rural household income per capita, and urban household income per capita. This study uses regression analysis conditional on controlling key factors to estimate the effects of renewable energy consumption on welfare by accounting for heterogeneity and multicollinearity. The data is extracted from World Development Indicators (WDI), International Monetary Fund (IMF), Our World in Data (OWD), and General Statistics Office of Vietnam (GSO) covering period from 2002 to 2022. The findings provide insights for policymakers and energy and social planners, aiding the development of evidence-based strategies for a cleaner and more prosperous future.

Keywords Vietnam · Renewable energy consumption · Linear regression · Economic welfare

H. T. Huynh (✉) · H. H. Nguyen
Vietnam - The Netherlands Programme, University of Economics Ho Chi Minh City, Ho Chi Minh City, Vietnam
e-mail: huy.ht@vnp.edu.vn

H. H. Nguyen
e-mail: hoang.nh29@vnp.edu.vn

H. T. Huynh
International Institute of Social Studies (ISS), Erasmus University Rotterdam, Rotterdam, The Netherlands

P. K. Nam and A. Heshmati (eds.), *Recent Trends in Vietnam's Rapid Economic Development*, Frontiers in South and Southeast Asian Development Research,
https://doi.org/10.1007/978-981-97-6079-4_6

1 Introduction

1.1 Development of Renewable Energy in Vietnam

In recent years, the advancement of renewable energy in Vietnam has emerged as a compelling narrative within the nation's broader energy landscape. Figure 1 shows that renewable power is now 26.4% of total capacity at 20,165 MW in 2022. Renewables are thus Vietnam's third largest power source, behind coal at 25,312 MW (32.5% of the total) and hydropower at 22,544 MW (29.0%). As one of Southeast Asia's most dynamic and rapidly growing economies, Vietnam has recognized the pivotal role of renewable energy in achieving a sustainable, secure, and resilient energy future.

This introduction outlines Vietnam's journey toward utilizing renewable energy sources. Vietnam's rapid economic growth and industrialization have led to a surge in energy demand, primarily met by fossil fuels, raising concerns about energy security, environmental sustainability, and vulnerability to global energy market shifts. In response, Vietnam is implementing a multifaceted strategy to integrate renewable energy and transition to cleaner sources.

Vietnam's progress toward renewable energy development is marked by policy initiatives, technological progress, global collaborations, and a growing focus on environmental responsibility. This shift promises to not only reduce environmental impact but also drive economic growth, create jobs, and improve energy access for all. Looking into Vietnam's progress in renewable energy, this study explores policy frameworks, technology, challenges, opportunities, and the economic and

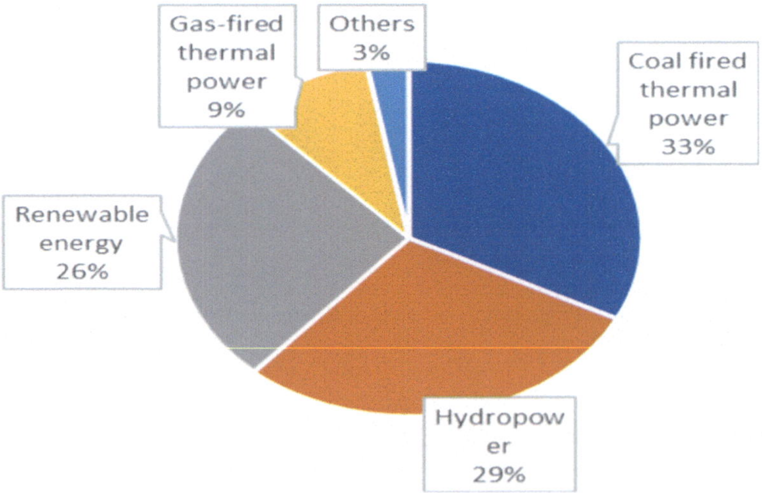

Fig. 1 Installed capacity breakdown in 2022 in Vietnam. *Source* nangluongvietnam.vn (Yuanta Research, Vietnam: Renewable Energy)

environmental effects. By studying Vietnam's experience, valuable insights can be gained for the global transition to cleaner, sustainable energy systems. This research aims to contribute to this discussion by examining Vietnam's unique path toward a renewable energy-powered future. The remaining parts of this introduction inform about the renewable energy and economic welfare, economic impacts of renewable energy consumption, energy security and energy independence, policy interventions and achievements, and outlook and research gaps all in Vietnam's context. Section 2 reviews the literature in the field. The methodology is discussed in Sect. 3. Section 4 discusses the estimation results, and the final Sect. 5 concludes and provides policy recommendations.

1.2 Renewable Energy and Economic Welfare

Vietnam started as an active participant in COP21 (referred to as the 2015 Paris Climate Change Conference with the objective of limiting global warming to under 2 °C) and has committed to acting against climate change. Their primary focus has been on advancing renewable energy. To accomplish this, the Vietnamese government has put in place various regulations and taxes. These measures have two main goals: to raise the share of renewable energy in the electricity supply and to tackle the difficulties of providing electricity to remote areas of the country where the grid is less accessible (Zimmer et al., 2015). Decision No. 2068/QD-TTg (2015), approving Vietnam's renewable energy development strategy to 2030, with a vision to 2050, underscores the multifaceted role of renewable energy, detailing it by increasing the amount of electricity generated from renewable energy sources from about 58 billion kWh in 2015 to 101 billion kWh in 2020, to about 186 billion kWh in 2030 and 452 billion kWh in 2050.

The proportion of electricity from renewable energy sources in the total national output will increase from 35% in 2015 to 38% in 2020; 32% in 2030; and 43% in 2050. Besides, raise in the share of households using efficient and clean stoves will rise from almost zero at present to about 30% in 2020 and around 60% in 2025; and from 2030, most of rural households will use high-quality and sanitary stoves. It not only focuses on expanding the scale and proportion of renewable energy sources in the energy supply, ensuring energy security, but also addresses the challenge of providing energy resources to rural areas. This approach contributes to the promotion of production development, resource-efficient and environmentally friendly resource utilization, and ultimately, at the national level sustainable development.

1.3 Economic Impacts of Renewable Energy Consumption

Assessing the direct economic ramifications of renewable energy consumption, a synthesis of various research endeavors is essential. These studies delve into multiple facets, including job creation within the renewable energy sector, the attraction of foreign investments, and the effect of renewable energy adoption on energy costs for businesses and consumers. For instance, according to a government report, especially concerning the transformation of wind power and solar power industries, the potential contribution to Vietnam's GDP is estimated to be as high as 70–80 billion USD, with the creation of approximately 90,000–105,000 direct jobs.

Table 1 presents the data on the share of different sources of energy in Vietnam's electricity generation by the end of 2016. Hydro and coal are the main sources, with capacities of 15,857 MW and 14,448 MW, respectively, making up two-thirds of the total electricity generation capacity. The rest of the capacity mainly consists of oil, gas, and diesel, while non-hydro renewables account for 5.8% of the total capacity, or 2418 MW (Nguyen et al, 2019). Hydroelectric power is a significant energy source, with low operating costs, minimal emissions, and high flexibility to meet changing electricity demand (Nguyen-Tien et al., 2018). The Renewable Global Status Report (Dwyer & Teske, 2018) ranks Vietnam among the countries that have experienced large increases in hydropower capacity in recent years. Vietnam is the fifth-largest country in the world in terms of new hydroelectric installations. The upcoming Lai Chau province plant will be Vietnam's third-biggest hydropower facility (Dwyer & Teske, 2018).

Besides that, there are three stages of development of Vietnam's power market to encourage more use of renewable energy, as stated in Decision No.63/2013/QD-TTg dated November 8, 2013. The first stage, which ended by 2014, aimed to end the monopoly in Vietnam's power market and created a competitive power generation market. The second stage involved testing a wholesale market in 2015–2016, with

Table 1 Composition of fuels for power production in Vietnam, 2016, and planned to 2020 (in MW and percentage)

Power source	Capacity (MW)	Percent	Percent projected 2020
Hydropower	15,857	37.6	22.0
Coal-fired power	14,448	34.3	43.2
Oil-fired power	1370	3.3	2.9
Gas-fired power	7502	17.8	20.5
Renewable	135	0.2	3.0
Other	2283	5.4	NA
Import	540	1.2	NA
Total	42,135	100.0	100.0

Source: Nguyen et al (2019)

plans to make it fully competitive by 2021. The third and final stage plans to introduce a fully competitive retail market. It remains to be seen whether these actions will effectively attract more investors to these markets.

1.4 Energy Security and Independence

Recent years have witnessed a growing proportion of clean energy sources, such as solar and wind power, in Vietnam's energy mix. This shift has enabled the diversification of energy sources and reduced dependence on imported energy, thereby bolstering the nation's energy security. Hoang Tien Dung, the director of the Ministry of Industry and Trade's Department of Electricity and Renewable Energy, has emphasized the critical role of clean energy in the energy transition process. This shift holds paramount importance in all economic activities and is a pivotal factor affecting Vietnam's economic recovery. In the realm of evolving costs and pricing trends, solar energy serves as a prime example of decreasing costs. According to IRENA (2015), solar PV module prices dropped by about 75% from 2009 to 2014. Moreover, the most cost-effective large-scale solar PV projects can produce electricity at $0.08 per kWh without any financial support, while fossil fuel-based power costs between $0.045 and $0.140 per kWh (IRENA, 2016). Another area experiencing growth is onshore wind power, with the lowest-cost wind power projects worldwide delivering electricity at $0.05 per kWh in 2016 (IRENA, 2016).

Given these shifting cost dynamics in renewable energy, policymakers in Vietnam are contemplating the establishment of national targets for its long-term development. Achieving this objective necessitates continuous assessment of clean energy integration, enabling active participation from communities, consumers, and renewable energy investors. Vietnam's energy production costs must also be benchmarked against other energy sources, both domestically, regionally, and globally. In this context, clean renewable energy is expected to become more competitive than traditional energy sources.

1.5 Policy Interventions and Achievements

The Vietnam Government revised the overall power development program (PDP 7) in 2016 to shift energy resources from fossil fuels and coals to renewable sources for achieving energy security, climate change mitigation, environmental protection, and long-term socioeconomic development goals. Currently, the share of renewable energy components in Vietnam differs by sources. Vietnam has a renewable energy resource potential of 359,000 MW per year; however, its production capacity as of 2018 was merely 2120 MW. In 2020, MoIT reported that the government had a policy to support tax incentives, flexible investment models, and investor and entrepreneur encouragement to invest in building systems and creating renewable energy in Vietnam.

There are various obstacles that affect the interest of potential investors and the advancement rate of renewable energy. There are some difficulties as follows: (1) the overall infrastructure and system, especially the transmission grid, have not kept up with the development pace of sources in renewable energy; (2) there are not enough energy storage systems and backup sources to integrate renewable energy on a large scale; (3) some policies about renewable energy development have not been in place for a long time; (4) there is no mechanism to attract investment capital for renewable energy; and (5) in Vietnam, the development of renewable energy projects is not studied comprehensively.

An examination of government policies and incentives intended to foster renewable energy adoption in Vietnam reveals their pivotal role in driving growth in the sector. For instance, the feed-in tariff (FIT) policy, introduced in Vietnam in 2017, has played a crucial role in incentivizing renewable energy investments. Such policies serve as instrumental tools in creating a conducive environment for the renewable energy industry to thrive.

A compelling aspect of the research lies in specific case studies and empirical evidence from Vietnam, which exemplify the tangible effects of renewable energy consumption on economic welfare. For instance, an analysis of the Tra Vinh Wind Power Project (2022) serves as a pertinent example. This case illustrates the positive economic impact of renewable energy projects in Vietnam, showcasing tangible outcomes such as increased local employment opportunities and the development of essential infrastructure.

1.6 Outlook and Research Gaps

Vietnam has promulgated some policies and guidelines to motivate the development of renewable energy. Moreover, on February 11, 2020, the Politburo released Resolution No. 55-NQ/TW (The Communist Party of Vietnam, 2020), which sets out the strategic direction for Vietnam's national energy development until 2030, with a vision extending to 2045. This resolution underscores the necessity of innovative policies to tap into the renewable energy potential within the country. The purpose is to reduce reliance on foreign-sourced energy sources and instead focus on exploiting domestic renewable resources from solar and wind energy. Expecting that the government's framework for supporting the advancement of renewable energy sources will attract some investors, motivating them to participate actively in research and investment activities for renewable energy projects.

In Vietnam, some policies designed to promote development of renewable energy have played a pivotal role in Vietnam's recent successes, both in the wind and solar energy sectors. These strategies incentivize investment in renewable energy by guaranteeing favorable pricing compared to market rates for manufacturers. What's more, manufacturers engage in long-term contracts, which, through the feed-in tariff (FIT) mechanism, serve to mitigate capital risks in renewable energy ventures. Furthermore, the revised FIT program started soon after the government declared its plan to double power generation in the next ten years, with the goal of increasing the share of renewable energy to 20%, thereby reducing reliance on coal-fired thermal power.

The Prime Minister approved the outline of the 18th National Energy Development Plan at the end of 2019, slated for completion by the end of 2021, spanning the period from 2021 to 2030 and envisioning developments extending to 2045. This master plan places considerable emphasis on fostering the growth of renewable energy and attracting investment, marking these as two pivotal priorities.

The Ministry of Industry and Trade submitted Report No. 544/TTr-BCT dated January 21, 2020, to the Prime Minister, in addition to preparing the National Energy Development Plan. The report suggested the launch of a pilot proposal for a direct renewable electricity trading mechanism. The pilot project aims to allow electricity producers to sell and deliver electricity directly to corporate customers, without the involvement of state-owned utilities. Some critics have expressed doubts about the restricted scope of this Pilot Program, but the project by the Ministry of Industry and Trade is a positive step in the development of renewable energy in Vietnam. This demonstrates Vietnam's commitment to nurturing solar energy and implementing supportive measures to retain the interest of investors in the renewable energy sector. Future research endeavors should delve into emerging technologies, such as energy storage and smart grids, and their role in enhancing the integration of renewable energy into Vietnam's energy system. Additionally, refining existing policies and exploring avenues for international partnerships will be instrumental in facilitating the sustainable growth of renewable energy in Vietnam, consequently, its influence on economic welfare.

2 Literature Review

The interplay between economic welfare and renewable energy consumption has emerged as a central theme in the global discourse on sustainable development. Scholars have long recognized the potential of renewable energy sources to act as catalysts for economic growth.

According to United Nation, renewable energy consumption defined that renewable energy consumption is the use of energy sources that are derived from natural resources that can be replenished or regenerated, such as wind, solar, biomass, and hydro. According to the European Union, share of renewable energy consumption is the proportion of energy that is derived from natural resources that can be replenished or regenerated, such as wind, solar, biomass, hydro, and geothermal, in the total amount of energy used by a country or region.

In recent years, there has been a growing emphasis on the significance of renewable energy to deal with the environmental impacts and to satisfy the energy demands for economic growth. Therefore, research exploring the link between the development of economy and renewable energy consumption has appeared in academic literature.

Fang (2011) used OLS regression to study data in China from 1978 to 2008 to analyze the effects of renewable energy consumption (REC) and share of renewable energy consumption (SREC) on economic well-being. This study has shown that RECs have a positive impact on economic welfare, while SRECs have a negative impact on welfare indicators. Using panel data and using cluster analysis, for EU countries from 2007 to 2017, Simionescu et al. (2020) show that there is a causal relationship from GDP per capita to the share of renewable energy; this shows the potential for using renewable energy in developed countries.

Karimi et al. (2021) used nonlinear ARDL approach including the bounds testing approach to cointegration and the asymmetric method to analyze the relationship between economic growth, renewable energy consumption, and CO2 emissions in Iran in 2017. This study has shown that growth in GDP is positively related to an increase in the use of renewable energy. Besides, the study also shows the statistical significance of the capital and labor resource variables. Hashmi et al. (2022) show that monetary policies promote renewable energy consumption in the short run and long run. Magazzino et al. (2022) used several panel data tests of five economies in Scandinavian countries from 1990 to 2018 to evaluate the causal relationship between renewable energy, CO_2 emissions, and GDP growth. This study shows that renewable energy consumption does not negatively affect GDP growth.

3 Methodology

3.1 Economic Welfare and Indicators

Economic well-being is a standard indicator to measure the level of economic prosperity. Gross domestic product (GDP) and other indexes reflecting on welfare of population are tools to measure economic prosperity. Almost all research models the demand of energy using GDP as a proxy for income, and in IEA's economic models, GDP is the main factor of the demand for energy. Fang (2011) concluded that there are four factors used to measure economic welfare including per capita annual income of rural households, per capita annual income of urban households, GDP, and GDP per capita. These indicators reflect the national and individual of economic well-being.

3.2 Cobb–Douglas Production Function

The Cobb–Douglas production function is a common tool in economics, which was used to analyze the relationship between inputs and outputs. The general form of the function is written as:

$$Q = AL^{\alpha}K^{\beta},$$

where Q is total production; K and L are quantity of capital and labor inputs in turn; A is total factor productivity; and α and β are the output elasticities of labor and capital, respectively.

3.3 The Data and Model

The purpose of this empirical work is to investigate the effect of renewable energy consumption on economic well-being. A linear regression model was applied with panel data. According to Fang (2011), linear regression is applied to estimate models and is able to present acceptable estimates for the independent variables. Based on the context in Vietnam, we chose our dependent variables as GDP, GDP per capita, per capita annual income of rural households, and per capita annual income of urban households to represent economic welfare.

To estimate the influence of renewable energy consumption, we based on Cobb–Douglas functional form of production and considered some independent variables to fit with the context and data in Vietnam. Therefore, we specified the semi-logarithmic form of a Cobb–Douglas as:

$$\ln Y_i = \varphi + \alpha \ln \mathrm{REC} + \beta\, \mathrm{SRE} + \gamma \ln K + \delta \ln L + \varepsilon, \tag{1}$$

where Y_i are GDP ($i = 1$, Model 1), GDP per capita ($i = 2$, Model 2), rural household per capita annual income ($i = 3$, Model 3), and urban household per capita annual income ($i = 4$, Model 4), respectively; REC is renewable energy consumption; SRE is share of renewable energy consumption; K is the gross capital formation; L is total number of labors (over 15 years old); ε is an error term; and φ, α, β, γ, δ are unknown parameters to be estimated.

The dataset was collected from public sources from 2002 to 2022. The list of variables, their measurement unit, and sources are reported in Table 2.

4 Empirical Results and Discussion

4.1 Descriptive Data Analysis

Table 3 shows the descriptive statistics of the variables such as GDP, GDP per capita, rural household income per capita, urban household income per capita, renewable energy consumption, share of renewable energy consumption, gross capital formation, and labor force. The features include mean values, sum values, minimum and maximum values, and number pf observations.

Table 2 Variables with measurements

Variable	Measurement/unit	Source
GDP (GDP)	Billion dollars	International Monetary Fund (IMF)
GDP per capita (GPC)	Dollars	International Monetary Fund (IMF)
Rural household per capita annual income (IR)	Thousand VND/month	General Statistics Office, Vietnam (GSO)
Urban household per capita annual income (IU)	Thousand VND/month	General Statistics Office, Vietnam (GSO)
Renewable energy consumption (REC)	TWh	Our World in Data (OWD)
Share of renewable energy (SRE)	% of total final energy consumption	World Development Indicators (WDI)
Gross capital formation (*K*)	Billion dollars	World Development Indicators (WDI)
Labor force (*L*)	Thousand employees	General Statistics Office, Vietnam (GSO)

Table 3 Descriptive statistics

	GDP	GPC	*K*	*L*	IR	IU	REC	SRE
Mean	197	2137	62	50,263	1761	3398	52	0.34
Minimum	45	547	12	40,716	275	547	17	0.16
Maximum	406	4087	123	55,767	3864	6022	131	0.52
Sum	4147	44,880	1295	1,055,513	36973	71358	1102	7.19
Count	21	21	21	21	21	21	21	21

4.2 Multicollinearity and Heteroskedasticity Issues

Using OLS estimation method can cause imperfect multicollinearity and heteroskedasticity issues. There are two popular ways to detect these issues including Pearson's pairwise correlation test (Pwcorr) and variance inflating factor (VIF). Gujarati (2009) suggests that the rule of thumb is that high correlation coefficients (usually believed to be $\pm$ 0.8) suggest high multicollinearity. Wooldridge (2015) suggested that the VIF below 10 is not a serious problem. Returning to Pearson's correlation test in Table 4, there is a high correlation coefficient in all the variables, which suggests high multicollinearity. As Table 5, the VIF value in some variables including "ln REC," "ln K," "ln L," and "Sre" shows a high value with above 10. Thus, we can conclude that there is multicollinearity problem in the OLS model.

To address the multicollinearity issue, there are a range of solutions to tackle multicollinearity issues such as dropping variable, transforming of variables, principal component analysis (PCA), "do nothing," and using Ridge regression. Gujarati

Table 4 Pearson's pairwise correlation test

	ln K	ln L	ln REC	SRE
ln K	1.00			
ln L	0.94	1.00		
ln REC	0.95	0.85	1.00	
SRE	– 0.94	– 0.80	– 0.91	1.00

Table 5 Variance inflating factor (VIF) test

Variable	ln REC	ln L	ln K	SRE
VIF test	11.4	16.9	65.3	13.9

Table 6 Breusch–Pagan test for heteroskedasticity

	Form of function	p-value
Model 1	$\ln Y_i = \varphi + \alpha \ln \text{REC} + \beta\, \text{SRE} + \gamma \ln K + \delta \ln L + \varepsilon$ H$_0$: Constant variance	0.68
Model 2		0.61
Model 3		0.60
Model 4		0.06

(2009) suggests that multivariate statistical techniques such as Ridge regression are often employed to tackle the problem of multicollinearity. Thus, we chose Ridge regression to handle multicollinearity in these models without transforming any of the variables. Table 7 shows some dominant differences of the data performed by OLS regression and Ridge regression. As we can see, Ridge regression gives more statistically significant coefficients than OLS regression method, and the sign of coefficients is similar between both of regression methods.

Regarding to heteroskedasticity issues, we use Breusch–Pagan (BP) test to detect heteroskedasticity. Table 6 shows the BP test, it indicates that OLS regression and Ridge regression give the same p-values in Models 1, 2, 3, 4, and the results show that they do not suffer from problem of heteroskedasticity, because there is no evidence of heteroskedasticity in these models at 10% significant level.

4.3 Models' Estimation

Based on the data and Eq. 1, we have estimated four models as below for the different dependent variables:

$$\ln \text{GDP} = -16.30 + 0.24 \ln \text{REC} + 0.84 \ln L + 0.48 \ln K \\ - 0.01\, \text{SRE (Model 1)}.$$

Table 7 Comparison between OLS and Ridge regression

Independent variables	Dependent variables							
	GDP		GDP per capita (GPC)		Per capita annual income of rural households (IR)		Per capita annual income of urban households (IU)	
	OLS coefficient	Ridge coefficient	OLS coefficient	Ridge coefficient	OLS coefficient	Ridge coefficient	OLS coefficient	Ridge coefficient
Renewable energy consumption (REC)	0.23**	0.24**	0.19**	0.20**	0.56***	0.51***	0.2	0.23**
Number of employee (L)	0.69	0.84*	0.75	0.90*	2.83**	2.48***	3.62*	3.03***
Gross capital formation (K)	0.52**	0.48***	0.51**	0.47***	0.11	0.21*	0.3	0.29***
Share of renewable energy consumption (SRE)	− 0.01*	− 0.01*	− 0.00	− 0.01	− 0.02*	− 0.02**	− 0.01	− 0.01*

Note $^{*}p < 0.10$, $^{**}p < 0.01$, $^{***}p < 0.001$

$$\ln \text{GPC} = -14.30 + 0.20 \ln \text{REC} + 0.90 \ln L + 0.47 \ln K - 0.01\ \text{SRE (Model 2)}.$$

$$\ln \text{IR} = -26.26 + 0.51 \ln \text{REC} + 2.48 \ln L + 0.21 \ln K - 0.02\ \text{SRE (Model 3)}.$$

$$\ln \text{IU} = -32.49 + 0.23 \ln \text{REC} + 3.03 \ln L + 0.29 \ln K - 0.01\ \text{SRE (Model 4)}.$$

4.4 *Statistical Test of the Models*

Based on the Ridge regression results reported in Table 8, we summarize the coefficients of four models. In general, most of coefficients of variables including renewable energy consumption (REC), number of employees (*L*), gross capital formation (*K*), and share of renewable energy consumption (SRE) are statistically significant at the 10% level of significant.

Table 8 Ridge regression results

Independent variables and parameters	Dependent variables (Economic welfare)			
	GDP	GDP per capita (GPC)	Per capita annual income of rural households (IR)	Per capita annual income of urban households (IU)
Renewable energy consumption (REC)	0.24** (0.17)	0.20** (0.17)	0.51*** (0.22)	0.23** (0.20)
Number of employee (*L*)	0.84* (0.19)	0.90* (0.19)	2.48*** (0.20)	3.03*** (0.18)
Gross capital formation (*K*)	0.48*** (0.37)	0.47*** (0.36)	0.21* (0.32)	0.29*** (0.13)
Share of renewable energy consumption (SRE)	– 0.01* (0.18)	– 0.01 (0.18)	– 0.02** (0.21)	– 0.01* (0.19)
Intercept	– 16.30* (11.24)	– 14.30* (10.91)	– 26.26 (10.89)	– 32.49* (7.58)
R^2	0.99	0.99	0.99	0.91
R^2 adjusted	0.99	0.99	0.98	0.90

Notes Standard error in parentheses, $*p < 0.1$, $**p < 0.01$, $***p < 0.001$

In particular, the number of employees has the highest elasticity among the factors observed. This shows the strong relationship between economic welfare and the number of employees. Total renewable energy consumption is statistically significant in all models, which confirms the strong impacts of renewable energy consumption on national and individual economic welfare. When renewable energy consumption increases, it contributes to an increase of GDP, GDP per capita, rural household per capita annual income, and urban household annual per capita annual income. The coefficients of gross capital formation are significant and positive; it implies that economic welfare has a positive relationship with the elasticity of gross capital formation. Remarkably, although the elasticity of the share of renewable energy consumption is insignificant in Model 2, the negative coefficient in all models shows that the share of renewable energy consumption is inversely proportional with all dependent variables including GDP, GDP per capita, and per capita income of rural households and urban households.

4.5 Impact of REC on Economic Welfare

In accordance with Decision No. 2068/QD-TTg issued by the Prime Minister on November 25, 2015, titled "Approving Vietnam's Renewable Energy Generation Strategy to 2030, vision to 2050," the government outlines a national medium-term and long-term renewable energy strategy.

By the strategy, around 2030 Vietnam continues to develop and use renewable energy while fostering growth within the renewable energy sector. The overall goal is to increase the total renewable energy sources to 62 million tons of oil equivalent (TOE) by 2030. This includes developing hydropower to perform the task of reserve, adjust demand, and improve response capacity with a capacity of 2.400 MW. Priority is placed on utilizing biomass for electricity production, with the total biomass energy projected to reach 32.2 million TOE. Priority will be given to developing wind power sources on land, with an expected output of 16 billion kWh. Solar power is also focused on, estimated at about 35.4 billion kWh.

Looking further ahead, by approximately year 2050, the aim is to increase total renewable energy to 138 million TOE. This entails expanding hydropower capacity to 8000 MW and increasing the biomass share to 70%, resulting in a total biomass energy output of 62.5 million TOE. Furthermore, long-term plans include the exploration and development of offshore wind power sources and continental shelf projects from 2023 to 2050, aiming for an expected output of 53 billion kWh. Solar power is anticipated to contribute significantly, with an estimated output of 210 billion kWh by 2050.

Renewable energy consumption helps to reduce the dependence on imported fossil fuels, which can lower the trade deficit, increase the foreign exchange reserves, and enhance the energy security of the country. Thus, renewable energy helps in fostering the environmental and social sustainability of the energy system, by reducing greenhouse gas emissions, air pollution, water consumption, land use conflicts, and health impacts. These benefits can improve the quality of life and well-being of the population, as well as avoid the costs of environmental degradation and climate change mitigation.

The results analyzed from the data are appropriate with these objectives of the government and benefits of renewable energy consumption expressed above; we can see that output elasticity of REC shown in Table 8 is appropriate. It is evident that when renewable energy consumption increases, it will contribute to a rise in GDP, GDP per capita, per capita annual income of rural households, and per capita annual income of urban households. We found that when REC increases by 1%, GDP increases by 0.24%, GDP per capita increases by 0.20%, rural household per capita income increases by 0.51%, and urban household per capita annual income increases by 0.23%.

4.6 Relationship Between Share of Renewable Energy Consumption (SRE) and Economic Welfare

The analysis of share of renewable energy consumption reveals that an increase in SRE will have a negative impact on economic welfare. When SRE rises by 1-unit, the per capita annual income of rural households drops at the largest rate, approximately 2.0%. This impact is smaller in comparison with GDP and the per capita annual income of urban households, which experience the nearly equal percentage decrease of 1.0%. The results also suggest that the share of renewable energy does not impact GDP per capita. These negative effects can be explained by several reasons, as explained below.

Cost of Investment in Development of Renewable Energy

The high upfront capital costs and long payback periods of some renewable energy projects, especially those that require large-scale infrastructure or complex technologies. A project of development in using renewable energy takes a lot of time; this may lead to additional costs including cost of labor and capital. The International Renewable Energy Agency (IRENA) estimates that investment costs for renewable energy projects in 2022 will increase by an average of 15–25% compared to 2020 (Nga, 2023). According to analysis by Vietnam Joint Stock Commercial Bank for Foreign Trade Securities Company (VCBS), the reason for high initial costs comes from the increasing price trend of input materials necessary for the production process, including wind power equipment and solar panels. Moreover, due to the problem of supply scarcity and supply chain disruption, the trend of reducing production costs has not been realized. Moreover, the report of VCBS presented that investment costs for renewable energy projects are still high compared to those in other countries due to conditions specific to Vietnam. Besides, Fang (2011) stated that cost of supply renewable energy is higher than other conventional forms of energy.

The cost burden can fall on households or the public budget, affecting national or individual incomes.

The potential negative externalities or trade-offs of some renewable energy sources, such as land use conflicts, water consumption, biodiversity impacts, or social acceptance issues should be considered. These factors can increase the environmental or social costs of renewable energy projects and create opposition or resistance from stakeholders or communities toward them. Consequently, this has a negative impact on the welfare of households.

The variability and intermittent of some renewable energy sources, such as wind and solar, depend on weather conditions and diurnal cycles. These characteristics can create challenges for grid integration and reliability, as well as increase the need for backup generation or storage systems. These additional costs can reduce the economic viability and efficiency of renewable energy projects, thus affecting national welfare.

Government Policies

There continues to be a lack of synchronization in policy, including pricing policies and complex procedures. Additionally, lack of public awareness and acceptance of renewable energy sources may result in social or environmental conflicts, resistance, or opposition. For example, in 2021, in Ben Tre province, fearing the impact of the wind power plant, many households did not allow construction, causing investors to lose over 100 billion VND.

Besides, there is a lack of clear and consistent policies and regulations that support renewable energy development and integration, such as feed-in tariffs, net metering, power purchase agreements, tax incentives, and environmental standards. For instance, on March 14, 36 businesses investing in wind power and transitional solar power (projects that do not operate commercially in time to enjoy fixed preferential prices for 20 years) sent a document to the Prime Minister, outlining recommendations to overcome inadequacies in the electricity generation price mechanism (Tam, 2023) . These inadequacies discourage investment and innovation in renewable energy sources, which often require more capital-intensive and long-term projects than conventional energy sources.

Consequences

The share of renewable energy, measured as a percentage of total final energy consumption, is decreasing due to a more increase in non-renewable production, despite the government's encouragement of renewable energy development.

In sum, the factors identified and discussed above reduce people's economic welfare, even inversely and proportional to the GDP.

5 Conclusion and Policy Implications

In recent years, renewable energy production and consumption are gaining immense popularity in Vietnam, receiving more attendant of government and its agencies. Generally, the data in Vietnam have demonstrated the existence of significant relationship between greater renewable energy consumption and economic welfare of the population. The results of empirical work indicate that 1% increase in renewable energy consumption leads to increase in GDP by 0.24%, per capita annual income of urban households by 0.23%, GDP per capita by 0.20%, and per capita income of rural household by 0.51%.

However, this study finds an inverse proportional relationship between the share of renewable energy consumption and economic well-being. This negative association is explained by several practical reasons, including cost-effectiveness and lack of policies as explained above.

To reduce the negative impacts of the share of renewable energy consumption on economic welfare, we should consider some solutions as below:

- Market of renewable energy consumption: The government should encourage priority investment and use of renewable energy in a variety of fields.
- Incentive policy: Ministries should coordinate to promulgate a reasonable pricing policy about electricity produced by renewable sources. This directly affects the revenue and profit of the organizations, which is related to GDP growth and welfare of the nation and individuals. Government promulgates some supporting policies, including tax, capital, and interest rates to support and protect the benefits of investors.
- Management frameworks: The government should develop and adopt more transparent and consistent policies and regulations that support renewable energy development and integration, based on best practices and international standards. Besides, the government should design a quality standard framework about input and output of renewable energy and create some legal frameworks to troubleshoot and simplify processing and procedures to develop investment projects in renewable energy sources.
- Human resources: The government should enact mechanism for training and developing expertise in human resources as well as encourage universities to design training programs to train high-tech students. Moreover, the government should conduct international cooperation to improve domestic human resources capacity.

Renewable energy consumption can have a profound effect on increasing GDP and economic well-being, but it also requires appropriate policies and strategies to overcome the challenges or barriers that may hinder its development and sustainable consumption. The policies listed above assist our country in being proactive in all aspects such as technology, capital, and output to develop the renewable energy industry. Moreover, this helps enterprises to enhance their competitive capability and save costs, contributing to the development of GDP and impacting positively the environment, health, and economic welfare of the population.

References

Dwyer, S., & Teske, S. (2018). Renewables 2018 global status report. In *Renewables 2018 global status report*.

Fang, Y. (2011). Economic welfare impacts from renewable energy consumption: The China experience. *Renewable and Sustainable Energy Reviews, 15*(9), 5120–5128.

General Statistics Office. *Average income per capita per month at current prices divided by urban, rural and by region*. PX Web—General Statistics Office of Vietnam (gso.gov.vn).

General Statistics Office. *Labor force aged 15 and over by gender and by urban and rural areas*. PX Web—General Statistics Office of Vietnam (gso.gov.vn).

Gujarati, D. N. (2009). *Basic econometrics*. Prentice Hall.

Hashmi, S. M., Syed, Q. R., & Inglesi-Lotz, R. (2022). Monetary and energy policy interlinkages: The case of renewable energy in the US. *Renewable Energy, 201*, 141–147.

International Renewable Energy Agency (IRENA). (2015). *Renewable power generation costs in 2014*. Renewable Power Generation Costs in 2014 (irena.org).

International Renewable Energy Agency (IRENA). (2016). *Planning for renewable future: Long-term modelling and tools to expand variable renewable power in emerging economies*. Planning for the renewable future Long-term modelling and tools to expand variable renewable power in emerging economies AVRIL findings (irena.org).

Karimi, M. S., Ahmad, S., Karamelikli, H., Dinç, D. T., Khan, Y. A., Sabzehei, M. T., & Abbas, S. Z. (2021). Dynamic linkages between renewable energy, carbon emissions and economic growth through nonlinear ARDL approach: Evidence from Iran. *PLoS ONE, 16*(7), e0253464.

Magazzino, C., Toma, P., Fusco, G., Valente, D., & Petrosillo, I. (2022). Renewable energy consumption, environmental degradation and economic growth: The greener the richer? *Ecological Indicators, 139*, 108912.

Nga, T. (2023). Journal of construction. *The cost of investing in renewable energy in Vietnam depends largely on the global market.* Chi phí đầu tư năng lượng tái tạo ở Việt Nam phụ thuộc phần lớn vào thị trường toàn cầu (tapchixaydung.vn).

Nguyen, N. T., Ha-Duong, M., Tran, T. C., Shrestha, R. M., & Nadaud, F. (2010). Barriers to the adoption of renewable and energy-efficient technologies in the Vietnamese power sector. *GMSARN International Journal, 4*(2), 89–104.

Nguyen, P. A., Abbott, M., & Nguyen, T. L. T. (2019). The development and cost of renewable energy resources in Vietnam. *Utilities Policy, 57*, 59–66.

Nguyen-Tien, V., Elliott, R. J., & Strobl, E. A. (2018). Hydropower generation, flood control and dam cascades: A national assessment for Vietnam. *Journal of Hydrology, 560*, 109–126.

Prime Minister of Vietnam. (2015). *Decision No. 2068/QD-TTg dated November 25, 2015 of the Prime Minister approving the development strategy of renewable energy of Vietnam by 2030 with a vision to 2050.* Decision 2068/QD-TTg of Prime Minister date issued 25/11/2015 (luatvietnam.vn).

Simionescu, M., Strielkowski, W., & Tvaronavičienė, M. (2020). Renewable energy in final energy consumption and income in the EU-28 countries. *Energies, 13*(9), 2280.

Tam, B. (2023). Journal of Nhandan. *It is necessary to soon have a policy to resolve solar power prices.* Cần sớm có chính sách giải quyết về giá điện mặt trời (nhandan.vn).

The Communist Party of Vietnam. (2020). *Resolution of the Political Bureau on orientation of Vietnam's national energy development strategy through 3030 with a vision toward 2045*. Resolution No. 55-NQ/TW 2020 orientation of National Energy Development Strategy through 2030 (luatvietnam.vn).

United Nations. *What is renewable energy?* What is renewable energy? | United Nations.
Wooldridge, J. M (2015). *Introductory econometrics: A modem approach.* Cengage Learning.
Yuanta Research. *Vietnam: Renewable energy.* 20230130-Energy-sector-note-edited.pdf (yuanta.com.vn).
Zimmer, A., Jakob, M., & Steckel, J. C. (2015). What motivates Vietnam to strive for a low-carbon economy? On the drivers of climate policy in a developing country. *Energy for Sustainable Development, 24*, 19–32.

Huynh Thanh Huy holds a background in chemical technology and business administration, with experience working in companies within the fields of agriculture and public health. Currently, he is pursuing a Master of science in Applied Economics, the program is a cooperation between Ho Chi Minh City University of Economics and ISS International Institute of Erasmus University Rotterdam, Netherlands.

Nguyen Huy Hoang, currently a master's student in applied economics at the University of Economics Ho Chi Minh city, holds a degree in business administration with a logistics major from Ton Duc Thang University. He began his career in a trading company with a focus on purchasing and exporting. In 2019, he transitioned to agency work, gaining diverse experience in creative, event, and talent management. Now, pursuing his master's, he is shifting toward a career in business analytics, showcasing his adaptability and commitment to growth in dynamic fields.

Part III
Banks, Finance and Development

Chapter 7
Bank Equity as a Predictor of Economic Growth: Evidence from Vietnam

Pham Quoc Tien

Abstract The equity market is often regarded as a thermometer of the economy thanks to its unique ability to not only accurately reflect current conditions, but also provide predictions of future trends. Specifically, this predictive power stems from the foundation that the equity market is significantly influenced by a wide range of macroeconomic variables. This paper aims to inspect such predictability by examining the correlation between the economic crisis and the underperformance of banking equity. This research is conducted as a replication of "Banking crises without panic" (Baron et al. in Q J Econ 136:51–113, 2021) but focuses mainly on the context of Vietnam. The research methodology used in this study is based on the local projection specification, with some adjustments for the specific context. Vietnam's financial market has grown rapidly around three key pillars: bank credit, equity, and bond markets. Although the analysis did not yield statistically significant results, several important conclusions can still be drawn. These findings are expected to be valuable for policymakers, financial investors, and other stakeholders aiming to understand and predict economic development. The government should particularly focus on developing the equity market, as it can serve as both an additional funding source and a platform that reflects market expectations.

Keywords Bank equity · Equity market · Economic growth · Banking crisis · Predictability · Bank equity crash · Panics

1 Introduction

The usage of debts as a financial tool proved to be beneficial and played a significant role in their economy as it enabled individuals to finance wars, build economies as well and develop smooth businesses. Indeed, debts have resulted in the development

P. Q. Tien (✉)
Vietnam - the Netherlands Programme, University of Economics Ho Chi Minh city, Ho Chi Minh City, Vietnam
e-mail: Tien.pq@vnp.edu.vn

P. K. Nam and A. Heshmati (eds.), *Recent Trends in Vietnam's Rapid Economic Development*, Frontiers in South and Southeast Asian Development Research,
https://doi.org/10.1007/978-981-97-6079-4_7

of a new form of social association, where creditors and debtors are bound together in a network of financial responsibility. Naturally, such a relationship has led to the need for a central institution to manage this network, and this is what banks are responsible for. Accordingly, banks play a pivotal role in any economy, serving as the backbone of financial systems and driving economic growth. Not only hypothetical theories but also empirical studies contended that banks and other financial intermediaries' offerings are essential for promoting economic growth and advancing businesses, industries as well and entire nations.

However, debts around the world have been on the rise over the last decade. Cascading crises in recent years have triggered a sharp acceleration of this trend. As a result, global debt has surged over five times since 2000, far outstripping the tripled global GDP growth (United Nations, 2023). Globally, debt reached a record of USD 92 trillion by 2022. Developing countries owed almost 30% of the total, of which roughly 70% was attributable to China, India, and Brazil. In addition, debt has increased faster in developing countries compared to developed countries over the last decade. Rogoff (2022) highlighted that many emerging markets and most low-income developing economies are in a state of debt distress and are experiencing significant constraints on their fiscal space. The rise of debt has mainly been due to growing development financing needs—exacerbated by the COVID-19 pandemic, the cost-of-living crisis, and climate change—and by limited alternative sources of financing. Renovating the growth model that relies on excessive debts as an advancement catalyst when it becomes obsolete and inhibits growth is considered a strategically crucial task in many countries (Pham & Pham, 2014). Today, more than 3.3 billion people live in countries that spend more on interest payments than on education or health. A world of debt disrupts prosperity for people and the planet (United Nations, 2023).

Vietnam, located in Southeast Asia, has emerged as one of the fastest-growing economies in the region and the world. From a central-planned economy to a dynamic market-oriented system, Vietnam has experienced a remarkable economic transformation by capitalizing on its strengths, implementing structural reforms, and embracing globalization to fuel its rapid growth. Overall, Vietnam is one of a few countries that have been successful in achieving dual goals of fighting the COVID-19 pandemic and reviving socioeconomic development. It would be remiss not to acknowledge the contribution of the banking system led by the State Bank of Vietnam, all aimed at maintaining a stable macroenvironment and sustaining the growth rate. In opposition, there are still some debates that associate growth with abundant credits, which is also evidenced by the out-performance of the banking sectors and the others during the pandemic.

Although the debates remain controversial, it has already been revealed that bank credit serves as a primary source of funding for the entire economy. In addition, Vietnam is still in the process of heavily relying on capital accumulation to maintain its economic growth. Indeed, Vietnam possesses large enterprises operating in capital-intensive industries, whereas the government continues to pursue the goal of transforming the country into an industrial society over the coming decade (Leung, 2010). According to Le (2022), the top 25 banks have already accounted for 87%

of the total credit outstanding. In fact, despite recent remarkable developments, both the domestic equity and bond markets are considered immature and still require additional time to share a role of financing the economy along with bank credit.

Such a situation has raised concerns about the sustainability of economic growth when bank credits serve as the sole engine. The development of the Vietnamese economy has been largely driven by the expansion of inputs (Nguyen, 2022). Nevertheless, this study's objective is not only to emphasize the importance of the banking system but also to provide empirical evidence in terms of the Vietnam context. In summary, this study may aim to answer questions as follows:

- What is the importance of the banking system to the short-term and long-term prospects of the economy in Vietnam as an emerging market?
- To what extent does the Vietnamese equity market reflect expectations about economic growth? How does a decline in terms of stock prices predict change in macroeconomic variables?
- In terms of economic impact, which sectors, whether financial or non-financial, would have a greater and more noteworthy influence in the Vietnam context?

The objective of this analysis is to investigate the predictability of the equity market, specifically focusing on banking equity crashes, and their ability to anticipate declines in certain economic variables. The paper is structured into six sections including (i) introduction, (ii) literature review, (iii) data collection, (iv) research methodology, (v) finding and discussion, and (vi) conclusion and recommendation, which adhere to the common structure of a research paper. Notably, in addition to comprehending the usual regression model, the author also examines the dynamics before and after the bank equity crash through visualization.

2 Literature Review

Both financial development and economic growth have been popular topics widely researched in academia. Scholars have extensively studied the relationship between these two concepts, seeking to understand their dynamics and interactions. These studies in this area have yielded valuable insights into the role of financial development in promoting economic growth and the mechanisms through which it can contribute to a nation's prosperity.

The correlation between equity market and economic development is always a complex relationship that can vary depending on various factors and time frames. While there can be a general positive association between these variables over the long term, it is important to recognize that short-term fluctuations and market dynamics can lead to divergences or temporary disconnections between the two. It is worth mentioning that this statement is supported not only by theoretical frameworks but also by empirical evidence. On the one hand, Cornell (2010) stated that the performance of the equity market should be inextricably linked to economic development.

By examining the source of long-term economic development as well as the relationship between equity earnings and GDP growth, respectively, he finally concluded that over the long run, investors should not expect real equity return to exceed roughly 4% which is also an average growth rate of the developed world. Masoud (2013) affirmed the positive relationship between the equity market and economic development, and this association was further extended to the short-term dimension by considering the wealth effect on investment. On the other hand, Ritter (2004) argued that such a correlation is likely to be negative due to an increase in capital or labor input does not significantly enhance the profitability or dividends of existing corporations, and retaining monopoly positions, which are crucial for technological advancements, is often challenging for firms. Although there may not be a substantial long-term correlation between the equity market and the current period growth rate, a consistent relationship does exist between equity returns and the expectation of future GDP (Wade & May, 2013).

The correlation becomes more intricate when considering the impact of bank equity, as this specific sector is closely related to macroeconomic variables. According to Ross (1997), the development of the banking system plays a crucial role in facilitating the efficient movement and distribution of capital, fostering economic transactions, and promoting the growth of capital accumulation and technology, which ultimately contribute to driving economic expansion. From another perspective, countries that have underdeveloped financial markets, lacking a robust connection between savings and investments, typically experience sluggish economic growth and are prone to recessions and macroeconomic instability. However, the evolution of the financial system does not consistently follow a stable trajectory. During certain periods characterized by uncertainty, financial crises can emerge, leading to a failure of the financial system to effectively support economic growth (Loayza & Ranciere, 2006; Prochniak & Wasiak, 2017).

Additionally, including the equity market in the model adds complexity to an already controversial topic among researchers. Due to important pair-wise interaction within the three variables, several studies have been conducted to comprehend the relationships' dynamic and interconnection. For example, although there is a strong unidirectional causal flow observed from banking development to the equity market and from the equity market to economic growth, the study did not identify any causality between banking development and economic growth, applying to South Africa's context (Nyasha & Odhiambo, 2015). Furthermore, this relationship was further affirmed as these authors who conducted the same research focusing on Kenya (Nyasha & Odhiambo, 2016).

In addition to the above studies, the findings of Naceur and Ghazouani (2007) further support the notion that there is no substantial relationship between banking development and equity markets and economic growth. More specifically, the association between banking development and economic growth is even negative after controlling for the equity market. In contrast, Kim and Lin (2013) put forth the argument that banking development has a greater impact on economic growth in low-income countries, while the equity market is more advantageous for growth in high-income than low-inflation economies. Additionally, the study unveiled the coexistence of a positive impact of banking development on the equity market but a negative influence of the equity market on banking development.

With the increasing popularity of equity markets, certain researchers have started utilizing their extensive infrastructure as an alternative source of information on macroeconomic variables, replacing traditional databases. Through the usage of the GMM model, Cole et al. (2008) concluded that equity returns of the banking sector can predict future economic growth. Additionally, they also found that much of the predictive power of bank equity return is captured by a series of country-specific and banking institutional characteristics.

In summary, the correlation between variables above exhibits highly dynamic patterns, making it challenging to establish a singular interpretation that applies universally. Therefore, when assessing the correlation, it is crucial to consider the specific context and other relevant characteristics that may influence the relationship between the variables. For instance, the association between the equity market and economic growth tends to be sustained over a sufficiently long period, but it is susceptible to fluctuations over shorter time frames, even for banking equity. Furthermore, this correlation is significantly diminished in countries where the equity market is underdeveloped as compared with the dominance of the banking sector as the primary funding channel.

3 Data Collection

This section describes the process of gathering and constructing the historical database used in the analysis. The author discusses the following types of variables including equity return and macroeconomic variables. All variables are quarterly and focus only on the Vietnamese context throughout 2016–2023. Due to the limited availability of data, the author intentionally shortened the time horizon from years to quarters in comparison to the original study (Baron et al., 2021).

Bank and non-financial equity return

Despite its rapid growth in recent years, the Vietnamese equity market is currently classified as a frontier market Morgan Stanley Capital International (MSCI) in 2023 as it faces some challenges including low market capitalization and insufficient liquidity and transparency. Besides that, one of the other factors influencing the process of upgrading its rank to emerging markets is institutional underdevelopment. However, such limitation has been gradually resolved as the Ho Chi Minh Stock Exchange introduced ten new indexes based on different sectors in 2016. Particularly, constituent stocks included in these indexes have represented more than 80% of total equity market capitalization. All databases in terms of index prices are captured and reported daily on the website of the Ho Chi Minh Stock Exchange.

To capture the returns of bank equities, the author utilizes the price of the Vietnam Financials index, which is convenient due to its being readily available. Despite constituents regarding security and insurance firms, the index is still highly dominated by bank equity, comprising almost 90% of its total market capitalization. The inclusion of non-financial equity returns in the model serves the purpose of accounting for additional relationships that cannot be solely attributed to bank equities. Therefore, from the remaining nine indexes, the author intentionally selected one based on specific criteria such as low pair-wise correlation and high market capitalization (see Table 1). As a result, the returns of non-financial equities were represented by selecting the Vietnam consumer staples index. Both sectors' returns are collected quarterly and expressed in real terms.

GDP and Bank Credit-to-GDP

All databases regarding macroeconomic variables are captured and reported on the website of the General Statistics Office of Vietnam. Particularly, real GDP is calculated by adjusting nominal GDP for inflation. It is the same CPI used to deflate equity returns in the previous section. Similarly, bank credit-to-GDP is not directly recorded but requires making some minor calculations. All variables are collected quarterly and expressed in real terms.

Summary Statistics of Variables

As anticipated, the variability in the distribution of equity returns is significantly greater when compared to the fluctuations observed in macroeconomic variables. Remarkably, in the context of Vietnam, bank credit-to-GDP has demonstrated a consistent upward trend, with no quarters experiencing a decline, throughout the entire review period. In contrast, the distribution of GDP growth in Vietnam displayed pronounced variability, along with a notable feature of negative skewness. See Table 2.

4 Research Methodology

This section describes the process of examining the predictive power of large bank equity decline for subsequent economic outcomes such as real GDP and bank credit-to-GDP. In addition, the scope also expands to control non-financial equities to capture all the potential relationships, representing the whole equity market. The author aims to emphasize that the equity declines, either bank or non-financial, should not be dismissed as mere market fluctuations but rather recognized as potentially significant sources of information. By revealing that declines in bank equity often precede severe economic outcomes, the study provides a basis for utilizing the equity market as a tool for analyzing and predicting future banking and economic crises.

Therefore, the analysis is structured into three sub-categories including: (i) GDP and credit dynamic around bank equity crash, (ii) bank equity decline and future GDP growth, and (iii) bank equity decline and future bank credit growth. The initial section provides a qualitative overview, while the subsequent two sections offer quantitative models that enable precise measurement of the relationship.

Table 1 Pair-wise correlations across sector indices

Pair-wise correlation		VNCOND	VNCONS	VNENE	VNFIN	VNHEAL	VNIND	VNIT	VNMAT	VNREAL
Vietnam consumer discretionary	VNCOND									
Vietnam consumer staples	VNCONS	0.43								
Vietnam energy	VNENE	0.03	0.37							
Vietnam financials	VNFIN	0.90	0.42	0.16						
Vietnam health care	VNHEAL	0.90	0.33	(0.10)	0.88					
Vietnam industrials	VNIND	0.64	0.65	0.57	0.68	0.56				
Vietnam material	VNMAT	0.91	0.15	(0.06)	0.89	0.89	0.46			
Vietnam technology	VNIT	0.85	0.44	0.16	0.94	0.82	0.68	0.80		
Vietnam real estate	VNREAL	0.76	0.60	(0.03)	0.72	0.68	0.48	0.56	0.77	
Vietnam utilities	VNUTI	0.83	0.60	0.24	0.76	0.73	0.60	0.73	0.64	0.66

Table 2 Statistical distribution of variables

	GDP	CRE	R^B	R^N
Vars	1	2	3	4
N	30	30	30	30
Min	(0.02)	0.05	(0.18)	(0.18)
Max	0.05	0.09	0.46	0.27
Range	0.08	0.04	0.64	0.45
Mean	0.02	0.06	0.04	0.01
Median	0.02	0.06	0.01	0.01
Standard deviation	0.01	0.01	0.15	0.10
Standard error	0.002	0.002	0.02	0.01
Skewness	(1.76)	0.43	0.80	0.60
Kurtosis	7.96	(0.87)	0.38	0.74

GDP and credit dynamic around bank equity crash

To initiate the investigation, the study begins by analyzing the evolution of real GDP and bank credit-to-GDP during periods of bank equity crashes in comparison to periods without such a large decline. Throughout the study, an "equity crash" is defined as a quarterly decline exceeding 5% in the value of equities. To accommodate a shorter period, the author adjusts by lowering the threshold to 5% quarterly, or 20% annually, from the previous threshold of 15% of the original study (Baron et al., 2021). The aforementioned criteria are uniformly applied to both bank and non-financial equity consistently. As a result, we have summarized the number of bank and non-financial equity crashes from 2016 to 2023 are 5 and 4 times, respectively.

The analysis calculates the average cumulative change in log real GDP and bank credit-to-GDP about a year before the bank equity crashes. For given variables, each movement is plotted from four quarters before a bank equity crash ($t = -4$) to four quarters after the crash ($t = 4$). Time $t = 0$ is defined as the quarter of the bank equity crash. For reference purposes, the author also includes a plot depicting the average dynamics during normal periods without equity crashes.

Bank equity decline and future GDP/bank credit growth

Within this sub-category, the study formally investigates the predictability of significant declines in bank equity about subsequent GDP and bank credit-to-GDP. To account for flexible estimation and potential non-linearity, the author also employs the Jorda (2005) local projection specification to estimate the predictability of bank equity declines for horizons $h = 1, 2, 3$, and 4.

$$\Delta_h \text{GDP}_{t+h} = \sum_j \beta_j^h 1\left[R_t^B \in B_j\right] + \sum_j \delta_j^h 1\left[R_t^N \in B_j\right] + \pi^h X_t \varepsilon_t^h \quad (1)$$

where $\Delta_h \mathrm{GDP}_{t+h}$ is real GDP growth from quarter t to t + h. $1\left[R_t^B \in B_j\right]$ is an indicator variable for whether the bank equity return in quarter t is within a range defined by bin B_j. The indicator $1\left[R_t^N \in B_j\right]$ is similarly defined but for non-financial equity returns. To examine the predictability across the full distribution of returns, the study includes eight evenly spaced bins, B_j, for both bank and non-financial returns: less than – 15%, – 15% to – 10%, – 10% to – 5%, – 5% to 0%, 0% to 5%, 5% to 10%, 10% to 15% and greater than 15%. The excluded bin refers to the range of returns between 0 and 5%, which the author considers as returns observed during "normal" periods. In Eq. (1), the model includes controls for contemporaneous (i.e., t – 1 to t) and lagged real GDP growth and the change in bank credit-to-GDP. Additionally, it incorporates lags of the bank and non-financial equity return bins, represented by the variable X_t. The author proposes the usage of two lags instead of three of the instructions to achieve better accuracy in estimating the model.

The main focus here lies on the sequence of local projection impulse responses $\{\beta_j^h\}$, which illustrate the predictive capability of bank equity returns. These responses are derived by considering the influence of non-financial returns as well as current and previous economic conditions. It is important to note that after accounting for contemporaneous non-financial returns, declines in bank equity can be attributed to two distinct sources. Firstly, they may indicate the current period's loan losses incurred. Secondly, since equity prices are forward-looking, they may also reflect the equity market's expectation of future losses. Consequently, the impulse responses not only capture the influence of current bank losses on the overall economy, stemming from the impact on banks' ability to lend to businesses and households but also account for the expected interactions between future economic downturns and forthcoming bank losses. It is worth noting that bank equity may provide informative insights beyond the banking channel for various reasons. For instance, declines in bank equity may also indicate the macroeconomic repercussions of household balance sheet distress since households are directly affected by bank lending.

For ex-positional purposes, the study substitutes the eight return bins with an indicator variable denoting whether a bank equity crash has occurred, specifically defined as a quarterly decline of below –5% quarterly, $1\left[r_t^B \leq -5\%\right]$. In this particular model, the author intentionally analyzes horizons of two- and four-quarters-ahead.

$$\Delta_h \mathrm{CRE}_{t+h} = \sum_j \beta_j^h 1\left[R_t^B \leq -5\%\right] + \sum_j \delta_j^h 1\left[R_t^N \leq -5\%\right] + \pi^h X_t \varepsilon_t^h \quad (2)$$

The entire process subsequently includes bank credit-to-GDP as the dependent variable, systematically examining the relationship between these variables and evaluating whether a bank equity crash can effectively predict a slowdown in credit growth.

5 Findings and Discussion

GDP and credit dynamic around bank equity crash

In order to assess the predictability of bank equity, the author has generated initial visual representations showcasing the accumulated changes in economic variables for both situations, considering both the presence and absence of the crash. The comparative analysis spans a time frame of eight quarters, encompassing four quarters prior to the crash and four quarters following the crash.

The analysis shown in Fig. 1 suggests that there is no significant distinction in the growth rate of both real GDP and bank credit-to-GDP variables during the quarters leading up to the crash. However, after that time, a noticeable disparity emerged and has continued to expand ever since. Surprisingly, the version that experienced the bank equity decline exhibited higher growth. Within one year following the bank equity crash, there has been a notable widening disparity in GDP, exceeding 3%, with the gap persisting as early as two quarters after the crash. Despite the crash of the equity market, the correlation between financial development and economic growth, as illustrated by real GDP and bank credit-to-GDP, remains intact and unaffected. It appears that the continuous credit expansion, which is partly responsible for the crash, acts as a significant driving factor for economic development.

The typical sequence of events can be summarized as follows. As GDP growth decelerates, there is a requirement to depend on borrowing to fuel economic expansion. As a consequence, the government imposes policies to promote credit expansion and lead to a rise in the bank credit-to-GDP ratio, which is often noticed two quarters before an equity market crash. In anticipation of better future performance, the bank equity increases. The debt-driven mechanism effectively stimulates economic growth. Although there is a subsequent decline in equity prices due to overvaluation, it does not hinder the growth of economic indicators as the process continues.

Bank equity decline and future GDP/bank credit growth

The author further delves into the potential causation by incorporating the equity crash caused by non-financial along with the banking sector (see Figs. 2 and 3). In addition, the decline is also categorized into separate bins encompassing all the

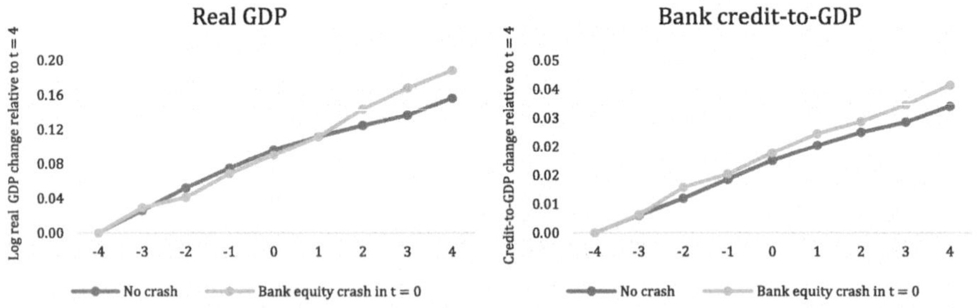

Fig. 1 Dynamic of output and credit around bank equity crash

quarterly changes in equity. The four-quarter period continues to serve as the chosen time frame to accurately reflect the level of predictability.

As previously mentioned, the correlation between bank equity returns and economic growth remains uncertain, with varying effects on the direction of the growth rate in the year following a bank equity crash. In addition, the magnitude of the decline in bank equity returns does not consistently correspond to the observed effects on the difference in growth rate. Especially, two quarters after the crash, the GDP growth rate started to accelerate, which is consistent with the earlier analysis. Similarly, such ambiguous analysis can be extended to the relationship between a bank equity crash and the bank credit-to-GDP ratio.

In comparison to its counterpart, the non-financial equity crash appears to have a more pronounced impact, as all bins exhibit a consistent direction, particularly evident since the third quarter. However, the analysis does not provide conclusive evidence of a definite slowdown in the growth rate one year after an equity crash. In contrast, when examining the bank credit-to-GDP ratio, the average drop of 6.3 percentage points indicates a noticeable decrease primarily attributed to an actual decline in bank credit (see Table 3).

The correlation is ultimately materialized by employing a regression model that incorporates lagged variables with a time lag of two quarters and four quarters, respectively. Additionally, the model also controls for the effect of the non-financial sector along with the primary variables of the banking crash (see Table 4).

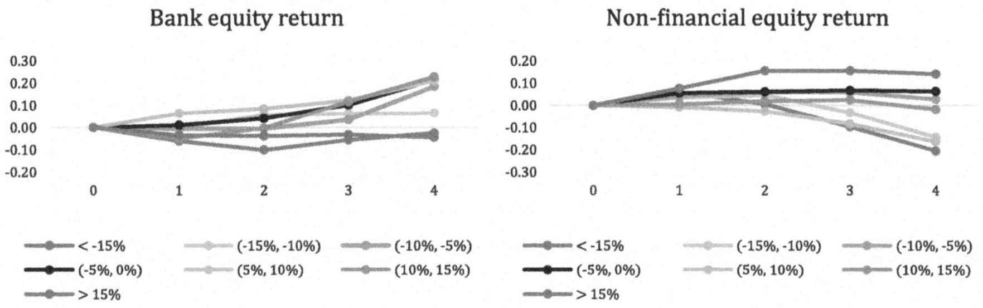

Fig. 2 Bank equity crash and output gaps

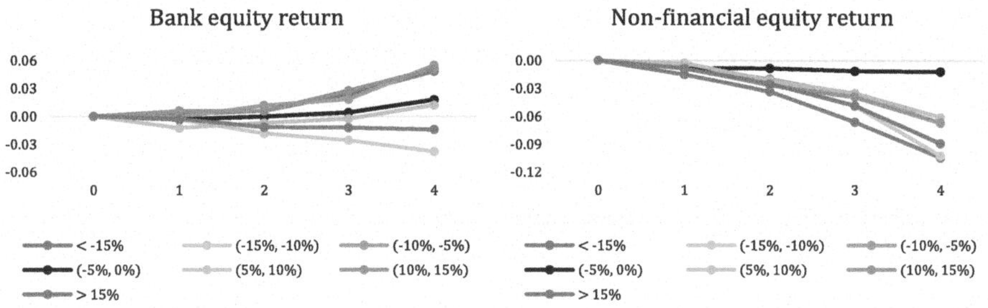

Fig. 3 Bank equity crash and credit contraction

Table 3 Bank equity crash and output gaps

	Real $GDP_{t,\,t+2}$		Real $GDP_{t,\,t+4}$	
	(1)	(2)	(3)	(4)
Bank equity crash	0.01 [1.41]	0.002 [0.14]	0.003 [0.18]	− 0.009 [− 0.34]
Non-financial equity crash	− 0.01 [− 1.42]	− 0.03* [− 1.96]	− 0.04* [− 1.91]	− 0.045 [− 1.36]
Controls		✓		✓
Adj. R^2 (within)	0.12	0.45	0.12	0.47
N	28	28	28	28

Table 4 Bank equity crash and credit contraction

	Credit-to-$GDP_{t,\,t+2}$		Credit-to-$GDP_{t,\,t+4}$	
	(1)	(2)	(3)	(4)
Bank equity crash	− 0.0006 [− 0.27]	− 0.0018 [− 0.65]	− 0.0029 [− 0.64]	0.0006 [0.21]
Non-financial equity crash	− 0.0026 [− 1.07]	0.0001 [0.05]	− 0.0106** [− 2.16]	− 0.0037 [− 1.07]
Controls		✓		✓
Adj. R^2 (within)	0.0481	0.5056	0.1755	0.8711
N	28	28	28	28

Similarly, the regression model analysis in Tables 3 and 4 further supports the notion that there is no significant causal relationship between a bank equity crash and macroeconomic variables including GDP growth rate and the bank credit-to-GDP ratio. Even with the inclusion of control effects, neither a time horizon of two quarters nor one year yields statistically significant results. In contrast, concerning non-financial equity crashes, there are certain instances where meaningful correlations between dependent and independent variables can be observed. However, it is important to note that the number of such cases is relatively minimal, and even when present, the level of significance, if any, is also small. This outcome, combined with the earlier analysis featuring different bins, broadens the model to encompass all the changes in the equity market, to reinforce the idea of a widespread absence of correlation.

6 Conclusion and Recommendations

The model applied to the Vietnam context does not provide evidence of a statistically significant relationship between a bank equity crash and macroeconomic variables including GDP growth rate and the bank credit-to-GDP ratio. However, several notable findings emerge from the analysis. Firstly, there is an identifiable conventional process leading up to a bank equity crash. Additionally, the analysis suggests that non-financial equity has a more pronounced effect on the estimation of economic growth compared to bank equity.

The absence of a statistically significant relationship can be primarily attributed to the underdevelopment of the Vietnamese equity market, characterized by a lack of depth, liquidity, efficiency, and transparency. This underdevelopment poses significant challenges when using stock prices as reliable indicators for future equity market projections. Furthermore, the market's inefficiency and lack of transparency result in information asymmetry, making it difficult to accurately assess companies' fundamentals and predict future trends based solely on stock prices.

Overall, the underdeveloped equity market hampers the ability to make informed decisions and accurately forecast future outcomes based on stock price movements. Similarly, the current development of the banking industry introduces difficulties in using it as a predictor of macroeconomic trends. The government frequently relies on the banking sector to make necessary adjustments and stimulate economic growth. Rather than relying solely on the banking industry for accurate projections, policymakers turn to it as a mechanism to implement measures that can positively impact the economy and drive economic growth.

The equity market plays a vital role in every economy, serving as a fundamental pillar alongside the banking sector in the overall financial market structure. To maximize the potential of the equity market, it should be cultivated not just as a funding channel that complements the banking sector, but also as a dynamic platform that accurately reflects the market's expectations. Furthermore, the government must foster and respect the autonomy of the banking sector while assuming the oversight function of a supervisor.

In expanding on the need for further research, it is important to recognize that the analysis conducted in this study represents a preliminary exploration into the relationship between bank equity and GDP growth in Vietnam. To exploit the full potential of this analysis, additional research is required to delve deeper into various aspects. By undertaking more extensive research, policymakers, financial investors, and other stakeholders will have access to a more nuanced and comprehensive understanding of the role of bank equity in estimating the effects of macroeconomic variables in Vietnam.

References

Baron, M., Werner, E., & Xiong, W. (2021). Banking crises without panics. *The Quarterly Journal of Economics, 136*(1), 51–113.

Cole, R. A., Moshirian, F., & Wu, Q. (2008). Bank stock returns and economic growth. *Journal of Banking & Finance, 32*(6), 995–1007.

Cornell, B. (2010). Economic growth and equity investing. *Financial Analysts Journal, 66*(1), 54–64.

Jorda, O. (2005). Estimation and inference of impulse responses by local projections. *The American Economic Review, 95*(1), 161–182.
Kim, D., & Lin, S. (2013). Interrelationships among banks, stock markets and economic growth: An empirical investigation. *Applied Economics, 45*(31), 4385–4394.
Le, D. (2022). Banking sector outlook in Vietnam: Opportunities and challenges. *FiinGroup: Enlighten the Market.* https://fiingroup.vn/upload/docs/Banking_Sector_Outlook_in_Vietnam-Opportunities_and_Challenges_FiinResearch.pdf
Leung, S. E. (2010). Vietnam: An economic survey. *Asian-Pacific Economic Literature, 24*, 83–103.
Loayza, N. V., & Ranciere, R. (2006). Financial development, financial fragility, and growth. *Journal of Money, Credit and Banking, 38*(4), 1051–1076.
Masoud, N. (2013). The impact of stock market performance upon economic growth. *International Journal of Economics and Financial Issues, 3*(4), 788–798.
Naceur, S., & Ghazouani, S. (2007). Stock markets, banks, and economic growth: Empirical evidence from the MENA region. *Journal of Economic Literature, 21*, 297–315.
Nguyen, P. T. (2022). The impact of banking sector development on economic growth: The case of Vietnam's transitional economy. *Journal of Risk and Financial Management, 15*(8), August, 1–18.
Nyasha, S., & Odhiambo, N. (2015). The impact of banks and stock market development on economic growth in South Africa: An ARDL-bounds testing approach. *Journal of Contemporary Economics, 9*, 93–108.
Nyasha, S., & Odhiambo, N. (2016). Banks, stock market development and economic growth in Kenya: An empirical investigation. *Journal of African Business, 18*(1), 1–23.
Pham, T. T., & Pham, Q. T. (2014). *The relationship between the renovation of growth model and the restructure of the economy.* https://tapchitaichinh.vn/moi-quan-he-giua-doi-moi-mo-hinh-tang-truong-va-tai-cau-truc-nen-kinh-te.html
Prochniak, M., & Wasiak, K. (2017). The impact of the financial system on economic growth in the context of the global crisis: Empirical evidence from the EU and OECD countries. *Empirica, 44*, 295–337.
Ritter, J. R. (2004). Economic growth and equity returns. *Journal of Pacific-Basin Finance, 13*(5), 489–602.
Rogoff, K. (2022). Emerging market sovereign debt in the aftermath of the pandemic. *Journal of Economic Perspectives, 36*(4), 147–166.
Ross, L. (1997). Financial development and economic growth: Views and agenda. *Journal of Economic Literature, 35*, 668–726.
United Nation. (2023). *A world of debt.* https://unctad.org/publication/world-of-debt
Wade, K., & May, A. (2013). GDP growth and equity market returns. *Schroders Investment Management Limited.* https://prod.schroders.com/en/sysglobalassets/schroders/sites/pensions/pdfs/gdp-growth-and-equity-market-returns-feb2013.pdf

Pham Quoc Tien current role is to identify and evaluate business opportunities to enhance the financial performance of his company. He is also an active member of the CFA Institution and CMA (Australia) Association. As a lifelong learner, Tien's pursuit of a master's program in Economics is driven by his desire to gain a deeper academic understanding to enrich his knowledge and insights in the field.

Chapter 8
Measuring Technological Progress and Productivity Growth in Vietnam's Banking Industry

Ung Trieu Gia Bao

Abstract The relationship between the banking system and other entities impacts the overall national economy. This connection has grown stronger over the past few decades. Assessing individual banks' performance is important for understanding their market position and providing useful insights for practitioners. This study assesses performance of 17 commercial banks in Vietnam from 2017 to 2022 by employing the Malmquist productivity index and data envelopment analysis (DEA). The assessment covers seven dimensions of bank performance, including operating expenses, assets, liabilities, and deposits as inputs, with loans, bad debt, and profit before tax as outcomes. Utilizing the Malmquist productivity method, the study indicates that banks' total productivity growth indices, which are then decomposed into technological and efficiency changes. According to the Malmquist index results, most banks experienced a decline in productivity from 2017 to 2022, showing reductions in both technical change and productivity indexes. This research offers a thorough examination of the performance of commercial banks in Vietnam, providing insights for managers in the banking sector. The findings bring implications for sustainable development and offer strategic recommendations at the bank's managerial level.

Keywords Decision analysis · Commercial bank · Malmquist productivity index · Technological progress · Data envelopment analysis (DEA)

U. T. G. Bao (✉)
Vietnam - the Netherlands Programme, University of Economics Ho Chi Minh City, Ho Chi Minh City, Vietnam
e-mail: bao.utg@vnp.edu.vn

Erasmus University, Rotterdam, the Netherlands

P. K. Nam and A. Heshmati (eds.), *Recent Trends in Vietnam's Rapid Economic Development*, Frontiers in South and Southeast Asian Development Research,
https://doi.org/10.1007/978-981-97-6079-4_8

1 Introduction

In 2022, the banking industry faced significant challenges due to global turmoil, particularly from the COVID-19 pandemic. However, the year also marked a crucial period for recovery, with supportive measures and financial aid implemented through economic stimulus initiatives. These measures aimed to protect businesses, citizens, and the vital banking sector, which supports nearly all economic activities. Despite the upheaval, the banking industry showed positive signs of recovery and effectively responded to the challenges posed by the pandemic. Despite facing turbulence, the pivotal function of banks has been underscored in latest years, as they played a crucial function by providing financial assistance to customers, employees, and society at large (Batten & Vo, 2019). The State Bank of Vietnam (SBV) reported noteworthy figures that held significance for the entire economy. Key indicators included a relatively low inflation rate (averaging 3.15%), a high economic growth rate of 8.02%, a accredit increase of 14.5%, and stable foreign exchange markets, with the Vietnamese dong depreciating by 3.5% and a 1% increase in interest rates. Vietnam was also removed from the US Department of the Treasury's list of countries under advanced monitoring for currency manipulation, acknowledging the State Bank of Vietnam's adept management of monetary and exchange rate policies.

To address economic challenges, timely solutions were implemented, including adjustments to deposit interest rate in VND for terms less than six months at credit institutions increased by 0.8–2.0% per year. Concurrently, the maximum lending interest rates were raised twice, resulting in a total increase of 2.0% per year. These measures aimed to control inflation, stabilize the foreign currency market, and provide flexibility to adapt to market fluctuations, thereby contributing to macroeconomic stability. Additionally, the monitoring of deposit interest rates, which had reached their peak, prompted some banks to surpass the 12% mark, leading to an increase in the lending rate. Credit institutions also underwent revisions to reduce operating costs, administrative procedures, and unnecessary expenses, creating room to lower lending interest rates and alleviate the financial burden on citizens and businesses.

Understanding the key factors influencing banking activities during and after financial crisis is essential for tailoring public policies, regulations, and management practices. This enables the recognition and application of appropriate guidelines to proactively address banking issues. Assaf et al. (2019) emphasize that the efficiency of banks in pre-crisis periods, often overlooked, significantly contributes to overall bank efficiency. Consequently, we utilize Malmquist productivity models to evaluate the temporal performance of Vietnamese commercial banks over the period spanning from 2017 to 2022, focusing on seven dimensions: net income, deposits, liabilities, loans, operating expenses, assets, loans, and bad debt. The selection of these dimensions is grounded in extensive investigation and support from experts, researchers, and studies within the banking industry, as detailed in Tables 1 and 2.

Table 1 Common input and output factors in previous banking studies

No.	Authors (Citation)	Input factors	Output factors	# of DMUs	Research scopes
1	Jablonsky et al. (2004)	Employees Operating expense Space	Number of accounts Number of transactions Savings	81	Illustrating the efficiency in productivity of branches in the Czech Republic
2	Emrouznejad and Anouze (2010)	Assets Equity Deposit	Loan Profit	36	Evaluating the efficiency and productivity of the banking sector in the Gulf Cooperation Council countries
3	Lin and Chiu (2013)	Fixed assets Operating expense Capital	Non-interest income Interest income Profit	30	Examining the performance evaluation of domestic banks in Taiwan
4	Fujii et al. (2014)	Employees Deposits Fixed assets	Acquired assets Customer loans Bad loans	24	Analyzing technical efficiency and productivity growth within the Indian banking sector
5	Wang et al. (2014)	Employees Fixed assets	Total deposits Income before tax Total credit	117	Assessing the efficiency of the Chinese commercial banking system
6	Wanke et al. (2016)	Total costs Employee costs	Total deposits Income before tax Total credit	117	Evaluating the productive efficiency of banks in Mozambique
7	Mahmoudabadi and Emrouznejad (2019)	Employees Fixed assets Non-operating costs Interest expenses	Bank facilities Interest income Non-interest income	37	Assessing the operational efficiency, service effectiveness, and social effectiveness of commercial banks in Iran
9	Sáez-Fernández et al. (2021)	Staff expenses Non-earning assets Equity Customer deposits Market liabilities	Loan Securities	124	Evaluating the technical performance of banks in Brazil
10	This paper	Assets Deposits Operating expenses Liabilities	Loan Bad debt Income before tax	17	Assessing the technological and productivity growth of commercial banks in Vietnam

Table 2 Catalog of premier commercial banks in Vietnam

DMUs	Abbreviation	Banks	Profit before tax in 2022 (million VND)	Ranking by 2022 net profit before tax
B1	CTG	Vietinbank	20.946	6
B2	BID	BIDV	23.009	3
B3	VCB	Vietcombank	37.368	1
B4	ACB	ACB	17.114	7
B5	STB	Sacombank	6.339	11
B6	SHB	SHBank	9.686	9
B7	MBB	Military Bank	22.729	4
B8	VPB	VPBank	21.220	5
B9	OCB	Orient Commercial	4.389	15
B10	MSB	Vietnam Maritime	5.787	12
B11	TPB	TPBank	7.828	10
B12	HDB	HDBank	10.268	8
B13	TCB	Techcombank	25.567	2
B14	LPB	LienViet Post Bank	5.689	13
B15	SSB	SEABANK	5.068	14
B16	EIB	Export Import Bank	3.709	16
B17	BAB	Bac A Bank	832	17

Source iboard.ssi.com.vn

Our chosen dimensions are based on a data set available on Harvard Dataverse,[1] a reliable platform for researchers seeking information and data. Bank operations involve resource utilization across multiple dimensions such as operating expenses, liabilities, deposits, assets (input variables), generating various output like bad debt, profit before tax, and loans. Consequently, the evaluation must consider multiple inputs and outputs simultaneously. Given the complex nature of a bank's operations and absence of a readily available analytical representation for the relationship between inputs and outputs, data envelopment analysis (DEA) emerges as a suitable approach to address these concerns. DEA is instrumental in assisting active research areas by revealing patterns of efficiency and efficiency changes over time for each bank. It also identifies inefficient banks that require improvement and highlights banks that can serve as a role model or benchmark for the Vietnamese banking industry, offering valuable insights for both researchers and practitioners.

In this study, we utilized the Malmquist productivity index measurement incorporated within the data envelopment analysis (DEA) framework to examine a sample of 17 commercial banks in Vietnam over the period from 2017 to 2022. The assessment encompassed two distinct dimensions: inputs (consisting of operating expenses, liabilities, deposits, and assets of banks) and outputs (including bad debt, profit

[1] https://library.harvard.edu/services-tools/harvard-dataverse.

before tax, and loans of banks), aiming to evaluate the performance of the banks. The Malmquist model was applied to analyze the overall rates of productivity development within the banks, revealing the patterns of efficiency changes over time. To identify the factors influencing efficiency change, the Malmquist indexes were decomposed into two components: technical efficiency change (catch-up) and technical change (frontier-shift). Frontier is measured as in the sample best-performing banks. This decomposition provides insights into the individual banks' performance evolution based on their efforts, as well as the collective impact of prevailing trends on the entire group.

This study seeks to fill certain gaps present in the current literature. Through the utilization of the suggested DEA model, our goal is to provide more resilient and thorough insights into the Vietnamese banking industry (Avkiran, 2015; Avkiran & Cai, 2014; Dang-Thanh, 2012; Mohtashami & Ghiasvand, 2020; Paradi & Zhu, 2013). This, in turn, serves as a practical guide for practitioners to enhance awareness of the position and circumstances. It provides a foundation for more effective strategies for improving efficiency and advancing sustainability within the banking industry.

The subsequent sections of this paper include a literature review in Sect. 2, the theoretical framework in Sect. 3, data collection with the choice of decision making units (DMUs) in Sect. 4, the empirical results in Sect. 5, and the conclusion with policy implications in Sect. 6.

2 Literature Review

Efficiency in a financial institution or bank is characterized by its capacity to achieve results with minimal extra effort and resources. This is gauged by how closely a production unit approaches its production possibility frontier, a collection of points that optimally combine inputs to produce one unit of output (Kablan, 2009).

Various methods are available to assess the effectiveness of banks, classified into (1) profit and cost efficiency (Assaf et al., 2019), (2) aspects like operating expenses, loans, interest expenses, interest/non-interest revenue (Banker et al., 2010), and more complex dimensions including (3) service quality (Paradi et al., 2018), and (4) system uncertainty (Avkiran, 2018), among other factors. While commonly employed efficiency measurements method tends to concentrate on simple financial ratios, they come with several shortcomings. Faello (2015) highlighted that financial ratios may be deceptive as they do not account for factors like product mix or input prices.

An alternative method involves focusing on the production function or cost functions of banks, where the estimated function is considered an optimal representation of the banking system (Worthington, 2010). The objective is to minimize cost to produce a given level of output or to maximize output for a given level of inputs. The service industry minimizes the cost of providing service which is exogenously given yet possible to influence the demand. This parametric estimate is derived from a model with specific confidence intervals and deviations, making it statistically recognized. In the survey spending the years 1992–1997, Berger and Humphrey (1992) found that over 52% of researchers favored the parametric approach for measuring financial institutions' efficiency. The parametric approach allows to model behavior and use non-inputs and outputs characteristics of banks, market, and policy. However, it is important to note that this estimation makes notable assumptions about function forms especially when dealing with a small sample size. In such cases, non-parametric approach is often preferred.

In the evaluation of efficiency, there are various methodological approaches, and among them, data envelopment analysis (DEA) is a commonly used nonmetric method for measuring comparative efficiency and productivity across diverse areas and time periods. Rooted in mathematical optimization, DEA is especially effective for benchmarking units with multiple inputs and outputs. Its utilization extends to diverse contexts, where different versions of DEA are frequently used to assess the performance of entities called decision making units (DMU) like industrial sectors, countries, facilities, cities, and companies. A disadvantage of non-parametric approach is that bank-specific effects which are not accounted for can bias the measured degree of inefficiency of banks. The main advantage is not assuming strong assumptions such as functional forms.

The objective of the study is to employ Malmquist motto in constructing a comprehensive valuable evaluation framework specifically designed for fostering sustainable development within the banking industry. The practical contribution of the study lies in providing an in-depth understanding through the analysis of 17 commercial banks in Vietnam as a case study. Utilizing chosen indicators, we employed the Malmquist model to evaluate the banks' productivity growth over time, considering changes in performance, technology, and overall productivity. The practical importance of this study is apparent as it can aid decision-makers in gaining insights into their organization's standing within the banking sector, bringing a comprehensive understanding of overall efficiency and productivity of individual banks and the aggregate industry.

3 Theoretical Framework

3.1 Mathematical Modeling Framework

Essentially, the study introduces a modeling framework designed to measure productivity advancement and evaluate the performance of decision making units (DMUs), exemplified by the case study involving 17 Vietnam commercial banks, incorporating four inputs and three outputs, as illustrated in Fig. 1.

The Malmquist model functions as a valuable tool to evaluate the banks' productivity growth across two periods, relying on three indices: changes in technical efficiency, technological advancements, and overall productivity. DEA is a non-parametric method where both inputs and outputs play a significant role in determining the outcome. Previous research indicates that a business needs to modify or decrease inputs (input or cost-oriented minimization) while enhancing or expanding

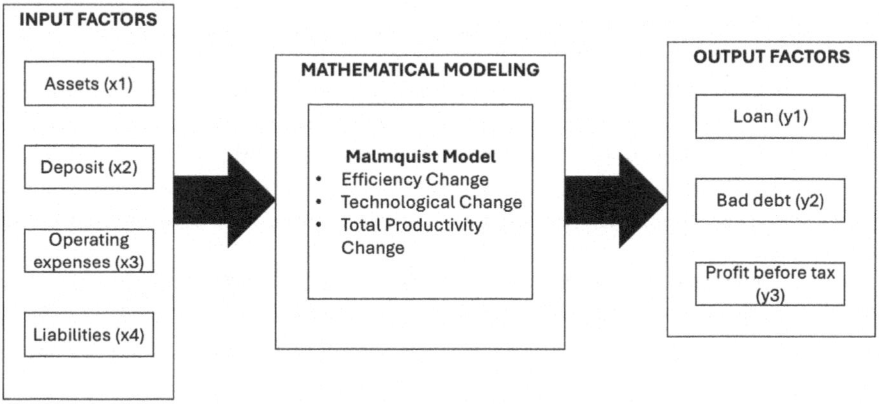

Fig. 1 Research's multi-input multi-output modeling framework

outputs (output-oriented maximization), particularly concerning financial indices (Charnes et al., 1979; Wang et al., 2020). Consistent with the study's aim and considering the typically employed input and output factors in evaluating banking system performance (as delineated in Table 1), four inputs and three outputs were used in this research, detailed as below.

Input factors

1. Assets ($\times 1$): The cumulative valuation of assets held by the bank encompasses various items that possess potential liquidity and value, such as real estate, tradable assets, loans extended to customers, and deposits held by the bank at its headquarters.
2. Deposits ($\times 2$): The overall sum of customer deposits with the bank and deposits with others.
3. Operating expenses ($\times 3$): Expenditures borne by banking entities, covering items like remuneration and benefits, legal fees, and information technology expenses.
4. Liabilities ($\times 4$): Applications that the bank is eventually required to settle, encompassing loans from the headquarters, customer deposits, change liabilities, and non-performing loans.

Output factors

1. Loan ($y1$): It belongs to the function of consumers, entrepreneurs, or lending companies, showcasing their capability to offer financial services.
2. Bad debt ($y2$): It is referred to debt that cannot be collected. It is a part of operating a business if that company allows customers to use credit for purchases.
3. Profit before tax ($y3$): It is a profitability measure that provides for greater comparability among companies that pay a varying amount of taxes.

3.2 Pearson Correlation

In earlier research, the Pearson correlation coefficient has commonly been utilized to depict the linear association between two variables. Here, + 1 signifies a complete positive linear relationship, 0 indicates no linear relationship, and − 1 denotes a total negative linear relationship (Le & Wang, 2017). It should be noted that Pearson correlation coefficient measures only pairwise direct correlation relationships and is unconditional of third factors' indirect effects.

Isotropy is a crucial assumption in DEA data analysis. Prior to applying the DEA model, the correlation between inputs and outputs is examined, requiring it to be a complete positive linear relationship. The calculation of Pearson's formula (r) with factor (u) and (v) is expressed as Eq. (1) (Wang et al., 2021a, 2021b).

$$r_{uv} = \frac{\sum_{i=1}^{n} u_i v_i - \frac{\sum_{i=1}^{n} u_i \sum_{i=1}^{n} v_i}{n}}{\sqrt{\left(\sum_{i=1}^{n} u_i^2 - \frac{\left(\sum_{i=1}^{n} u_i\right)^2}{n}\right)}}, \tag{1}$$

where n is the sample size: u_i, v_i are the sample's positions related to DMU i.

3.3 DEA Malmquist Model

The calculation of the catch-up index (C), representing technical efficiency, the frontier-shift index (F), indicating technological changes, and the Malmquist Productivity Indicator (MPI), is performed as outlined in Eqs. (2)–(5) (Wang et al., 2021a, 2021b).

$$C = \frac{d^2\left((u_i, v_i)^2\right)}{d^1\left((u_i, v_i)^1\right)} \tag{2}$$

$$F = \left[\frac{d^1\left((u_i, v_i)^1\right)}{d^2\left((u_i, v_i)^1\right)} \times \frac{d^1\left((u_i, v_i)^2\right)}{d^2\left((u_i, v_i)^2\right)}\right]^{\frac{1}{2}} \tag{3}$$

$$\text{MPI} = C \times F = \frac{d^2\left((u_i, v_i)^2\right)}{d^1\left((u_i, v_i)^1\right)} \times \left[\frac{d^1\left((u_i, v_i)^1\right)}{d^2\left((u_i, v_i)^1\right)} \times \frac{d^1\left((u_i, v_i)^2\right)}{d^2\left((u_i, v_i)^2\right)}\right]^{\frac{1}{2}} \tag{4}$$

$$\text{MPI} = \left[\frac{d^1\left((u_i, v_i)^2\right)}{d^1\left((u_i, v_i)^1\right)} \times \frac{d^2\left((u_i, v_i)^2\right)}{d^2\left((u_i, v_i)^1\right)}\right]^{\frac{1}{2}}. \tag{5}$$

Let (u_i^1, v_i^1) represent the data envelopment analysis (DEA) model unit DMU$_i$ at stage 1, (u_i^2, v_i^2) denote DMU$_i$ at stage 2, and the efficiency score of the DMU$_i$ $\left(u_i^1, v_i^1\right)^{t_1}$ is assessed by the technological frontier t_2: $d^{(t_2)}\left((u_i, v_i)^{t_1}\right)$.

Based on the equations presented earlier, the indicators of frontier-shift, catch-up, and Malmquist productivity for DMI$_i$ demonstrate progress, consistency, or deterioration as the values exceed 1, equal 1, or drop below 1, representing progress, unchanged, and regress, respectively, during the transition from stage 1 to stage 2. This observation is supported by the provided evidence.

4 Case Study

4.1 *The Choice of DMUs*

This research centers on assessing the operational effectiveness of Vietnam's prominent commercial joint-stock banks. Specifically, the analysis encompasses the 17 commercial banks that wield significant influence over the Vietnam banking stock market. All these banks are listed on the Ho Chi Minh Stock Exchange (HOSE) (SSI, 2023), as indicated in Table 2.

4.2 *Data Collection*

In this investigation, data spanning the period from 2017 to 2022 was utilized. A diverse set of input and output factors, comprising fundamental financial indicators, was considered. The inputs included assets ($\times 1$), deposits ($\times 2$), operating expenses ($\times 3$), and liabilities ($\times 4$), while the outputs consisted of loans ($y1$), bad debt ($y2$), and profits before tax ($y3$). The data were compiled from the major commercial banks' annual financial statement reports of listed on the Vietnam stock market. All measurements are presented in billions of Vietnamese dongs (VND), and the detailed statistical information for each respective year is comprehensively presented in Table 3.

Table 3 Analysis of distribution of inputs and outputs for each year, 2017–2022 (in billions VND)

Period	Statistics	Input factors				Output factors		
		*a*1	*a*2	*a*3	*a*4	*b*1	*b*2	*b*3
2017	Max	1,202,284	859,985	64,492	1,153,449	86,6885	23,675	11,341
	Min	84,300	53,205	4757	78,160	36,212	35,1612	164,429
	Avg	363,061	252,496	19,173	340,542	231,102	4601	3810
	SD	367,960	260,408	17,292	351,577	254,051	6137	3706
2018	Max	1,313,037	989,671	72,757	1,258,486	988,738	23,538	18,269
	Min	97,029	60,362	6247	89,946	48,762	488	622
	Avg	398,343	282,521	22,619	371,445	262,516	5592	5039
	SD	389,681	295,019	20,036	372,027	285,400	6785	4834
2019	Max	1,489,957	1,114,162	83,183	1,412,304	1,116,997	19,496	23,122
	Min	107,889	69,142	8040	100,074	63,594	1235	933
	Avg	448,945	319,885	25,766	416,005	303,362	4593	6556
	SD	432,772	330,359	21,651	409,352	315,952	4730	5949
2020	Max	1,516,685	1,226,673	85,483	1,437,039	1,214,295	21,369	23,049
	Min	117,189	86,442	8254	108,825	79,340	628	734
	Avg	496,619	360,534	26,759	458,152	342,707	4751	7539
	SD	448,598	362,035	21,639	423,502	343,765	5086	6498
2021	Max	1,761,695	1,380,397	76,428	1,675,366	1,354,632	16,244	27,388
	Min	119,791	93,440	8520	110,740	84,598	655	908
	Avg	578,164	399,441	25,363	530,605	394,609	5307	9943
	SD	502,389	411,968	19,391	475,325	382,702	4889	7778
2022	Max	2,120,609	1,473,598	89,914	2,016,419	1,522,221	25,137	373,68
	Min	128,793	96,904	9604	118,993	94,120	513	1038
	Avg	680,989	441,694	30,816	622,857	457,582	6155	13,397
	SD	622,022	439,304	23,472	589,234	434,230	6465	10,164

Source Calculated by the author

5 Result and Analysis

5.1 Pearson Correlation Coefficient Test

Utilizing Eq. (1), Table 4 presents the Pearson coefficient values for the factors of DMUs in the years from 2017 till 2022. The Pearson correlation coefficient falls within the range of − 1 to + 1.

Correlation coefficients ranging from 0.5050 to 0.9970 indicate positive correlations among the input and output factors, establishing them as suitable variables for the DEA model (specifically, the Malmquist model). This signifies that the gathered

Table 4 Correlation coefficients among factors

Period	Factors	Input factors				Output factors		
		× 1	× 2	× 3	× 4	*y*1	*y*2	*y*3
2017	Asset	1						
	Deposits	0.9945	1					
	Operating expenses	0.9645	0.9624	1				
	Liabilities	0.9998	0.9952	0.9642	1			
	Loans	0.9846	0.9823	0.9876	0.9849	1		
	Bad debt	0.5404	0.5826	0.6143	0.5402	0.5499	1	
	Income before tax	0.8119	0.7702	0.7700	0.8047	0.7690	0.3209	1
2018	Asset	1						
	Deposits	0.9955	1					
	Operating expenses	0.9701	0.9619	1				
	Liabilities	0.9996	0.9964	0.9702	1			
	Loans	0.9899	0.9859	0.9883	0.9913	1		
	Bad debt	0.6256	0.6186	0.6900	0.6304	0.6603	1	
	Income before tax	0.6806	0.6594	0.5759	0.6673	0.5974	0.2428	1
2019	Asset	1						
	Deposits	0.9954	1					
	Operating expenses	0.9725	0.9658	1				
	Liabilities	0.9996	0.9964	0.9730	1			
	Loans	0.9913	0.9856	0.9872	0.9924	1		
	Bad debt	0.8432	0.8306	0.9254	0.8460	0.8829	1	
	Income before tax	0.7409	0.7169	0.6502	0.7268	0.6689	0.4346	1
2020	Asset	1						
	Deposits	0.9941	1					
	Operating expenses	0.9628	0.9623	1				
	Liabilities	0.9995	0.9957	0.9644	1			
	Loans	0.9909	0.9896	0.9836	0.9924	1		
	Bad debt	0.7777	0.78692	0.90451	0.7836	0.8350	1	
	Income before tax	0.7192	0.6671	0.6035	0.6992	0.6486	0.3284	1
2021	Asset	1						
	Deposits	0.9910	1					
	Operating expenses	0.9796	0.9655	1				
	Liabilities	0.9992	0.9937	0.9808	1			
	Loans	0.9953	0.9925	0.9876	0.9970	1		
	Bad debt	0.7175	0.6664	0.7946	0.7108	0.7316	1	
	Income before tax	0.6976	0.6427	0.6075	0.6714	0.6363	0.4358	1
2022	Asset	1						

(continued)

Table 4 (continued)

Period	Factors	Input factors				Output factors		
		× 1	× 2	× 3	× 4	*y*1	*y*2	*y*3
	Deposits	0.9942	1					
	Operating expenses	0.9750	0.9658	1				
	Liabilities	0.9992	0.9969	0.9750	1			
	Loans	0.9957	0.9938	0.9862	0.9969	1		
	Bad debt	0.5162	0.4707	0.6129	0.5050	0.5395	1	
	Income before tax	0.7854	0.7337	0.7215	0.7630	0.7407	0.4807	1

Source Formulated by the author

data adhere to isotropic conditions, affirming their suitability for application in the methodology outlined in this paper.

5.2 *Malmquist Productivity Index (MPI)*

The MPI proves to be an exceptionally valuable metric for assessing performance across various sectors, including but not limited to the automobile industry, medical, finance, insurance, and education. Reviewing the outcomes in Table 5, the calculated average Malmquist index for decision making units (DMUs) is calculated as 1.1157 (> 1), indicating that the majority (15 DMUs: B1, 2, 3, 4, 6, 7, 8, 9, 10, 11, 12, 14, 15, 16, and 17) show improvement in aggregate factor productivity. The general performance of the majority of DMUs displayed fluctuation throughout the study period (2017–2022).

On average, B10 (Vietnam Maritime Bank) recorded the highest MPI value of 1.4504, although its performance was not entirely stable. Conversely, B5 (Sacombank) recorded the lowest average MPI value of 0.9512, signifying it as the least efficient (or inefficient) bank throughout the entire period of 2017 to 2022. It is not worthy that none of the DMUs demonstrated a stable MPI performance, likely influenced by the impact of COVID-19 and the potential onset of a recession.

In each stage, the majority of banks exhibit effectiveness, specifically 11 DMUs (B2, 3, 4, 6, 7, 9,10, 11, 12, 15, 17) during 2017–2018, 10 DMUs (B1, 5, 9,11, 12, 13, 14, 15, 16, 17) during 2018–2019, 8 DMUs (1, 4, 7, 8, 9, 10, 14, 16) during 2019–2020, 14 DMUs (B1, 3, 4, 5, 6, 7, 8, 10, 12, 13, 14, 15, 16, 17) during 2020–2021, and 11 DMUs (B2, 3, 6, 7, 8, 9, 10, 12, 14, 15, 16) during 2021–2022. The average value of the Malmquist productivity index (MPI) across all DMUs was 1.1157, with the highest value observed in the period 2017–2018 and the lowest value of 1.0198 in 2019–2020. Particularly noteworthy was B10-Vietnam Maritime Bank, which exhibited exceptional performance with an MPI of 2.4762 during 2017–2018, well above the benchmark of 2.0. On the other hand, B17–Bac A Bank demonstrated the lowest performance with an MPI of 0.4389 during 2019–2020.

Table 5 Malmquist productivity indices (2017–2022)

DMUs	Banks	2017–2018	2018–2019	2019–2020	2020–2021	2021–2022	Average
B1	Vietinbank	0.9116	1.1509	1.0824	1.1835	0.7261	1.0109
B2	BIDV	1.0788	0.9568	0.9071	0.9554	1.2187	1.0233
B3	Vietcombank	1.1740	0.9364	0.9588	1.1477	1.0747	1.0583
B4	ACB	1.5614	0.5780	1.6946	1.3108	0.6809	1.1651
B5	Sacombank	0.5207	1.0791	0.9997	1.2196	0.9371	0.9512
B6	SHBank	1.9916	0.4842	0.9939	1.3324	1.2494	1.2103
B7	Military Bank	1.1723	0.9921	1.0094	1.0898	1.1602	1.0847
B8	VPBank	0.9759	0.9457	1.1246	1.2287	1.1492	1.0848
B9	Orient Commercial	1.3002	1.0057	1.0904	0.9459	1.1200	1.0924
B10	Vietnam Maritime	2.4762	0.9187	1.3881	1.4371	1.0320	1.4504
B11	TPBank	1.2867	1.1854	0.9722	0.8705	0.9759	1.0581
B12	HDBank	1.0238	1.3446	0.9264	1.1481	1.0963	1.1078
B13	Techcombank	0.9686	1.0743	0.6314	1.3006	0.976	0.9901
B14	LienViet Post Bank	0.9349	1.245	1.0277	1.1735	1.1603	1.1082
B15	SEABANK	1.4184	1.4135	0.9282	1.3488	1.1731	1.2564
B16	Export Import Bank	0.8625	1.0172	1.1639	1.0354	1.6316	1.1421
B17	Bac A Bank	1.1433	2.2853	0.4389	1.112	0.8867	1.1732
	Average	1.2235	1.0948	1.0198	1.1670	1.0734	1.1157
	Maximum	2.4762	2.2853	1.6946	1.4371	1.6316	1.4504
	Minimum	0.5207	0.4842	0.4389	0.8705	0.6809	0.9512

6 Conclusion and Policy Recommendations

The significance of the Vietnamese commercial banking system lies in its role in facilitating credit provision to businesses, underscoring the importance of maintaining stability within the banking sector for the overall economy. This study employs data envelopment analysis (DEA) efficiency and Malmquist productivity index assessments to analyze the efficacy of Vietnamese banks, with particular focus on the pre-COVID-19 period. The analysis specifically encompasses the performance evaluation of 17 Vietnamese commercial banks from 2017 to 2022, considering four input factors (deposits, liabilities, assets, operating expenses) and three output factors (profit before tax, loans, bad debt). Through the computation of bank-level Malmquist productivity indexes, valuable insights regarding the productivity levels and growth rates of these banks over time are obtained. The volatility of these indexes aids in identifying the sources of efficiency enhancements stemming from technological advancements and regional changes, depending on the contextual factors at the group level.

As depicted in Table 5, most banks (88%) achieved average MPIs above 1.0 during the study period, indicating a balance between technological and technical performance leading to progressive outcomes. The average MPI values of the banks fluctuated throughout the whole study period, reflecting improvements in the balance of technical and technological performance. The nature of MPI is evidently influenced by the technical capabilities inherent in the banking sector.

In conclusion, this study makes several contributions. Methodologically, it employs the DEA (Malmquist productivity) approach to offer a robust evaluation of the financial sector, presenting a comprehensive picture of financial performance and productivity improvement. Practically, the results provide an encompassing view of the strength of the leading 17 commercial banks in Vietnam. As customer expectations change and technological capacities advance, banks are facing challenges, especially with the increasing competition from bank startups utilizing technology for unique customer experiences in banking and financial services. In this context, this study provides financial decision-makers with valuable insights into the industry's current situation and key drivers, especially amid the changes brought by the global pandemic.

References

Assaf, A. G., Berger, A. N., Roman, R. A., & Tsionas, M. G. (2019). Does efficiency help banks survive and thrive during financial crises? *Journal of Banking and Finance, 106*, 445–470. https://doi.org/10.1016/j.jbankfin.2019.07.013

Avkiran, N. K., & Cai, L. (2014). Identifying distress among banks prior to a major crisis using non-oriented super-SBM. *Annals of Operations Research, 217*, 31–53. https://doi.org/10.1007/s10479-014-1568-8

Avkiran, N. K. (2015). An illustration of dynamic network DEA in commercial banking including robustness tests. *Omega, 55*, 141–150. https://doi.org/10.1016/j.omega.2014.07.002

Avkiran, N. K. (2018). Measuring the systemic risk of regional banks in Japan with PLS-SEM. *Theoretical Economics Letters, 8*, 2024–2037. https://doi.org/10.4236/tel.2018.811132

Batten, J. A., & Vo, X. V. (2019). Determinants of bank profitability-evidence from Vietnam. *Emerging Markets Finance and Trade, 55*(1), 1–12. https://doi.org/10.1080/1540496X.2018.1524326

Banker, R. D., Chang, H., & Lee, S. Y. (2010). Differential impact of Korean banking system reforms on bank productivity. *Journal of Banking and Finance, 34*, 1450–1460. https://doi.org/10.1016/j.jbankfin.2010.02.023

Berger, A. N., & Humphrey, D. B. (1992). Measurement and efficiency issues in commercial banking. In *Output measurement in the service sectors* (pp. 245–300). University of Chicago Press.

Charnes, A., Cooper, W. W., & Rhodes, E. (1979). Measuring the efficiency of decision-making units. *European Journal of Operational Research, 2*, 429–444. https://doi.org/10.1016/0377-2217(78)90138-8

Dang-Thanh, N. (2012). Measuring the performance of the banking system: Case of Vietnam (1990–2010). *Journal of Applied Finance and Banking, 2*, 289–312.

Emrouznejad, A., & Anouze, A. L. (2010). Data envelopment analysis with classification and regression tree—A case of banking efficiency. *Expert Systems, 27*, 231–246. https://doi.org/10.1111/j.1468-0394.2010.00516.x

Faello, J. (2015). Understanding the limitations of financial ratios. *Academy of Accounting and Financial Studies Journal, 19*(3), 75–85.

Fujii, H., Managi, S., & Matousek, R. (2014). Indian bank efficiency and productivity changes with undesirable outputs: A disaggregated approach. *Journal of Banking and Finance, 38*, 41–50. https://doi.org/10.1016/j.jbankfin.2013.09.022

Jablonsky, J., Fiala, P., Smirlis, Y., & Despotis, D. K. (2004). DEA with interval data: An illustration using the evaluation of branches of a Czech bank. *Central European Journal of Operations Research, 12*(4), 323–337.

Kablan, S. (2009). Banking efficiency and financial development in sub-Saharan Africa (SSA). *African Finance Journal, 11*(2), 28–50.

Le, T. N., & Wang, C. N. (2017). The integrated approach for sustainable performance evaluation in value chain of Vietnam textile and apparel industry. *Sustainability, 9*, 477. https://doi.org/10.3390/su9030477

Lin, T. Y., & Chiu, S. H. (2013). Using independent component analysis and network DEA to improve bank performance evaluation. *Economic Modelling, 32*, 608–616. https://doi.org/10.1016/j.econmod.2013.03.003

Mahmoudabadi, M. Z., & Emrouznejad, A. (2019). Comprehensive performance evaluation of banking branches: A three-stage slacks-based measure (SBM) data envelopment analysis. *International Review of Economics & Finance, 64*, 359–376. https://doi.org/10.1016/j.iref.2019.08.001

Mohtashami, A., & Ghiasvand, B. M. (2020). Z-ERM DEA integrated approach for evaluation of banks & financial institutes in stock exchange. *Expert Systems with Applications, 147*(3), 113218. https://doi.org/10.1016/j.eswa.2020.113218

Paradi, J. C., & Zhu, H. (2013). A survey on bank branch efficiency and performance research with data envelopment analysis. *Omega Journal, 41*(1), 61–79. https://doi.org/10.1016/j.omega.2011.08.010

Paradi, J. C., Sherman, H. D., & Tam, F. K. (2018). Bank branch benchmarking with quality as a component. *Data envelopment analysis in the financial services industry* (pp. 159–184). Springer.

Sáez-Fernández, F. J., Picazo-Tadeo, A. J., & Jiménez-Hernández, I. (2021). Performance and risk in the Brazilian banking industry. *Heliyon, 7*, e06524. https://doi.org/10.1016/j.heliyon.2021.e06524 [PubMed]

SSI. (2023). Annual financial report, extracted from https://iboard.ssi.com.vn

Wang, C.-N., Dang, T.-T., Nguyen, N.-A.-T., & Le, T.-T.-H. (2020). Supporting better decision-making: A combined grey model and data envelopment analysis for efficiency evaluation in E-commerce marketplaces. *Sustainability, 12*, 10385. https://doi.org/10.3390/su122410385

Wang, C.-N., Nguyen, T.-L., & Dang, T.-T. (2021a). Analyzing operational efficiency in real estate companies: An application of GM (1, 1) and DEA Malmquist model. *Mathematics, 9*, 202. https://doi.org/10.3390/math9030202

Wang, C.-N., Nguyen, T.-L., Dang, T.-T., & Bui, T.-H. (2021b). Performance evaluation of fishery enterprises using data envelopment analysis—A Malmquist model. *Mathematics, 9*, 469. https://doi.org/10.3390/math9050469

Wang, K., Huang, W., Wu, J., & Liu, Y. N. (2014). Efficiency measures of the Chinese commercial banking system using an additive two-stage DEA. *Omega, 44*, 5–20. https://doi.org/10.1016/j.omega.2013.09.005

Wanke, P., Barros, C. P., & Emrouznejad, A. (2016). Assessing productive efficiency of banks using integrated Fuzzy-DEA and bootstrapping: A case of Mozambican banks. *European Journal of Operational Research, 249*, 378–389. https://doi.org/10.1016/j.ejor.2015.10.018

Worthington, A. C. (2010). Frontier efficiency measurement in deposit-taking financial mutuals: A review of techniques, applications, and future research directions. *Annals of Public and Cooperative Economics, 81*(1), 39–75. https://doi.org/10.1111/j.1467-8292.2009.00405

Ung Trieu Gia Bao , an enthusiast of becoming a financial analyst, having worked in various financial positions across multiple companies. Currently, he is pursuing a master's degree in applied economics, in a joint program created between University of Economics Ho Chi Minh city and Erasmus University Rotterdam.

Chapter 9
Comparative Analysis of Remittances's Impact on Vietnam's Economy

Duc Duy Ngo

Abstract In recent years, labor export from Vietnam has evolved from its traditional role to alleviate poverty and generate employment for the population. Instead, it is increasingly viewed as a source of rising remittances. According to the latest data, Vietnam dispatches approximately 100,000 workers abroad annually, resulting in remittances exceeding 3 billion USD annually. This substantial influx significantly contributes to the country's GDP. To gain a more precise and comprehensive understanding of how remittances have impacted Vietnam's economic development over the past two decades and beyond, this research employs an ARDL bounds testing approach for cointegration and an error correction model derived from ARDL to assess the impacts of remittances on the Vietnam's economy. The framework, proposed by Pesaran et al. (J Appl Econ 16:289–326, 2001), allows for the analysis of both the long-term trends and short-term dynamics among the variables. These findings can add to the existing literature on the relationship between remittances and economic growth. With dataset collected from 2000 to 2022, this study provides up-to-date empirical evidence on whether remittances and financial development complement or substitute each other in driving GDP growth.

Keywords Remittances · GDP · Economic growth · Labor export · Financial development · ARDL method · Vietnam

1 Introduction

Remittances are defined as financial or material contributions sent by migrants to their families, relatives, or friends in their home country. According to the World Bank's definition, remittances encompass all current transfers of money or goods between resident and non-resident individuals, irrespective of the sender's income source and the relationships between households (whether they are related or not).

D. D. Ngo (✉)
Vietnam—the Netherlands Programme, University of Economics Ho Chi Minh City, Ho Chi Minh City, Vietnam
e-mail: duy.nd@vnp.edu.vn

P. K. Nam and A. Heshmati (eds.), *Recent Trends in Vietnam's Rapid Economic Development*, Frontiers in South and Southeast Asian Development Research,
https://doi.org/10.1007/978-981-97-6079-4_9

Remittances offer numerous benefits to individuals as well as the economy of the recipient country, particularly in developing nations (Lubambu, 2014). Typically, remittances are sent by overseas diaspora or migrant workers to support their loved ones and families. For individuals and households, these remittances constitute a source of income that helps cover expenses and improves living standards (Ratha, 2005).

For the economy, as emphasized by Ravallion (1997), remittances play a significant role in reducing poverty and alleviating hunger, especially in developing countries. This is reflected in various indicators, such as increased income and increased spending on education, healthcare, and food. Furthermore, remittances have been assessed as having positive effects on economic growth, such as serving as an investment resource, supporting economic development, and improving international balance of payments (Hao & Long, 2017).

According to the expenditure multiplier model, each dollar of remittance received by households contributes to boosting the retail market, increasing demand for goods and services, thus promoting economic growth, and creating employment opportunities (Ratha, 2005). Giuliano and Ruiz-Arranz (2009) asserted that remittance flows help develop the financial systems of countries with underdeveloped financial infrastructure, thereby stimulating economic growth. Research by Aggarwal et al. (2011) suggested that as remittance flows increase, it leads to a rise in deposits and credit at financial institutions, fostering financial system development. Remittances can also become a source of investment in the form of bank deposits, which banks use as funds for lending in housing construction projects. Alternatively, households can directly purchase stocks in housing construction companies, and increase the pool of funds available for investment in the housing sector. The increased investment capital has the effect of reducing interest rates for loans in housing projects, making the cost of buying or renting homes more affordable, and increasing the supply of housing in the market.

From the early years of the twenty-first century until 2022, Vietnam has witnessed a substantial economic growth, accompanied by a significant surge in remittances flowing into the country. This surge propelled Vietnam to become one of the world's largest recipients of remittances. Notably, remittances emerged as a substantial source of external private finance for Vietnam compared to other financial inflows such as foreign direct investment (FDI) and official development assistance (ODA). Remittances have demonstrated greater stability and predictability over time. Consequently, remittances have been playing a significant role in the Vietnamese economy, especially given the backdrop of an enduring trade deficit, elevated government expenditures, a substantial gap in funding, and variabilities in FDI and ODA as proportions of GDP. Significantly, in some years, the share of remittances in GDP surpassed that of FDI. According to the World Bank's forecast, remittances to developing countries may experience a slight decrease due to global economic downturn, but overall, they are expected to continue rising.

However, the impact of remittances on Vietnam's economic growth remains a subject of debate, and the most recent research on this topic in the country is outdated. Therefore, this paper investigates the effect of remittances on economic growth in

Vietnam during the period from 2000 to 2022 to emphasize its roles in this country growth and development. This research is divided into two primary findings. Firstly, it revealed a positive and statistically significant correlation between remittances and economic growth in the country, both in the short term and the long term. Secondly, the study highlighted that remittances have effectively served as an alternative to traditional financial services in driving economic growth. These findings might contribute valuable insights into the debate on remittances roles in GDP growth, exploring whether remittances and financial development independently or jointly influence GDP growth in recipient countries.

The rest of this research is outlined as follows. Section 2 reviews the literature. Section 3 presents the methodology used and empirical results are discussed in Sect. 4. The conclusion and policy implications of the result are provided in Sect. 5.

2 Literature Review

The relationship between remittances and economic growth is debated among researchers, with mixed results fueling ongoing discussions among policymakers. First, many studies show the vague relationship between remittances and the receiving nation's GDP. In a study conducted by Chami et al. (2008), which analyzed data from 108 countries spanning the period of 1970 to 2004 using the instrumental variable method, it was found that the direct impact of workers' remittances on economic growth is not always clearly positive. Additionally, this study revealed that when workers' remittances are considered in conjunction with the depth of the financial system, a higher ratio of remittances to GDP, combined with a more developed financial system, might be associated with lower economic growth rates. This was indicated by the consistently negative and significant coefficients on interaction terms in most analyses.

In 2005, the International Monetary Fund (IMF) conducted a study utilizing the instrumental variable method, focusing on the total remittance variables, which includes workers' remittances, employee compensations, and migrant transfers. The paper's findings suggest an absence of a statistically significant association between economic development and whole remittances. This lack of clear connection is not unique to this study. Giuliano and Ruiz-Arranz (2009) found that remittances do promote economic growth, but only in countries with less developed financial systems. This is evidenced by significant negative coefficients on interaction terms, suggesting that remittances play a more important role in growth when their financial systems are in low-quality conditions.

On the contrary, several studies have also discovered a positive impact of remittances on economic growth in receiving countries. Some of these studies have revealed a positive association between remittances and financial development, thereby fostering economic growth. For example, Aggarwal et al. (2011) looked at data from over 100 developing countries between 1975 and 2007 and found that money sent home by migrant workers (remittances) boosted the amount of money saved in banks (deposits) and the amount loaned out to businesses (credit) in those countries. In simpler terms, remittances exhibit a positive correlation with financial development in the recipient countries.

Similar to the research conducted by the IMF (2005), which utilized total remittances and applied the ordinary least squares (OLS) method, Faini (2006a, 2006b) conducted a regression analysis on a dataset comprising 68 countries observed from 1980 to 2004. The research found that remittances seemed to boost economic growth at first but when they dug deeper using a more rigorous method (instrumental variable method), the positive effect was not statistically significant anymore. This suggests the initial positive finding might be due to other factors correlated with remittances, not remittances themselves. This idea of remittances helping growth is also supported by another study by Catrinescu et al. (2009), which looked at 114 countries from 1991 to 2003 and found a positive link between total money sent home country and GDP. Adding to this confirmation of support, a World Bank (2006) study also contributed to the discussion with positive results. They analyzed data from 67 countries between 1991 and 2005 and found that money sent home by migrant workers had a positive effect on economic growth in those countries. Orozco (2004) also reported a positive relationship between remittances and financial development in developing countries, attributed to the theory that funds channeled through financial institutions might encourage recipients to access and utilize other financial products and services. Additionally, Aggarwal et al. (2011) found that increases in remittances could lead to growth in the volume of deposits and credit intermediated by financial institutions, thereby fostering financial sector development. Ultimately, these findings indicate that financial development and economic growth are interconnected and often mutually reinforced in a country's economy. In other words, there is a positive correlation between remittances and financial development in the countries receiving remittances.

Several studies back the idea that remittances can boost economic growth, and Pakistan is no exception. Javid et al. (2012) found strong evidence that money sent home by overseas workers has a positive and significant impact on Pakistan's economic development. They empirically test data from 1973 to 2010 using the ARDL approach. Pakistan-specific research also offers mixed results. In another related study, Waheed and Aleem (2008) found an interesting pattern in the short term, remittances seem to have a positive impact on economic growth in Pakistan. However, their study suggests this effect might not hold true in the long run, with remittances potentially hindering growth. In contrast, Ahmed et al. (2011) using a different approach, found evidence that remittances have a consistently positive effect on Pakistan's growth, both in the short and long run.

These studies mentioned above collectively contribute to a better understanding of the complex dynamic relationships between remittances and economic growth in Pakistan, highlighting the nature of this relationship and its variations over different time that is multifaceted varying on regions and type of economy. In the case of Vietnam, as a developing country and a remittance recipient country, the pattern for correlation between remittances inflow and GDP growth is not thoroughly analyzed and should be updated on a yearly basis.

3 Methodology

Data Collection: The study collects time series data for real GDP (lnGDP) and remittances inflow (lnREM) in Vietnam spanning from the year 2000 to 2022 from Vietnam General Statistics Office (GSO) and IMF database including 23 yearly observations. In general, the data shows a progressive trend for remittances inflow over two decades, with last year's figure that had doubled compared to the first observed year. At the same point, the GDP of Vietnam grew nearly ten times over the time. The data collected from annual reports in IMF and GSO might be slightly different. The study applies logarithm transformation to the continuous variables, facilitating data handling and analysis.

Testing Steps:

To ensure stationarity, the study performs the first level of differencing on both lnGDP and lnREM. Using the first difference data, the study conducts the Augmented Dickey-Fuller (ADF) tests to confirm stationarity. However, to account for potential lags and improve model robustness, more complex models' formulation and estimation are needed.

Further examination of this model, the study employs the autoregressive distributed lag (ARDL) method to evaluate the short-term and long-term connections between the remittance volume and the GDP of Vietnam. The ARDL technique, initially developed by Charemza and Deadman (1992), underwent refinement in subsequent research conducted by Pesaran et al. (2001), as well as Pesaran and Shin (1995). The ARDL model is well-suited for analyzing time series data, especially when the dataset has a limited number of observations. In fact, according to the results of Badeeb and Lean (2017), Makuyana and Odhiambo (2019), one of the most advantages of ARDL test is that it is more robust and performs better for small sample size of data. Thus, this test is suitable for this research because the dataset is small, with only 23 observations needed to estimate the ARDL model.

Besides, the ARDL method can optimize the lag length by considering the Akaike Information Criterion (AIC) value. This approach involves simultaneously estimating the short- and long-term components within the ARDL model, effectively addressing issues related to endogeneity and serial correlation. These favorable characteristics make the ARDL technique a reliable choice for obtaining accurate estimations. Furthermore, the ARDL model allows for estimation when dealing with both stationary and non-stationary data series (Fayissa & Nsiah, 2010; Khalid, 2012).

The ARDL model is outlined in three stages: the generalized model and ARDL models for long-term and short-term remittance effects on the economy, as outlined below.

A. **The generalized model**: The relationship between remittances and Vietnam's economic growth is structured as follows:

$$\text{GDP} = f(\text{REM}) \tag{1}$$

where gross domestic product (GDP) in Vietnam collected as time series data from 2000 to 2022 obtained from the General Statistical Office (GSO).

REM (Personal remittances inflows) in the period of 2000–2022 collected from International Monetary Fund (IMF). *Given all unit in billion United State Dollar (USD).

The extension of Eq. 1 in natural logarithm form is:

$$\ln \mathrm{GDP}_t = \alpha_0 + \alpha 1 \ln \mathrm{REM}_t + \varepsilon_t \tag{2}$$

As the natural logarithm of GDP (lnGDP) and remittances (lnREM) was computed to ensure the linearity of the variables with ε_t is the white noise.

B. **ARDL model for long-term effect**: To estimate the long-term impact of remittances inflows on economic growth in Vietnam using ARDL unrestricted error correction models, Eq. (3) is implemented as follows:

$$\Delta \ln \mathrm{GDP}_t = \propto_0 + \propto_1 \Delta \ln \mathrm{REM}_{t-1} + \sum_{i=1}^{k} \Delta \propto_2 \Delta \ln \mathrm{REM}_{t-1} + \lambda \mathrm{ECT}_{t-1} + \varepsilon_t \tag{3}$$

where $\propto_0$ is the intercept, the subscript t indicates time period, Δ is the first difference. The error correction term (ECT) is the residual part of the regression results of the long-term coefficients in the ARDL model conducted earlier, ε_t is the white noise, and K is the optimal number of lags.

The first step involves a statistical test (F-test or Wald-test) to see if there's a long-term connection between the variables in Eq. (3). This test works by assuming the effects of past changes in the independent variables (like remittances) disappear after a certain period.

Null hypothesis (H0) to be tested is: There is no long-run relationship or cointegration among GDP and remittances in the natural logarithm of the REM variable in the model.

$$\mathrm{H0} : \propto 1 = 0$$

Alternative hypothesis (H1): There exists a long-run relationship or cointegration among the variables in the model.

$$\mathrm{H1} : \propto 1 \neq 0$$

The null hypothesis suggests that both variables do not have a stable, long-term relationship, while the alternative hypothesis suggests that they do have such a relationship. The ARDL test is used to determine whether there is evidence of cointegration between the variables, indicating a long-term connection.

Table 1 Summary statistics of the variables in natural logarithm

	lnREM	lnGDP
Var	1	2
N	23	23
Mean	1.73	4.97
SD	0.74	0.76
Median	2.07	5.14
Minimum	0.10	3.68
Maximum	2.58	2.35
Range	2.48	2.35
Skewness	-0.88	-0.36
Std. Dev.	0.16	0.16

C. **ARDL model for short-term effect**: To estimate the short-term impact of remittances on Vietnam's economic growth using ARDL error correction regression, Eq. (4) is carried out as follows:

$$\Delta \ln \text{GDP}_t = \propto_3 + \sum_{t=1}^{p} \Delta \propto_4 \Delta \ln \text{REM}_{t-1} + \varepsilon_t \quad (4)$$

4 Empirical Results

4.1 Descriptive Statistics

Table 1 presents summary statistics for the variables used in the empirical analysis of the ARDL model.

In the dataset, remittance in natural logarithm form has an average of about 1.73 and a moderate standard deviation (SD) of approximately 0.74 while its counterpart has an average of roughly 4.97 and a standard deviation of about 0.76. The data shows some variability in both variables. 'lnREM' ranges from approximately 0.10 to 2.58, with a leftward skewness (− 0.88), and 'lnGDP' has a range from approximately 3.68 to 6.03, with a slight leftward skewed (− 0.36) and light tails (− 1.34 kurtosis). The standard error (SE) of the mean estimate for both variables is around 0.16.

4.2 ADF Test for Stationary

To transform the non-stationary time series data into a stationary form, differencing techniques were applied to remove serial correlation and achieve stationarity. The

Table 2 ADF test for stationary results

Variable	Dickey-Fuller statistic	Lag order	*p*-value	Stationary at 10%% significance level
diff_lnGDP	– 4.097	2	0.019	Yes
diff_lnREM	– 3.882	2	0.029	Yes

resulting differenced variables are labeled as Diff_lnGDP and Diff_lnREM. Table 2 presents the results of the Augmented Dickey-Fuller (ADF) tests conducted to assess the stationarity of these variables.

Table 2 displays the results of unit root tests for the variables at the first difference level. In the Augmented Dickey-Fuller test, the null hypothesis (H0) is that the series has a unit root, indicating non-stationarity. The *p*-values for both "Diff_LnGDP" and "Diff_REM" are lower than the chosen significance level of 10%. Consequently, we reject the null hypothesis for both variables. This implies that both "Diff_LnGDP" and "Diff_REM" are stationary at the integrated order of 1 written as $I(1)$.

In practical terms, this means that a differencing of the original series once (taking the 1st difference) has made these variables stationary, which is a prerequisite for many time series analyses. Given that both variables are now stationary at $I(1)$, it is appropriate to use the Autoregressive Distributed Lag (ARDL) technique for cointegration analysis. This approach allows us to examine the impact of remittances on GDP in Vietnam from 2000 to 2022 while accounting for the potential long-run relationship between these variables.

4.3 ARDL Estimation Results

Table 3 summarizes the lag order selection process for both "lnGDP" and "lnREM" variables using the Akaike Information Criterion (AIC). Each row represents a combination of lag orders, and the associated AIC test value is provided. Researchers typically select the lag order combination with the lowest AIC value as it represents the best trade-off between model fit and its complexity.

From the results, the 4–2 lag order combination was selected because it minimizes the AIC test value, indicating that it strikes a balance between accurately capturing the data's patterns and keeping the model parsimonious.

The ARDL regression analysis was performed to examine the relationship between the natural logarithm of GDP (lnGDP) and the natural logarithm of remittances (lnREM) using a model with lag orders (4, 2). The results are presented in Table 4.

Based on the results presented in Table 4, the model's overall fit is excellent, with an adjusted R-squared value of 0.9983, indicating that a high proportion of the variability in lnGDP can be explained by the model. The joint F-statistic is

Table 3 AIC test results for lag order selection

lnGDP lag order	lnREM lag order	AIC
4	2	– 80.979
4	3	– 80.179
4	4	– 78.521
5	5	– 77.664
1	0	– 71.444
1	1	– 69.449
3	5	– 66.073
2	2	– 65.687
3	4	– 63.901
2	1	– 62.968
3	3	– 62.010

Table 4 ARDL regression results

Variable	Coefficient	*t*-value	Pr(> |*t*|)
Intercept	1.115***	5.997	8.97e-05
L(lnGDP, 1)	0.347	2.189	0.051
L(lnGDP, 2)	0.029	0.157	0.877
L(lnGDP, 3)	– 0.153	– 0.845	0.416
L(lnGDP, 4)	0.516**	3.657	0.003
lnREM	0.246**	4.327	0.001
L(lnREM, 1)	0.115	1.896	0.084
L(lnREM, 2)	– 0.136*	– 2.793	0.017
R-squared: 0.999 Adjusted *R*-squared: 0.998	F-stat 1,513 on 7 and 11 Degrees of freedom	*p*-value: 1.63e−15	

Notes Where * is significance level at 10%, ** is at 5% and *** is at 1%. *L* indicate lagged variable, ln log transformed, and the number after a variable name indicates the lag length

highly significant (*p*-value: 1.63e−15), suggesting that the model's slopes are jointly statistically significant and different than zero.

The next step involves assessing whether the chosen ARDL model exhibits long-run relationships between the dependent and independent variables. This assessment is carried out through the application of the Bounds F-test to investigate the presence of cointegration, as illustrated in Table 5.

The null hypothesis tested is that there is no cointegration. Since the p-value is extremely low (close to zero), we reject the null hypothesis. This suggests that there is a possibility of cointegration between the variables in the model, indicating a long-term relationship between two variables lnGDP and lnREM (see Table 6).

Table 6 summarizes the estimated coefficients, standard errors, *t*-values, and *p*-values for the intercept term and the lnREM variable in the long-run ARDL model.

Table 5 ARDL bound test results

Bound F-Test (Wald) for no cointegration)				
Estimate model	F-stat	*p*-value	Critical values	
			Lower bound I(0)	Upper bound *I*(1)
ARDL (4, 2)	17.595	1e−06	4.037	4.785

Table 6 ARDL test results for long-term effect

Term	Estimate	Std. error	*t*-value	Pr(> |*t*|)
Intercept	4.281	0.239	17.859	1.79E−09
lnREM	0.868	0.074	11.615	1.62E−07

In the long run, the intercept term has a substantial positive multiplier effect of approximately 4.281 (SE = 0.239), indicating that a one-unit change in the natural logarithm of remittances (lnREM) corresponds to a 4.281-unit change in the natural logarithm of GDP (lnGDP), while other factors remain constant. This relationship is highly significant with a t-value of 17.859.

Similarly, for the lnREM variable, there is a long-run multiplier effect of approximately 0.868 (SE = 0.074), implying that a one-unit change in lnREM results in a 0.868-unit change in lnGDP, with other factors held constant. This relationship is statistically significant, as indicated by a t-value of 11.615.

Hence, both the intercept and lnREM have significant long-term impacts on lnGDP, highlighting the importance of remittances in influencing economic growth in Vietnam.

From the ARDL model for short-term effects, the results are presented in Table 7. This table summarizes the coefficient estimates, *t*-values, and *p*-values for each variable in the error correction model (ECM) for the ARDL (4, 2) model specified.

In particular, the ECM results reveal a significant and robust long-term relationship between remittances (lnREM) and GDP growth (lnGDP) in Vietnam. The

Table 7 ARDL model for short-term effect

Variable	Estimate	*t*-value	Pr(> |*t*|)
Intercept	1.115***	6.707	0.000
d(*L*(lnGDP, 1))	− 0.391***	− 3.099	0.009
d(*L*(lnGDP, 2))	− 0.362***	− 3.160	0.008
d(*L*(lnGDP, 3))	− 0.516***	− 4.440	0.000
d(lnREM)	0.246***	6.395	3.43E−05
d(*L*(lnREM, 1))	0.136**	2.937	0.0124
ECT (Error Correction)	− 0.260***	− 6.196	4.62E−05

t statistics in parentheses: * $p< 0.05$, ** $p< 0.01$, *** $p< 0.001$
Notes d indicate differenced variable, ln log transformed and the number indicated the number of lags

intercept is statistically significant, underscoring the existence of a meaningful long-term connection between these variables. Lagged GDP growth and remittances exhibit significant impacts on current GDP growth, emphasizing the role of historical economic performance and remittance inflows in shaping the country's economic growth trajectory.

Furthermore, the presence of a significant error correction term indicates that any short-term deviations from the long-term equilibrium between remittances and GDP growth are corrected over time. This cointegration relationship underscores the importance of remittances as a driver of economic growth in Vietnam, supported by a well-fitting model with a high R-squared value of approximately 0.906. This is affirming the model's capacity to explain a substantial portion of GDP growth variability even after considering lagged effects.

5 Conclusion and Policy Implications

Conclusion: The results indicate that during the period from 2000 to 2022, remittances have played a significant role in promoting economic growth in Vietnam. The long-term cointegration relationship between remittances and economic growth shows stability in this relationship. Furthermore, remittances have a positive impact on economic growth not only in the short term but also in the long term. The effects are stronger accounting for dynamic multiplicative effect.

Policy Implications: The study provides several policy recommendations aimed at not only attracting more remittances but also enhancing their role in stimulating economic growth in Vietnam.

Firstly, Vietnam's government should prioritize the labor export activities, especially to work in countries with developed industrial sectors. This will not only provide Vietnamese laborers with opportunities to enhance their professional skills, improve their work ethics, and gain knowledge from access to advanced technologies but also enable them to earn higher incomes compared to domestic income levels. They can also help the Vietnamese industry to increase their export. Consequently, labor export activities can increasingly contribute to larger remittance inflows in the future and transfer of advanced technology and knowledge to workers and firms in Vietnam. Furthermore, labor export is also a means to alleviate unemployment pressures on the Vietnamese labor market.

Relevant authorities should implement measures to direct and promote the transition of remittances into productive sectors, creating goods and services that benefit society. This strategic shift can empower the impact of remittances on Vietnam economic development. In addition, there should be measures in place to restrict the flow of remittances into areas like the speculative investment areas like foreign stock market, real estate, and gold. Such restrictions can help curb speculative behavior, prevent asset bubbles, and maintain a better macroeconomic stability.

There is also a need to further enhance the quality-of-service channels for remittance transfers to Vietnam, such as the banking system and financial institutions, to create even more favorable conditions for overseas Vietnamese and Vietnamese laborers abroad to send money back to their home country. In addition, it is essential to continue implementing policies that harness the potential sources of remittances by intensifying efforts to promote the country's image, providing regular updates on economic development, economic reform policies, and timely information about positive changes in the investment environment to the overseas Vietnamese community. This will help to attract more remittances to Vietnam in the form of investments and contributions to production and business activities soon.

References

Aggarwal, R., Demirguc-Kunt, A., & Peria, M. (2011). Do remittances promote financial development? *Journal of Development Economics, 96*(2), 255–264.

Ahmed, J., Zaman, K., & Ali Shah, I. (2011). An empirical analysis of remittances-growth nexus in Pakistan using bounds testing approach. *Journal of Economics and International Finance, 3*(3), 176–186.

Badeeb, R. A., & Lean, H. H. (2017). Financial development, oil dependence, and economic growth: Evidence from the Republic of Yemen. *Studies in Economics and Finance, 34*(2), 281–298.

Catrinescu, N., Leon-Ledesma, M., Piracha, M., & Quillin, B. (2009). Remittances, institutions and economic growth. *World Development, 37*(1), 81–92.

Chami, R., Barajas, A., Cosimano, T., Fullenkamp, C., Gapen, M., & Montiel, P. (2008). *Macroeconomic consequences of remittances*. International Monetary Fund, Occasional Paper 259.

Charemza, W., & Deadman, D. F. (1992). *New directions in econometric practice*. Edward Elgar Publishing.

Faini, R. (2006a). *Migration and remittances: The impact on the countries of origin*. University of Rome.

Faini, R. (2006b). Foreign aid and fiscal policy (CEPR Discussion Paper No. 5721). Centre for Economic Policy Research.

Fayissa, B., & Nsiah, C. (2010). Can remittances spur economic growth and development? Evidence from Latin American Countries (LACs). Middle Tennessee State University, Department of Economics and Finance Working Paper Series.

Giuliano, P., & Ruiz-Arranz, M. (2009). Remittances, financial development, and growth. *Journal of Development Economics, 90*(1), 144–152.

Hao, D. T. K., & Long, D. T. T. (2017). The impact of remittances on economic growth. *Banking Journal*, May 2017.

International Monetary Fund. (2005). *World economic outlook: Globalization and external imbalances*. The International Monetary Fund.

Javid, M., Arif, U., & Qayyum, A. (2012). Impact of remittances on economic growth and poverty. *Academic Research International, 2*(1), 433–447.

Khalid, A. K. (2012). The link between remittances and economic growth in Pakistan: A boon to economic stability. *British Journal of Economics, Management, and Trade, 2*(3), 167–185.

Lubambu, K. M. K. (2014). The impacts of remittances on developing countries [Report]. *European Parliament's Committee on Development*. https://doi.org/10.2861/57140

Makuyana, G., & Odhiambo, N. M. (2019). Public and private investment and economic growth in Malawi: An ARDL-bounds testing approach. *Economic Research-Ekonomska Istraživanja, 32*(1), 673–689. https://doi.org/10.1080/1331677X.2019.1578677

Orozco, M. (2004). *Remittances to Latin America and the Caribbean: Issues and perspectives on development*. Organization of American States.

Pesaran, M. H., & Shin, Y. (1995). *An autoregressive distributed lag modelling approach to cointegration analysis* (Vol. 9514, pp. 371–413). Department of Applied Economics, University of Cambridge.

Pesaran, M. H., Shin, Y., & Smith, R. J. (2001). Bounds testing approaches to the analysis of level relationships. *Journal of Applied Econometrics, 16*, 289–326.

Ratha, D. (2005). Remittances: A lifeline for development. *Finance and Development, A Quarterly Magazine of the IMF, 42*(4).

Ravallion, C. (1997, 2006). World Bank weakly relative poverty report (1997, 2006).

Waheed, A., & Aleem, A. (2008). Workers' remittances and economic growth: Empirical evidence from Pakistan. *Journal of Social Science and Humanities, 47*(1), 1–12.

World Bank. (2006). *Global economic prospects: Economic implications of remittances and migration.* https://documents1.worldbank.org/curated/en/507301468142196936/841401968_200510327112047/additional/Globaleconomic-prospects-2006-economic-implications-of-remittances-and-migration.pdf

Duc Duy Ngo is a dedicated professional with a Bachelor's degree in English Language for Business and International Business. With two years at the New Zealand Visa Application Center, he developed a strong understanding of visa processes and customer service challenges. As a Migrant Services Assistant at the International Organization for Migration (IOM) since 2018, he provides administrative support and client services, primarily for Canadian visa applications. His commitment to positive change, combined with his global perspective, informs his ongoing research on migrant issues and economic growth in Vietnam.

Part IV
Manufacturing and Service Industries

Chapter 10
Relationships Between Innovation and Firm Performance in Vietnam's Manufacturing and Services Industries

Ngoc-Thanh Pham

Abstract Innovation is widely considered a key driver for economic growth and firm's competitiveness. While not a new concept, innovation has become an essential element for obtaining competitiveness in the ever-changing environment and speeding up the economy's development. This study aims to investigate the connections between innovation and firm performance in Vietnam, considering four types of innovation—product, process, organizational, and marketing—across two main industries: manufacturing and services. The study employs a sample of 965 firms, comprising of 666 manufacturing firms and 299 services firms. Data was obtained through a survey conducted in Vietnam between November 2014 and April 2016, as part of the World Bank's Enterprise Survey project. Estimation of a knowledge production function sheds light on the innovation behaviour of firms and its impacts on their performance, growth, and survival. The results will have implications for public policies supporting innovation and performance of manufacturing and service firms.

Keywords Innovation · Firm performance · Manufacturing industry · Services industries

1 Introduction

In recent years, business firms in almost all areas of industry have faced increasing competition, especially in developing countries where firms must compete with foreign competitors possessing the latest knowledge, skills, and technology. Therefore, innovation is not only a decisive factor for success, but also a key determinant of business growth and survival. Many studies have placed great emphasis on the effect of innovation on a firm's competitiveness and performance. For example, fierce

N.-T. Pham (✉)
Vietnam - the Netherlands Programme, University of Economics Ho Chi Minh City, Ho Chi Minh City, Vietnam
e-mail: thanh.pn@vnp.edu.vn

P. K. Nam and A. Heshmati (eds.), *Recent Trends in Vietnam's Rapid Economic Development*, Frontiers in South and Southeast Asian Development Research,
https://doi.org/10.1007/978-981-97-6079-4_10

competition requires firms to be more innovative to obtain competitive advantages over local and foreign rivals (Rosli & Sidek, 2013). Innovation is very important for enterprises themselves in increasing competitiveness, creating a value, determining the long-term survival, and raising productivity (Iuliia, 2022; Lööf & Heshmati, 2003, 2006; Nam et al., 2017). Moreover, in the dynamic landscape of contemporary markets, failure to innovate can lead to obsolescence and loss of market share, as existing products are susceptible to changing customer needs and tastes, new technologies, shortened product life cycles, and increased international competition. Hence, it is widely acknowledged that all firms, regardless of their size or sector, should prioritize innovation to not only compete but also to thrive in the competitive market.

Among developing economies, Vietnam has a big domestic market with around 100 million population, a great number of natural resources, and an inexpensive and disciplined and organized labour force. The country has achieved remarkable economic development in the last two decades, increasing per capita domestic product (GDP) from $97 USD from 1990 to $4100 USD in 2022, reducing poverty, and improving living standards for majority of the population. However, traditional sources of growth have weakened, and it is time for Vietnam to gradually shift towards innovation-based productivity gains including indigenous innovation for more sustainable and inclusive growth in the future. Unfortunately, Vietnam's innovation pillar has been in the lowest position in terms of value since 2010–2011. Recently, Vietnam ranked 48 out of 132 economies in the Global Innovation Index 2022 by the World Intellectual Property Organization (WIPO, 2022). However, little research has been conducted on the link between innovation and firm performance. Specifically, there is a need for empirical evidence on the link between innovation and firm performance at the firm level.

In the context of Vietnam's industry, manufacturing firms have played a crucial role in the country's economic growth and the improvement of employment conditions. Although it has recently been considered a manufacturing hotspot in Southeast Asia, Vietnam needs to boost its innovation to compete in both global and regional market, given that the country has an established status as a newer member among its neighbours. Innovation can enhance employees' manufacturing competence and skills, while also helping firms sharpen their competitive advantage by differentiating their products and creating value for customers.

On the other hand, the service sector accounted for 41.3% of the gross domestic product (GDP) of Vietnam. This sector has consistently remained the largest contributor to Vietnam's economy in recent years. A large share of the services produced are exportable. For services firms, innovation is also crucial in building competitive advantage and staying ahead of national and regional competitors.

There are few studies on innovation at firm level in Vietnam. Some studies focus innovation and its effect on firm performance of manufacturing and supporting industries (Canh et al., 2019; Nham et al., 2016). Other studies examine impacts of innovation on SME (Long & Anh, 2017). This study aims to fill the gap in the literature by examining the effectiveness of four innovation types (product, process, organizational, and marketing) of manufacturing and services industries in Vietnam. The study involves an analysis of 996 firms surveyed in Vietnam between November 2014 and April 2016, as part of the World Bank's Enterprise Survey project. The empirical study uses regression analysis with some control variables producing some interesting results. Consistent with existing literature, our research indicates a robust correlation between marketing innovation and enhanced productivity among Vietnamese firms. Conversely, process innovation exhibits a negative impact on productivity, while the remaining two types of innovation show no impact on productivity levels. The results have also highlighted the impacts of other influencing factors namely firm size and firm age.

The remainder of the paper is organized as follows: The first section summarizes the relevant literature and outlines the development of four research hypotheses. The research methodology section describes the data and presents the research model. The findings are discussed, and some implications are offered in the four and fifth sections.

2 Literature Review

2.1 Innovation

Innovation is crucial for the success, survival and growth of any firm (Damanpour, 1996; Jayani et al., 2018). The capability to innovate is key for firms to remain competitive and renew themselves in response to changes in the market environment (Joakim & Sofia, 2012). Porter (1990) identifies innovation as: '*a new way of doing things that is commercialized*'. In broadest term, Schumpeter (1934) defines innovation as "the driving force for development". In his definition, Vyas (2009) proposed five manifestations of innovation: the creation of new products (radical innovation) or qualitative improvements in existing products (incremental innovation), the use of new industrial processes, the opening of new markets, the development of new sources of raw materials or other inputs, and the establishment of new forms of industrial organization. Innovation is classified into two types: radical and incremental innovation, according to its degree. Radical innovation involves significant changes in products, services, or processes, resulting in a drastic transformation in the industry (Yadav et al., 2023). On the other hand, incremental innovation focuses on continuous and progressive improvements, optimizing operations and performance (Felipe et al., 2023). Apart from the degree of innovation, The Oslo Manual (OECD, 2005), which provides global guidelines for innovation activities, has classified innovation at the firm level into four types: product, process, organization, and marketing innovations.

2.2 Firm Performance

Corporate performance is often associated with organizational effectiveness, but it is essential to differentiate between the two. Venkatraman and Ramanujam (1986) proposed a clear scope of organizational effectiveness and company performance through a framework of three concentric circles. The first circle encompasses organizational effectiveness, which includes business performance, firm performance, and financial performance. The second circle delves into the essence of business performance, encompassing financial and operational performance. The third circle focuses solely on financial performance. Here, business performance is a component of both operational and financial performance, contributing to the overall effectiveness of the firm's organization.

The multidimensional nature of firm performance implies that assessment cannot rely solely on financial metrics like sales or profit. Intter et al. (2003) underscore the significance of non-financial performance measures, including customer satisfaction, firm innovation capabilities, product quality, and employee satisfaction. For this research, due to limited data access, performance is measured using financial methods.

2.3 Product Innovation and Firm Performance

Product innovation refers to the development and introduction of new or improved products to the market. It involves creating novel features, functionalities, or designs that meet customer needs and preferences. Product innovation is often regarded as a direct measure of a firm's innovation efforts among the different types of innovation. Product innovation has positive and significant short-term and long-run effects on firm profitability, which, however, vary across industries (Stoneman et al., 2018). Nham et al. (2016) observed that product innovation had a limited effect on innovative performance, while the other three categories—process, organizational, and marketing innovation—exerted a more pronounced influence on the innovative outcomes within the supporting industry sector. Based on the reviewed literature, product innovation is an important performance indicator. Therefore, we should include it in our first hypothesis formulated as follows:

H1. *Product innovation is positively correlated with firm performance.*

2.4 Process Innovation and Firm Performance

Process innovation involves adopting a new or notably enhanced method for production or delivery of products. This includes significant changes in techniques, equipment and/or software. Process innovation has been found to have varying effects on firm performance.

Some studies find a preferable effect of process innovation over its product counterpart. Hall et al. (2009) reveals that factors such as firm size and investment in research and development (R&D) play pivotal roles as drivers of product and process innovations for Italian small and medium enterprises (SMEs). Waheed (2011) performed a similar examination using a sample of firms in Bangladesh and Pakistan and found that process innovation has a greater influence on productivity compared to its product counterpart. Other study found the opposite result as product innovation, not process innovation affects firms' productivity (Cassiman el al., 2010).

In summary, prior studies reviewed in this section tend to suggest that process innovation is a more important driver of firm performance for SMEs in developing countries than for larger firms in developed countries. Therefore, in our case of Vietnam, process innovation should be included in our second hypothesis.

H2. *Process innovation is positively correlated with firm performance.*

2.5 Organization Innovation and Firm Performance

The OECD defines organizational innovation as the implementation of a new or significantly changed organizational method in the business practice, workplace organization, or external relations of the institutional unit. It involves the adoption of new strategies, structures, and systems that promote creativity, collaboration, and flexibility. Organizational innovation can manifest in various forms, such as the introduction of new management practices, changes in organizational culture, the implementation of new technologies, or the development of new business models. By fostering a culture of innovation and providing the necessary resources and support, organizational innovation can enhance a firm's ability. Firms with more organization capital and capacity have a greater number of patents and receive more citations on their patents, indicating the importance of organization capital in the innovation process (Ute et al., 2019). Although organizational innovation does not directly influence firm performance, it can improve the overall ability of the firm, leading to better performance. Therefore, it should be included in the third hypothesis.

H3. *Organizational innovation is positively correlated with firm performance.*

2.6 Marketing Innovation and Firm Performance

Marketing innovation refers to the adoption of a fresh marketing approach that include significant changes in product design or packaging, product placement, product promotion, and pricing tactics. Marketing innovations are aimed at better addressing customer needs, opening new markets, or newly positioning of a firm's product on the market, with the objective of increasing the firm's sale of the products. Marketing innovation has a positive impact on firm performance, including innovative, production, market, and financial performances (Gürhan et al., 2011). Therefore, marketing innovation is added in our fourth hypothesis.

H4. *Marketing innovation is positively correlated with firm performance.*

3 Research Methodology

3.1 Data and Sample

The sample firms were extracted from Vietnam—Enterprise Survey 2015, where we selected firm that belong to manufacturing and services industries in Vietnam. The standard Enterprise Survey topics include firm characteristics, firm performances, financing, corruption, infrastructure, and innovation issues. After deleting observations with missing values, our final sample size includes 965 firms. Among them, 666 is manufacturing firms and remaining 299 is services firms.

The innovation module is quite different for manufacturing and services firms. The test variable is a firm's innovative activities proxied by fours type of innovation based on the following four survey questions:

(1) Product Innovation: During the last three years, has this establishment introduced new or significantly improved products or services? (Yes/No/Don't answer)
(2) Process Innovation: During the last three years, has this establishment introduced any new or significantly improved methods of manufacturing products or offering services? (Yes/No/Don't answer)
(3) Organizational Innovation: During the last three years, has this establishment introduced any new or significantly improved organizational structures or management practices? (Yes/No/Don't answer)
(4) Marketing Innovation: During the last three years, has this establishment introduced new or significantly improved marketing methods? (Yes/No/Don't answer).

We define a firm as innovative for each type of innovation if their answer to the corresponding survey question is Yes and Zero otherwise. Out of 965 firms surveyed, 475 answered Yes to at least one of the innovation questions. Specifically, for each type of innovation, we found that 290 (32%) answered Yes to product innovation, 302 (33%) answered Yes to process innovation, 164 (18%) answered Yes to organizational innovation, and 272 (30%) answered Yes to marketing innovation.

To evaluate a firm's performance, several measures are considered, including total sales and total profit. However, these financial measures have their limitations. Profit data is often incomplete, and profits may be underreported in many developing countries. Therefore, the total sale could be used as proxy for firm performance.

Note that a firm can answer Yes to these questions even if the firm only slightly modifies its product, adopts a new product from overseas, or simply copies a product from another domestic firm. If the product is new or improved to that firm, the firm can answer Yes to the questions. In that sense, the understanding of "innovation" is broader than one might think. However, the implication for the return on innovation remains unchanged: in an environment where a firm can freely copy a product and claim it as a new, innovative product, the return on its "innovation" is not likely to be high. This applies not only to those who originally come up with the products, but also to those who copy them. Protection of intellectual property rights and enforcement of business law differ among countries which weakens propensity to invest in innovation.

3.2 Research Model

Drawing on the relevant literature, we selected the following models to test the previously established hypotheses:

$$Y(\text{Total Sale}_t) = \alpha + \beta_j(\text{Innovation activities}) + \sum \text{Control variables} + \varepsilon \quad (1)$$

where Total Sale_t represents total sale of last completed fiscal year.

Innovation is analysed under 4 types: Product, Process, Organization, and Marketing represented by the subscript j. Each dummy variable is equal to one if the answer for a survey question is yes and zero otherwise.

1. Product_Innovation: one if the firm introduced new or significantly improved products or services during the last three years and zero otherwise.
2. Process_Innovation: one if the firm introduced any new or significantly improved methods of manufacturing products or offering services during the last three years and zero otherwise.
3. Organization_Innovation: one if the firm introduced any new or significantly improved organizational structures or management practices and zero otherwise.
4. Marketing_Innovation: one if the firm introduced new or significantly improved marketing methods and zero otherwise.

The main regression (Eq. 1) of this study also included control variables that can affect firm performance. They were firm size, firm age, firm sales, percent (%) of export from sales, market type, listing status, subsidiary status, industrial dummy (reference group: manufacturing). The detailed explanation for each variable is as follows:

- *Firm size:* measured as the natural logarithm of the number of employees.
- *Firm age:* measured as the natural logarithm of firm age.
- *Export:* measured as the percentage ratio of exports to sales.
- *Domestic:* coded as one if the main market is domestic and zero otherwise.
- *Subsidiary:* coded as one if the firm is part of a larger firm and zero otherwise.

4 Data and Estimation

4.1 Descriptive Statistics

According to Table 1, firms are interested in engaging in process innovation, product innovation, and marketing innovation, with an average value of 0.3, or roughly 30%. The low value of 0.18 for organizational innovation probably indicates that organizational activities require more resources and knowledge and are more involved, and it is also harder to measure it's impact.

Table 2 shows the Pearson correlation between each pair of the variables from Column 1 to Column 9. The independent variables *Product_inno, Organizational_inno were* significantly correlated with the dependent variable *Total sales with correlation value* (0.11) and (0.15) at *1% level. Marketing_inno* had a slightly positive correlation (0.07) whereas correlation between Process_inno and Total sale was not significant. Several control variables also showed a positive correlation with *Total sales*: *Employees* (0.69), *Export* (0.24), Firm age (0.22). Finally, firms belong to a

Table 1 Descriptive statistics of the data

Statistic	N	Mean	St. Dev	Minimum	Maximum
product_inno	965	0.31	0.46	0	1
process_inno	965	0.32	0.47	0	1
organizational_inno	965	0.18	0.38	0	1
marketing_inno	965	0.30	0.46	0	1
employees	965	201.65	1011.15	2	17,000
establish_year	965	2002.19	9.75	1902	2014
domestic_sale	965	82.08	33.99	0	100
export	965	12.02	28.44	0	100
subsidiary	965	1.92	0.28	1	2
firm_type	965	1.56	0.86	1	3
industry	965	30.09	13.90	15	72

larger firm had a negative correlation with Total sales (– 0.26) and firms' operation on domestic market only had a negative correlation with Total sale (– 0.23). Correlation matrix shows that pairwise correlation is not very high.

4.2 Regression Results

Table 3 shows the regression results using OLS method over total sample, all hypotheses were estimated by looking at p-value of each variables estimated coefficient.

These results suggest that *Process_Innovation* had a significantly negative effects on *Total sales whereas Marketing_Innovation* was likely to have significantly positive effects on *Total sales.* The coefficient estimates on *Process_Innovation and Marketing_Innovation* was -0.28 and 0.23, respectively. Other two types of innovation such as *Product_Innovation* and *Organizational*_Innovation had insignificant effects on *Total sales.* Among the control variables, *Employees* had positive coefficient ($\beta = 0.93$), and subsidiary ($\beta = -0.59$).

The main results suggested that marketing innovation such as the introduction of new or significantly improved marketing method can increase the firm performance, while the firm performance may suffer after adopting new or significantly improved methods. The Variance Inflation Factor's results are all lower than 10 for the model above, which confirms that multicollinearity is not likely to be a real concern.

5 Discussion

This study aimed to test the effects of four different innovation on manufacturing and services firms in Vietnam. As mentioned earlier, four types of innovation—product, process, organizational, and marketing—are found to be statistically significant drivers of firm performance. However, when the interaction of these innovation types and control variables are introduced, this study shows that the introduction of new or significantly improved marketing method had positive effect on total sales measuring financial performance. New or improved marketing method increases the total sales by improving product awareness, reaching new market segment, or reminding existing customers. The positive relation between marketing innovation and total sales implies that firms can benefit from modification of marketing methods on the market.

On the other hand, the adoption of new or significantly improved methods leads to negative total sales. There were some possible reasons why process innovation was negatively related to total sales. First, it may take time to observe the effect of process innovation of the production on firm performance. Process innovation may require the introduction of new machinery of equipment in manufacturing firms and for services firms it could be adapting new methods, or new customer services

Table 2 Pearson correlation coefficients

	sale_t	product_ inno	process_ inno	organizational_ inno	marketing_ inno	employees	firm_age	export	subsidiary	domestic	industry
sale_t	1.00	0.07^{*}	– 0.02	– 0.01	0.01	0.63^{***}	0.31^{***}	0.10^{**}	-0.12^{***}	-0.09^{**}	– 0.05
product_inno	0.07^{*}	1.00	0.50^{***}	0.27^{***}	0.43^{***}	0.04	0.09^{**}	0.06	0.00	-0.09^{**}	– 0.05
process_inno	– 0.02	0.50^{***}	1.00	0.32^{***}	0.47^{***}	0.01	0.04	0.05	0.01	– 0.05	-0.07^{*}
organizational_ inno	– 0.01	0.27^{***}	0.32^{***}	1.00	0.37^{***}	0.04	0.07^{*}	0.05	– 0.01	-0.07^{*}	– 0.03
marketing_ inno	0.01	0.43^{***}	0.47^{***}	0.37^{***}	1.00	– 0.01	0.02	– 0.02	0.01	0.01	0.04
employees	0.63^{***}	0.04	0.01	0.04	– 0.01	1.00	0.21^{***}	$0.18^{** *}$	-0.14^{***}	-0.13^{***}	– 0.03
firm_age	0.31^{***}	0.09^{**}	0.04	0.07^{*}	0.02	0.21^{***}	1.00	0.03	-0.17^{***}	-0.09^{**}	-0.07^{*}
export	0.10^{**}	0.06	0.05	0.05	– 0.02	0.18^{***}	0.03	1.00	– 0.06	-0.66^{***}	-0.23^{***}
subsidiary	-0.12^{***}	0.00	0.01	– 0.01	0.01	-0.14^{***}	-0.17^{***}	– 0.06	1.00	0.04	-0.00
domestic	-0.09^{**}	-0.09^{**}	– 0.05	-0.07^{*}	0.01	-0.13^{***}	-0.09^{**}	-0.66^{***}	0.04	1.00	0.25^{***}
industry	– 0.05	– 0.05	-0.07^{*}	– 0.03	0.04	– 0.03	-0.07^{*}	-0.23^{***}	– 0.00	0.25^{***}	1.00

Note Significant at 1% (***), 5% (**) and 10% (*) level of significance

Table 3 Regression results: the effect of innovation on firm's performance

	Dependent variable: log(sale_t)
product_inno	0.011
	(0.124)
process_inno	− 0.280**
	(0.125)
organizational_inno	− 0.009
	(0.137)
marketing_inno	0.228*
	(0.126)
log(employees)	0.934***
	(0.040)
log(firm_age)	0.069
	(0.088)
subsidiary	− 0.595***
	(0.177)
export	− 0.002
	(0.002)
domestic	0.107
	(0.140)
Constant	21.194***
	(0.472)
Observations	965
R^2	0.482
Adjusted R^2	0.478
Residual std. error	1.445 (df = 955)
F-statistic	98.919*** (df = 9; 955)
Note:	*$p < 0.1$; **$p < 0.05$; ***$p < 0.01$

programmme. Adaptation often requires multiple rounds of trial and error, which can negatively impact firm productivity and performance. Kraft (1990) show that a new or significantly improved equipment or technique based on up-to-date knowledge may have negative effects on firm performance when the working environment supports such changes.

Another possible reason for weak or negative effects was the fact that the sample used in this study majority of firms is SME firms and belong to low and medium tech sector. According to Hirsch-Kreinsen et al. (2005), rather than process innovation, organizational innovations may play a critical role in firm performance in low and medium-tech industries.

References

Canh, N. T., Liem, N. T., Thu, P. A., & Nguyen, V. K. (2019). The impact of innovation on the firm performance and corporate social responsibility of Vietnamese manufacturing firms. *Sustainability, 11*(13), 3666. https://doi.org/10.3390/SU11133666

Cassiman, B., Golovko, E., & Martinez-Ros, E. (2010). Innovation, exports and productivity. *International Journal of Industrial Organization, 28*, 372–376.

Croitoru, A. (2013). Schumpeter, J.A., 1934 (2008). *The theory of economic development: An inquiry into profits, capital, credit, interest and the business cycle* (R. Opie, Translated from the German). New Brunswick (U.S.A) and London (U.K.): Transaction Publishers.

Damanpour, F. (1996). Organizational complexity and innovation: Developing and testing multiple contingency models. *Management Science, 42*(5), 693–716. https://doi.org/10.1287/mnsc.42.5.693

Felipe, M.-C., & Canova-Barrios, C. (2023). An approach to the concepts of radical, incremental, and disruptive innovation in organizations. *Región Científica, 2*(1), 202324. https://doi.org/10.58763/rc202324

Gürhan, G., Gündüz, U., Kemal, K., & Lütfihak, A. (2011). Effects of innovation types on firm performance. *International Journal of Production Economics, 133*(2), 662–676. https://doi.org/10.1016/J.IJPE.2011.05.014

Hall, B. H., Lotti, F., & Mairesse, J. (2009). Innovation and productivity in SMEs—Empirical evidence for Italy. *Small Business Economics, 33*, 13–33.

Hirsch-Kreinsen, H., Jacobson, D., Laestadius, S., & Smith, K. (2005). Low and medium technology industries in the knowledge economy: The analytical issues. In H. Hirsch-Kreinsen, D. Jacobson & S. Laestadius, (Eds.), *Low-tech innovation in the knowledge economy* (pp. 11–30). Peter Lang.

Ittner, C. D., Larcker, D. F., & Randall, T. (2003). Performance implications of strategic performance measurement in financial services firms. *Accounting, Organizations and Society, 28*(7–8), 715–741. https://doi.org/10.1016/S0361-3682(03)00033-3

Iuliia, K. (2022). Increasing the competitiveness of enterprises under the conditions of digitalization. *Innovation and Sustainability Series*. https://doi.org/10.31649/ins.2022.4.101.108

Jayani, R. P., Rajapathirana, & Yan, H. (2018). Relationship between innovation capability, innovation type, and firm performance. *Journal of Innovation & Knowledge, 3*(1), 44–55.https://doi.org/10.1016/J.JIK.2017.06.002

Joakim, B., & Sofia, B. (2012). Assessing firm capabilities for innovation. *International Journal of Knowledge Management Studies, 5*(1/2), 171–184. https://doi.org/10.1504/IJKMS.2012.051970

Kraft, K. (1990). Are product and process innovations independent of each other? *Applied Economics, 22*, 1029–1038.

Long, P. D., & Anh, H. T. M. (2017). Innovation and productivity of Vietnamese small and medium enterprises: Firm level panel data evidence. *International Journal of Economics and Financial Issues, 7*(3), 226–232.

Lööf, H., & Heshmati, A. (2003). The link between firm-level innovation and aggregate productivity growth: A cross-country examination. *Research Evaluation, 12*(2), 131–147.

Lööf, H., & Heshmati, A. (2006). On the relationship between innovation and performance: A sensitivity analysis. *Economics of Innovation and New Technology, 15*(4/5), 317–344.

Nam, T. H., Tuan, N. P., & Van Minh, N. (2017). Critical successful factors for innovation in Vietnamese firms. *Journal of Industrial Engineering and Management, 10*(3), 522–544.

Nham, P. T., Nguyen, N., Pham, G., Nguyen, T., & Bich, N. (2016). The effects of innovation on firm performance of supporting industries in Hanoi–Vietnam. *Journal of Industrial Engineering and Management, 9*(2), 413–431.https://doi.org/10.3926/JIEM.1564

OECD (2005) *The measurement of scientific and technological activities Oslo manual. Guidelines for collecting and interpreting innovation data* (3rd ed.). OECD EUROSTAT. https://doi.org/10.1787/9789264013100-en

Porter, M. E. (1990). *The competitive advantage of nations*. Free Press.
Rosli, M. M., & Sidek, S. (2013). The impact of innovation on the performance of small and medium manufacturing enterprises: Evidence from Malaysia. *Journal of Innovation Management in Small and Medium Enterprises, 2013*, 885666.
Stoneman, P., Bartoloni, E., & Baussola, M. (2018). Product innovation and firm performance. *The Microeconomics of Product Innovation*, Oxford, online edn, Oxford Academic, March 22, 2018.
Ute, S., Petra, A., Petra, A., Alain, D., & Alain, D. (2019). Goal multiplicity and innovation: How social and economic goals affect open innovation and innovation performance. *Journal of Product Innovation Management, 36*(6), 721–743. https://doi.org/10.1111/JPIM.12511
Venkatraman, N., & Ramanujam, V. (1986). Measurement of business performance in strategy research: A comparison approach. *Academy of Management Review, 11*(4), 801–814.
Vyas, V. (2009), *Innovation and new product development by SMEs: An investigation of Scottish food and drinks Industry*, Edinburgh Napier University, Ph.D. Thesis, Edinburgh.
Waheed, A. (2011). *Innovation and firm-level productivity: Econometric evidence from Bangladesh and Pakistan*; UNU-MERIT.
World Intellectual Property Organization (WIPO). (2022). *World intellectual property indicators 2022*. WIPO. https://doi.org/10.34667/tind.47082
Sanjeev, K. Y., Samadhiya, A., Kumar, A., Majumdar, A., Garza-Reyes, J. A., & Luthra, S. (2023). Achieving the sustainable development goals through net zero emissions: Innovation-driven strategies for transitioning from incremental to radical lean, green and digital technologies. *Resources Conservation and Recycling, 197*, 107094. https://doi.org/10.1016/j.resconrec.2023.107094

Ngoc-Thanh Pham is a product manager for a tech firm in Ho Chi Minh, Vietnam, where he turns ideas into real products, overseeing their journey from the start to when they reach customers. Using his knowledge, he understands market needs, user preferences, and technology to create products that people demand. Holding a B.Sc. in Computer Sciences and pursuing an M.Sc. degree in Applied Economics, he is believed in the synergy between combining data-driven approaches and technological innovation, supporting the creation of a sustainable firm that optimizes operations, reduces environmental impact, fosters innovation, and enhances social responsibility.

Part V
Economic Development and Welfare

Chapter 11
Governance Quality, Infrastructure Development, and Income Inequality in Vietnam's Provinces

Dương Duy Lâm and Võ Ngọc Tường Vy

Abstract This study examines the effects of governance quality and infrastructure development on reducing income inequality in the provinces/districts of Vietnam. Panel data from population of 63 provinces in Vietnam over a 3-year period (2018–2020) is collected, with the GINI index serving as the proxy for income inequality. The study utilizes the fixed effects estimation method with robust standard errors to investigate the relationship between investment in development infrastructure, governance quality, and income inequality. The findings support the hypotheses that governance quality and infrastructure development are negatively correlated with income inequality. The study highlights the need to redirect investment away from industrial development and toward other infrastructure projects to effectively close the income gap and improve living standards in the provinces. However, the study acknowledges limitations in data availability, suggesting the need for further research to explore specific income segments and causality relationships to inform more targeted policy implications for local governance in Vietnam.

Keywords Governance quality · Infrastructure development · Income inequality

1 Introduction

Income inequality is a persistent challenge faced by many countries, including Vietnam. It refers to the unequal distribution of income among individuals or households within a society. High levels of income inequality can have adverse effects on social cohesion, economic stability, and sustainable and inclusive development. Addressing income inequality requires a comprehensive understanding of its determinants and potential effective policy interventions without reducing individuals work incentives.

D. D. Lâm (✉) · V. N. T. Vy
Vietnam - the Netherlands Programme, University of Economics Ho Chi Minh City, Ho Chi Minh City, Vietnam
e-mail: lam.dd@vnp.edu.vn; vy.vnt@vnp.edu.vn

P. K. Nam and A. Heshmati (eds.), *Recent Trends in Vietnam's Rapid Economic Development*, Frontiers in South and Southeast Asian Development Research,
https://doi.org/10.1007/978-981-97-6079-4_11

There are two contributing factors of inequality reduction that draw avid interests of this study. Investment in development infrastructure plays a crucial role in promoting economic growth and improving living standards in countries around the world. It includes various sectors such as transportation, housing, energy, telecommunications, and social infrastructure. The allocation and effectiveness of investment in development infrastructure can have significant implications for socioeconomic outcomes, including income inequality (Giang & Pheng, 2014). Governance is also a significant contributor to addressing almost every socioeconomic issue. Under effective control of the governors, investment flows smoothly and is distributed efficiently across provinces, facilitating the active employment market in the area. With better job opportunities, people have access to better income sources and income generation, thus income dispersion is gradually reduced.

This study aims to examine the relationship between investment in development infrastructure and income inequality in the context of provinces in Vietnam. The objective is to narrow down the literature gap on the topic of income inequality by examining the impacts of governance quality and development infrastructure on income inequality. By focusing on this specific relationship, the study seeks to shed light on the potential impacts of infrastructure investment on income distribution patterns and its inter-regional variations within the country. Understanding how investment in development infrastructure influences income inequality is essential for policymakers. It can inform the design and implementation of strategies that promote more equitable and inclusive economic growth and reduce disparities. By identifying the specific types of infrastructure investment that have the most significant effects on income inequality, policymakers can prioritize and allocate resources effectively to promote both within and between provinces equality.

The study hypothesizes that investment in development infrastructure can have both direct and indirect effects on income inequality. Directly, infrastructure projects that enhance access to economic opportunities, such as transportation networks or industrial zones, may contribute to income generation and reducing income disparities. Indirectly, investment in social infrastructure, such as education and healthcare facilities, can improve human capital and lead to more equitable income distribution. By focusing on the relationship between investment in development infrastructure and income inequality, this study aims to provide valuable insights for policymakers at national and province levels in Vietnam. The findings can guide the allocation of resources toward infrastructure projects that have the potential to reduce income inequality effectively. However, it is important to acknowledge the limitations of data availability and the need for further research to explore the specific mechanisms and causal relationships between infrastructure investment and income inequality in Vietnam. Such research can inform more targeted policy interventions and contribute to more inclusive and sustainable development resulting in reduced inequality.

This research consists of 5 sections as follows. Section 1 is an introduction—an overview of the study. Section 2 is the literature review—a critical analysis of current literature on related topics. Section 3 is the methodology—specific procedures used to identify, select, and analyze data. Section 4 describes the data analysis, findings, and discussion of statistical results. Finally, Sect. 5 provides a conclusion and recommendation for further research.

2 Literature Review

2.1 Infrastructure Development and Income Inequality

The relationship between investment in development infrastructure and income inequality has been the subject of scholarly investigation in various contexts. Several studies have found a negative correlation between infrastructure investment and income inequality. Chotia and Rao (2017), for example, conducted a study investigating the scope of the Brazil, Russia, India, China, and South Africa (BRICS) nations to provide valuable insights into the interrelationships between infrastructure development, poverty, and income inequality. Through its rigorous empirical analysis and robust findings, the study contributes to the existing literature on the subject and provides a foundation for evidence-based policymaking in the realms of infrastructure development, poverty alleviation, and inclusive growth in the BRICS context. To achieve this objective, Chotia and Rao (2017) utilize a comprehensive dataset spanning the period from 1991 to 2014. The dataset encompasses key variables such as per capita household consumption expenditure, rural–urban inequality measured by the agricultural-to-industrial value-added ratio, and real GDP per capita. In addition, the study constructs an infrastructure development index using principal component analysis (PCA) and incorporates control variables such as trade openness and the consumer price index. To analyze the relationships between these variables, the authors employ various statistical techniques. These include panel unit root tests, which assess the stationarity of the variables, co-integration tests to examine the long-run relationships, and Panel Dynamics Ordinary Least Squares (PDOLS) estimation for estimating long-run coefficients. Additionally, panel Granger causality analysis is conducted to investigate the causal relationships among the variables. The Chotia and Rao (2017) study examines how infrastructure, inequality, and poverty are linked in the BRICS nations. The results indicate that there is a persistent connection between the variables in the long term. This suggests that both economic growth and infrastructure development have important contributions to reducing poverty. Additionally, the research identifies a temporary causal relationship, where economic growth and infrastructure development influence poverty reduction, as well as from economic growth to rural–urban inequality. The robustness of the empirical results is tested through various methods. Individual exclusion of the top-performing nations does not alter the findings, suggesting the high reliability of the results. Moreover, conducting analyses with sub-samples of data (panels) further confirms the robustness of the findings.

Besides, another significant contribution to the literature on the effects of infrastructure development is the research conducted by Calderón and Serven (2004) providing valuable insights into the relationship of interest subjects. The authors employ a comprehensive dataset covering 121 countries over the period from 1960 to 2000 and utilize instrumental variable techniques to address potential endogeneity issues. The main conclusions of the study can be summarized as follows: Firstly, the presence of a substantial positive impact on long-term economic growth is evident when considering infrastructure quantity, as indicated by infrastructure stocks. This finding remains consistent across various measures of infrastructure and estimation techniques. However, the relationship between infrastructure quality and economic growth demonstrates less consistency, potentially attributed to the high correlation between quantity and quality metrics. Secondly, both infrastructure quantity and quality exhibit a consistent and negative influence on income inequality.

The study finds that larger infrastructure stocks and improved quality of infrastructure services contribute to reducing income inequality. Additionally, the inclusion of safe water access as an infrastructure indicator further enhances the positive impact on income equality. Third, the study provides evidence of a causal relationship between infrastructure, growth, and inequality by controlling for reverse causation and conducting various statistical tests to ensure the robustness of the results. Furthermore, the study conducts illustrative experiments to demonstrate the economic significance of the findings. For example, the authors simulate scenarios where countries in Latin America and the Caribbean catch up with the infrastructure levels of regional leaders. The results show that achieving higher infrastructure development levels would lead to substantial per capita growth gains ranging from 1.1–4.8% per annum and reductions in Gini coefficients between 0.02 and 0.10.

Inequality is multi-dimensional but the monetary dimension measured as income inequality is dominating. The other dimensions include housing, education, health, longevity, and utilities. The inclusion of water access in these scenarios further contributes to reducing income inequality. Overall, Calderón and Servén's (2004) study emphasizes the importance of infrastructure development in promoting economic growth and reducing income inequality. It suggests that investing in infrastructure can be a win–win strategy for poverty reduction, as it not only raises overall income levels but also has a greater positive impact on the income of the poor. These findings align with the objectives of the essay, which explores the impacts of investment in development infrastructure on income inequality in Vietnam. By incorporating the insights from Calderón and Serven (2004), one can provide a solid theoretical foundation and contribute to the existing literature on the topic.

On the other hand, Akomea-Frimpong et al. (2023) investigates the application of public–private partnerships (PPPs) for achieving sustainability in infrastructure projects in Ghana. From a practical standpoint, the study informs the measures and strategies implemented to achieve sustainable infrastructure in Ghana. It highlights the need to address climate change, ensure facility resilience, and establish effective regulations and financial support mechanisms. Policy-wise, the study emphasizes the importance of enacting regulations and policies that govern PPP arrangements to promote sustainable development. It is important to note that the results of this study are specific to Ghana and should be understood in the context of the country's unique circumstances. However, the findings contribute to the growing body of knowledge regarding the significance of the PPP model in achieving sustainable public infrastructure projects with effects on inequality and poverty.

Overall, studies have contributed to the growing body of knowledge on the relationship between investment in development infrastructure and income inequality. They provide a solid theoretical foundation and valuable insights into the impacts of infrastructure development on economic growth, poverty reduction, and income distribution. By incorporating these insights into our research, we can contribute to the existing literature and provide a comprehensive analysis of the effects of infrastructure investment on income inequality in your specific context, namely Vietnams provinces.

2.2 Governance Quality and Income Inequality

Acemoglu et al. (2005), as well as North (1989), identified effective institutions or governance as the driving force behind economic growth. According to Drzeniek-Hanouz (2015), both private and public institutions have significant potential for promoting long-term economic development. This viewpoint was reinforced by Dossou et al. (2023), who provided empirical evidence confirming that economic institutions can improve market efficiency, thereby contributing to overall economic growth. Recent research has widened the focus on the impact of governance quality and institutions efficiency on economic growth to include broader socioeconomic development, with a particular emphasis on addressing income inequality as a top priority. With extended series of research, Ofori et al. (2021, 2022a, 2022b, 2023) concluded that governance of high quality can contribute to facilitation of a better income distribution. However, the literature has recorded that quality of institutions has a dual impact on reducing income inequality.

Sou and Vinnicombe (2021) posited that the contribution of good governance to the reduction of income inequality by minimizing transaction cost which in turn improves foreign direct investment (FDI) attractiveness and creates job opportunities. Accessing the income gap the same way, Dossou et al. (2023) proved that by creating a harmonic environment, quality institutions can help foster mutual trust between public and private investors, which in turn offer greater employment opportunities. Agreeing with them, Ofori et al. (2022a, 2022b, 2023) added that by minimizing criminal rate and boosting investors' confidence, good governance spontaneously facilitates job market and addresses income inequality. On the other hand, research also proved that bad governance can be an obvious contributor to the exacerbation of income inequality. Reasons suggested by Sou and Vinnicombe (2021) pointed out that with the impuissance of the governance, corruption levels would be rampant and damage the income distribution. In a similar view, Xu et al. (2021) stated that one of the worst consequences of detrimental governance is to undermine political and economic stability, resulting in retarding the economic growth and enlarging the income gap.

2.3 The Case of Vietnam

In the case of Vietnam, there is a lack of extensive research on the specific relationship between investment in development infrastructure and income inequality. This represents a research gap that needs to be addressed. By conducting a study on this topic in the context of Vietnam, we can contribute to filling this gap and provide valuable insights into the impacts of infrastructure investment on economic growth and income inequality in the country. To gain a comprehensive understanding of the relationship between investment in development infrastructure and income inequality in Vietnam, it is necessary to review studies that analyze income distribution, poverty levels, and the impacts of infrastructure development initiatives in the country. These studies can provide insights into the specific mechanisms through which infrastructure investment affects income distribution and inequality in the Vietnamese context.

3 Methodology

3.1 Research Approach

The study applied the correlational and non-experimental quantitative research to link empirical observation and mathematical expression of quantitative relationships. In doing so, firstly we provide descriptive analysis of the data. Next, we conduct panel data analysis by random and fixed effects together with Hausman test to select the best model. We continue by performing some diagnostic tests to detect heteroskedasticity, autocorrelation and cross-sectional dependence. Treatment for any possible defects is coming up next and we finalize the regression.

3.2 Sampling Method

The study collects panel data from population of 63 provinces in Vietnam over a 3-year period (2018–2020). The data includes information on governance quality, infrastructure development and income inequality, and some other control variables.

Data on infrastructure development is obtained from government reports, development plans, and official statistical sources. Income inequality data is collected from national surveys and statistical databases. Additional data on provincial competitiveness, housing and industrial land use are sourced from relevant government agencies and research institutions.

3.3 Variable Measurement

The measurements of the dependent, independent, and control variables are described as follows:

Income Inequality: In the analysis of income inequality, the GINI index is employed to approximate the magnitude of inequality. The GINI index serves as a quantitative metric that gauges the extent to which the distribution of income or consumption among individuals or households within an economy diverges from an ideal state of complete equality. It provides a measure of the degree of disparity present in the distribution, reflecting the deviations from a perfectly equal allocation. A Gini index of 0 represents perfect equality, while an index of 100 implies perfect inequality. A disadvantage of the GINI measure is that it does not provide any information of distribution of inequality across population and spaces, unless it is computed for each province separately.

Governance Quality: As the scope of the research is province level, Governance Quality will be proxied by the Provincial Completeness index (PCI), provided annually by PCIVietnam—an organization co-founded by the Vietnam Chamber of Commerce and Industry (VCCI) and The United States Agency for International Development (USAID). The PCI is constructed in a three-step sequence, referred to as "the 3 Cs": (1) Collect business survey data and published data sources, (2) Calculate ten sub-indices and standardize to a 10-point scale, and (3) Calibrate the composite PCI as the weighted mean of ten sub-indices with a maximum score of 100 points.

To represent the levels of infrastructure development in Vietnam, we use a group of two variables, namely Industrial land use (INDLAND) and Housing (HOU). The measurement of these variables are as follow:

Industrial Land Use (INDLAND): We collected the total land area used for industrialization of each province. Data is publicly available on the General Statistics Office of Vietnam. The data measurement unit is measured in hectares.

Housing (HOU): Housing is measured by the total housing area completed annually by provinces. Data is publicly available on the General Statistics Office of Vietnam. The data measurement unit is square meters.

Moreover, we also utilize the *Index of industrial production (IIP)* and *Gross regional domestic product (GRDP)* as control variables. Data for those variables is reported on the General Statistics Office of Vietnam.

3.4 Analytical Framework

The fixed effects regression estimator is employed to investigate the relationship between investment in governance quality, infrastructure development, and income inequality. This technique is suitable for panel data analysis as it accounts for time and province-specific heterogeneity effects, controlling for potential confounding factors. Besides the sample is same as the population and fixed effects is an obvious choice compared with Random Effects model.

To ensure the validity and reliability of the findings, robustness checks is conducted. Various statistical tests are employed to assess the robustness of the model and address potential endogeneity issues.

The model of this study is expressed as:

$$\mathrm{GINI}_{\mathrm{it}} = \alpha_1 + \beta_1 \mathrm{PCI}_{\mathrm{it}} + \beta_2 \mathrm{INDLAND}_{\mathrm{it}} + \beta_3 \mathrm{HOU}_{\mathrm{it}} + \beta_4 \mathrm{IIP}_{\mathrm{it}} + \beta_5 \mathrm{GRDP}_{\mathrm{it}} + \varepsilon_{\mathrm{it}}.$$

4 Data Analysis, Findings, and Discussion

4.1 Descriptive Data

Table 1 provides a summary of the investigated variables, including GINI as the dependent variables, Provincial Competitiveness, Industrial Land Use, and Housing Area as independent variables. The dataset consists of 189 observations for each variable, collected manually from various available public data sources in Vietnam in the period between 2018 and 2020.

Income dispersion, assessed by GINI index, of Vietnamese provinces observed in the period ranged within 23 and 50%, explained by the standard deviation at only 5.6% varied between the average score of 36.4%. This generally summarizes the situation of income inequality across provinces in Vietnam, which is still under effective control to fall within a safe, efficient, and suitable threshold for high growth.

Observations of the competitiveness variable produces average scores around 64.4 and standard deviation of 2.8. Lowest score was recorded at 58.2, and the most

Table 1 Descriptive statistics of all variables, NT = 63 × 3 = 189 observations

Variables	Definition	Mean	Std dev	Minimum	Maximum
GINI	GINI coefficient	0.364	0.056	0.236	0.501
PCI	Provincial competitiveness index	64.453	2.800	58.157	75.086
INDLAND	Industrial land use	31.369	15.955	8.800	82.400
HOU	Housing area	1727.190	1591.901	364.000	10,422.000
IIP	Index of industrial production	109.388	10.658	73.100	188.500
GRDP	Gross regional GDP	65.861	40.720	26.070	309.620

competitive reach was up to 75.1. In the group of independent variables that represent the infrastructure development, industrial land area, and housing area reported huge gaps between the top and the bottom figures. For area of land use for industrial purposes, the mean is 31.4 thousand hectares with standard deviation of 16 thousand hectares. For new housing areas built, provinces with the largest added value reach 10 thousand square meters, compared to the lowest one with only 364 square meters.

4.2 Multicollinearity Test

Multicollinearity generally occurs when there are high correlations between two or more predictor or explanatory variables in a model, GINI in current case. In other words, one predictor variable can be used to predict the other. This creates redundant information, skewing the results in a regression model (Glen, 2015). Multicollinearity reduces the precision of the estimated coefficients, which weakens the statistical power of your regression model. The *p*-values to identify independent variables that are statistically significant may no longer be trust-worthy (Frost, 2017).

Variance Inflation Factor (VIF) and correlation coefficient tests are employed to check if multicollinearity exists in the sample. The numerical value for VIF tells what percentage the variance is inflated for each coefficient. The VIF value bigger than 5 implies high correlations between independent variables (Everitt & Skrondal, 2010). Table 2a displays the VIF values for the explanatory variables. The range of VIF values is from 1.07 to 1.44, indicating that there is little or no multicollinearity in the dataset. The mean VIF is calculated to be 1.27, further supporting the absence of significant multicollinearity.

In general, an absolute correlation coefficient of larger than 0.7 between pairs of two predictors indicates the presence of multicollinearity (Molala, 2019). Furthermore, Table 2b presents the pairwise correlation matrix of the explanatory variables. The correlation coefficients do not exceed 0.7, providing additional evidence that multicollinearity is not a concern in the dataset used in this study.

Table 2a Variance inflation factor of explanatory variables

Variable	VIF	1/VIF
INDLAND	1.44	0.695543
HOU	1.42	0.703833
PCI	1.07	0.935847
Mean VIF	1.27	

Table 2b Correlation matrix of explanatory variables, Obs = 189

	PCI	INDLAND	HOU	IIP	GRDP
PCI	1.0000				
INDLAND	0.1943	1.0000			
HOU	0.1899	0.5188	1.0000		
IIP	– 0.0408	0.0528	0.0552	1.0000	
GRDP	0.4140	0.1637	0.2392	– 0.1311	1.0000

4.3 Model Testing

Fixed Effects Model (FEM), Random Effects Model (REM), and Pooled Ordinary Least Square (OLS) are three basic approaches to analyze panel data. To select the best model for estimation of variations in the dependent variable GINI Index, we conduct the necessary tests described as followed (Table 3).

To validate the selection of the FE model, the Hausman (1978) test was employed. We present the Hausman test results for model 1 with Chi-square test value of 40.202 and p-value equals 0.000. The obtained p-value of 0.000 indicates the rejection of the null hypothesis, which assumes no systematic difference between the coefficients in

Table 3 Regression results

GINI index	Pooled OLS	Random effects	Fixed effects
Governance quality	– 0.007***	– 0.009***	– 0.007***
	(0.001)	(0.001)	(0.002)
Industrial land use	0.00005	– 0.0002	– 0.005***
	(0.0003)	(0.0004)	(0.001)
Housing	– 0.00001***	– 0.00001**	– 0.00003***
	(0.000003)	(0.000004)	(0.00001)
Industrial production	– 0.0004	0.0002	0.0001
	(0.0003)	(0.0003)	(0.0002)
GRDP	– 0.0001	– 0.0002	– 0.001**
	(0.0001)	(0.0002)	(0.0004)
Constant	0.867***	0.943***	1.097***
	(0.095)	(0.093)	(0.102)
Observations	189	189	189
R-squared	0.262		0.450
Production control	Yes	Yes	Yes
Categorical factor	No	RE	FE
Number of province		63	63

Standard errors in parentheses, $^{***}p < 0.01$, $^{**}p < 0.05$, $^{*}p < 0.1$

Table 4 Robustness checks

	Heteroskedasticity	Autocorrelation	Cross-sectional dependence
Chi-squared test value	47,092.18	1.227	0.832
p-value	0.000	0.272	0.405

the two FE and RE models. This suggests the presence of correlation between the individual effects and other regressors, making the Random Effect (RE) model inconsistent and biased. Consequently, the fixed effects (FE) model is deemed consistent and unbiased but not efficient, and more suitable for the analysis. A joint F-test for significance of individual province effects also shows that the effects are different than zero suggesting fixed effects preferred to Pooled OLS estimation method.

In summary, the analysis revealed no significant multicollinearity in the dataset. The fixed effects (FE) model was selected as the most appropriate approach based on the Hausman test results, indicating the presence of correlation between individual effects and other regressors rendering suitability of the Random Effects (RE) model.

4.4 Robustness Check

Before conducting analysis of the estimation results, we have to make sure that we meet certain conditions to which we can come up with the best linear unbiased estimator (BLUE) possible. In this section, we will perform several statistical tests that help detect some common defects that violate the Classical Linear Regression Model (CLRM) assumptions (Frost, 2018). The assumptions are linearity of parameters, full rank, exogeneity of predictors, independently, identically, and normally distributed error terms.

By employing Modified Wald test for groupwise heteroskedasticity, Wooldridge test for autocorrelation and Pesaran's test of cross-sectional independence, we detect heteroskedasticity in our model. The test results are presented in Table 4.

4.5 Statistical Results

The tests conducted in the last section suggest that our data is heteroskedastic, inefficient, and potentially give misleading inferences (Kmenta, 1986). The Robust standard errors are utilized in the fixed effects model as to its ability to eliminate the phenomenon. Table 5 presents the results of the model using robust standard errors to control for the effects of heteroskedasticity. Theoretically, the results are more consistent, reliable, and prone to less errors than the normal fixed effects model.

Overall, the use of the robust standard errors has made some changes in the estimation results. The key independent variables all have estimated coefficients with

Table 5 Fixed effects model with robust standard errors, dependent variable is GINI income inequality

Variables	Fixed effects (robust)	Fixed effects
Governance quality	– 0.007***	– 0.007***
	(0.002)	(0.002)
Industrial land use	– 0.005***	– 0.005***
	(0.002)	(0.001)
Housing	– 0.0003***	– 0.0003***
	(0.00001)	(0.00001)
Industrial production	0.0001	0.0001
	(0.0002)	(0.0002)
GRDP	– 0.001	– 0.001**
	(0.001)	(0.0004)
Constant	1.097***	1.097***
	(0.098)	(0.102)
Observations	189	189
R-squared	0.450	0.450
Number of province	63	63
Production control	Yes	Yes
Robust standard errors	Yes	No
Categorical factor	FE	FE

Notes Standard errors in parentheses, ***$p < 0.01$, **$p < 0.05$, *$p < 0.1$

the significant level less than 5%, while none of the control variables are statistically significantly different than zero. The results reveal that both Governance quality and Infrastructure development contribute to the elimination of the income gap across provinces in Vietnam. We find that every 10 points improvement in Provincial Competitiveness reduces the income dispersion by 7 percentage points of GINI inequality. This implies that the quality of local governance plays an important role against income inequality. Regarding the variables proxying the infrastructure development, housing establishment accelerate the process of narrowing the income dispersion by 1 percentage point of GINI for every thousand square meters, whilst the figures for increase in land area used for industrialization is 0.5 percentage point of GINI in response for a thousand hectares of land.

4.6 Discussion

In this study, the primary objective was to examine the factors influencing income inequality in a panel dataset of provinces in Vietnam. The analysis utilized a fixed effects regression model and conducted several diagnostic tests to ensure the validity of the results. Additionally, a heteroskedastic Random Effects model using Feasible Generalized Least Squares (FGLS) regression was implemented to address heteroskedasticity in the data.

The findings of the study can be summarized as follows, with a focus on the importance of infrastructure:

Infrastructure Development and Income Inequality: The analysis demonstrated a statistically significant relationship between housing establishment and income inequality. An increase in housing establishment, measured by the area in square meters, was associated with decreases in income inequality by both measures. This suggests that promoting housing development can contribute to narrowing income disparities.

Industrialization and Income Inequality: The analysis revealed a statistically significant negative relationship between the area used for industrialization (INDLAND) and income inequality. This implies that an increase in the area dedicated to industrialization facilitates the reduction of income disparities. While industrialization is important for economic growth, policymakers can consider its double impacts on income inequality and develop strategies to fully derive the benefits.

Governance Quality and Income Inequality: The study also found a significant negative relationship between provincial competitiveness index (PCI) and income inequality. A 10-point improvement in provincial competitiveness was associated with a 7-percentage point reduction in GINI index. This highlights the importance of enhancing the quality of local governance and promoting competitiveness in addressing income disparities.

Overall, the findings emphasize the significance of infrastructure development, including industrialization and housing establishment, in reducing income inequality. Additionally, provincial competitiveness and the careful management of industrialization play important roles in addressing income disparities across provinces. Policymakers can utilize these findings to prioritize investments in infrastructure, promote competitiveness, and design policies that ensure equitable access to the benefits of industrialization.

It is worth to mention that, the findings here are based on average effects. Income inequality can be vast between provinces. Policies should target both inequality between and within provinces by employing redistribution of state and provincial tax revenues to achieve inclusive growth and higher within and between province equality.

5 Conclusions

5.1 Summary of Findings

The main aim of this study is to expound the possible impacts of Local governance quality and Infrastructure development on reducing Income inequality in the context of Vietnam's provinces. To investigate the relationship, this study collects a panel data from 63 provinces in Vietnam for a 3-year period from 2018 to 2020. GINI index is chosen to be the proxy for the dependent variable in the fixed effects regression estimator with the use of robust standard errors, whereas Provincial Competitiveness Index, Industrial Land Use, and Housing play the role of independent variables helping to explain variation in income inequality. The regression produces the results that accept the two stated hypotheses: Governance quality and Infrastructure development are between regional equality enhancing by being negatively correlated with Income inequality.

5.2 Policy Implications

By employing the robust standard errors, this study has successfully eliminated the effects of the existing panel data deficiencies, which is heteroscedasticity, and enhanced the validity and reliability of the findings. In addition to strengthening empirical evidence and filling theoretical gaps in the context of Vietnam, this study puts forward an intriguing suggestion for local policymakers. The results of this paper raise the awareness to enhance focus for the development plan, with the direction to improve current living standards and aim for sustainable development.

In details, the following policy implications can be considered:

Enhance Provincial Competitiveness: Given the significant negative relationship between provincial competitiveness (PCI) and income inequality, policymakers should focus on improving the quality of local governance and promoting competitiveness within provinces. This can be achieved through measures at the province levels such as reducing bureaucratic barriers, streamlining regulatory processes, and fostering an environment conducive to entrepreneurship and innovation.

Invest in Infrastructure Development: Promoting housing development initiatives can contribute to narrowing income disparities by ensuring affordable and adequate housing options for all income groups supported at both national and province levels.

Ensure Dynamics Industrialization: With the importance of industrialization to economic growth, policymakers can benefit from its potential double impact on income inequality. The results obtained from this study suggest the need for policies that promote sustainable industrialization to help facilitate inequality moderation. This can be achieved by implementing measures such as investing in workforce development, tax and mitigation incentives or Public–Private Partnerships (PPP), etc., financed and supported at both province and national levels.

Social Safety Nets and Redistribution: To complement the above policies, it is important to establish social safety nets and redistributive measures to support vulnerable populations and mitigate the impact of income disparities. This can include targeted welfare programs, progressive taxation policies, and investments in education and healthcare to ensure equal access to opportunities and basic services.

Monitoring and Evaluation: It is crucial for policymakers to continuously monitor and evaluate the impact of implemented policies on income inequality. Regular assessments can help identify areas of success and areas that require further attention or adjustments. Monitoring should involve collecting relevant data on income distribution, infrastructure development, provincial competitiveness, and other relevant indicators to inform evidence-based policymaking and conduct necessary regulatory adjustments.

5.3 Limitations of the Research

This study has limitations and leaves room for further improvements. First, a better and in-depth analysis can be put into the proxy of Income Inequality. Income inequality is multi-dimensional. Construction of multi-dimensional inequality can be a better measure than single dimensionally measure inequality. The use of multiple indexes that also measure inequality can help to provide a multi-dimensional view of its relationship toward Governance Quality and Infrastructure Development. Furthermore, causality relationships have not been touched on. This is rooted from the other limitation—the limited public data sources available in Vietnam. The obtainability of data has severely hindered the research scope and the dept of the study with limited dataset.

5.4 Future Research Directions

Despite the numerous limitations, this study provides valuable insights into the relationship between local governance quality, infrastructure development, and income inequality in Vietnam. Building on this research, future studies can explore the following directions.

First, researchers can investigate causal relationships by employing experimental designs, instrumental variable approaches, or quasi-experimental methods to determine the causal impact of local governance and infrastructure on income inequality.

Second, additional factors that may influence income inequality, such as education levels, healthcare access, social welfare programs, and regional economic disparities, should be considered to provide a more comprehensive and deep understanding of income inequality determinants.

Third, extending the analysis to a longer period can capture the dynamics of income inequality and examine how the relationships between variables may change over time, providing insights into the long-term impacts of local governance and infrastructure development. The changes also can be decomposed in to within and between province components and how they change over time measuring governance performance and implemented local and central government's policy effects.

Fourth, conducting subnational analysis at the district or community level, can reveal how local governance and infrastructure initiatives affect income disparities within smaller geographic areas, enabling targeted interventions for specific regions or communities.

Fifth, comparative analysis can be conducted to compare the findings from Vietnam with other countries or regions, offering a broader perspective on the relationship between local governance, infrastructure, and income inequality.

Lastly, supplementing quantitative analysis with qualitative research methods, such as interviews or focus groups, can provide insights into the experiences and perceptions of individuals affected by income inequality and local governance policies, contributing a nuanced understanding of social and cultural factors influencing income distribution.

By addressing these research directions, future studies can contribute to a deeper understanding of the complex interplay between local governance, infrastructure development, national efforts and goals, and income inequality. Moreover, they can inform evidence-based policy decisions aimed at reducing income disparities and promoting inclusive economic growth.

References

Acemoglu, D., Johnson, S., & Robinson, J. A. (2005). Institutions as a fundamental cause of long-run growth. In A. Philippe & D. Steven (Eds.), *Handbook of economic growth* (pp. 385–472), Elsevier.

Akomea-Frimpong, I., Xiaohua, J., Robert, O., & Kukah, A. S. (2023). Public-private partnerships for sustainable infrastructure development in Ghana: A systematic review and recommendations. *Smart and Sustainable Built Environment, 12*(2), 237–257. https://doi.org/10.1108/SASBE-07-2021-0111

Calderón, C. A., & Serven, L. (2004). The effects of infrastructure development on growth and income distribution. *Annals of Economics and Finance, 15*(2). https://doi.org/10.1596/1813-9450-3400

Chotia, V., & Rao, N. V. M. (2017). Investigating the interlinkages between infrastructure development, poverty and rural–urban income inequality: Evidence from BRICS nations. *Studies in Economics and Finance, 34*(4), 466–484. https://doi.org/10.1108/SEF-07-2016-0159

Dossou, T. A. M., Kambaye, E. N., Bekun, F. V., & Eoulam, A. O. (2023). Exploring the linkage between tourism, governance quality, and poverty reduction in Latin America. *Tourism Economics, 29*(1), 210–234.

Drzeniek-Hanouz, M. (2015, January 2). *Why institutions matter for economic growth.* Worlds Economic Forum. https://www.weforum.org/agenda/2015/01/why-institutions-matter-for-economic-growth/
Everitt, B. S., & Skrondal, A. (2010). *The Cambridge dictionary of statistics.* Cambridge University Press.
Frost, J. (2017). *Multicollinearity in regression analysis: Problems, detection, and solutions.* Statistics by Jim. https://statisticsbyjim.com/regression/multicollinearity-in-regression-analysis/
Frost, J. (2018). *7 classical assumptions of ordinary least squares (OLS) linear regression.* Statistics by Jim. https://statisticsbyjim.com/regression/ols-linear-regression-assumptions/
Giang, D. T. H., & Pheng L. S. (2014). Critical factors affecting the efficient use of public investments in infrastructure in Vietnam. *Journal of Infrastructure Systems, 21*(3). https://doi.org/10.1061/(ASCE)IS.1943-555X.00002
Glen, S. (2015). *Multicollinearity: Definition, causes, examples.* Statistic How To. https://www.statisticshowto.com/multicollinearity/
Hausman, J. A. (1978). Specification tests in econometrics. *Econometrica, 46*(6), 1251–1271. https://doi.org/10.2307/1913827
Kmenta, J. (1986). Generalized linear regression model and its applications. *Elements of Econometrics* (pp. 607–650). Macmillan.
Molala, R. (2019). Correlation and collinearity—How they can make or break a model. ClairVoyantSoft. https://blog.clairvoyantsoft.com/correlation-and-collinearity-how-they-can-make-or-break-a-model-9135fbe6936a
North, D. C. (1989). Institutions and economic growth: An historical introduction. *World Development, 17*(9), 1319–1332. https://doi.org/10.1016/0305-750X(89)90075-2
Ofori, I. K., & Asongu, S. A. (2021). ICT diffusion, foreign direct investment and inclusive growth in Sub-Saharan Africa. *Telematics and Informatics, 65*, 101718. https://doi.org/10.1016/j.tele.2021.101718
Ofori, I. K., Cantah, W. G., Afful, B., Jr., & Hossain, S. (2022b). Towards shared prosperity in sub-Saharan Africa: How does the effect of economic integration compare to social equity policies? *African Development Review, 34*(1), 97–113. https://doi.org/10.1111/1467-8268.12614
Ofori, I. K., Dossou, T. A. M., & Akadiri, S. A. (2023). Towards the quest to reduce income inequality in Africa: Is there a synergy between tourism development and governance? *Current Issues in Tourism, 26*(3), 429–449. https://doi.org/10.1080/13683500.2021.2021157
Ofori, I. K., Osei, D. B., & Alagidede, I. P. (2022a). Inclusive growth in Sub-Saharan Africa: Exploring the interaction between ICT diffusion, and financial development. *Telecommunications Policy, 46*(7), 102315. https://doi.org/10.1016/j.telpol.2022.102315
Sou, J. P. U., & Vinnicombe, T. (2021). Does governance quality matter for FDI-led tourism development? A supply-side perspective. *Tourism Economics, 29*(4), 135481662110528. https://doi.org/10.1177/13548166211052814
Xu, C., Han, M., Dossou, T. A. M., & Bekun, F. V. (2021). Trade openness, FDI, and income inequality: Evidence from sub-Saharan Africa. *African Development Review, 33*(1), 193–203. https://doi.org/10.1111/1467-8268.12511

Dương Duy Lâm is a master's student in the field of Applied Economics, specializing in Finance and currently interested in Behavioral Finance and Development Economics. Driven by his passion to explore the insights between economic factors and their social/human responses, he expects to bring a fresh and analytical perspective to the discipline, showcasing a commitment to connect field knowledge and real-world economic scenarios.

Võ Ngọc Tường Vy, a master's student in Development Economics, combines her academic knowledge with practical experience in technology finance services. Driven by a passion for sustainable economic development, she seeks to bridge theory and practice, identify opportunities, and implement growth strategies to contribute to Vietnam's progress.

Chapter 12
The Roles of Human Capital Dynamics and Health Status in Vietnam's Economic Growth

Nguyen Viet Ngan and Lam Nguyen Do Khoa

Abstract Education and health represent essential pillars that serve as fundamental objectives and vital components of development. They are integral to enhancing human capacity, which lies at the heart of a nation's progress and growth. Thus, several studies have focused on the relationship between human capital and economic growth, particularly emphasizing education, and health as crucial development factors. However, most existing studies have mainly explored the one-way interrelation between these developmental factors and economic growth. Hence, this study examines the bidirectional relations of human capital, specifically regarding health and education, on economic growth in Vietnam. The results are based on the 2SLS estimation method and panel data covering 2020–2022. The result highlights the significance of both productivity enhancing dimensions of human capital. Specifically, education and health positively affect Vietnam's GDP growth. This finding, new to Vietnam, highlights the partial substitution of variables when measuring human capital and its quality dimensions. It contributes to existing literature and underscores the importance of these variables in assessing human capital's impact on growth. Local researchers and policymakers can use this insight to develop better policies for Vietnam's future prosperity.

Keywords Human capital · Education · Health · Economic growth · Vietnam

N. V. Ngan (✉) · L. N. Do Khoa
Vietnam - the Netherlands Programme, University of Economics Ho Chi Minh city, Ho Chi Minh City, Vietnam
e-mail: ngan.nv@vnp.edu.vn

L. N. Do Khoa
e-mail: khoa.lnd@vnp.edu.vn

P. K. Nam and A. Heshmati (eds.), *Recent Trends in Vietnam's Rapid Economic Development*, Frontiers in South and Southeast Asian Development Research,
https://doi.org/10.1007/978-981-97-6079-4_12

1 Introduction

Human capital, encompassing knowledge, skills, health, and education, is critical for economic growth (Mankiw et al., 1992; Romer, 1986). At its core, economic growth relies on labor productivity, the cornerstone for competitiveness and long-term prosperity. Health and education are vital components of human capital, influencing productivity and steering economic growth in the era of advanced stage of automation, robotization and artificial intelligence, as well as twin transitions of digitalization and environmental sustainability.

In the modern economy, human capital receives special attention for sustainable development, contributing significantly to a country's economic progress (Mankiw et al., 1992). With a growing population and transformative demographic shifts since 1976, Vietnam is well-positioned to maximize its workforce potential. The shift from low-skilled to high-skilled resources, evident in labor productivity growth surpassing the ASEAN average, signifies a promising trend.

However, challenges lie ahead, with Vietnam's "golden population" period ending by 2040 and the demographic landscape undergoing significant changes. Recognizing the paramountcy of labor productivity and human capital, Vietnam faces a call to action. EuroCham suggests cultivating high-caliber human capital, accelerating administrative reforms, and upgrading infrastructure to fortify economic standing.

Education and health represent essential pillars that are vital components of development. They are integral to enhancing human capacity, which lies at the heart of progress and growth. Several studies have focused on the relationship between human capital and economic growth, emphasizing education, and health as crucial development factors. However, most existing studies have explored the one-way interrelation between these factors and economic growth. This study examines the bidirectional correlation of human capital, namely health and education, on economic growth in Vietnam. The estimation results are based on the 2SLS estimation method and panel data covering 2020–2022. The result highlights the significance of both productivity enhancing dimensions of human capital. It contributes toward existing literature and emphasizes the importance of considering these variables when assessing human capital's growth impact. Accordingly, local researchers and policymakers can utilize this finding to have better policies striving for inclusive development and prosperity in the future.

As Vietnam stands at the crossroads of economic progress, policymakers must grasp the impact of human capital, particularly in form of health and education. The study uses endogenous growth model techniques to explore correlations between health, education, and economic growth in Vietnam. The findings aim to inform government decisions and policies, providing insights into the dynamic influences of these elements on Vietnam's developmental trajectory and guiding resource allocation adjustments.

The rest of this study is as follows. Section 2 reviews the literature. The data and model are described in Sect. 3. The empirical results and its analysis are performed in Sect. 4. Section 5 concludes the study and provide implications of the results for promoting economic growth in Vietnam.

2 Literature Review

2.1 Theoretical Background

Since the dawn of macroeconomic analysis, detecting factors that drive economic growth has posed significant challenges. While Adam Smith hinted at the connection between development and the labor force, further analyses were required. Malthus proposed a framework for dynamic economic growth, suggesting nations move toward a steady per capita income phase. Despite Malthus's 19th-century proposition, fertility rates have declined to very low levels contrary to predictions. Solow's neoclassical exogenous growth model (1956) introduced a perspective explaining GDP growth based on external factors. However, it needs refinement to account for variations in growth rates among nations.

In the late 1980s, economists like Lucas (1988) and Romer (1986) restructured the neoclassical growth model, emphasizing endogenous variables for sustained growth. Schultz (1961) highlighted the importance of investing in human capital, while Uzawa (1965) emphasized its significance in fostering economic growth. Mankiw et al. (1992) extended Solow's neoclassical growth model to include human capital, which was later modified by Knowles and Owen (1995) to incorporate health and education. They enhanced the Solow model by introducing an explicit human capital accumulation process, developing a convergence equation relating output increments to investment rates for both physical and human capital. The rapid technological change, openness, information technology, robotization and artificial intelligence, and their nexus are among new dimensions of economic development, growth, and its modeling.

2.2 The Role of Human Capital in Economic Growth

Human capital, encompassing skills, knowledge, health, and education within a society, is foundational in economics (Becker, 1964). Recognized as a critical determinant of economic growth and development (Romer, 1986), it positions individuals as active contributors rather than passive inputs in production. Education, crucial in developing skills and knowledge, prepares individuals for effective participation in a modern economy (Schultz, 1961). Simultaneously, health directly influences productivity and longevity, impacting an individual's economic engagement (Bloom & Williamson, 1997). The multifaceted nature of human capital extends beyond formal education to on-the-job training, experiential learning, healthcare access, and migration patterns (Becker, 1964), necessitating comprehensive policies.

Empirical evidence establishes the profound impact of human capital on economic growth. In endogenous growth models, it is a powerful driver, leading to increased productivity, innovation, and financial performance in countries with higher human capital levels (Ogundari & Awokuse, 2018). Health is found to have a more significant effect than education, emphasizing their irreplaceable roles (Ogundari & Awokuse, 2018). Investment in education, healthcare, and skills development is vital for economic growth and is applicable globally (Psacharopoulos & Patrinos, 2018).

Vietnam's economic success is attributed to significant investments in human capital, particularly in education and healthcare, and infrastructure and utilities, transforming it into a Southeast Asian economic powerhouse. Studies on Vietnam economy underscore the positive impact of human capital, with primary education identified as a dominant factor (Phan et al., 2020; Tran, 2010). However, advancement in technology implies investment in higher and specialized education to strengthen technological knowledge and human capital.

2.3 The Linkage Between Education and Economic Development

Numerous studies confirm the role of education in fostering economic growth. Barro (2002), which analyzed data from 100 countries, unveiled a positive correlation between GDP per capita's growth rate and education levels, suggesting that education could enhance a country's annual growth rate by 0.44%. Similarly, Azam and Ahmed (2010) found that education and health significantly impact Pakistan's economic development. They noted that a 1.4% increase in primary and intermediate school enrollment could result in a 40% increase in GDP per capita for wealthy countries over the next 25 years. These findings underscore the pivotal role of educational attainment and quality in economic growth, making it a critical consideration for policy recommendations in Vietnam. Oxaal and Baden (1997) stated that the school enrollment ratio is linked to a nation's productivity. Educated individuals tend to be more productive themselves and positively influence the productivity of those they interact with (Blundell et al., 2000). Also, educational attainment correlates with economic development across different stages of a nation's development (Krueger & Lindahl, 2001). Countries with the lowest education levels experienced substantial growth benefits if the number of persons with schooling attainment increased. Moreover, among a sample of 19 OECD nations, Aghion et al. (2006) indicated the heightened significance of tertiary education in countries with advanced technological infrastructure.

While higher education holds more significance in developed and developing countries, secondary education has positively impacted growth in developing nations. For example, secondary education contributes positively to Malaysia's short- and long-term development (Tang & Lai, 2011). The study also showed a societal preference for education over healthcare in Malaysia, a trend attributed to societies with lower levels of education. Marquez-Ramos and Mourelle (2019) again verified this relationship. Their results showed a nonlinear correlation between these factors, meaning that secondary and tertiary education played instrumental roles in driving economic growth. However, they noted that the magnitude of this impact varies across different national and regional levels of education. Therefore, highlighting the complex interplay between educational attainment and economic development is essential.

However, these studies often implicitly assume that each additional year of schooling yields the same growth effects in knowledge and capabilities, regardless of educational quality. This underscores a limitation in quantity-based education metrics like years of schooling. Additionally, volume-based metrics, which rely on the educational system alone, neglect other influential factors shaping human capital, such as the roles of family and culture. Given Vietnam's status as an emerging economy, primary education holds particular importance. This study follows the framework established by Li and Huang (2009) employing the student-to-teacher ratio to gauge the expenditure on education stock. We choose that ratio of primary level to justify the importance of primary education.

2.4 The Contribution of Health to Economic Growth

Positive health outcomes are integral to human capital development, significantly impacting productivity. Poor health can detrimentally affect work performance, as highlighted by Baldacci et al. (2008) study on child mortality, indicating a positive correlation between reducing child mortality and improvements in economic indicators like education and savings rates. Despite its intangible nature, health shares characteristics with tangible resources, necessitating investment and accumulation for flourishing.

Bloom et al. (2018) explored the multifaceted mechanisms of health that influence economic growth across various countries. In developing nations, a crucial mechanism emerges with the increase in life expectancy, fostering demographic transition and making investments in human capital pivotal. However, the health and economic growth relationship is more complete in industrialized countries. Challenges identified by Breyer et al. (2010) and Pauly and Saxena (2011) revolve around health benefits favoring the elderly population, potentially leading to increased dependency ratios and substantial healthcare expenditures, which may surpass productivity gains.

De Mello-Sampayo et al. (2014) study on health expenditure in OECD countries highlighted the impact of government health spending on medical costs, explaining about 65% of the increase. Private healthcare and demographics, including the percentage of the population under 15 and over 65, also play a role. Unidirectional relationships between healthcare spending and economic development, as noted by Gerdtham et al. (1992) and Braendle and Colombier (2016), emphasize the pivotal role of economic progress in healthcare costs. Meanwhile, bidirectional causal relationships have been identified in various studies, such as Wang (2011), Amiri and Ventelou (2012), Chaabouni et al. (2016), Chaabouni and Saidi (2017), and Mehrara and Musai (2011) underlining the intricate dynamics between healthcare spending and economic growth.

3 Data and Model Description

This study examines the relationship between regional economic growth and physical and human capital accumulation. The focus is on assessing real GDP per capita growth at the regional level (RGDP), with the Provincial Competitiveness Index (PCI) as a control variable. Recognizing potential endogeneity in education and health variables, the authors employ the two-stage least squares estimation method, using lagged values of health and education as instruments.

The explanatory variables include lag RGDP, the investment savings ratio (IN), and workforce growth (WG). The investment savings ratio represents the investment share of GDP, acting as a proxy. Furthermore, the study considers a set of total depreciation rate (5%) and maintains technological advancement as a constant factor, aligning with established methods (Mankiw et al., 1992). This comprehensive approach aims to unravel regional economic growth's nuanced dynamics, accounting for physical and human capital dimensions.

As a result, the model is specified as:

$$\begin{aligned}\mathrm{RGDP}_{\mathrm{it}} &= \beta_0 + \beta_1\,\text{Workforce Growth} + \beta_2\text{PCI} + \beta_3\text{Physical Investment}\\ &+ \beta_4 RGDP_{\mathrm{it}-1} + \beta_5\text{Life Expectancy}_{\mathrm{it}} + \beta_6\text{Doctor ratio}_{\mathrm{it}}\\ &+ \beta_7\text{Student\_teacherPrimary}_{\mathrm{it}} + \beta_7\text{Student\_teacherSecondary}_{\mathrm{it}}\\ &+ \beta_8\text{Student\_teacherTertiary}_{\mathrm{it}} + + \mathrm{u}_{\mathrm{it}}\end{aligned}$$

This study examines the relationship between regional economic growth and key factors using panel data from all 63 provinces in Vietnam for the years 2020 and 2022. The variables include economic growth rates (RGDP), investment savings ratios, student–teacher ratios, health indicators, and control variables reflecting state governance capacity. This approach ensures a comprehensive analysis of the intricate relationship between economic growth, physical capital accumulation, and human capital investment. The data, sourced from the General Statistics Office of Vietnam, adheres to established academic practices, ensuring the reliability and validity of the research findings (see Table 1).

Table 1 Descriptive statistics of the province data, 2020–2022

Variables	Definition	Unit	Description	Article reference
lWG	Workforce growth	(%)	It is the combination of population growth rate, depreciation growth rate, and technological progress to be constant at 5% for all year	Li and Huang (2009), Mankiw et al. (1992)
lPCI	Provincial competitiveness Index	Index, based at 100	This variable is used to control for the fixed effect between provinces	Li and Huang (2009)
lIN	Share of Physical investment as % of GRDP	%	We derive the figure of physical investment in each region, then divide it by GRDP	Li and Huang (2009), Mankiw et al. (1992)
$RGDP_{t-1}$	Lag of RGDP		RGDP figure is taken with lag of 1 period	Li and Huang (2009)
lHL	Life expectancy		Average life expectancy of residents living in each province	Bloom et al. (2018), Li and Huang (2009)
lHD	Doctors per 10,000 people		This is the ratio of a doctor serving 10.000 people in region. This variable represents for health stock	Li and Huang (2009)
lEP	Student-to-teacher in primary schools ratio		The figure represents how many students are taught by one teacher. This variable relates to health stock	Li and Huang (2009)

(continued)

Table 1 (continued)

Variables	Definition	Unit	Description	Article reference
lES	Student-to-teacher in secondary schools ratio		The ratio tells us the number of students taught by one teacher in secondary schools	Li and Huang (2009)
lET	Student-to-teacher in tertiary schools ratio		The ratio tells us the number of students taught by one teacher in high schools	Li and Huang (2009)

4 Analysis of the Results

4.1 Descriptive Statistics

Table 2 summarizes the data analysis, while Table 3 presents statistics on critical variables, including GDP growth rates, health, and education factors across 63 provinces. Ho Chi Minh City exhibited the lowest average annual GDP growth rate at 3.0% between 2020 and 2022, while Ha Noi, the second-largest city, recorded an average growth rate of 5.7%. Ninh Thuan stood out with the highest growth rate at 13.18%.

Examining life expectancy reveals that Ba Ria Vung Tau had the highest average age at 76.43, and Lai Chau had the lowest at 67 years. Despite socio-economic differences, the life expectancy range across provinces was only 9.46 years, with an average lifespan of 73 years for Vietnamese citizens.

Table 3 also showcase regional student-to-teacher ratios from 2020 to 2022. In the North, student-to-teacher ratios in provinces like Gia Lai, Lang Son, and Kon Tum ranged from 12.9 to 14.32 across all three education levels. Ho Chi Minh City had the highest ratio at 48.76 students per teacher, while Thai Binh had the highest number of teachers per student at 24.9. On average, a teacher taught between 18 to 22 students annually in Vietnam during this period.

4.2 Results and Discussion

The research conducted a thorough analysis employing various statistical methods, including Ordinary Least Squares (OLS), Fixed Effects Model (FEM), and Random Effects Model (REM), as part of a rigorous analytical approach. The estimation results are presented in Table 2. Initially, the study focused on internal growth factors without considering human capital. Subsequent models delved into the relationship between human capital factors, particularly education and health, and

Table 2 Estimation results of the RGDP equation

Model	(1)	(2)	(3)	(4)	(5)	(6)	(7)
	OLS	OLS (1)	OLS (2)	OLS (3)	REM	FEM	2SLS
lWG	-0.226^{**}	-0.227^{**}	-0.211^{**}	-0.214^{**}	-0.214^{**}	-0.226^{**}	-0.237^{**}
	(0.067)	(0.067)	(0.068)	(0.068)	(0.068)	(0.082)	(0.074)
lPCI	0.504	0.609	0.419	0.562	0.562	1.047	− 0.253
	(1.304)	(1.314)	(1.313)	(1.331)	(1.331)	(1.871)	(1.498)
lIN	0.172	0.134	0.188	0.158	0.158	-1.723^{*}	0.109
	(0.117)	(0.125)	(0.120)	(0.126)	(0.126)	(0.811)	(0.143)
$RGDP_{t-1}$	0.164^{**}	0.161^{**}	0.154^{*}	0.151^{*}	0.151^{*}	-0.215^{**}	0.177^{**}
	(0.060)	(0.060)	(0.060)	(0.061)	(0.061)	(0.072)	(0.066)
lHL		0.314		− 0.127	− 0.127	− 6.820	0.715
		(2.211)		(2.389)	(2.389)	(24.555)	(2.902)
lHD		0.077		0.084	0.084	0.155	0.016
		(0.095)		(0.098)	(0.098)	(0.166)	(0.177)
lEP			− 0.215	− 0.203	− 0.203	1.025	− 0.717
			(0.357)	(0.373)	(0.373)	(2.213)	(0.602)
lES			0.579^{*}	0.568^{+}	0.568^{+}	1.286^{*}	− 0.581
			(0.282)	(0.292)	(0.292)	(0.492)	(0.511)
lET			− 0.375	− 0.522	− 0.522	1.008	2.231
			(0.553)	(0.590)	(0.590)	(1.601)	$(1.295)^{+}$
_cons	− 4.372	− 6.056	− 4.132	− 3.633	− 3.633	8.688	− 6.691
	(5.421)	(11.287)	(5.758)	(11.465)	(11.465)	(104.510)	(12.931)
N	189	189	189	189	189	189	189
R2	0.104	0.108	0.127	0.131		0.267	

Notes Standard errors in parentheses. $^{+}p < 0.10$, $^{*}p < 0.05$, $^{**}p < 0.01$

economic growth while addressing endogeneity through instrumental variable regression method with lagged variables. This comprehensive approach was motivated by the need to account for endogeneity challenges, given the study's focus on the correlation between regional economic growth and human capital investment. Additionally, the study recognized the unique data structure of panel data spanning multiple provinces over two years, prompting consideration of models like REM and FEM to accommodate individual-specific effects across regions. The systematic comparison of results from these models enhanced the credibility and reliability of the study's findings, contributing valuable insights to the academic exploration of human capital's role in regional economic growth.

Table 2 shows that the investment savings ratio (lIN) exhibits a significantly positive coefficient in the 2SLS model. However, this result is not statistically significant at conventional levels ($p < 0.05$) in the remaining models. This suggests a potential positive association between investment and economic growth, although further

Table 3 Summary of statistics of the variables by region, period 2020–2022, NT = 189 obs

Province	Summary of RGDP growth		Summary of Health_life		Summary of Edu_primary		Summary of Edu_second		Summary of Edu_teriary	
	Mean	Std. dev	Mean	Std. dev	Mean	Std. dev	Mean	Std. dev	Mean	Std. dev
An Giang	0.063	0.041	73.730	0.035	19.321	0.181	30.409	4.486	17.918	0.988
Ba Ria Vung Tau	0.104	0.126	76.430	0.035	30.231	0.500	24.914	0.759	17.040	0.193
Bac Giang	0.127	0.067	73.430	0.017	23.390	0.575	23.259	1.248	19.203	0.254
Bac Kan	0.071	0.032	72.587	0.006	21.811	0.389	19.299	1.497	16.457	0.652
Bac Lieu	0.094	0.057	74.647	0.064	19.859	0.115	43.857	10.990	23.173	0.620
Bac Ninh	0.042	0.023	74.190	0.121	22.612	0.731	22.549	1.178	18.689	3.019
Ben Tre	0.068	0.035	75.643	0.029	18.669	0.682	27.341	3.869	18.756	0.506
Binh Dinh	0.083	0.033	73.483	0.023	20.305	1.497	32.371	1.152	22.068	0.518
Binh Duong	0.038	0.017	74.750	0.000	28.950	0.623	29.834	2.729	17.860	0.698
Binh Phuoc	0.109	0.025	73.970	0.017	22.364	0.580	26.315	0.437	15.307	1.304
Binh Thuan	0.065	0.038	74.620	0.052	21.508	0.831	26.308	0.904	16.585	0.848
Ca Mau	0.071	0.097	75.183	0.110	20.934	0.215	32.206	1.747	18.235	0.440
Can Tho	0.062	0.096	75.857	0.098	19.317	0.885	26.665	5.733	17.523	0.099
Cao Bang	0.064	0.030	71.093	0.462	15.233	0.816	17.842	1.323	16.039	0.624
Da Nang	0.047	0.072	76.210	0.052	22.068	1.246	26.308	0.642	17.441	0.319
Dak Lak	0.101	0.025	71.277	0.248	22.774	0.809	25.076	1.789	17.613	0.418
Dak Nong	0.092	0.032	70.233	0.098	22.298	1.107	29.408	1.069	17.489	0.960
Dien Bien	0.074	0.046	68.440	0.000	16.017	0.582	28.679	0.862	15.932	0.790
Dong Nai	0.063	0.030	76.273	0.023	25.817	0.714	29.255	1.052	20.905	0.305
Dong Thap	0.065	0.060	74.767	0.098	20.981	0.516	40.335	6.081	17.961	0.466
Gia Lai	0.100	0.040	70.803	0.635	12.902	0.591	31.055	2.126	20.949	1.106
Ha Giang	0.060	0.029	74.693	0.006	29.127	0.798	23.730	1.748	16.082	0.869
Ha Nam	0.106	0.027	75.723	0.290	26.706	0.420	25.885	0.459	18.616	0.142
Ha Noi	0.057	0.040	72.737	0.127	19.466	0.801	25.986	1.788	21.540	0.434

(continued)

Table 3 (continued)

Province	Summary of RGDP growth		Summary of Health_life		Summary of Edu_primary		Summary of Edu_second		Summary of Edu_teriary	
	Mean	Std. dev	Mean	Std. dev	Mean	Std. dev	Mean	Std. dev	Mean	Std. dev
Ha Tinh	0.048	0.003	72.660	0.052	22.581	0.974	24.770	0.635	15.725	0.164
Hai Duong	0.094	0.061	74.837	0.006	29.170	0.950	24.908	2.524	21.058	0.822
Hai Phong	0.125	0.025	74.633	0.081	28.163	1.162	26.189	1.831	21.722	0.274
Hau Giang	0.113	0.093	75.537	0.006	20.139	0.202	41.313	11.560	19.080	0.458
Ho Chi Minh	0.030	0.053	76.317	0.124	21.117	0.347	48.758	26.728	19.315	0.054
Hoa Binh	0.059	0.042	68.653	0.219	25.134	1.235	15.609	7.135	16.659	0.372
Hung Yen	0.114	0.042	74.673	0.023	24.010	1.214	23.099	3.204	19.334	0.800
Khanh Hoa	0.074	0.129	73.793	0.237	20.781	1.254	26.136	1.303	18.436	0.155
Kien Giang	0.065	0.058	74.443	0.006	22.819	0.306	29.918	6.019	19.177	0.418
Kon Tum	0.097	0.036	67.890	0.208	24.440	0.895	22.081	0.672	14.342	0.500
Lai Chau	0.070	0.046	67.497	0.699	19.886	0.240	30.488	1.699	17.438	1.745
Lam Dong	0.087	0.065	73.277	0.012	28.422	0.549	25.673	1.050	16.501	0.512
Lang Son	0.073	0.024	72.440	0.017	22.793	0.912	18.794	1.716	15.967	0.182
Lao Cai	0.089	0.054	69.727	0.404	23.105	0.872	25.063	2.152	17.821	0.846
Long An	0.075	0.049	75.827	0.264	23.266	0.852	31.615	2.127	18.058	0.271
Nam Dinh	0.079	0.019	74.503	0.040	24.682	1.392	24.005	1.675	18.688	0.376
Nghe An	0.089	0.026	73.130	0.035	22.995	0.894	25.511	1.811	18.859	0.536
Ninh Binh	0.088	0.034	74.223	0.046	20.427	0.770	21.041	0.769	17.173	0.657
Ninh Thuan	0.138	0.035	73.067	0.127	19.360	0.688	28.068	1.316	17.657	0.299
Phu Tho	0.080	0.023	73.500	0.052	17.565	0.854	21.938	2.186	18.979	0.128
Phu Yen	0.061	0.043	73.537	0.029	22.989	0.720	25.284	1.330	18.632	0.351
Quang Binh	0.078	0.030	72.790	0.121	21.382	0.973	25.316	1.039	18.685	0.512

(continued)

Table 3 (continued)

Province	Summary of RGDP growth		Summary of Health_life		Summary of Edu_primary		Summary of Edu_second		Summary of Edu_teriary	
	Mean	Std. dev	Mean	Std. dev	Mean	Std. dev	Mean	Std. dev	Mean	Std. dev
Quang Nam	0.056	0.065	73.080	0.035	21.076	0.740	25.871	2.280	18.643	0.238
Quang Ngai	0.123	0.111	72.477	0.092	17.486	0.888	25.413	1.515	17.707	0.700
Quang Ninh	0.116	0.047	73.470	0.035	24.848	0.705	23.386	1.229	19.293	0.752
Quang Tri	0.076	0.031	68.923	0.652	20.701	1.005	25.242	0.808	16.219	0.210
Soc Trang	0.073	0.061	74.310	0.035	24.298	0.202	30.454	7.128	16.219	0.833
Son La	0.070	0.041	70.947	0.012	18.246	0.782	29.527	2.109	21.948	0.097
Tay Ninh	0.068	0.049	74.787	0.040	32.746	0.679	30.359	2.096	21.082	0.469
Thai Binh	0.098	0.034	75.243	0.289	15.982	0.418	21.828	1.991	24.964	0.381
Thai Nguyen	0.071	0.034	73.693	0.012	24.846	0.748	23.712	2.120	19.503	0.573
Thanh Hoa	0.121	0.058	73.427	0.006	25.199	1.221	26.911	1.269	19.447	0.697
Thua Thien Hue	0.067	0.040	72.110	0.346	25.505	1.049	28.088	1.228	17.168	0.048
Tien Giang	0.052	0.064	76.007	0.098	21.084	0.984	31.828	6.299	21.803	0.486
Tra Vinh	0.062	0.050	74.690	0.069	21.315	0.769	30.208	1.191	16.417	1.581
Tuyen Quang	0.090	0.027	72.213	0.058	16.273	0.632	26.229	2.092	18.077	0.432
Vinh Long	0.083	0.083	75.470	0.087	21.044	0.651	37.432	12.094	15.057	0.130
Vinh Phuc	0.077	0.039	74.240	0.208	27.205	0.823	27.592	2.192	18.707	2.801
Yen Bai	0.086	0.030	69.627	0.058	23.539	1.513	28.347	1.350	20.303	0.781
Total	0.080	0.050	73.372	2.199	22.369	3.861	27.411	6.993	18.432	2.174

investigation may be needed to establish its significance. Prior studies have highlighted that higher investment can drive economic growth by increasing capital accumulation and productivity (Barro & Lee, 2013). While this study's result suggests a similar trend, further research could explore the nuanced relationship between savings, investment, and growth in the Vietnamese context.

The positive coefficient for life expectancy (lHL) across models, except for the one without considering education variables (OLS (1)), suggests that life expectancy improvements positively impact economic growth in Vietnam. Although the statistical significance is not shown at conventional levels ($p < 0.05$), the positive coefficient for life expectancy remains a critical variable. Previous studies have indicated that improved health outcomes have significant economic benefits, although this analysis did not demonstrate statistical significance. Research has shown that better health, measured by life expectancy indicators, can lead to a more productive workforce, reduced absenteeism, and increased economic efficiency. Future research could explore specific health interventions that contribute most significantly to improved life expectancy and their implications in the Vietnamese context.

Similarly, the coefficient for the number of doctors per 10,000 individuals (lHD) is positive but not statistically significant across model specifications, though it expresses a positive relationship with economic growth. This suggests that the presence of doctors may be a minor driver of regional economic growth. However, the importance of healthcare accessibility on economic development cannot be overlooked. Access to healthcare services, including doctors, is a crucial aspect of human capital development. Although these variable lacks significance, it still deserves further attention, especially in evaluating the quality and effectiveness of healthcare services. In future research, it would be beneficial to explore the specific roles of healthcare infrastructure and quality in advancing economic growth in Vietnam.

The seemingly insignificant but noteworthy negative coefficient observed for student-to-teacher ratios at the primary (lEP) education levels provides valuable insights into the intricate relationship between basic education and economic growth. The coefficient of primary education expresses the antagonistic relationship in OLS, 2SLS, and REM, except for FEM. The contrasting positive relationship in FEM relative to other models implies that when the differences between provinces are fixed, the overall contribution of primary education on growth remains positive. That said, the unequal quality of primary education amongst provinces can drive growth rates. Although the relationship is insignificant, these findings underline the multifaceted nature of this connection, urging for a more nuanced exploration of educational quality as a catalyst for economic development.

On the other hand, all the models consistently emphasize that the increase in tertiary level (lET) could substantially increase economic growth. This discovery resonates with previous research emphasizing that higher education can yield social and private benefits (Power, 2015), highlighting the need for a comprehensive examination of regional average social and personal rates of return. Recent evidence further underscores the pivotal role of human capital in fostering economic advancement, with particular emphasis on the quality of education. In Vietnam, tertiary education is a milestone in preparing for university entrance, which is the most pronounced determinant of the quality of labor.

Rather than suggesting that increasing the number of teachers per student hampers progress, these results emphasize the necessity for a more profound analysis of educational quality. The significance of these ratios underscores the importance of the quality of education and its alignment with the evolving demands of the labor market. Consequently, future research endeavors should delve into the various factors influencing academic quality and its profound implications for economic growth, particularly within the dynamic educational landscape of Vietnam.

Another noteworthy finding is that the coefficient for workforce growth (lWG) signifies a negative association with growth on measures of all models. This discovery accentuates the potential challenges posed by rapid population growth, particularly in the context of an ageing population in Vietnam. As the population proliferates, limited resources and infrastructure may become overburdened, potentially hindering sustained economic progress. To promote sustainable economic growth in Vietnam, it becomes imperative to implement policies that effectively manage population dynamics. These policies may encompass initiatives such as family planning and skills development programs. The significance of the workforce growth rate as a variable underscores the critical importance of implementing such measures to navigate the complex demographic landscape and foster economic development effectively.

Moreover, while the coefficient for the provincial competitiveness index (lPCI) was positive across model specifications, it is essential to note that this result was statistically insignificant. This suggests that the local competitiveness index may not substantially influence regional economic growth in Vietnam. The lack of a significant correlation between the provincial competitiveness index (lPCI) and economic growth is a noteworthy finding, warranting further investigation into the factors that drive local competitiveness and how these factors interact with the dynamics of economic growth in Vietnam. This result aligns with the need for comprehensive research to understand better the nuanced relationship between regional competitiveness and economic development, as it has broader implications for regional policy and planning (Malesky et al., 2008).

Lastly, a strong and statistically significant correlation exists at the regional level between past and present economic growth, as evidenced by the positive coefficients for $RGDP_{t-1}$ (Mankiw et al., 1992). This substantial coefficient highlights the concept of path dependence in economic progress, indicating that regions with a history of robust growth are more likely to continue on an upward trajectory. This finding aligns with previous research emphasizing the importance of initial conditions and historical factors in shaping long-term economic development trajectories (Acemoglu et al., 2005; Comin & Hobijn, 2009). It underscores the enduring impact of past financial performance on current regional growth patterns. It emphasizes the need for policies that can break the cycle of persistent regional disparities in economic development (Rodríguez-Pose, 2013).

5 Conclusion and Implications

This study examines the relationship between human capital, comprising health and education, and regional economic growth in Vietnam. The findings highlight the crucial role of human capital investment and provide insights into the country's complex economic development dynamics.

The results indicate a positive impact of investment on Vietnam's economic growth, emphasizing the need for further research to deepen our understanding of this relationship. Improvements in life expectancy and healthcare accessibility are essential for enhancing worker productivity, while investments in higher education can significantly influence economic growth. Policymakers must prioritize family planning and skills development programs to address challenges posed by rapid population growth and an ageing demographic. The study highlights the need for more research on what drives regional competitiveness and how it interacts with economic growth, offering foundations for informed decision-making.

First, maintaining a solid commitment to healthcare policies is crucial for improving public health and developing human capital in Vietnam. The Health Insurance Law, introduced in 1992 and updated in 2008, has made healthcare services more affordable and accessible, resulting in increased health service utilization and improved health outcomes. Investments in healthcare infrastructure, particularly in remote areas, ensure equitable healthcare access for all citizens. Vietnam's health promotion and disease prevention programs, including efforts against infectious diseases, demonstrate its dedication to elevating human capital, positioning it for continued success and resilience.

Second, Vietnam's transformative journey to bolster its education system, particularly tertiary education, is paramount to national development. Aligning instruction with economic needs is crucial, and investments in medical education contribute to individual well-being and economic development. The Vocational Education and Training (VET) system, teacher training initiatives, and the establishment of pivotal universities showcase Vietnam's visionary approach to workforce development, contributing to enduring progress and global competitiveness.

Finally, Vietnam's effective population management policies, initiated in the late 1980s, have reduced fertility rates and maintained stable population growth. Policymakers should focus on supporting older workers with skills development, flexible retirement options, and tailored healthcare services. Infrastructure development, investment incentives, and job creation in less developed regions are vital to curb regional disparities and foster economic growth.

While the study provides empirical evidences, limitations include a restricted dataset and the absence of an assessment of potential methodology-related limitations. Future research should expand data sources and address potential methodological concerns like reverse causality.

Appendix

See Table 3.

References

Acemoglu, D., Johnson, S., & Robinson, J. A. (2005). Institutions as a fundamental cause of long-run growth. In *Handbook of economic growth* (pp. 385–472). https://doi.org/10.1016/S1574-0684(05)01006-3

Aghion, P., Meghir, C., & Vandenbussche, J. (2006). Growth, distance to frontier and composition of human capital. *Journal of Economic Growth, 11*(2), 97–127.

Amiri, A., & Ventelou, B. (2012). Granger causality between total expenditure on health and GDP in OECD: Evidence from the toda–yamamoto approach. *Economics Letters, 116*(3), 541–544. https://doi.org/10.1016/j.econlet.2012.04.040

Azam, M., & Ahmed, A. M. (2010). Role of human capital in economic development: Evidence from Pakistan. *Interdisciplinary Journal of Contemporary Research in Business, 2*(4), 220–233.

Baldacci, E., Clements, B., Gupta, S., & Cui, Qi. (2008). Social spending, human capital, and growth in developing countries. *World Development, 36*(8), 1317–1341.https://doi.org/10.1016/j.worlddev.2007.08.003

Barro, R. (2002). Quantity and quality of economic growth. In N. Loayza, R. Soto & N. Loayza (Series Editor), & K. Schmidt-Hebbel (Series Editor) (Eds.), *Economic growth: Sources, trends, and cycles* (1st ed., Vol. 6, chap. 5, pp. 135–162). Central Bank of Chile.

Barro, R. J., & Lee, J. W. (2013). A new data set of educational attainment in the world, 1950–2010. *Journal of Development Economics, 104*(C), 184–198. https://doi.org/10.1016/j.jdeveco.2012.10.001

Becker, G. S. (1964). *Human capital: A theoretical and empirical analysis, with special reference to education.* University of Chicago Press.

Bloom, D., & Williamson, J. (1997). *Demographic Transitions and Economic Miracles in Emerging Asia.* https://doi.org/10.3386/w6268

Bloom, D. E., Kuhn, M., & Prettner, K. (2018). Health and economic growth. *SSRN Electronic Journal.* https://doi.org/10.2139/ssrn.3301688

Blundell, R., Dearden, L., Goodman, A., & Reed, H. (2000). The returns to higher education in Britain: Evidence from a British Cohort. *The Economic Journal, 110*(461), 82–99. https://doi.org/10.1111/1468-0297.00508

Braendle, T., & Colombier, C. (2016). What drives public health care expenditure growth? Evidence from Swiss Cantons, 1970–2012. *Health Policy, 120*(9), 1051–1060. https://doi.org/10.1016/j.healthpol.2016.07.009

Breyer, F., Costa-Font, J., & Felder, S. (2010). Ageing, health, and health care. *Oxford Review of Economic Policy, 26*(4), 674–690. https://doi.org/10.1093/oxrep/grq032

Chaabouni, S., & Saidi, K. (2017). The dynamic links between carbon dioxide (CO_2) emissions, health spending and GDP growth: A case study for 51 countries. *Environmental Research, 158*, 137–144. https://doi.org/10.1016/j.envres.2017.05.041

Chaabouni, S., Zghidi, N., & Ben Mbarek, M. (2016). On the causal dynamics between CO_2 emissions, health expenditures and economic growth. *Sustainable Cities and Society, 22*, 184–191. https://doi.org/10.1016/j.scs.2016.02.001

Comin, D., & Hobijn, B. (2009). Technology diffusion and postwar growth. *NBER Macroeconomics Annual, 25*(1), 209–246. https://doi.org/10.1086/657531

De Mello-Sampayo, Felipa & de Sousa-Vale. (2014). Financing health care expenditure in the OECD countries: Evidence from a heterogeneous, cross-sectional dependent panel. *Panoeconomicus, 61*, 207–225.https://doi.org/10.2298/pan1402207m

Dinh, P. H., & Tu, D. H. (2016). Tac dong cua von con nguoi den tang truong kinh te Dong bang song Cuu Long. *Tap chi Phat trien Kinh te, 27*(2), 2–16.

Gerdtham, U. G., Søgaard, J., Andersson, F., & Jönsson, B. (1992). An econometric analysis of health care expenditure: A cross-section study of the OECD countries. *Journal of Health Economics, 11*(1), 63–84. https://doi.org/10.1016/0167-6296(92)90025-V

Knowles, S., & Owen, P. D. (1995). Health capital and cross-country variation in income per capita in the Mankiw-Romer-Weil model. *Economics Letters, 48*(1), 99–106. https://doi.org/10.1016/0165-1765(94)00577-O
Krueger, A. B., & Lindahl, M. (2001). Education for growth: Why and for whom? *Journal of Economic Literature, 39*(4), 1101–1136. https://doi.org/10.1257/jel.39.4.1101
Li, H., & Huang, L. (2009). Health, education, and economic growth in China: Empirical findings and implications. *China Economic Review, 20*(3), 374–387. https://doi.org/10.1016/j.chieco.2008.05.001
Lucas, R. E. (1988). On the mechanics of economic development. *Journal of Monetary Economics, 22*(1), 3–42. https://doi.org/10.1016/0304-3932(88)90168-7
Malesky, E. J., Minh, D. N., Hai T. N., Anh, T. T. V., Tuan, D. A., & Lan, D. D. (2008). Provincial economic governance and its impact on local competitiveness. Business issues bulletin vietnam, 26. Retrieved September 17, 2023, from http://documents.worldbank.org/curated/en/981781468317981533/Provincialeconomic-governance-and-its-impact-on-local-competitiveness
Mankiw, N. G., Romer, D., & Weil, D. N. (1992). A contribution to the empirics of economic growth. *The Quarterly Journal of Economics, 107*(2), 407–437. https://doi.org/10.2307/2118477
Marquez-Ramos, L., & Mourelle, E. (2019). Education and economic growth: An empirical analysis of nonlinearities. *Applied Economic Analysis, 27*(79), 21–45. https://doi.org/10.1108/AEA-06-2019-0005
Mehrara, M., & Musai, M. (2011). Granger causality between health and economic growth in oil exporting countries. *Interdisciplinary Journal of Research in Business, 1*(8), 103–108.
Nelson, R., & Phelps, E. (1966). Investment in humans, technological diffusion, and economic growth. *The American Economic Review, 56*, 69–75.
Ogundari, K., & Awokuse, T. (2018). Human capital contribution to economic growth in Sub-Saharan Africa: Does health status matter more than education? *Economic Analysis and Policy, 58*, 131–140. https://doi.org/10.1016/j.eap.2018.02.001
Oxaal, Z., & Baden, S. (1997). Gender and development definitions, approaches and implications for policy. *BRIDGE Institute of Development Studies, 40*, 1–32.
Pauly, M. V., & Saxena, A. (2011). Health employment, medical spending, and long-term health reform. *Cesifo Economic Studies, 58*(1), 49–72. https://doi.org/10.1093/cesifo/ifr030
Phan, T. B. N., Tran, T. H. L., & Luong, T. T. (2020). Nguon von con nguoi va tang truong kinh te cap do tinh-thanh pho tai Viet Nam. *Tap chi nghien cuu Kinh te va Kinh doanh Chau A, 29*(8), 5–17. http://jabes.ueh.edu.vn/Home/SearchArticle?article_Id=69249ab9-e4d2-4519-9714-1b6f9f2db18b
Power, C. (2015). Higher education: The engine of development. In *Education in the Asia-Pacific Region: Issues, concerns and prospects* (pp. 163–186). https://doi.org/10.1007/978-981-287-221-0_10
Psacharopoulos, G., & Patrinos, H. A. (2018). Returns to investment in education: A decennial review of global literature. *Education Economics, 26*, 1–14. https://doi.org/10.1080/09645292.2018.1484426
Rodríguez-Pose, A. (2013). Do institutions matter for regional development? *Regional Studies, 47*(7), 1034–1047. https://doi.org/10.1080/00343404.2012.748978
Romer, P. M. (1986). Increasing returns and long-run growth. *Journal of Political Economy, 94*(5), 1002–1037. http://www.jstor.org/stable/1833190
Schultz, T. W. (1961). Investment in human capital. *The American Economic Review, 51*(1), 1–17. https://www.jstor.org/stable/1818907
Smith, A. (1976). An inquiry into the nature and causes of the wealth of nations. *The Glasgow Edition of the Works and Correspondence of Adam Smith, Vol. 2: An Inquiry into the Nature and Causes of the Wealth of Nations, Vol. 1*. https://doi.org/10.1093/oseo/instance.00043218
Solow, R. M. (1956). A contribution to the theory of economic growth. *The Quarterly Journal of Economics, 70*(1), 65–94.

Tang, C. F., & Lai, Y. W. (2011). The causal relationship between health and education expenditures in Malaysia. Theoretical and Applied Economics, Asociatia Generala a Economistilor din Romania—AGER, *0*(8(561)), 61–74.
Tran, T. D. (2010). Vai tro von con nguoi trong cac mo hinh tang truong. *Tap Chi Nghien Cuu Kinh Te, 393*, 3–10.
Uzawa, H. (1965). Optimum technical change in a aggregative model of economic growth. *International Economic Review, 6*(1), 18–31. https://doi.org/10.2307/2525621
Wang, K. M. (2011). Health care expenditure and economic growth: Quantile panel-type analysis. *Economic Modelling, 28*(4), 1536–1549. https://doi.org/10.1016/j.econmod.2011.02.008.

Nguyen Viet Ngan is a graduate student of M.Sc. in Economics at UEH. She works at Hoan My Medical Corporation as a Digital Copywriter, serving healthcare services for Vietnamese people. Her research interests include health economics, financial markets and macroeconomic policies. She received a bachelor's degree in Marketing from the University of Economics of Ho Chi Minh City.

Lam Nguyen Do Khoa is a graduate student of M.Sc. in Economics at UEH. He works at Yuanta Securities as a training department staff member, serving investment education for Vietnamese investors. His research interests include welfare economics, financial inclusion, financial market and macroeconomic policies. He received a bachelor's degree in finance from Ho Chi Minh University of Banking.

Chapter 13
Population Growth and Urbanization in Vietnam

Nhu Nam Do and Quang Dong Quan Le

Abstract This study provides an empirical analysis of the established trends in population growth and urbanization in Vietnam. It aims to offer insights into underlying implications of Vietnam's changing demographic landscape, and its correlation with urbanization and sustainable development. The paper demonstrates that while the country's population has been growing at a slower pace, Vietnam's urbanization rate has been increasing rapidly. The stylized facts of urbanization's drivers include natural population growth, inter-provincial migration owing to industrialization, socio-economic and geo-political factors, as well as statistical effects derived from Vietnam government's administrative urban planning policies. Adopting a panel data regression approach, the analysis examines the correlation between urbanization and economic development in Vietnam's 63 provinces during the 2007–2022 period. The results show that rapid urbanization and slowing population growth pose several development policy implications for the country. These include aging population, urban labor market quality, and labor supply–demand imbalance, as well as navigating rural–urban socio-economic welfare and infrastructure development. The challenges also include issues such as empowerment of migrating women, delayed marriage age and low fertility rate, unemployment in urban areas, high dependency ratio, and concentration of low-skill employment in rural underdeveloped areas.

Keywords Population growth · Urbanization · Sustainable economic development · Vietnam's inter-provincial growth

N. N. Do (✉) · Quang D. Q. Le
Vietnam—the Netherlands Programme, University of Economics Ho Chi Minh City, Ho Chi Minh City, Vietnam
e-mail: nam.dn@vnp.edu.vn

Quang D. Q. Le
e-mail: quan.lqd@vnp.edu.vn

P. K. Nam and A. Heshmati (eds.), *Recent Trends in Vietnam's Rapid Economic Development*, Frontiers in South and Southeast Asian Development Research,
https://doi.org/10.1007/978-981-97-6079-4_13

1 Introduction

The implications of Vietnam's population growth and urbanization in the last three decades are multifaceted. Urbanization in Vietnam has mainly been driven by natural population growth, inter-provincial migration that entails socio-economic driving forces, such as economic growth and the establishment of Special Economic Zones or Industrial Zones, as well as administrative influences from urban planning policies (GSO & UNFPA, 2020). In turn, urbanization has played a crucial role in driving Vietnam's economic development, through increasing investments and employment in key industries and services, thereby reducing poverty. However, this rapid process necessitates effective urban planning and sustainable development strategies to address overall social welfare, in particular housing security and affordability, public infrastructure, gender and income equality, and environmental sustainability. This study aims to examine Vietnam's urban development, highlight implications for evidence-based policymaking, as well as propose a strategic framework for sustainable urban development.

The empirical analysis utilizes panel data covering Vietnam's 63 provinces during the 2007–2022 period, in which the causes of urbanization are investigated from 2007, and the correlation between economic growth, urbanization, and other designated socio-economic attributes is analyzed during the 2018–2022 period. The data and relevant insights are obtained from the annual reports and the Population and Housing Census conducted by the General Statistics Office of Vietnam, as well as from Vietnam's Ministry of Construction, Vietnam Chamber of Commerce, and Industry (VCCI), and the United Nations Population Fund (UNFPA). The provincial list and its regional classification are provided in Appendix for the reader's reference.

We seek to specify and estimate two key models, with the first model aiming to analyze the effects of natural population growth, migration, and administrative effects on urbanization. The second model seeks to understand how urbanization, as well as other socio-economic factors, fosters economic growth. The models are estimated by panel data regression approach. We find in our random effects model, which covers the 2007–2022 period, that natural growth, migration, and administrative effects are three key urbanization drivers, in which migration is further affected by each province's attractiveness in growth and industrialization, labor market, and infrastructure development. Our adopted fixed effects model demonstrates the positive relationship between urbanization, measured by population proportion, and economic development, measured by Gross Regional Domestic Product per capita (GRDP), in Vietnam's 63 provinces during the 2018–2022 period. However, through use of a squared variable in the specified model to capture nonlinearity, the model also predicts a turning point after which excessive urbanization could dampen growth.

The paper begins with a review of urbanization's key concepts, as well as previous relevant findings. In this section, we also present related descriptive analyses on Vietnam's recent trends of population growth, migration, and urban administrative polices. Then, we introduce our dataset, from which we conduct a panel data regression analysis of Vietnam's urbanization driving forces. Further, we utilize our panel data to estimate the relationship between Vietnam's urbanization, among other independent variables, and economic growth. We then conclude with summarized findings, urbanization-related socio-economic challenges, and corresponding policy recommendations in response to the Vietnam's shifting demographics.

2 Review of Key Concepts and Findings on Vietnam's Urbanization

GSO and UNFPA (2020) attributed the key driving factors of urbanization in Vietnam to population growth, within and between provinces migration, and administrative policies. Nguyen and Nguyen (2018) and Fatima (2022) identified positive correlation between urbanization and economic growth in Vietnam and neighboring countries. Furthermore, urbanization casts an indirect impact on education and infrastructure investment, which in turn influences economic growth (Dao, 2020; Heshmati & Rashidghalam, 2020; Kadyraliev et al., 2022). Throughout this section and the following analyses, we analyze the above causes and consequences of urbanization in Vietnam's 63 provinces during the period 2007–2022.

2.1 Key Concepts

Population growth refers to the year-over-year growth rate of population size in percentage. The concept of urbanization could be measured by the population living in areas classified as "urban" or an "agglomeration" area. Urbanization can be defined as the ongoing process of population shift from rural-to-urban areas, resulting in a progressive rise in the population proportion residing in urban settings (GSO & UNFPA, 2020). Three key factors influence this urbanization process. Firstly, natural population growth rate of urban areas occurs when the birth rate in urban centers exceeds the death rate, leading to a net population growth in these areas. This intrinsic growth contributes to the increasing urbanization trend. Rural-to-urban migration is the second factor which can be spurred by various socio-economic factors, including population growth itself, employment opportunities, better access to services such as education and healthcare, and higher overall living standards. Lastly, administrative effects, such as the expansion or reclassification of urban areas, can also influence urbanization statistics (GSO & UNFPA, 2020).

Further, an urban agglomeration is defined as "the actual population residing within the boundaries of a contiguous territory inhabited at urban density levels, irrespective of administrative demarcations" (United Nations, 2006). Meanwhile, a metropolitan area is all-encompassing, entailing both the urban agglomeration and any "adjacent regions with lower settlement density that are equally subject to the direct influence of the city" (United Nations, 2006). These concepts are helpful in elucidating the positive externalities as spillover effects, as well as an increasing inter-provincial migration trend, from urban to surrounding areas, including both urban and rural.

However, urbanization studies of developing countries pose certain challenges that extend beyond classification discrepancies. Urban population data remains an obstacle to capture fully and accurately (Nguyen & Nguyen, 2018). Further, the results of population censuses often tend to underestimate the true urban population due to substantial mobility patterns that are frequently intricate to regulate (Cohen, 2004).

Bloom et al. (2010) elucidated fundamental methodologies utilized in urbanization statistics, also employed in this paper. A common gauge for assessing urbanization rate involves calculating the proportion of the population residing in urban areas (URB_t) relative to the total population residing in both urban and rural regions ($\mathrm{PU}_t + \mathrm{PR}_t$), where PU signifies the urban population, PR denotes the rural population, and the subscript t indicates time. This measure is mathematically expressed as follows:

$$\mathrm{URB}_t = \left(\frac{\mathrm{PU}_t}{\mathrm{PU}_t + \mathrm{PR}_t}\right) \times 100.$$

2.2 *Urbanization in Vietnam: An Overview*

Within the scope of this study, we approach urbanization based on classification categories by the Vietnam's government, in particular the Ministry of Construction and the General Statistics Office of Vietnam. Urban units in Vietnam are classified into Special-class and class-I to V cities, based on designated administrative and socio-economic criteria (Ministry of Construction, 2013). Urbanization analyses in this paper are mainly conducted on an inter-provincial level, while adding general insights into urbanization on an urban-class level, nationwide level, and regional level. Regional-level analysis divides the country into six main regions of Red River Delta, North Central and Central Coastal areas, Northern midlands and mountain areas, Central Highlands, Southeast and Mekong River Delta (GSO & UNFPA, 2021).

The official data estimated by GSO in 2022 yields a less than 40% urban population level, while rural population is approximately 62.5%. The population census as of April 1, 2019, which is subject to certain inconsistency due to data collection methods, indicated that Vietnam had a total urban population of 39.4 million individuals, 49% of which reside in special-class cities and class-I cities, totaling 19.3 million people. A quarter of the urban population, or 9.6 million people, live in class-IV and class-V cities. Overall, the urban population proportion in Vietnam has demonstrated a rapidly increasing trend, from around 20% in 1995 to approach the 40% level in 2022 (GSO & UNFPA, 2020).

2.3 *Driving Forces of Urbanization in Vietnam*

As previously mentioned, besides natural population growth, urbanization in Vietnam results from rural-to-urban migration, economic development, and administrative decisions (GSO & UNFPA, 2020). Past findings have elaborated their hypotheses on the driving forces of urbanization in Vietnam. We will conduct a summary and descriptive analysis of these forces prior to our model estimation in Sect. 4.

Natural Population Growth

During the last decade, Vietnam's population has witnessed a decreasing growth rate. A time series, bivariate plot demonstrates an upward trend in Vietnam's urbanization rate, whereas natural population growth rate, on the left axis, has stabilized around 1.1% level, before dropping to below 1% in recent years. It has been predicted that the Vietnamese population will become an "aged population" in 2036, when the 65 + age group accounts for 14% of total population. Furthermore, the country's "demographic window," with decreasing fertility and stable old-age group, is predicted to end by 2039 (Andrews & Philips, 2005; GSO & UNFPA, 2021; United Nations, 2004). These demographics trends pose challenges for the Vietnam's government to navigate sustainable population growth and urbanization strategy to maintain its workforce and facilitate long-term economic growth. Furthermore, with the country's 40% urbanization rate, as well as rural population's lower marriage age and higher child dependency ratio, natural population growth is expected to take place more in rural areas, thus exhibiting a slightly negative correlation with urbanization (GSO, 2021). In overall, we can observe in Fig. 1 that Vietnam's urbanization rate surpassing population growth rate since 2004, and that the two series have lacked a significantly positive relationship ever since, a matter into which we will investigate with a panel data regression model, with an expected small and negative coefficient.

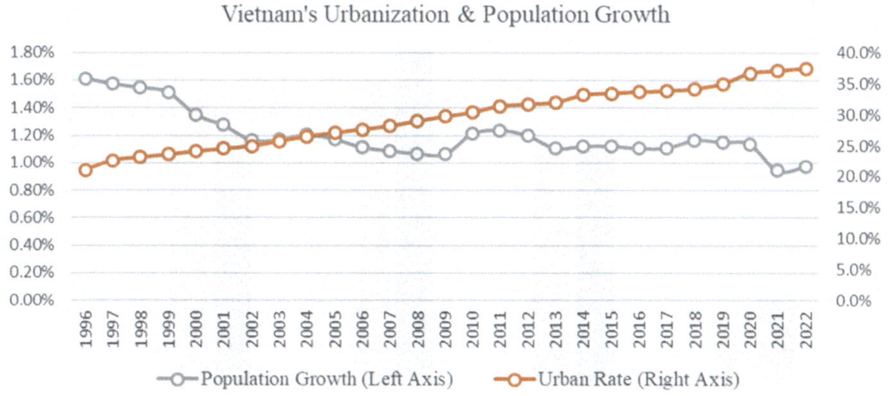

Fig. 1 Vietnam's urbanization and population growth, 1996–2022

Migration

Secondly, migration data, measured within a designated time frame, refers to the relocation of individuals from one geographic unit to another, thus playing a crucial role in driving demographic dynamics. This role is further pronounced in countries with relatively stable fertility and mortality rates such as Vietnam (GSO & UNFPA, 2020). The GSO & UNFPA survey (2020) delineates four key migration trajectories based on prior and current habitual residence: rural-to-rural migration (R–R), rural-to-urban migration (R–U), urban-to-rural migration (U–R), and urban-to-urban migration (U–U). Considering rural-to-urban migration as urbanization's driving force is consistent with prevalent theories for urbanization (Bodo, 2019; Fatima, 2022).

In fact, previous population censuses of Vietnam showed rural-to-rural migration as the main migration pattern. However, in 2019, urban-to-urban migration has emerged predominant against the four migration streams, as demonstrated in Fig. 2.

The process of migration significantly influences the trajectory of urbanization through socioeconomic enhancement. This shift can be understood under Vietnam's developing country context, where most of the population resides in rural areas. As the economy undergoes industrialization and modernization, migration from rural-to-urban areas has been a natural phenomenon and the main migration flow. However, in the 2009–2019 period, this migration flow has reverted to a decreasing trend. Meanwhile, urban-to-rural migration has continuously and comprehensibly maintained the smallest share of migration flow with minimal changes. Despite the recent "urban exodus" trend among youths, it is assumed that these demographic shifts do not account for a large proportion of migration flow. Moreover, the youths under this flow also shift their residence to "less-urbanized" areas, which are nonetheless classified as urban, thus adding to U–U migration instead (Long, 2020; OECD, 2015).

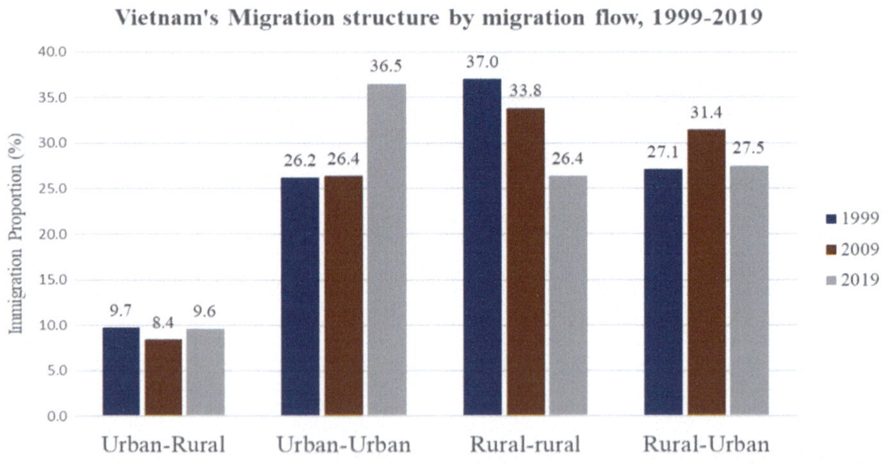

Fig. 2 Vietnam's migration structure by migration flow, 1999–2019

Therefore, over the past three decades, there has been a noticeable trend of decreasing out-rural migration flow, while urban migration has witnessed a rising pattern. This structural shift is attributable to various factors, including improved job opportunities and living conditions in rural areas. This enhancement is an outcome of small and medium industrial zones' expansion, under the backdrop of government policies that facilitate rural economic development, and the creation of "new rural areas" (IFAD, 2016). These policies, implemented effectively in numerous regions, have contributed to improved conditions in rural areas. Additionally, the robust development of cities, coupled with enhancements in transportation and infrastructure, has stimulated labor movement among cities and regions. This trend is consistent with the abovementioned positive externalities of urbanization spillover effect theory, as well as with policy recommendations of rural–urban sustainable development and equality (Fatima, 2022; McKenzie & Sasin, 2007). The survey also highlights a positive relationship between U–U migration between provinces with high economic growth, such as in the Southeast region, referring to improved labor mobility from economic development (GSO & UNFPA, 2020). With the new migration landscape, we expect a small positive coefficient of migration on urbanization, since we expect recent increases in U–U and U–R migration to crowd out the positive effect that R–U migration has on urbanization.

On the regional level, the 2019 migration landscape also demonstrates new demographic shifts. In 1999 and 2009, the Central Highlands were commonly known for positive net migration rate. However, in the 2019 Census, the Central Highlands has become an outmigration region, leaving the Red River Delta and the Southeast the only two net immigrant regions of Vietnam. The Mekong River Delta is the region with the largest negative net migration rate, with all provinces with negative net migration rates located there. Notably, in the 2009 Census, the Southeast region's migration rate peaked at nearly 120%, demonstrating rapid urbanization pace in an exuberant economic zone. 12 out of Vietnam's 63 provinces and cities experienced positive net migration rates. Among them, Binh Duong province stood out with the highest positive net migration rate at 200.4%, attracting over 489,000 immigrants in 2009–2019 period, notably in the Mekong River Delta (GSO & UNFPA, 2020).

On the other hand, in contrast to the 2009 Census, Thai Nguyen, Bac Ninh, and Long An provinces have changed from outmigration to immigration. Notably, the net migration rate of Bac Ninh province has changed from − 12.6‰ in 2009 to 85.3% in 2019. This province's change likely resulted from rapid development of new industrial zones and Foreign Direct Investment (FDI) attraction in the past ten years, thereby drawing a large workforce from other localities to live and work (GSO & Ministry of Construction, 2023c; UNFPA, 2020). The case of Bac Ninh substantiates a two-way, reverse causality between economic growth, including industrial accompanied with foreign and public investment, and urbanization. It also demonstrates geographical advantage when the province aims to become centrally run as a satellite city of Hanoi capital (Ministry of Construction, 2023c). There are also six provinces moving from immigration to outmigration that demonstrate the impact of urban agglomeration economies, where people migrate to nearby urban economic zones for work (World Bank, 2020).

On an urban-class level, the average immigration rate to urban areas in the country is 123.1%, equivalent to that of class-I cities but nearly four times higher than in rural areas. Therefore, migrants, excluding the emigration factor, constitute 12.3% of the population aged 5 + in urban areas, referred to as urbanization rate (GSO & UNFPA, 2020). Special-class and class-III cities face high immigration pressure. The former witnesses an influx of nearly 200 immigrants for every 1,000 residents, which is 2.7 times higher than the national average, and 5.3 times higher than rural areas. This phenomenon is attributable to substantial infrastructure development investments in recent years, including the establishment of many industrial zones and export processing chains in class-III cities, attracting an inflow of migrant workers (GSO & UNFPA, 2020). Less-urbanized class-IV and V cities only face immigration pressures equivalent to rural areas. This relationship between urbanization and economic growth will be further studied in the following sections on an inter-provincial level.

Administrative

While natural and mechanical population growth data remained relatively stable as demonstrated in the previous section, administrative decisions are believed to have affected approximately 4.1 million rural residents, shifted into urban areas. This is equivalent to 10.4% of the urban population in Vietnam in 2019. Even class-IV or class-V urban centers now have 700 communes with 6.3 million people, accounting for 16% of Vietnam's urban population. Compared with the 2009 Population Census, Vietnam's total number of communal administrative units increased by 94 units. The total number of wards and townships increased by 259 units.

Thus, administrative factors have contributed to a total of 26.4% of the urban population nationwide, or 10.4 million people. The communes recognized as urban centers, which are primarily located in the North Central and Central Coastal areas, account for nearly one-third of the shifted population during the census five-year gap (GSO & UNFPA, 2020). This change is consistent with the Government's and Ministry of Construction's urban planning (Ministry of Construction, 2023b). The most noteworthy adjustment that has a large effect on provincial urbanization rate is the merge of Ha Tay province, along with parts of Vinh Phuc and Hoa Binh, into Hanoi in 2008 (Bui et al., 2012). Following this merger, Hanoi's urban population rate dropped significantly from above 60% level to only above 40%. The city aims to enhance and reinforce its urban position by raising urbanization rate to over 60% by 2025, and to pre-merge level of 65–75% by 2030 (Ministry of Construction, 2023a).

It is thus important to recognize these exogenous factors in affecting the data regarding urban cities' legal and administration classification in Vietnam (Nguyen & Nguyen, 2018). In our following panel data regression analysis, we include administrative factors based on the annualized average urban population per one administrative on a commune level of the province and expect a positive coefficient owing to the administrative upgrade of rural-to-urban communes during the 1996–2022 period.

2.3.1 Urbanization and Economic Growth: Findings and Applications for Vietnam

Prior papers have identified a strong correlation between the level of urbanization and per capita GDP (Henderson, 2003). Policies that facilitate positive urbanization, aimed at fostering economic growth clustered in special economic zones, are prevalent across developing nations, including Vietnam (Friedmann, 2006; GSO & UNFPA, 2020). These influences range from population relocation plus demographic impacts to economic structure transition, job facilitation, poverty mitigation, and the fostering of sustainable development. In essence, urbanization has integrated into the economic growth framework, catalyzed by the Vietnamese government's economic reforms since the late 1980s (GSO & UNFPA, 2020). Consequently, urbanization has emerged as crucial facets of the nation's population and development research. In fact, it has been found that no country has achieved middle-income status without undergoing industrialization and urbanization. Similarly, no economy has attained high-income status without exuberant cities (World Bank, 2009). Even though the migration into cities brings about chaotic pressure on development, particularly in developing countries, such urbanization is often deemed imperative.

Bertinelli and Black (2004) elaborated diverse channels through which urbanization creates an impact on economic growth. Cities play a crucial role in the socioeconomic structure of developed and developing economies through educational services, employment opportunities, and healthcare access. Educational capital is pivotal in building a nation's capacity to innovate and advance technologies (Aghion & Howitt, 2009). Urbanization facilitates external economies of scale, curtails transaction costs, and enables internal specialization within firms, thus decreasing production expenses (Fujita et al., 1999; Krugman, 1991; Kumar & Kober, 2012). Concentrating populations and businesses in urban agglomeration facilitates more convenient and inclusive access to finance, encourages entrepreneurial initiatives, and creates a diverse local market (Glaeser et al., 2010).

An urban agglomeration's success relies on its ability to create an active and stable job market, which eventually enhances overall workforce skills (Bacolod et al., 2010). Spillover effects also arise from R–U migration through channels such as remittances, urban–rural interactions with knowledge and skill transfer, thus augmenting financial and human resource quality in rural areas, referred to as positive externalities (McKenzie & Sasin, 2007).

However, urbanization also causes unfavorable consequences in both urban and rural areas. Diseconomies of scale in large cities can negatively affect other urban centers in the hierarchy by diverting resources from smaller cities (Henderson, 2002). It has even been observed that agglomeration supports economic growth up to a certain level, after which diseconomies of scale's negative influences could deteriorate growth (Brulhart & Sbergami, 2009). Further, excessive urbanization could create pressure on infrastructure and sustainable socio-economic growth in terms of urban housing conditions, income equality, unemployment rate, rural dependency ratio, urban's late, and small marriage trend that leads to aging population, as well as the labor force's lower average qualification to do simple jobs (Alam et al., 2007; GSO & UNFPA, 2020; GSO, 2021).

Besides findings to the two directions above, studies also found no definitive evidence that urbanization influences economic growth (Bloom et al., 2008). Fay and Opal (2000) documented instances of urbanization without corresponding growth in developing economies in the late twentieth century. These findings contrast with the prevailing notion that there exists either a positive or negative relationship between urbanization and economic growth. Bloom et al. (2008) reiterated the need to re-evaluate the relationship between urbanization and economic growth against the backdrop of urbanization ideas prevalent in developing countries.

Regarding Vietnam, Nguyen and Nguyen (2018) conducted an empirical study on the urbanization and economic growth correlation with data of ASEAN countries, including Vietnam, from 1993 to 2014. Utilizing Granger causality, fixed effect, and random effect models, a causal relationship between urbanization and economic growth is substantiated. Their findings demonstrate that urbanization has a significant positive impact on ASEAN economic development. Dao (2020) provided empirical evidence of the widely concerned hypothesis that education, particularly primary and secondary schooling, has a positive effect on economic growth, measured by total factor productivity and GDP growth.

This paper focuses on the relationship in Vietnam's 63 provinces using panel regression methods. From preliminary review and descriptive findings, we expect urbanization to have a positive effect on economic growth, prior to a certain level. Further, we observe that Vietnam's higher urban-class cities witness higher unemployment and fewer low-skill jobs, while most rural employment stems from agricultural and low-skill simple jobs (GSO & UNFPA, 2020). Figure 3 illustrates this which reflects competitive job markets in urban agglomerate economies and an imbalance of labor force quality between urban and rural areas. This important socio-economic issue shall be further discussed in Sect. 5.

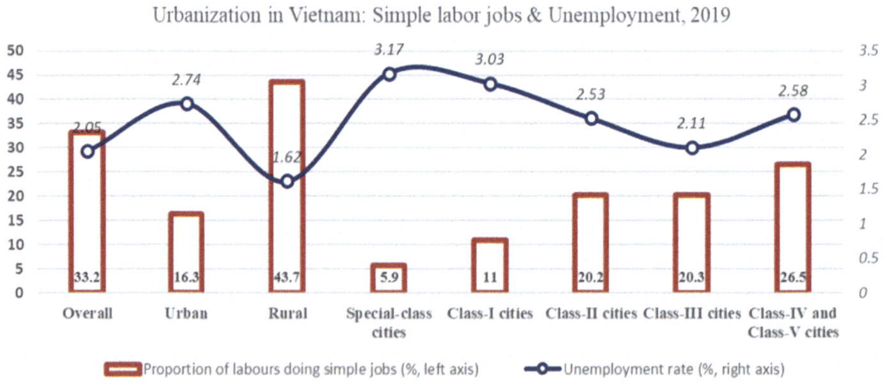

Fig. 3 Urbanization in Vietnam: low-skill simple jobs and unemployment, 2019

3 Methodology and Data

3.1 Methodology Review

In this section, we briefly review relevant methodologies employed by past studies that investigate urbanization and growth in developing economies. Heshmati and Rashidghalam (2020) conducted an inter-provincial urbanization analysis in China, in which they found significant inter-provincial disparities stemming from unbalanced urban infrastructure allocations. The study utilized composite indices of urban infrastructure, covering 15 socio-economic components. Their inter-provincial approach with indices processing is partially adapted in our panel data regression analysis of Vietnam's 63 provinces. Kadyraliev et al. (2022) also demonstrated how transport infrastructure investment stimulated economic development, including sustainable rural development, as well as affected the achievement of SDGs. Chang and Brada (2006) investigated urbanization in China, whose empirical evidence demonstrates that less-urbanized economies have been prevalent in recent global economic growth. Lewis (2014) examined the relationship between urbanization and economic growth in Indonesia, using time series data from 1960 to 2009 and panel data of Indonesia's sub-regions. The findings propose that urbanization is positively correlated with economic growth, yet the rate of change of urbanization negatively affects Indonesia's economic growth. In his model, dynamic panel regression estimates further clarify the level and significance of negative impact. The estimation results also suggest that the diseconomies effects of urban population growth are connected to inadequate local public infrastructure spending. As a policy proposal, it is necessary that regional governments increase infrastructure investment to negate the adverse effects of rapid urbanization on economic growth.

Fatima (2022) conducted a pooled, static, and dynamic panel regression analysis of urbanization and economic growth in South Asian countries, whose findings demonstrate the positive impact of urbanization on economic growth, while policy recommendations include reducing R–U migration barriers, enhanced infrastructure, and equal benefits, with an emphasis of good regional governance. This paper will focus on the relationship in Vietnam's 63 provinces using suitable panel regression methods. Fatima (2022) posited that the impact of urbanization on economic growth could be nonlinear, thus including an additional variable of squared urbanization rate in their estimation model. This approach is also adapted by this paper, in which we could comprehensibly observe a correlation between the urbanization rate and its squared term.

3.2 Data

In the previous and last sections of this paper, we used bivariate and meta-analyses to understand migration and urbanization in the context of socioeconomic and demographic factors at the provincial level. Descriptive data and relevant visualizations are obtained via Vietnam's General Statistics Office (GSO) data portal and statistical yearbook, as well as from GSO & UNFPA (2020). In the latter, data is collected from Vietnam's 2019 Population and Housing Census, which then becomes further restricted to the survey of respondents' households. While the census spans a populace exceeding 96.2 million individuals, the supplementary survey executed for the UNFPA report acts as a representative sample, covering 9% of households across Vietnam, which offers further insights into demographic shifts, particularly migration dynamics (GSO & UNFPA, 2020). Limitations exist in that the survey data only covers immigration cases and excludes emigration.

For the panel regression section, the paper uses data of Vietnam's 63 provinces from 1995 to 2022. All data are obtained from GSO, except for provincial competitiveness index (PCI), which was obtained from published dataset on "PCI Vietnam" website, released by Vietnam Chamber of Commerce and Industry (VCCI) in collaboration with USAID (PCI, 2022).

The paper presents two main panel regression models, the first of which aims to analyze the effects of natural population growth, migration, and administrative classifications on urbanization, while the second investigates the effects of urbanization and other relevant factors on economic growth.

For the first model, data of Vietnam's 63 provinces from 2007 to 2022 are used. The four variables are described in Table 1, while their descriptive statistics are presented in Table 2. Owing to the lack of available data for urban population per each administrative unit, we measured the effects of administrative policies on urbanization by dividing urban population by total commune-level administrative units to account for the number of administrative units relative to the urban population size.

For the second model, data of Vietnam's 63 provinces from 2018 to 2022 is used. Tables 3 and 4 present its variables and descriptive statistics.

Table 1 Description of variables (model 1) driving forces of urbanization URB

Variable name	Description	Unit
URB *(dependent variable)*	Urban population proportion by province	%
Nat_Growth	Natural population growth by province (natural birth – natural death rate)	%
Migration	Net migration by province	%
URB_Units	Urban population divided by total number of commune-level administrative units by province	Persons/Unit

Table 2 Descriptive summary statistics (model 1) determinants of URB

	Obs	Mean	SD	Min	Max	Range	SE
Province	1008	–	–	–	–	–	–
Year	1008	–	–	2007	2022	15	–
URB	1008	27.47	16.88	7.66	87.45	79.80	0.53
Nat_Growth	1008	1.01	0.35	0	2.09	2.09	0.01
Migration	1008	– 0.17	0.86	– 2.72	7.46	10.18	0.03
URB_Units	1008	2.90	3.85	0.38	25.58	25.20	0.12

Table 3 Description of variables (model 2), GRDP

Variable name	Description	Unit
GRDP_PC *(dependent variable)*	*(log of)* Gross regional domestic product per capita by province	Million VND/year
URB	Urban population proportion by province	%
URB_sq	Urban population proportion by province, squared	%
Retail_Rev	*(log of)* Total retail + consumer services Revenue (current price)	Trillion VND
Unemp	Unemployment rate of labor force at working age by province	%
Pop_Growth	Year-over-year population growth	%
PCI	Provincial competitiveness index by VCCI and USAID	Index
Pop_Dense	*(log of)* Population density	Persons/squared kilometer

Table 4 Descriptive summary statistics (model 2), GRDP

	Obs	Mean	SD	Min	Max	Range	SE
Province	315	–	–	–	–	–	–
Year	315	–	–	2018	2022	4.00	–
GRDP_PC	315	4.14	0.44	3.26	5.82	2.55	0.03
URB	315	0.30	0.17	0.10	0.87	0.78	0.01
URB_sq	315	0.12	0.16	0.01	0.76	0.76	0.01
Retail_Rev	315	3.83	0.91	1.51	6.96	5.45	0.05
Unemp	315	2.41	1.43	0.08	9.41	9.33	0.08
Pop_Growth	315	0.94	0.93	– 1.22	6.41	7.63	0.05
PCI	315	64.32	3.11	55.12	73.40	18.28	0.18
Pop_Dense	315	5.73	0.99	3.91	8.41	4.50	0.06

3.3 Regressions

The paper employs panel regression analysis methods to investigate the correlation between population growth and urbanization, as well as test the significance of urbanization's impact on economic growth in Vietnam's provinces. As mentioned earlier, we first regress the effects of natural population growth, migration, and administrative effects on urbanization rate in Vietnam's 63 provinces from 2007 to 2022. Then, we regress urbanization rate, its squared variables, and five other socio-economic variables against economic growth, measured by the natural log of GRDP per capita.

For each regression, we employ three regression models, including a Pooled ordinary least squares, fixed effects (static), and random effects (dynamic) model. We then conduct a post-regression Hausman test to determine whether the dynamic model is mis-specified.

For pre-regression testing, we tested for possible multicollinearity between the two models' independent variables using correlation matrix and variance inflation factor (VIF). We posit a preliminary hypothesis that model 2 will contain a pair of variables that display multicollinearity, namely urbanization and urbanization squared. Tables 5 and 6 depict the Pearson correlation, while Tables 7 and 8 display the VIF values, among the variables of model 1 and model 2, respectively.

Table 5 Correlation matrix of regression model 1, urbanization

Variables	Migration	Nat_Growth	URB_Units
Migration	1.000		
Nat_Growth	0.328	1.000	
URB_Units	0.522	0.015	1.000

Table 6 Correlation matrix of regression model 2, GRDP

Variables	URB	URB_sq	Retail_Rev	Unemp	Pop_Growth	PCI	Pop_Dense
URB	1.000						
URB_sq	0.969	1.000					
Retail_Rev	0.575	0.541	1.000				
Unemp	0.365	0.349	0.255	1.000			
Pop_Growth	0.291	0.348	0.016	-0.162	1.000		
PCI	0.437	0.424	0.500	0.263	-0.004	1.000	
Pop_Dense	0.375	0.398	0.689	0.170	0.045	0.417	1.000

Table 7 Variance inflation factor of regression model 1, urbanization

VIF collinearity statistics		
URB	URB_sq	Retail_Rev
1.038	1.039	1.016

Table 8 Variance inflation factor of regression model 2, GRDP

VIF collinearity statistics						
URB	URB_sq	Retail_Rev	Unemp	Pop_Growth	PCI	Pop_Dense
8.312	8.171	1.729	1.036	1.038	1.255	1.476

We observe that the values of VIF of variables in both models are low, mainly below 2 and smaller than 4. Both models also demonstrate low multicollinearity in the correlation matrix, where all correlations are within reasonable level, being smaller than 0.80. Notably, we observe a slight negative correlation between population growth and unemployment. The exception of urbanization and its squared term in model 2 stands out as hypothesized. With the usage of panel data and squared variables for nonlinear relationship testing, the probable multicollinearity between urbanization and its squared term can be ignored (Nguyen & Nguyen, 2018).

4 Model Estimation

4.1 Driving Forces of Urbanization in Vietnam

The three applicable estimation methods for model 1 driving forces of urbanization are specified according to the model specification below. As they are like the three estimation methods applied to model 2 determinants of GRDP, we will further discuss the three estimation methods' discrepancies and applications in the presentation of model 2.

Pooled OLS:

$$\text{URB} = \beta_0 + \beta_1\text{Nat\_Growth} + \beta_2\text{Migration} + \beta_3\text{URB\_Units} + \mu_{\text{it}}$$

Fixed effects (within-group, without intercept):

$$\text{URB} = \beta_1\text{Nat\_Growth} + \beta_2\text{Migration} + \beta_3\text{URB\_Units} + \mu_{\text{it}}$$

Random effects:

$$\text{URB} = \mu + \beta_1\text{Nat\_Growth} + \beta_2\text{Migration} + \beta_3\text{URB\_Units} + \mu_{\text{it}}.$$

From the modeling framework above, with the data collected from GSO, processed by the authors, and estimated in R program, we yield the output for the three estimation methods (pooled OLS (1), fixed effects (2), and random effects (3)), presented in Table 9.

Table 9 Estimation result of model 1 (dependent variable: URB)

Variables:	(Pooled OLS 1)	(Fixed effects 2)	(Random effects 3)
Intercept	12.749***		19.677***
	(0.887) (< 2.2e−16)		(1.026) (< 2.2e−16)
Nat_Growth	2.642***	− 1.825***	− 1.743***
	(0.746) (0.000)	(0.378) (0.000)	(0.378) (0.000)
Migration	− 1.572***	0.320*	0.342*
	(0.356) (0.00001)	(0.167) (0.055)	(0.166) (0.039)
URB_Units	4.070***	3.253***	3.316***
	(0.075) (< 2.2e−16)	(0.079) (< 2.2e−16)	(0.075) (< 2.2e−16)
#Obs	1008	1008	1008
R-squared	0.793	0.651	0.664

Column 1 indicates pooled OLS model. Columns 2 and 3 indicate panel regression with fixed effects on province and year, and random effects, respectively
Standard error reported underneath coefficient. *p*-value reported underneath Standard error
Signifying significance level: *** for 0.1%; ** for 1%, * for 5%.

Results shown in Table 9 demonstrate consistent output between our models, while discrepancies in coefficients are noted between pooled OLS and our two panel regressions. Since the pooled OLS assumes the error term is not autocorrelated and homoscedastic, while our variables are non-stochastic and strictly exogenous, we find its applications limited in this study. Our pooled OLS model's output was also inconsistent with prior descriptive and literature findings, regarding migration's positive and natural growth's negative effects on urbanization rate in Vietnam's 63 provinces.

After estimation, we proceed to investigate whether the FE or RE model is more suitable to use through the Hausman test (1978). In the Hausman test, we employ the null hypothesis that both models are equally effective, while the alternative hypothesis states that the fixed effect model is consistent and unbiased while the random effects model is mis-specified inconsistent and biased. Since our test's *p*-value is larger than 0.10, we do not reject the null hypothesis. Therefore, our first regression leans toward utilizing our random effects model which is consistent, unbiased, and efficient, as displayed in column 3 of Table 9.

Specification test	Test-statistic (chi-squared)	*p*-value
Hausman	2.247	0.522

4.2 Urbanization and Economic Growth in Vietnam

The variables used in modeling relationship between urbanization and economic growth were defined and described in Sect. 3, where we computed the natural logarithm of GRDP, retail revenue, and population density, while including a squared variable of urbanization to test for nonlinear trend. The model is developed with adaptations of panel data of Vietnam's 63 provinces, adapted from previous relevant studies (Fatima, 2022; Nguyen & Nguyen, 2018). The overall model estimated by pooled OLS, fixed effects, and random effects then is specified as follows:

$$\begin{aligned}\mathrm{GRDP_PC} =&\beta_0 + \beta_1\mathrm{URB} + \beta_2\mathrm{URB\_sq} + \beta_3\mathrm{Retail\_Rev}\\ &+ \beta_4\mathrm{Unemp} + \beta_5\mathrm{Pop\_Growth} + \beta_6\mathrm{PCI} + \beta_7\mathrm{Pop\_Dense}.\end{aligned}$$

To control the heterogeneous and unobserved factors in the model, the fixed effects (FE) model is often employed, in which the original intercept β_0 is replaced by α_i that measures the individual effect components of within-group variations.

$$\begin{aligned}\mathrm{GRDP\_PC} = &\alpha_i + \beta_1\mathrm{URB} + \beta_2\mathrm{URB\_sq} + \beta_3\mathrm{Retail\_Rev} + \beta_4\mathrm{Unemp}\\ &+ \beta_5\mathrm{Pop\_Growth} + \beta_6\mathrm{PCI} + \beta_7\mathrm{Pop\_Dense} + \mu_{\mathrm{it}}.\end{aligned}$$

However, among fixed effect methods, we employ the within-group model, where we subtract the average of variables across time, with time-invariant parameters, from the original FE model, which will eliminate the fixed effects estimator α_i.

$$\begin{aligned}\mathrm{GRDP\_PC} = &\beta_1\mathrm{URB} + \beta_2\mathrm{URB\_sq} + \beta_3\mathrm{Retail\_Rev} + \beta_4\mathrm{Unemp}\\ &+ \beta_5\mathrm{Pop\_Growth} + \beta_6\mathrm{PCI} + \beta_7\mathrm{Pop\_Dense} + \mu_{\mathrm{it}}.\end{aligned}$$

Secondly, we employ the random effect (RE) model that assumes across-group variation is random and the individual specific random component, as well as the idiosyncratic disturbance, is normally distributed. This model utilizes the generalized least squares estimation method, and yields the functional form as follows:

$$\begin{aligned}\mathrm{GRDP\_PC} = &\mu + \beta_1\mathrm{URB} + \beta_2\mathrm{URB\_sq} + \beta_3\mathrm{Retail\_Rev} + \beta_4\mathrm{Unemp}\\ &+ \beta_5\mathrm{Pop\_Growth} + \beta_6\mathrm{PCI} + \beta_7\mathrm{Pop\_Dense} + \mu_{\mathrm{it}}.\end{aligned}$$

From the above tri-variation estimation framework, with the data collected from GSO, processed by the authors, and estimated in R program, we yield the following regression output (Table 10).

Due to the utilization of panel data across Vietnam's 63 provinces from 2018 to 2022, we have employed the appropriate models of fixed effects and random effects. In the post-regression Hausman test, the value of the chi-squared test-statistic is 126 with 7 degrees of freedom, yielding a *p*-value smaller than 0.05. The null hypothesis, as stated in Sect. 4.1, that both the FE and RE models are equally effective

Table 10 Estimation result of regression 2 (dependent variable: GRDP_PC)

Variables	(Pooled OLS 1)	(Fixed effects 2)	(Random effects 3)
Intercept	0.040		1.141***
	(0.346)		(0.259)
URB	0.031***	0.020***	0.023***
	(0.003)	(0.004)	(0.004)
URB_sq	– 0.026***	– 0.014*	– 0.018***
	(0.004)	(0.008)	(0.005)
Retail_Rev	0.013	0.509***	0.348***
	(0.026)	(0.037)	(0.034)
Unemp	– 0.006	0.003	– 0.000
	(0.011)	(0.004)	(0.004)
Pop_Growth	0.105***	0.004	0.005
	(0.018)	(0.007)	(0.008)
PCI	0.037***	0.012***	0.017***
	(0.005)	(0.002)	(0.002)
Pop_Dense	0.161***	0.340*	0.005
	(0.021)	(0.168)	(0.042)
#Obs	315	315	315
R-squared	0.665	0.700	0.613

Column 1 indicates pooled OLS model. Columns 2 and 3 indicate panel regression output with fixed effects and random effects, respectively

Standard error reported underneath coefficient

Signifying significance level: *** for 0.1%; ** for 1%, * for 5%; * for 10%

is thus rejected. Therefore, we will interpret the result based on the primary FE model estimation output.

Specification test	Test-statistic (chi-squared)	*p*-value
Hausman test	126	< 0.000

4.3 Interpretation of Estimation Results

For our first regression, the output and post-regression testing determined that the random effects model was accepted. In this model, we observe that all independent variables are significant at 0.1% significance level, except for migration, which is significant at 5% significance level. We also substantiated our earlier hypotheses derived from Sect. 2, where natural population growth weighed a downward pressure on urbanization, due to Vietnam's current urbanization rate of 40%, as well as rural areas' tendency to have lower marriage age and higher birth rate, reflected in higher dependency ratios (GSO, 2021). We could then assume that a larger part of Vietnam's natural birth population is concentrated in rural areas, who then migrate to urban settings, or whose rural areas could be identified as urban from administrative changes. We also note that, since this variable is significant, we proceeded to use total annualized population growth rate for each province in our second regression, which also includes urbanization as an independent variable, to avoid multicollinearity.

Migration has a small, positive effect on urbanization. This is consistent with previous findings described in Sect. 2, where recent trends of urban–urban and urban–rural migration have crowded out the rural–urban migration source that adds positively to urbanization. We could conclude that migration's effect on urban population has been mixed. Administrative factors, measured by total urban population divided by total commune-level administrative units of each province, proved significant, with a large, positive coefficient. For each additional urban person per unit, a province's urbanization rate increases by 3.31 percentage points.

For the estimation result of the FE model of the second regression, with economic growth, measured by natural log of GRDP growth, as the dependent variable, we observe firstly that there are five statistically significant variables, including URB, URB_sq, Retail_Rev, PCI, and Pop_Dense. The urbanization variable is significant with a low *p*-value of 0.0000325, while its squared variable is significant at 10% significance level. This particular outcome, along with that of population density variable, is consistent with previous relevant studies reviewed in this paper (Fatima, 2022; Nguyen & Nguyen, 2018). As hypothesized in related studies and this paper's descriptive analyses, urbanization has a significantly positive impact on economic growth. When a province in Vietnam has a higher urban population proportion, its GRDP increases. Notably, the nonlinear trend is also demonstrated, as the URB_sq variable is significant and shows a negative impact on economic growth. Other significant variables demonstrate that total retail and consumer services revenue, PCI index, and population density all positively impact economic growth of the province.

The natural population growth does not show a significant impact on urbanization and neither does unemployment. Furthermore, urbanization and its squared variables demonstrate a relatively high beta coefficient, demonstrating its pivotal role in facilitating economic growth. For each additional percentage point in urbanization rate, GRDP per capita increases by approximately 2%. However, with negative squared effect, this impact is non-linear and could be at a slowing rate, hinting at a possible threshold at which urbanization becomes an economic growth hindrance, consistent with previous studies (Arouri et al., 2014; Lewis, 2014; Nguyen & Nguyen, 2018); Kolomak, 2012). This potential threshold, if applicable, could be calculated by the squared equation, ceteris paribus, with the maximum value at: $\frac{\beta 1}{2*(-\beta 2)}$.

Therefore, the Vietnam's government should focus on urbanization's positive impact on economic growth, while devising prudential policies that ensure sustainable and equal development, which shall be analyzed in the following section.

5 Urbanization in Vietnam: Challenges and Policy Implications

As Vietnam faces key period of demographic structural changes that bring about urbanization and socio-economic shifts, analysis of the causes, impacts, and relationships of urbanization presents relevant findings that aid policy proposals. From the above research, we have observed a positive relationship between urbanization and economic growth, despite a possible reversal threshold through our fixed-model estimation. Thus, we will investigate the side-effects of urbanization on demographic and labor market structures, which result in several policy implications for Vietnam's sustainable development.

Firstly, as migration is one of urbanization's main causes, Vietnam's policies need to ensure that development policies at regional and local levels account for the migrant population's role in urbanization, to adapt to changing demographic factors and leverage migrants' positive socio-economic contributions. Additionally, based on our inter-provincial analysis, budgets for local municipalities need to be based on their migrant pressure for sustainability. Among that, especially in highly urbanized areas, given their young migrants aged 20–39, it is crucial to provide welfare support including social security and special attention to female and ethnic migrants who face more challenges developing in their destinations. This is accomplished by establishing mechanisms for migrants' access to social housing options, educational resources to decrease the low-skill job proportion. Addressing these demographic structures requires implementing policies that prioritize women in job creation and vocational training, with the aim of decreasing female unemployment rate and increasing female skilled occupations.

Secondly, Vietnam's governments should recognize the impact of migration on departure and destination areas, particularly when the country is facing an aging population issue. While popular, urbanized in-migrant areas face migrant pressure on social security and economic inequality, rural areas exhibit population aging, higher dependency ratios, and increased social needs and healthcare demands. Consequently, national account allocations to local governments should address these factors to bridge the inequality gap between in-migrant and out-migrant provinces, as well as between the old and the young, the urban and the rural (Heshmati & Rashidghalam, 2020).

The dependency ratio demonstrates each urban-class population's socio-economic pressure, cast from the old-age and child upon the working-age segment. This ratio is determined by the urban cities' fertility and mortality rates, as well as migration patterns (Rodriguez, 1988). Rural and small urban settings face higher fertility rates that grow population without migration in working age (GSO & UNFPA, 2020). Notably, rural areas overall face a 50% dependency ratio, where one person in working-age faces dependency from two old-age and child inhabitants. Thus, one could hypothesize that the working-age population residing in rural areas face more pressure in maintaining overall social well-being for elders and children in their areas. This pressure could be eased by urban–rural knowledge and resource transfer because of prior rural–urban migration (McKenzie & Sasin, 2007).

The dependency ratio also poses a crucial question regarding Vietnam's population growth and demographics. It has been predicted that the Vietnamese population will become an "aged population" in 2036 when the 65 + age group accounts for 14% of total population, while the country's "demographic window," with decreasing fertility and stable old-age group, ending by 2039 (Andrews & Philips, 2005; GSO & UNFPA, 2021; United Nations, 2004). With an increasing dependency ratio trend, Vietnam faces policy challenges to tackle development sustainability, particularly balanced development between urban and rural areas.

It is also observed that individuals in special-class cities enter their first marriage at around 27.5 years old, which is 2.5 years higher than corresponding age groups in class III-V cities. This delayed marriage trend in urban areas is attributable to greater pressures of employment, income, and the trade-off for education and training clearly witnessed in urban settings compared to rural regions (Duong, 2023; GSO & UNFPA, 2020).

This socio-economic pressure is in turn manifested in labor force quality. Special-class cities possess the largest share of labor force holding university degrees or higher qualifications. A quarter of special-class cities' 15-and-older population holds advanced degrees, which is 5.5 times higher than rural areas (GSO & UNFPA, 2020). Accordingly, to achieve balanced urban–rural development in Vietnam, aligned with aging demographic issue, public policies for less-urbanized areas' socioeconomic development are essential to encourage skilled individuals with qualifications to come and work in rural and smaller urban centers.

Apart from labor force education and vocational quality, other socio-economic challenge associated with urbanization are unemployment, as earlier described in Sect. 2. As a developing country, the unemployment rate in Vietnam appears consistently low, especially when measured against more developed economies. This phenomenon is attributable to the modest income base (Nguyen, 2016). Vietnam's labor supply displays a persistent willingness to seek employment opportunities and accept jobs that differ from their preferences or expertise. This reflects the mindset and need to provide for themselves and their close ones (GSO & UNFPA, 2020).

Vietnam's 2019 Population Census shows that the unemployment rate among individuals aged 15 + is 2.05%. Among these, the significant difference between urban and rural areas is noteworthy. In urban areas, the unemployment rate is considerably higher at 2.74%, whereas unemployment in rural areas is notably lower at 1.62%. Special-class cities exhibit the highest rate at 3.17%, followed by class-I cities with a rate of 3.03% (GSO & UNFPA, 2020). This discrepancy underscores the complex dynamics of employment in Vietnam. Migrants flock to urban agglomerations for work, leading to a larger workforce and higher ratio of qualified workers, nonetheless increasing the unemployment rate in these areas as well. This issue reflects the substantial employment pressure on urban centers to create job opportunities, especially for young workers. Addressing this issue would not only contribute to economic development but also help mitigate social issues stemming from underemployment.

On the other hand, special-class cities, where the unemployment rate is the highest, witness the lowest proportion of workers in low-skilled jobs. This reflects the nature of Vietnam's labor force, where most people are classified as "employed" residing in rural areas work in agricultural or low-skilled jobs. This poses questions regarding future workforce's quality and economic structure that depends on outsourced manufacturing and assembling, rather than innovation and high-skilled expertise. Approximately, one-third of Vietnam's workforce is engaged in low-skilled jobs. This proportion varies significantly between urban and rural areas, with urban areas recording a rate of 16%. Rural areas, with only 12.2% of technical qualifications ratio for population aged 15 +, see a substantial share of workers in low-skilled jobs, reaching 43.5% (GSO & UNFPA, 2020). This is nearly three times higher than in urban areas in general. This trend reflects Vietnam's distinct rural employment characteristics, where low-skilled jobs are primarily in agricultural, forestry, and fishing activities. Thus, rural areas face fewer job opportunities with lower incomes, resulting in acceptance of low-skilled or undesirable jobs.

However, in recent years, higher-skilled job categories are starting to dominate the fastest growing occupations. Thus, the high unemployment rates that raise concerns regarding skill mismatch between labor supply and demand could be gradually reflected in Vietnam's job market transition, particularly in foreign-owned and domestic, private sectors (Demombynes & Testaverde, 2018). In terms of gender, females come across more challenges in job search, as their unemployment rate continues to overweigh that of males across all urban centers' classes (GSO & UNFPA, 2020). Research concerning Vietnam's key labor market aspects observes a similar issue, where women and ethnic minorities have lower probability of wage jobs. Those who receive job income also face income inequality issues, despite the declining wage gap for women (Demombynes & Testaverde, 2018).

6 Conclusion

A balanced growth relation between urban and rural areas needs to be achieved for Vietnam to avoid the reversal threshold after which urbanization turn to become an economic hindrance. In our study, we have provided descriptive and regression analysis to demonstrate the causes and effects of urbanization. Natural population growth, migration, and administrative factors all have a significant effect on urbanization, which in turn influences economic growth. While urbanization normally fosters growth, it poses sustainable development challenges regarding social welfare, labor force quality and unemployment, urban's higher marriage age and lower fertility and rural' s higher dependency ratio and lower service availability.

Aside from urban investment that benefits major cities, the Vietnam's government should devise balanced investment strategies for smaller city classes and rural provinces to promote sustainable development. This investment strategy will lower migrants' socioeconomic pressure on urban agglomerates. Meanwhile, Vietnam's urban development legal framework should be constantly adapted and developed, given the ever-growing urban population, to avoid concentrated investments that overlap or become inadequate in important development initiatives. This should be reflected in nationwide urban–rural infrastructure development, as well as balanced national account allocations between provinces and cities to maintain equality in provincial development opportunities.

Appendix

List of 63 cities and provinces with matching regions as subjects of study in the paper

Index	Province name	Region
1	Hà Nội	Red River Delta
2	Vĩnh Phúc	
3	B´ăc Ninh	
4	Quảng Ninh	
5	Hải Dương	
6	Hải Phòng	
7	Hưng Yên	
8	Thái Bình	
9	Hà Nam	
10	Nam Định	
11	Ninh Bình	
12	Hà Giang	Northern midlands and mountain areas
13	Cao B`ăng	
14	B´ăc Kạn	
15	Tuyên Quang	
16	Lào Cai	
17	Yên Bái	
18	Thái Nguyên	
19	Lạng Sơn	
20	B´ăc Giang	
21	Phú Thọ	
22	Điện Biên	
23	Lai Châu	
24	Sơn La	
25	Hòa Bình	
26	Thanh Hóa	North Central and Central Coastal areas
27	Nghệ An	
28	Hà Tĩnh	

(continued)

(continued)

Index	Province name	Region
29	Quảng Bình	
30	Quảng Trị	
31	Th`ưa Thiên—Huế	
32	Đà N˜ăng	
33	Quảng Nam	
34	Quảng Ngãi	
35	Bình Định	
36	Phú Yên	
37	Khánh Hòa	
38	Ninh Thuận	
39	Bình Thuận	
40	Kon Tum	Central Highlands
41	Gia Lai	
42	Đ´ăk L´ăk	
43	Đ´ăk Nông	
44	Lâm Đồng	
45	Bình Phư´ơc	Southeast
46	Tây Ninh	
47	Bình Dương	
48	Đồng Nai	
49	Bà Rịa—Vũng Tàu	
50	TP. Hồ Chí Minh	
51	Long An	Mekong River Delta
52	Tiền Giang	
53	Bến Tre	
54	Trà Vinh	
55	Vĩnh Long	
56	Đồng Tháp	
57	An Giang	
58	Kiên Giang	
59	Cần Thơ	
60	Hậu Giang	
61	Sóc Trăng	
62	Bạc Liêu	
63	Cà Mau	

References

Aghion, P., & Howitt, P. (2009). *The economics of growth.* MIT Press.

Alam, S., Fatima, A., & Butt, M. S. (2007). Sustainable development in Pakistan in the context of energy consumption demand and environmental degradation. *Journal of Asian Economics, 18*(5), 825–837.

Andrews, G. J., & Philips, D. R. (Eds.). (2005). *Ageing and place: Perspectives, policy, practice.* Routledge.

Arouri, M., Ben Youssef, M., Cuong, N. V., & Soucat, A. (2014). Effects of urbanization on economic growth and human capital formation in Africa. *PGDA Working Paper No. 119.*

Bacolod, M., Blum, B. S., & Strange, W. C. (2010). Elements of skill: Traits, intelligences, education, and agglomeration. *Journal of Regional Science, 50*(1), 245–280.

Bertinelli, L., & Black, D. (2004). Urbanization and growth. *Journal of Urban Economics, 56*(1), 80–96.

Bloom, D. E., Canning, D., & Fink, G. (2008). Urbanization and the wealth of nations. *Science, 319*(5864), 772–775.

Bloom, D. E., Canning, D., Fink, G., Khanna, T., & Salyer, P. (2010). Urban settlement: data, measures, and trends. *UNU-WIDER Working Paper No. WP2010/12, Working Paper Series.* World Institute for Development Economic Research (UNU-WIDER).

Bodo, T. (2019). Rapid urbanisation: Theories, causes, consequences and coping strategies. *Geographical Studies, 2*(3), 32–45.

Brulhart, M., & Sbergami, F. (2009). Agglomeration and growth: Cross-country evidence. *Journal of Urban Economics, 65*(1), 48–63.

Bui, D. D., Kawamura, A., Tong, T. N., Amaguchi, H., & Trinh, T. M. (2012). Aquifer system for potential groundwater resources in Hanoi, Vietnam. *Hydrological Processes, 26*, 932–946. https://doi.org/10.1002/hyp.8305

Chang, G. H., & Brada, J. C. (2006). The paradox of China's growing under urbanization. *Economic Systems, 30*(1), 24–40.

Cohen, B. (2004). Urban growth in developing countries: A review of current trends and a caution regarding existing forecasts. *World Development, 32*(1), 23–51.

Dao, B. (2020). Education and economic growth in Vietnam. *Journal of Education and Practice, 11*(6), 10–22.

Demombynes, G., & Testaverde, M. (2018). Employment structure and returns to skill in Vietnam: Estimates using the labor force survey. *World Bank Policy Research Working Paper No. 8364.* Available at SSRN: https://ssrn.com/abstract=3139156

Duong, T. M. (2023). Navigating personal priorities: Marriage indifference among Vietnamese youth. OSF Preprints. https://doi.org/10.31219/osf.io/7adbk

Fatima, Z. (2022). *An empirical analysis of urbanization and economic growth in South Asian countries.* Unpublished. Microsoft Word—Zanib My_Final_thesis Edited (1).docx (diva-portal.org).

Fay, M., & Opal, C. (2000). Urbanization without growth: a not so uncommon phenomenon. *Policy Research Working Paper No. 2412.* World Bank.

Friedmann, J. (2006). Four theses in the study of China's urbanization. *International Journal of Urban and Regional Research, 30*(2), 440–451.

Fujita, M., Krugman, P., & Mori, T. (1999). On the evolution of hierarchical urban systems. *European Economic Review, 43*(2), 209–251.

Glaeser, E. L., Rosenthal, S. S., & Strange, W. C. (2010). Urban economics and entrepreneurship. *Journal of Urban Economics, 67*(1), 1–14.

GSO. (2021). *Major findings: The 1/4/2021 time—point population change and family planning survey.* General Statistics Office, Hanoi. https://www.gso.gov.vn/en/highlight/2022/12/major-findings-the-1-4-2021-time-point-population-change-and-family-planning-survey/

GSO & UNFPA (2020). *The population and housing census 2019: Migration and urbanization: Situation, trends and differences.* Ha Noi, Viet Nam. https://vietnam.unfpa.org/sites/default/files/pub-pdf/di_cu_va_do_thi_hoa_eng.pdf

GSO & UNFPA. (2021). *The population and housing census 2019: Population ageing and older persons in Viet Nam*. General Statistics Office, Hanoi. https://www.gso.gov.vn/wp-content/uploads/2021/08/Dan-so-gia-hoaEN.pdf

Hausman, J. A. (1978). Specification tests in econometrics. *Econometrica, 46*(6), 1251–1271. https://doi.org/10.2307/1913827

Henderson, V. (2002). Urban primacy, external costs, and quality of life. *Resource and Energy Economics, 24*(1–2), 95–106.

Henderson, V. (2003). The urbanization process and economic growth: The so what question. *Journal of Economic Growth, 8*(1), 47–71.

Heshmati, A., & Rashidghalam, M. (2020). Measurement and analysis of urban infrastructure and its effects on urbanization in China. *Journal of Infrastructure Systems, 26*(1). https://doi.org/10.1061/(ASCE)IS.1943-555X.0000513

IFAD. (2016). Policy case study: Viet Nam—Review of experience of the National Target Program for new rural development. https://www.ifad.org/es/web/knowledge/-/publication/policy-case-study-viet-nam-review-of-experience-of-the-national-target-program-for-new-rural-development

Kadyraliev, A., et al. (2022). Investment in transport infrastructure as a factor of stimulation of economic development. *Transportation Research Procedia, 63*, 1359–1369.

Kolomak, E. (2012). Urbanization and economic development in Russia. In *ERSA Conference Papers No. ersa12p82*. European Regional Science Association.

Krugman, P. (1991). Increasing returns and economic geography. *Journal of Political Economy, 99*(3), 483–499.

Kumar, A., & Kober, B. (2012). Urbanization, human capital, and cross-country productivity differences. *Economics Letters, 117*(1), 14–17.

Lewis, B. D. (2014). Urbanization and economic growth in Indonesia: Good news, bad news and (Possible) local government mitigation. *Regional Studies, 48*(1), 192–207.

Long, N. (2020). *Urban exodus, a new trend among young Vietnamese*. VnExpress. https://e.vnexpress.net/news/life/trend/urban-exodus-a-new-trend-among-young-vietnamese-4175501.html

McKenzie, D., & Sasin, M. (2007). Migration, remittances, poverty, and human capital: conceptual and empirical challenges. *Policy Research Working Paper No. 4272*. The World Bank.

Ministry of Construction. (2013). Classification of urban criteria. https://moc.gov.vn/en/news/45813/classification-of-urban-criteria.aspx

Ministry of Construction. (2023a). Hanoi strives to raise urbanisation rate to 75% by 2030. http://moc.gov.vn/vn/tin-tuc/1273/77496/hanoi-strives-to-raise-urbanisation-rate-to-75-by-2030.aspx

Ministry of Construction. (2023b). Workshop on "consultation on appraisal urban and rural system planning for the period 2021–2030, with a vision to 2050". http://moc.gov.vn/vn/tin-tuc/1274/77599/workshop-on-consultation-on-appraisal-urban-and-rural-system-planning-for-the-period-2021---2030--with-a-vision-to-2050-318.aspx

Ministry of Construction. (2023c). Bac Ninh ordered to become a city with modern industry, high technology. https://moc.gov.vn/en/news/77508/bac-ninh-ordered-to-become-city-with-modern-industry-high-technology.aspx

Nguyen, H. M., & Nguyen, L. D. (2018). The relationship between urbanization and economic growth: An empirical study on ASEAN countries. *International Journal of Social Economics, 45*(2), 316–339. https://doi.org/10.1108/IJSE-12-2016-0358

Nguyen, H. Q. (2016). Relationship between economic growth, unemployment and poverty: Analysis at provincial level in Vietnam. *International Journal of Economics and Finance, 8*(12), 113–119.

OECD. (2015). Key issues affecting youth in Viet Nam. https://www.oecd.org/dev/inclusive-societies-development/youth-issues-in-vietnam.htm

PCI. (2022). The provincial competitiveness index. PCI. Available at: The provincial competitiveness index (PCI) (pcivietnam.vn)

Rodriguez, A. (1988). The dependency ratio and optimum population growth: The total utility case. *Journal of Population Economics, 1*(2), 141–156.
United Nations. (2004). *World POPULATION to 2300.*
United Nations. (2006). *World urbanization prospects: The 2005 revision population database.* UN.
World Bank. (2020). *Vietnam's urbanization at a crossroads: Embarking on an efficient, inclusive, and resilient pathway*, Other Urban Studies. The World Bank. https://doi.org/10.1596/34761
World Bank. (2009). *World development report 2009: Reshaping economic geography.* The World Bank.

Nhu Nam Do holds a Bachelor of Economics and Finance from Royal Melbourne Institute of Technology (RMIT). He is currently working in Vietnam's banking industry as a business analyst for Commercial Banking function. His research areas of interest include Vietnam's sustainable socio-economic development and financial markets. He is currently pursuing MSc study in Applied Economics at the University of Economics, Ho Chi Minh City (UEH) – Vietnam - the Netherlands Programme.

Quang Dong Quan Le has a bachelor's degree in Economics and Management from Toulouse I University. Post-graduation, she served as a research assistant at Vietnam Center of Research in Economics, Management, and Environment, under the supervision of Manh-Hung NGUYEN (Ph.D). She has 13 years of working experience, with exposure in hospitality, customer service, and marketing. She is currently operating her own business in consulting and managerial services. She is currently pursuing MSc study in Applied Economics at the University of Economics Ho Chi Minh City (UEH) – Vietnam-Netherlands Program.

Part VI
Productivity Growth

Chapter 14
The Relationship Between Intellectual Property Rights Protection and Economic Development in Vietnam

Tung Lam Ha

Abstract This study examines the relationship between intellectual property rights and economic development in Vietnam. Through Doi-Moi reform period, which is from mid to late 1980, Vietnam has made significant strides in transforming its economy to the adoption of free-market principles. The reforms implemented aimed to establish property rights protection, recognize private ownership, and provide a legal framework to protect these rights. In Vietnam, land-use rights are of utmost importance for individuals and businesses entering the market, particularly due to the country's historical reliance on agriculture. However, there is a growing alarm regarding the potential loss of highly skilled individuals, such as intellectuals, scientists, researchers, and creative professionals like musicians. This event happened due to their works and creations not being protected enough by law, specifically intellectual property rights laws. Currently, the framework surrounding intellectual property rights in Vietnam is relatively loose and it lacks enforcement measures, leading to minimal protection and enforcement of these rights. Intellectual property rights laws reform is also one of the three focus areas of the 2023 Vietnam government considering law reforms. Therefore, as discussion and analysis of historical and future relationship between property rights and economic development in Vietnam, this study will investigate these two rights' development based on main events and released new laws with the shifting in economic situation associated with Covid-19 or potential global or regional conflicts.

Keywords Intellectual property rights · Economic development · Doi-Moi reform · Vietnam

---

T. L. Ha (✉)
University of Economics Ho Chi Minh City, Ho Chi Minh City, Vietnam
e-mail: lam.ht@vnp.edu.vn

Vietnam - the Netherlands Programme, Ho Chi Minh City, Vietnam

P. K. Nam and A. Heshmati (eds.), *Recent Trends in Vietnam's Rapid Economic Development*, Frontiers in South and Southeast Asian Development Research,
https://doi.org/10.1007/978-981-97-6079-4_14

1 Introduction

This essay examines the relationship between intellectual property rights and economic development in Vietnam. The transformative journey of Vietnam's economy, which commenced during the mid to late 1980s through the Doi-Moi reform period, is symbolic of a nation embracing free-market principles. This pivotal era in Vietnam's history witnessed a series of reforms aimed at establishing robust property rights protection, acknowledging private ownership, and enacting a comprehensive legal framework to safeguard these rights. Among the various facets of property rights, land-use rights assume paramount significance, especially in a country with a deep-rooted agricultural heritage like Vietnam. Enforcement of land-use rights reform then supported the miracle growth of Vietnam in the past 30 years with real estate and infrastructure development as indisputable pillar.

Vietnam faces the threat of losing many highly skilled individuals, including intellectuals, scientists, researchers, and creative professionals like musicians. This emigration stems from a fundamental issue—insufficient protection of their intellectual creations and works under the prevailing legal framework, specifically in the realm of intellectual property rights. Vietnam's intellectual property rights laws are currently lax and lack strong enforcement, leading to poor protection of these rights.

The pressing need for reform in intellectual property rights laws has not gone unnoticed by the Vietnamese government. In fact, it ranks among the top three priority areas for legal reforms in 2023. Consequently, this research scrutinizes the historical and prospective interplay between property rights, encompassing intellectual property rights (IPRs), and the trajectory of economic development in Vietnam. We focus on key development events and the introduction of the new laws, while excluding factors like the Covid-19 pandemic and potential global or regional conflicts, to provide a clear analysis.

Section 2 explains the Doi-Moi reforms, the genesis property rights, and its importance to foster economic development. IPRs in Vietnam, the current landscape and challenges are presented in Sect. 3. This follows discussion of urgency of intellectual property rights reform in Sect. 4. Assessment of the impact on economic development is found in Sect. 5. Challenges and potential pitfalls are discussed in Sect. 6. The final section concludes.

2 The Doi-Moi Reforms and the Emergence of Property Rights

The implementation of the Doi-Moi reforms in the mid-1980s marked a significant turning point in Vietnam's socio-economic development. At this time, the nation transitioned from a centrally planned economy to one that embraced free-market principles. Central to this transformation was the recognition of the importance of property rights in fostering economic development.

During this era, Vietnam started a series of policy changes aimed at property rights reform. This included the recognition of private property ownership, a fundamental shift from the previous collectivist ideology. Individuals and entities were granted greater autonomy over their property, leading to an increase in economic activity as entrepreneurs and businesses gained the confidence to invest and innovate.

Land-use rights emerged as a central component of property rights in Vietnam. Historically, agriculture played a pivotal role in the Vietnamese economy, making land-use rights a critical factor in the economic landscape. The reforms in land-use rights allocation allowed farmers greater control over their land, thereby incentivizing increased agricultural productivity. This shift marked a turning point in Vietnam's agricultural sector, contributing significantly to the nation's economic growth.

3 IPRs in Vietnam: Current Landscape and Challenges

Vietnam's progress in economic development, driven by economic and legal reforms, has indeed been remarkable. Over time, it has become clear that establishing a solid foundation is crucial for people to thrive. In essence, acknowledging and protecting property rights, with land-use rights at the core, provides a strong basis for economic growth. However, a pressing issue persists, or we could say emerge strongly in the 4.0 industry age, where digital assets and artificial intelligence generated (or comprised) assets challenging the normal property rights, the inadequacy of Vietnam's IPRs framework. This section examines the current landscape of IPRs in Vietnam and lay out the possible challenges it has faced and may continue to face, many of which might not yet have the "correct" answer.

3.1 Lax Enforcement and Its Consequences

Despite Vietnam's reputation as a hub for innovation and creativity, its IPRs framework remains relatively loose and under-enforced. This inherent weak enforcement has resulted in losing of intellectual asset "creators", which may include:

Piracy and Infringement: Creative professionals like artists, musicians, writers, and software developers face widespread piracy and intellectual property infringement. Despite their efforts to create innovative works, they often struggle to protect their creations. Counterfeit products and unauthorized reproductions of copyrighted content flood the market, causing significant financial losses and discouragement among creators.

Innovation and Research: Innovators and inventors find themselves in a precarious position. The limited protection afforded to their intellectual creations dissuades them from investing in research and development. The fear of seeing their inventions copied or their ideas stolen looms large, leading to a reluctance to embark on pioneering projects. Consequently, this hampers the nation's potential for technological advancement and the creation of cutting-edge products and services.

All the problems above are existing problems without challenging from open-source AI or digital asset, and the problems is more damaging for the economy when considering the losing economic benefits of applied technology in manufacturing, chips, clean energy, circular energy, etc., "running out" of the country. Companies would be less likely to invest in research in generally, or research in Vietnam. This would reduce Vietnam's chance of achieving its goal of becoming a global technology hub and a developed country.

3.2 Deterrents for Foreign Investment and Technology Transfer

Beyond the domestic ramifications, Vietnam's lax IPRs framework poses a significant deterrent to foreign investment and technology transfer.

Foreign Companies' Hesitation: Foreign companies, while recognizing Vietnam's burgeoning market potential, are often cautious about entering the Vietnamese market or engaging in collaborations with local entities. This wariness stems from the risk of intellectual property theft, as they fear that their proprietary technologies and innovations may be vulnerable to exploitation. This hesitance translates into missed opportunities for Vietnam to attract foreign investment and to leverage external expertise.

Technology Diffusion and Global Integration: The integration of Vietnam into the global innovation ecosystem faces impediments due to the underdeveloped IPRs environment. Effective technology diffusion from foreign companies into the local economy is stymied, thereby hindering the nation's ability to keep pace with global technological advancements. As a result, Vietnam's long-term competitiveness in the international arena remains compromised.

The urgency of addressing these challenges cannot be overstated. While Vietnam's economic development trajectory is promising, the lack of robust IPRs protection threatens to stunt its growth potential. Without tangible reforms in this crucial area, the nation risks squandering its creative and innovative potential and missing out on the economic benefits of a thriving intellectual property ecosystem.

Even though the challenges seem to be dire, the actual reform may be very different than what we expected. The comparison or learning figure of Vietnam is our considered successful predecessor, China. The following section will explore Ginarte and Park (1997) model, the research on what and how China treats IPRs and enforcements, the relationship between proposed reforms in IPRs laws, and their potential impact on Vietnam's economic development. The proactive steps taken in this regard signify a pivotal moment in Vietnam's quest for economic progress and global recognition in the realm of intellectual property protection.

4 IPRs Reform: Urgent Need or Still in the Future

Vietnam stands at a pivotal point in its economic development and urgently needs comprehensive reform of its IPRs. Recognizing the indispensable role of IPRs in fostering economic growth and innovation, the Vietnamese government has taken a bold step by prioritizing this vital issue in its legislative agenda for 2023. This commitment reflects a keen awareness of the shortcomings within the current legal framework and the imperative to bring Vietnam in alignment with international standards in intellectual property protection. However, to have the objective view of this question, we can look at international standards and commonly used index, using China as a case study.

4.1 IPRs Index: Ginarte and Park Model

Ginarte and Park (1997) used econometric analysis to investigate the empirical variables affecting their index. Their research showed that numerous important factors were positively connected with the durability of patent rights over time and across nations. Real GDP per capita, the percentage of GDP devoted to research and development (R&D), the degree of openness to international commerce, and a metric used to measure how free the market was from arbitrary and opaque government rules were some of these factors. Additionally, they discovered that patent rights were positively and significantly impacted by human capital, as shown by the ratio of secondary school attendance in a previous time. Habib et al. (2019) empirically analyze whether human capital, intellectual property rights, and research and development expenditures are important for total factor productivity.

These findings suggest that the evolution of patent rights is responsive to increasing demands for protection. This is because countries with higher levels of R&D investment and human capital tend to have stronger patent rights indexes. The intriguing aspect of their research is the positive influence of trade openness, which can be interpreted in various ways. It may indicate that open economies are more inclined to provide robust protection for IPRs (IPRs) because these protections help safeguard access to a broader range of consumer choices. Alternatively, it could suggest that in open economies, international trade and innovative endeavors interact positively, creating a greater demand for intellectual property protection.

Using this Ginarte and Park model, Sattar and Mahmood (2011) study 38 countries with different segments of income and development over the period of 1975–2005. They find out although IPRs have significant positive relation with the economic growth with increasing effect on higher income countries. The findings could mean the significant correlation between the IPRs and economic growth but not verify the causal impact. The challenging evidence will be the case of China.

4.2 IPRs in China: The Successful Predecessor

IPRs violations due to ignorance or lax enforcement have significantly impacted China's economy in the twenty-first century. Surprisingly, China takes advantage of it and leads rapid economic growth and innovation, particularly in the technology and manufacturing sectors. The list of factors includes wise trading policies, tax incentives, biggest market as well as cheap labor force with natural resource and more. As to spot the astounding element in the long list of why China success, China's ability to quickly adopt and adapt foreign technologies is stand out. This ability has been facilitated by lax enforcement, allowing foreign companies to "share" their technology and intellectual property with Chinese partners, sometimes unwillingly. This has allowed Chinese companies to rapidly acquire knowledge and develop their capabilities in areas like electronics, telecommunications, and manufacturing. However, this success has come at the expense of foreign companies who have seen their intellectual property stolen or used without proper compensation, leading to concerns about the sustainability of this model. International scrutiny and backlash have led to trade disputes, tariffs, and tensions between China and its trading partners.

China has success which proves the weak enforcement on IPRs to be an amazing "cheating" way in catching up and surpass in some of the technology. China must now face its long-term impacts of losing trust. Controlling key resources and market, China moves fast to be self-sufficient developed economic powerhouse.

The violations of IPRs due to ignorance or lax enforcement in China case therefore have played a double-edged role in supporting China's economy in the twenty-first century. While it has contributed to rapid economic growth and technological advancement, it has also led to international disputes and raised questions about the sustainability of China's economic model. By learning about China, Vietnam can better find its path to globalization.

Hong et al. (2022) analyze the evolution of the Chinese intellectual property rights system, the IPR legislation revisions and enforcement. The economic openness, economic development, and membership in the World Trade Organization induced radical changes in the laws and its enforcement. The study shows that patent law, trademark law, and copyright law have substantially enhanced since 2000. The Chinese IPR legislation, its development, and enforcements, as well as IPR infringement cases and their handling can be informative for Vietnam in its smooth and effective transformation of the national IPR system.

4.3 IPRs in Vietnam: A Very Different Branching

Vietnam has learnt and followed closely on China and other success nations' policies. However, in recent years, Vietnam may consider branching its policy of IPRs enforcement differently from China due to several reasons like development stages, internal market power, and market accessibility.

Vietnam and China are at different stages of economic development. China has already achieved a higher level of economic development and technological advancement. In contrast, Vietnam is still in the process of industrialization and catching up. As such, Vietnam may prioritize attracting foreign investment and technology transfer to accelerate its economic growth, making robust IPRs enforcement more attractive. IPRs' protection is mostly a part of international agreements and treaties. Adhering to these agreements can enhance Vietnam's global reputation, boost foreign investment, and promote technological advancements.

Moreover, no matter how closely Vietnam is to China, Vietnam's economic model and development strategies have branched different from China. Vietnam has smaller internal market as well as labor force. The Vietnamese economy is not yet an essential part of the global manufacturing and service industry. In fact, Vietnam is trying to be in the values creating chain of the Western world, learning from China's hurtful lessons. Despite dissimilarities between China and Vietnam, since main share of recent foreign direct investment to Vietnam is relocated from China, a deeper analysis of the challenges faced by China during the IPR evolution process can ease the IPR convergence to meet the Western world's standard.

Maintaining a reputation for respecting IPRs now plays a crucial factor in supporting Vietnam access global markets more easily. Many international companies are cautious about operating in regions with lax IPRs' enforcement due to concerns about their intellectual property being compromised, especially when it comes to high-value products and the locations of their research centers. Finding a balance between promoting national technology advancements and protecting international (and local) IPRs will be crucial for Vietnam's long-term economic success.

4.4 Bolstering the Legal Framework

The cornerstone of the proposed IPRs reform in Vietnam revolves around the strengthening of the legal framework governing IPRs. At present, the existing legal provisions are deemed insufficient to provide robust protection and clear guidance for intellectual property owners. Therefore, one of the key objectives of the reform is to revise and augment existing laws while introducing new legislation that comprehensively addresses the multifaceted aspects of IPRs.

These amendments and additions to the legal framework aim to create a more conducive environment for intellectual property owners to safeguard their creations. By clarifying ownership rights, delineating the boundaries of fair use, and establishing mechanisms for resolving disputes, the reforms will foster a more predictable and secure landscape for innovators, artists, and creators.

4.5 Enhancing Enforcement Mechanisms

One of the paramount challenges in Vietnam's IPRs landscape is the inadequacy of enforcement mechanisms. Recognizing this, the proposed reforms are committed to establishing more robust enforcement procedures. A fundamental element of this endeavor is the introduction of stricter penalties for IPRs infringement. By increasing the severity of penalties, such as fines and potential criminal charges, the government aims to create a strong deterrent against intellectual property theft and unauthorized reproduction. Moreover, enhanced coordination among law enforcement agencies will be pivotal in ensuring a swift and effective response to violations. This will not only protect the interests of intellectual property owners but also foster an environment where innovators can confidently invest in their creative endeavors without constant fear of piracy or infringement.

4.6 Fostering a Culture of Innovation

Central to the success of IPRs reform in Vietnam is the cultivation of a culture of innovation. These reforms aspire to provide greater incentives for research and development, which are the bedrock of economic progress in a knowledge-driven world. Vietnam's Property Strategy until 2030 and driving forces of intellectual property assets are analyzed in a report by the Intellectual Property Office of Vietnam (IPO, 2020). To achieve this, several measures are envisioned:

Encouraging Patent Applications: The reform aims to simplify and expedite the patent application process, reducing bureaucratic obstacles that have traditionally hindered inventors. This streamlined approach will empower innovators to protect their inventions efficiently.

Protecting Trade Secrets: Recognizing the importance of trade secrets, the reforms will offer more robust protection for confidential business information. This is crucial for industries where maintaining the secrecy of processes and formulations is paramount.

Supporting Innovation-Driven Businesses: Special attention will be directed toward nurturing businesses that rely on innovation. This includes offering financial incentives, grants, and resources to startups and enterprises committed to research and development (see Ha Nguyen & Huyen Vu, 2021).

4.7 International Alignment

In an increasingly interconnected global economy, harmonizing with international standards is essential. Vietnam's reform in IPRs acknowledges this imperative. The government seeks to align the nation's IPRs framework with international agreements and conventions. By doing so, Vietnam not only enhances protection for its domestic creators but also facilitates international cooperation and trade. This alignment with international standards can lead to reciprocal benefits, as it instills confidence in foreign investors and trading partners. A consistent and reliable IPRs regime enhances Vietnam's reputation as a destination for foreign investment and strengthens its position in the global marketplace.

In conclusion, the urgency of IPRs reform in Vietnam cannot be overstated. The proposed measures encompass strengthening the legal framework, enhancing enforcement, promoting innovation, and aligning with international standards. These reforms signal a clear commitment to fostering an environment where intellectual property is protected, innovation is incentivized, and Vietnam can fully participate in the global knowledge economy.

5 Assessing the Impact on Economic Development

The successful implementation of IPRs' reforms is expected to have far-reaching implications for Vietnam's economic development. Locke (2013) provides a review of the literature on the relationship between property rights and economic development. By providing stronger protection for intellectual creations and innovations, these reforms can unlock a wave of economic opportunities:

Attracting Foreign Investment: Strengthened IPRs will instill confidence in foreign investors, encouraging them to bring their capital and technologies to Vietnam. This influx of foreign investment can boost economic growth and create job opportunities. Janjua and Samad (2008) studied intellectual property rights and economic growth in middle-income developing countries.

Fostering Innovation Ecosystem: Robust intellectual property protection will incentivize domestic innovators and entrepreneurs to invest in research and development. This, in turn, can lead to the creation of new industries, products, and services, driving economic diversification.

Promoting Creative Industries: A more secure environment for intellectual property will nurture creative industries such as music, film, and literature. This can contribute not only to economic growth but also to the cultural enrichment of the nation.

Enhancing Trade Relations: Complying with international intellectual property standards will improve Vietnam's standing in global trade. This can facilitate trade agreements and partnerships, opening new export markets and opportunities.

6 Challenges and Potential Pitfalls

While IPRs' reform holds great promise, it is not without challenges and potential pitfalls. Several factors must be considered.

Firstly, striking the right balance between protecting IPRs and fostering access to knowledge and creativity is a delicate task. Overly stringent regulations may stifle innovation and hinder public access to essential information.

Secondly, effective enforcement of IPRs requires well-trained personnel and adequate resources. Building the capacity of relevant government agencies is crucial for the success of these reforms.

Thirdly, raising awareness among the public about the importance of IPRs and the consequence of infringement is essential. This can mitigate the prevalence of piracy and infringement.

Finally, international relations play a significant role. Vietnam must navigate its intellectual property reforms in the context of international relations. This includes addressing concerns from trading partners and ensuring compliance with international agreements.

7 Conclusion

In conclusion, the interplay between property rights, with a special emphasis on IPRs, and economic development in Vietnam is a multifaceted and dynamic relationship. The Doi-Moi reforms of the 1980s marked a pivotal moment in Vietnam's economic history, acknowledging the significance of property rights in fostering growth. However, while progress has been made in recognizing land-use rights, IPRs have languished in terms of protection and enforcement.

The urgency of reforming IPRs laws in Vietnam is underscored by the looming risk of losing highly skilled individuals and the government's commitment to address this issue in its 2023 legislative agenda. By strengthening the legal framework, enhancing enforcement mechanisms, and promoting innovation, Vietnam aims to unlock a new era of economic development.

While challenges and potential pitfalls exist, the potential benefits are immense, including attracting foreign investment, fostering innovation, promoting creative industries, and enhancing trade relations. Striking the right balance between protecting IPRs and promoting access to knowledge will be key to the success of these reforms.

As Vietnam charts its path toward economic development in 2024 and beyond, the evolution of property rights, particularly IPRs, will continue to play a defining role in shaping the nation's innovation capacity, technology, finance, and trade relations with Western nation determining Vietnam's future prosperity and global standing.

References

Ginarte, J. C., & Park, W. G. (1997). Determinants of patent rights: A cross-national study. *Research Policy, 26*(3), 283–301.

Ha Nguyen, T. T., & Huyen Vu, T. T. (2021). *Promoting the innovative startups in Vietnam through the network connecting startup ecosystem actors.*

Habib, M., Abbas, J., & Noman, R. (2019). Are human capital, intellectual property rights, and research and development expenditures really important for total factor productivity? An empirical analysis. *International Journal of Social Economics, 46*(6), 756–774. https://doi.org/10.1108/IJSE-09-2018-0472

Hong, J., Edler, J., & Massini, S. (2022). Evolution of the Chinese intellectual property rights system; IPR law revisions and enforcement. *Management and Organization Review, 18*(4), 755–787.

IPO. (2020). *Vietnam's intellectual property strategy until 2030: Driving force for development of intellectual property assets.* Accessed May 23, 2024 https://www.ipvietnam.gov.vn/web/english/network-of-tiscs-in-universities/institutes/-/asset_publisher/fHvn5xgrngSP/content/viet-nam-s-intellectual-property-strategy-until-2030-driving-force-for-development-of-intellectual-property-assets

Janjua, P. Z., & Samad, G. (2008). Intellectual property rights and economic growth: The case of middle-income developing countries. *The Pakistan Development Review, 46*(4), 711–722.

Locke, A. (2013). *Property rights and development: Property rights and economic development. Briefing Paper, April 2013.* Oversea Development Institute.

Sattar, A., & Mahmood, T. (2011). Journal article intellectual property rights and economic growth: Evidence from high, middle and low income countries. *Pakistan Economics and Social Review, 49*(2), 163–186.

Vietnam—Protecting intellectual property. International Trade Administration|Trade.gov. https://www.trade.gov/country-commercial-guides/vietnam-protecting-intellectual-property

Chapter 15
The Impacts of Trade and FDI on Total Factor Productivity Growth in Vietnam

Anh Ngoc Hai Nguyen and Long Hoang Vo

Abstract Studying Total Factor Productivity (TFP) growth and identifying its drivers have always been crucial for understanding Vietnam's economic development. Given Vietnam's extensive process of economic integration, international trade and inward Foreign Direct Investment (FDI) are recognized as having potential impacts on the country's productivity growth. This study examines the effects of trade and FDI on productivity growth across 24 Vietnamese provinces in the Four Key Economic Zones from 2015 to 2021. Using the DEA-Malmquist Productivity Index, the study decomposes TFP growth into two main components, efficiency change and technological change, aiming to provide a comprehensive evaluation of TFP growth in Vietnam. Additionally, the study employs a Generalized Method of Moments (GMM) technique to jointly examine the impacts of international trade and FDI on TFP growth. The findings show that FDI-induced spillover negatively impacts Vietnam's TFP growth, whereas international trade is a significant driver of TFP growth in Vietnam, regardless of the difficulties arising from the COVID-19 pandemics. These results highlight the importance of effectively managing FDI spillovers and leveraging trade to ensure sustainable productivity growth in Vietnam.

Keywords Productivity · DEA-Malmquist Productivity Index · Dynamic panel model · Trade · FDI · Vietnam

A. N. H. Nguyen · L. H. Vo (✉)
Vietnam—the Netherlands Programme, University of Economics Ho Chi Minh City, Ho Chi Minh City, Vietnam
e-mail: long.vh@vnp.edu.vn

A. N. H. Nguyen
e-mail: anh.nnh@vnp.edu.vn

P. K. Nam and A. Heshmati (eds.), *Recent Trends in Vietnam's Rapid Economic Development*, Frontiers in South and Southeast Asian Development Research,
https://doi.org/10.1007/978-981-97-6079-4_15

1 Introduction and Background

1.1 Introduction

Enhancing a country's economic development through increasing productivity remains a top priority on the agenda of nations. Consequently, extensive research is dedicated to studying the factors that impact Total Factor Productivity (TFP) growth. In the context of globalization and deepening international integration, the consideration of international trade and Foreign Direct Investment (FDI) becomes indispensable when examining their effects on TFP growth. Indeed, the relationship between international trade, FDI, and TFP has been substantiated through numerous studies in the literature.

Regarding the trade and productivity relationship, economic theory points to a positive trade and productivity nexus, as engaging in trade promotes advances in productivity. Trade is indicated to facilitate technology and knowledge spillover and the efficient allocation of resources across sectors, leading to increased aggregate productivity (European Central Bank, 2017). Apart from that, trade expansion is linked to economies of scale, resulting in improved productivity and TFP (Grossman & Helpman, 1991; Krugman, 1981). Furthermore, technological change is believed to be fostered through both imports and exports.

The association between FDI and productivity encompasses arguments for both positive and negative effects. On the one hand, FDI's positive impacts on TFP are considerably documented in the literature about "spillovers" of FDI. Particularly, FDI is considered a key driver of domestic economic development, impacting knowledge and capital transfers, advanced technology use, job creation, and infrastructure development (Gammoudi et al., 2016; Toone, 2013). The dependency theory, on the other hand, posits that the propagation of market capitalism through globalization entails the utilization of advanced technologies in exchange for relatively inexpensive labor. Consequently, economic development in host economies is negatively intertwined with foreign investment. Aitken and Harrison (1999) demonstrated that an increase in foreign presence may hurt the market share held by indigenous firms, compelling them to operate at a less efficient scale.

In the context of Vietnam, the role of TFP in the country's economic development is increasingly significant. According to the General Statistics Office (2020), the contribution of TFP to the economy increased from an average of 33.6% during the 2011–2015 period to approximately 43.5% during the 2016–2020 period. As a result, the nation has set a target to "Increase the contribution of science, technology, and innovation to growth, with TFP accounting for about 45% of GDP by 2025", as stated in "the National Assembly on the economic restructuring plan for the period 2021–2025". To achieve this goal, it is crucial to identify solutions to enhance the growth rate of TFP in Vietnam. In addition, as a country with a relatively high degree of economic integration, demonstrated by its openness level reaching 178.7% in 2022, it is essential to study the impact of international trade and investment on economic development in general and productivity growth in particular. Evidence is scarce regarding the examination of provincial-level effects. There is still limited research that has been conducted on simultaneously investigating the impacts of international trade and FDI on TFP growth in Vietnam.

Building upon the aforementioned growth background of Vietnam, with updated provincial-level data from 24 provinces in Vietnam, this study aims to contribute to the existing literature on the nexus of trades, FDI with its spillovers, and productivity growth amidst the challenges posed by the COVID-19 period. The results of this study underscore the importance of effectively managing FDI and leveraging trade to ensure sustainable and robust productivity growth in Vietnam. Moreover, the findings are expected to serve as a valuable reference for policymakers in optimizing international trade and FDI policies to foster TFP growth, thereby contributing to the country's overall economic development.

The remainder of the paper is structured as follows. The following section provides an overview of Vietnam's international trade and FDI attraction. Next, the literature review section presents the existing empirical research on this topic in Vietnam, both in separate studies and in joint examinations. The data section discusses the data used in this research, while the method section will provide a comprehensive explanation of the proposed methodological concept. Moving forward, the results section discusses the findings, including the estimation of TFP growth using the Malmquist Productivity Index in Vietnam, as well as a detailed examination of the impacts of international trade and FDI on TFP growth. The paper concludes with conclusions and policy recommendations.

1.2 Openness of Vietnam's Economy

Development of international trade performance of Vietnam during the period 2005–2022 is shown in Fig. 1. The trade openness index is computed based on the year 2000 value. The development, with a few exceptions, is positive.

Vietnam is regarded as one of the countries with the highest level of trade openness in the world. Over approximately two decades, Vietnam's trade openness has experienced a significant increase of nearly 49%, rising from 120.1% in 2005 to 178.7% in 2022. This trend serves as evidence of Vietnam's profound integration into the global economy.

Regarding Vietnam's import–export activities, there is a substantial growth in Vietnam's international trade volume over the past 27 years shown in Fig. 2, with a compound annual growth rate (CAGR) of 15.9%. Starting at only 13.6 billion USD in 1995, the trade balance has risen sharply up to 730.2 billion USD in 2022 (53 times higher). In addition, since 2016, Vietnam has always experienced a surplus situation, even during the COVID-19 pandemic period, with a trade surplus of nearly 4 billion USD in the 2020–2021 period. In 2022, FDI accounted for 74.3% and 65% of the export and import shares, respectively. This is attributed to Vietnam's low technological level, particularly in the domestic owned manufacturing sector, which has limited the creation of added value for products.

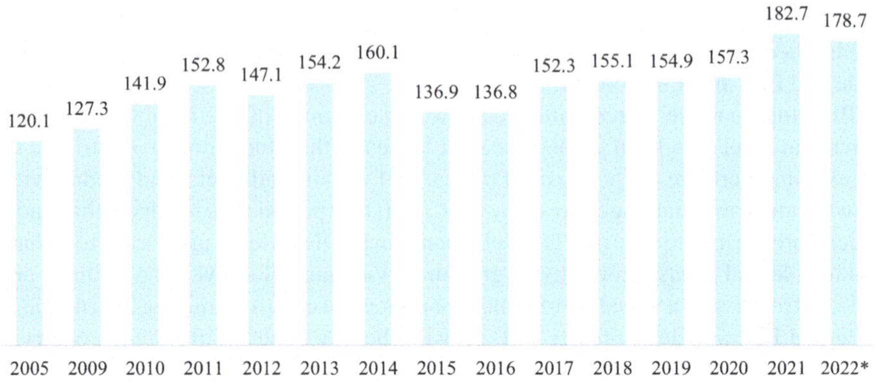

Fig. 1 Vietnam's Trade Openness in 2005–2022 (%). *The preliminary data for 2022. *Source* General Statistics Office of Vietnam

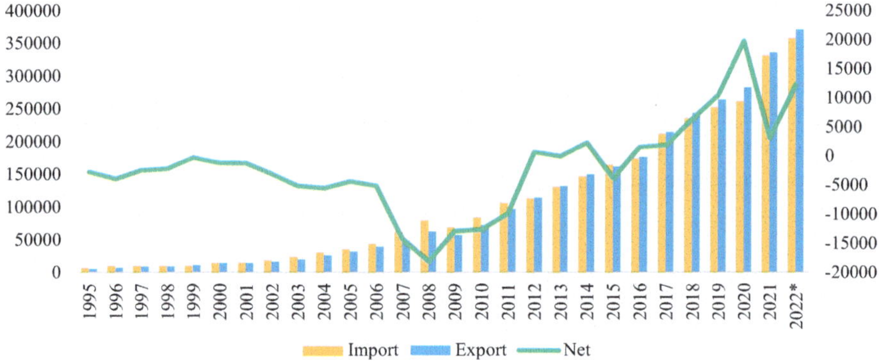

Fig. 2 Vietnam International Trade Situation in 1995–2022 (Million USD). *The preliminary data for 2022. *Source* General Statistics Office of Vietnam

Vietnam's Trading Relations

With a proactive and positive approach to international economic integration, Vietnam has actively engaged in negotiations and signed numerous bilateral and multilateral trade agreements since the 1990s. Particularly, Vietnam has expanded its relationship with around 230 countries and regions. Among them, China, Korea, ASEAN, Japan, the EU, and the USA have consistently remained the top major trading partners. On the other hand, Vietnam is considered to pro-actively participate in many Free Trade Agreements (FTAs). Up to now, Vietnam has had 15 effective FTAs and is currently negotiating two additional FTAs. Additionally, notable achievements include participation in the Comprehensive and Progressive Agreement for Trans-Pacific Partnership (CPTPP) and the EU-Vietnam Free Trade Agreement (EVFTA), which are considered new-generation FTAs. These types of FTAs

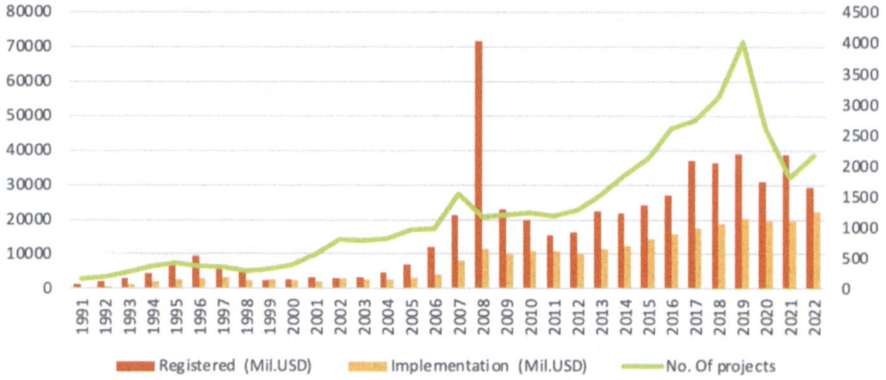

Fig. 3 FDI Attraction Situation in Vietnam (1991–2022), million USD. *Source* General Statistics Office of Vietnam

are believed to establish new standards and trade norms, thereby generating growth momentum for trade among member countries, including Vietnam (Phuong, 2022).

Over the past four decades (1986–2022), Vietnam has been regarded as a successful model in attracting FDI thanks to its attractive business environment, stable political foundation, and high economic growth potential. The total FDI during the period of 1991–2010 was around 20.7 billion USD. Meanwhile, the amount for the 2011–2022 period is approximately 9.4 times higher, reaching 194.4 billion USD, with an average annual inflow of 16.2 billion USD. As of 2022, the implemented FDI reached 22.4 billion USD, which is the highest record in the past five years (Fig. 3).

In general, over three decades, FDI has significantly influenced the Vietnamese economy, leading to notable effects such as fostering economic growth, enhancing employment opportunities, positively impacting exports, and contributing to the state budget. Furthermore, FDI has played a crucial role in creating a competitive environment that stimulates domestic firms to innovate, adopt modern technologies, and transform their business practices. Additionally, FDI has facilitated the transfer of technological advancements to domestic enterprises and has contributed to the improvement of labor quality in Vietnam.

2 Literature Review

Empirical studies of the impact of international trade and FDI on TFP growth in Vietnam are extensively examined. However, due to variations in methodologies, contexts, and data, the conclusions regarding the nexus between international trade, FDI, and TFP in Vietnam are diverse.

In terms of the trade-generated effects on productivity in Vietnam, several studies have identified a positive relationship between trade and TFP at the firm level. Huang and Yang (2016) argued that trade, especially export, has contributed to the growth of FDI firms' TFP in Vietnam. Similarly, Bach (2018) also confirmed the positive linkages between trade and productivity. In examining the localized effects of R&D spillovers in Vietnamese manufacturing, the findings show the crucial roles of trade-embedded foreign R&D spillovers from Japan, the USA, South Korea, and Germany in the manufacturing sector's TFP growth. As for the linkages of FDI-induced effect on TFP, the findings are mixed. On the one hand, some studies proposed that the FDI spillover effect positively influences TFP growth. To illustrate, by employing panel data that cover manufacturing firms over the period 2000–2005, Anwar and Nguyen (2013) explored that the presence of foreign firms was contributing to TFP growth in Vietnam via technological advancement. Le (2015) also proposed that FDI may contribute to boosting local productivity through spillovers, given the evidence on a panel data set covering the period 2005 to 2013. Besides firm-level studies, Huynh et al. (2021) proposed different results on the FDI-TFP growth nexus based on the provincial data level. Generally, the findings found that foreign presence has a positive direct effect on TFP. However, this effect is said to be indirect via the interaction effects of FDI with human capital. This means that better human capital enables provinces to internalize productivity spillover from foreign presence better.

On the other hand, Hien Huynh et al. (2019) found the negative linkages between FDI and TFP growth. By conducting the research on data from manufacturing firms in Vietnam from 2011 to 2015, the authors indicate that despite the benefit from FDI presence through robust backward spillover gained in all regions, and the gains are compensated for by a large magnitude of negative horizontal and forward spillover. This outcome implies the success of domestic firms as suppliers providing acceptable and competitive inputs for foreign firms. Apart from that, absorptive capabilities, especially in human capital, are proven to play a crucial role for FDI spillovers on TFP. This is explained by the consistent and positively robust result shown in the interaction effect of human capital and three spillover channels in the Red River Delta, which is a region featuring a good stock of human capital and highly educated workers. Moreover, similar results were also confirmed by the research of Phuong Nguyen and her partners (Nguyen et al., 2020). Specifically, the research examines the FDI's spillover effects on domestic productivity, using a sample of 537,772 enterprises operating in Vietnam in the 2007–2015 period. Accordingly, the presence of foreign entities is proven to negatively impact domestic firms' productivity, which outweighs the positive effects of technology spillovers (Nguyen et al., 2020).

FDI and trade also exhibit a reverse causality relationship in Vietnam. Many empirical studies have shown a positive correlation between FDI and International Trade (Anwar & Lan, 2011; Pham, 2012). However, there are also some findings showing only unilateral effects of FDI to import or export alone (Bhatt, 2013; Nguyen et al., 2012). On the reverse side, trade implied by Vietnam's participation in FTAs promotes inward FDI are also proved (Choi et al., 2021; Duong et al., 2021; Nguyen and Johnathan, 2002). Based on these considerations, there is a need for comprehensive studies on the relationship between trade, FDI, and TFP growth. However, the number of such studies in Vietnam remains limited. For instance, Ha (2017) conducted an extensive analysis of the relationship between Trade, FDI, and TFP growth in Vietnam, utilizing data from 63 provinces spanning the period of 2006–2014. The findings of this study indicated that both FDI and exports played significant roles in enhancing TFP growth in Vietnamese provinces.

It can be observed that the existing literature on the relationship between international trade, FDI, and TFP growth presents diverse conclusions due to variations in methodology and the subjects studied. In general, positive linkages between trade and TFP growth in Vietnam are mainly proposed in the previous research, particularly about FDI firms, together with the localized effects of trade-embedded R&D spillovers. Conversely, the findings regarding the impacts of FDI have shown both positive and negative impacts on TFP growth in Vietnam. Specifically, the positive effects of FDI on TFP growth are primarily reflected through its spillover effects related to technological advancement. Additionally, the relationship between FDI and TFP has been proven to be indirect, occurring through the interaction effects of FDI with human capital. On the contrary, despite the benefits gained from the presence of FDI through robust backward spillovers observed in all regions, these gains are indicated to be offset by a significant magnitude of negative horizontal and forward spillovers.

In terms of data and method, while numerous studies have examined the nexus between trade, FDI, and TFP at the national and firm levels, evidence regarding the provincial effect is scarce, particularly in the context of Vietnam. Moreover, there is insufficient research on the joint analysis of the effects of international trade and FDI on TFP in Vietnam, which seems to provide a more comprehensive understanding with the consideration of the interrelationship between trade and FDI. Building upon the identified research gap, this study aims to expand the literature, especially considering Vietnam's context, with a joint study of selected channels using updated provincial-level data from 24 provinces of Vietnam, which also took the COVID-19 pandemic period into account.

3 Methodology

Exploring TFP and its determinants among provinces in encouraged to implement policies that can improve outcomes and reduce production inefficiencies. TFP growth rate is calculated via the DEA-Malmquist Productivity Index as specified in Sect. 3.1. The index not only captures productivity changes over time but also assesses the efficiency of each decision-making unit (DMU) relative to its frontier. We consider that every province is a DMU that contributes to the total GDP of the countries. Next, we adopt static and dynamic models for panel data analysis to find factors driving TFP changes over time. Static panel models are applied with a preference for fixed-effects (FE) models after post-estimations. The fixed effect panel model is superior on the theoretical ground and fits with the panel dataset, as it controls time-invariant heterogeneity across countries and provides robust results to omit variable biases (Hausman & Taylor, 1981). Finally, we employ a dynamic panel model (as described in Sect. 3.2) with different GMM and relevant diagnostic tests to handle potential endogeneity among variables (trade openness and FDI).

3.1 DEA-Malmquist Productivity Index

We use the DEA approach for two main reasons. First, DEA is non-parametric and does not require a specific production function like Cobb–Douglas or translog. This avoids the limitations of parameter assumptions and data requirements found in functional-based methods. Second, DEA allows for breaking down overall efficiency and productivity into sub-components, providing a clearer understanding of efficiency dynamics and the factors influencing changes.

The data envelopment analysis method (DEA), developed by Charnes et al. (1978), refers to the use of a mathematical modeling method to calculate the optimal input–output rate of each DMU and evaluate the performance of decision unit by the distance between each DMU and the most efficient units. Meanwhile, the Malmquist Productivity Index is a non-parametric efficiency index developed by Sten Malmquist (1953) based on distance functions. Färe et al. (1992, 1994) then improved the model to measure the TFP change of a DMU between period t and $t+1$ based on DEA, as follows:

$$\begin{aligned}
\text{TFPCH} &= \text{Effch} * \text{Tech} = M^{t+1}\left(x^{t+1}, y^{t+1}, x^t, y^t\right) \\
&= \left[\frac{D^t\left(x^{t+1}, y^{t+1}\right)}{D^t(x^t, y^t)} \times \frac{D^{t+1}\left(x^{t+1}, y^{t+1}\right)}{D^{t+1}(x^t, y^t)}\right]^{\frac{1}{2}} \\
&= \left[\underbrace{\frac{D^{t+1}\left(x^{t+1}, y^{t+1}\right)}{D^t(x^t, y^t)}}_{\text{Effch}}\right] \times \left[\underbrace{\frac{D^t\left(x^{t+1}, y^{t+1}\right)}{D^{t+1}\left(x^{t+1}, y^{t+1}\right)} \times \frac{D^t\left(x^t, y^t\right)}{D^{t+1}(x^t, y^t)}}_{\text{Tech}}\right]^{\frac{1}{2}}.
\end{aligned}$$

The input, output variables, and distance function of t and $t+1$ are represented by x^t, y^t, and D^t and x^{t+1}, y^{t+1}, and D^{t+1}, respectively. TFP between two periods grows when the value of the index is larger than 1, indicating efficient use of inputs to generate optimal output quantities. By contrast, a decline of TFP is indicated as TFPCH < 1. The index can be decomposed the index into technical "efficiency change" (catching up), which reflects movements toward the efficient frontier, and "technological progress" (innovation) that reflects an expansion of production frontiers.

The unit converges toward the production frontier by effectively utilizing current technology when Effch > 1 and vice versa. Techch > 1 denotes the occurrence of technical progress or technological innovation, resulting in a positive shift in the production frontier. Techch < 1 reflects the low level of science and technology adaptation of DMUs to changes in the market environment. In short, a positive change is labeled as technological progress and a negative change technological regress.

3.2 Dynamic Panel Model with GMM

Allison (2009) suggested the inclusion of a lagged first-difference model (LFD) to tackle unobserved heterogeneity and reverse causality. The model is reformulated in terms of first differences, allowing a correlation of x_{it} between two preceding points in time with future values of idiosyncratic error term e_{it} after removing trait-like individual error term α_i (Anderson & Hsiao, 1981).

$$\begin{aligned} y_{it} &= \beta_1 x_{it} + \beta_2 Z_i + \alpha_i + \varepsilon_{it} \\ y_{it-1} &= \beta_1 x_{it-1} + \beta_2 Z_i + \alpha_i + \varepsilon_{it-1} \\ y_{it} - y_{it-1} &= \beta(x_{it-1} - x_{it-2}) + (\varepsilon_{it} - \varepsilon_{it-1}). \end{aligned}$$

In addition to the LFD model, dynamic panel models have been proposed using a lagged-dependent variable (LDV) as an explanatory variable to address endogeneity and elucidate the genuine association between dependent and independent variables over periods of time, as follows:

$$\begin{aligned} y_{it} &= \beta_1 y_{it-1} + \beta_2 x_{it} + \alpha_i + \varepsilon_{it}, \\ \Delta y_{it} &= \beta_1 \Delta y_{it-1} + \beta_2 \Delta x_{it} + \Delta \varepsilon_{it}. \end{aligned}$$

Arellano and Bond (1991) employed the generalized method of moments (GMMs), developed by Hansen in 1982, to introduce all preceding levels of the LDV ($y_{it-2}, y_{it-3} \ldots$) as instruments variable for Δy_{it-1}. Using this framework, Arellano-Bond (AB) dynamic panel model with different GMMs can yield us more consistent estimates in the context of reverse causality. Following the above discussion, our Arellano and Bond dynamic model incorporating one-year lag (1) and its first-differencing form (2) can be prescribed as follows:

$$\text{TFPCH}_{it} = c + \delta \text{TFPCH}_{i,t-1} + \sum_{j=1}^{J} \beta_i X_{it}^j + \sum_{k=1}^{K} \beta_k Y_{it}^k + \sum_{m=1}^{m} \beta_m \Delta Z_{it}^m + e_{it} \quad (1)$$

$$\text{with } \mathrm{e}_{it} = \alpha_i + \varepsilon_{it}$$

$$\Delta\text{TFPCH}_{it} = c + \delta \Delta\text{TFPCH}_{i,t-1} + \sum_{j=1}^{J} \beta_i \Delta X_{it}^j + \sum_{k=1}^{K} \beta_k \Delta Y_{it}^k$$

$$+\sum_{m=1}^{m} \beta_m \Delta Z_{it}^m + \Delta\varepsilon_{it} \tag{2}$$

where TFPCH denotes TFP growth rate of province i at time t and its lagged endogenous variable at time $t-1$, with $i = 1, \ldots, N$, and $t = i, \ldots, T$; c is the constant term; X_{it}^j, Y_{it}^k, Z_{it}^m are exogenous or endogenous explanatory variables; e_{it} is error term with unobserved province-specific effects α_i and idiosyncratic error $\varepsilon_{it} \sim N\left(0; \sigma_\varepsilon^2\right)$.

For a precise GMM specification, the number of instruments should be smaller than the number of groups. The estimate for the autoregressive term of the dependent variable should generate a value lower than the upward-biased OLS estimate and higher than the downward-biased fixed-effects. While the correlation of the residuals in first differences AR1 is tolerable, the detection of second-order serial correlation in differenced error term AR2 (rejecting the null hypothesis) implies the existence of omitted variables in the model (Arellano & Bond, 1991). The validity of instrument variables included in the model is confirmed by the Hansen test for overidentifying restrictions (Roodman, 2009). Failure to reject these null hypotheses supports the choice of instruments. Both values of the Hansen test and AR2 serial correlation test for the above dynamic panel model are also included in table of results. Additionally, the structure of our "small T-large N" panel dataset suggests carrying out the GMM dynamic model with endogenous instruments validated by post-estimations (Roodman, 2009).

4 Data and Variables Description

The dataset is a seven-year balanced panel data (2015–2021) with a sample of 24 provinces in key economic areas of Vietnam, consisting of 168 observations. Data availability has determined the sample size and its composition. Definitions of each variable and corresponding normalization in values are shown in Table 1. Data of gross domestic product (GDP), total working hours, yearly capital investment, growth rate of industrial production quantity, producer price index (PPI) are collected from annual publications of the General Statistical Office of Vietnam. Panel trade values, including imports and exports, are sourced from the yearly reports of the Vietnam Customs Statistics (2023). And yearly reports of FDI are reported by the Ministry of Planning and Investment (MPI, 2023). Number of patents is summarized by Intellectual Property Office of Vietnam (IP Vietnam, 2023). The COVID-19 dummy variable is accounted in our measurement to capture economic shocks during 2020–2021.

The growth rate of TFP between periods (TFPCH) and its components (Effch and Tech) are calculated by DEA-Malmquist Productivity Index analysis (using Gross regional domestic product as output, total working hours, and provincial capital stock as inputs). Observations of TFPCH dropped to 144 due to computation of the growth rate between periods. After estimation, the Index scores of TFP variables are exhibited in Tables 4 and 5, by year and by province, respectively. Stata software

Table 1 Definition of variables at the provincial level

Variable	Explanation	Measurement
lnGDP	Gross regional domestic product, PPI adjusted	Natural logarithm, billion VND
lnhours	Total working hours per year contributed by labor force at 15 years of age and above	Natural logarithm, hours
lncap	Capital stock of provinces, PPI adjusted	Natural logarithm, billion VND
lnFDI	Foreign direct investments by provinces, PPI and exchange rate adjusted	Natural logarithm, billion VND
Tradeopen	Trade openness of provinces, measured by total of import and export divided by adjusted GDP	% of adjusted GDP, percent
Patents	Number of technical solutions, inventions and industrial designs by provinces	Patents
Indus	Index for yearly growth rate of industrial quantity produced within a province	% of previous periods
Covid	Year of COVID-19 pandemic, 0: No Covid/1: present of Covid	Dummy variable
TFPCH	Growth rate of Total Factor Productivity (TFPCH) between periods, measured by DEA-Malmquist analysis; TFPCH = Effch*Tech, with efficiency change (Effch) and technical progress (Tech)	Growth rate scores index for the period of 2015–2021

version 17.0 and R-Studio version 2023.06.1 + 524 are utilized to conduct our growth measurements and its decomposition.

Capital calculation (*K*)

Capital stock data is not available at the provincial level, and only yearly capital investment is published in Vietnamese statistics. Using perpetual inventory methods, by accumulation of investment, the capital stock of province i at year t during 2015–2021 is calculated based on the annual flow of investments and annual depreciation rate, as follows:

$$K_{it} = I_{it} + (1 - \delta)K_{it-1}$$

where δ is a comprehensive depreciation rate of Vietnam's capital stock each year reported in Penn World Table during 1970–2019 (Feenstra et al., 2015). Unlike previous studies, we apply the Autoregressive Integrated Moving Average (ARIMA) model to calculate and forecast depreciation rate for the 2019–2021 period. We found that the depreciation rate of Vietnam's capital stock has averaged 5.6% since 1970, which is like the result of empirical studies in Vietnam (Le, 2009).

Following Sun and Heshmati (2010), the time series of capital stock during 2015–2021 is calculated based on initial capital stock in which data of investments are available. Therefore, a depreciated capital stock at the beginning of the observation period is evaluated as:

$$K_{it} = I_{it} + (1-\delta)I_{it-1} + (1-\delta)^2 I_{it-2} + \cdots$$
$$= \sum_{t}^{\infty} I_{it}(1-\delta)^t = I_{it}\sum_{t}^{\infty}\left[\frac{1-\delta}{1+g}\right]^t \approx I_{it}\left(\frac{1+g}{g+\delta}\right).$$

4.1 Descriptive Statistics

Table 2 summarizes the descriptive summary statistics of interested variables, including the number of observations, mean, median, standard deviation, minimum, and maximum during 2015–2021. A noteworthy observation centers on the uneven allocation of trade openness and patents, as well as quite high standard deviation of FDI and industrial production index among provinces and the time trend. This phenomenon signals heterogeneity among patents, trades, and FDI flows of investigated provinces that may affect efficiency and outcomes of them. Moreover, the mean level of national FDI inflows is reported at 13.466, unexpectedly higher than the mean level of 11.58 in key economic zones. The average level of trade openness within key economic regions stands at 1.621. This level notably surpasses the national average by 8.4 percentage points, as reported by the General Statistics Office (GSO).

It is apparent that TFP and GDP growth rates have been on a declining trajectory throughout the studied period. The mean index (TFPCH) value of 0.942 signifies a deterioration in efficiency year over year. The COVID-19 pandemic that happened

Table 2 Descriptive data

	N	Mean	Median	SD	Min	Max
lnGDP	168	11.698	11.395	0.835	10.442	14.035
lnhours	168	21.480	21.314	0.566	20.729	23.169
lncap	168	12.454	12.321	0.8302	11.030	14.874
TFPCH	144	0.941	0.941	0.063	0.708	1.214
lnFDI	168	11.586	11.661	1.466	6.824	13.832
Patent	168	11.273	1.000	36.422	0.000	245.000
Tradeopen	168	1.621	1.157	1.605	0.1528	8.860
Indus	168	107.573	107.980	7.098	85.710	135.500
Covid	168	0.285	0.000	0.453	0.000	1.000

Fig. 4 Average GDP growth rate, trade openness, and TFPCH. *Source* Authors' calculation

during 2020–2021 is considered to have exerted downward pressure on overall efficiency levels and GDP growth rate (Fig. 4). Therefore, an in-depth exploration into the determinants of TFP aims to enhance provincial efficiency and spur output growth rates in future periods.

4.2 *Correlation Analysis*

Table 3 shows the correlation between variables in this study. Multicollinearity is not severe when the correlation among variables is below 0.8 as a rule of thumb in multicollinearity diagnostics. The coefficients of all independent variables in the dynamic panel model do not exceed the threshold of 0.8 in this study. All Variance of Inflation Factor (VIF) results also advocate non-existence of multicollinearity for all values below 5, as suggested by Hair et al. (2021).

Table 3 Pairwise correlations—VIF

Variables	(1)	(2)	(3)	(4)	(5)	(6)	VIF
(1) TFPCH	1.000						
(2) lnFDI	– 0.137*	1.000					1.564
(3) Tradeopen	– 0.150*	0.416***	1.000				1.433
(4) Patent	– 0.002	0.352***	– 0.049	1.000			1.245
(5) Indus	0.051	– 0.029	0.172**	– 0.068	1.000		1.24
(6) Covid	0.005	0.091	0.061	0.071	– 0.268***	1.000	1.197

$^{***}p < 0.01$, $^{**}p < 0.05$, $^{*}p < 0.1$

Table 4 DEA-Malmquist Productivity Index by year

Year	TFPCH	Effch	Tech
2016	0.879	1.142	0.770
2017	0.981	0.984	0.997
2018	0.952	0.903	1.053
2019	0.952	1.060	0.898
2020	0.947	1.149	0.824
2021	0.937	0.975	0.961
Means	0.941	1.036	0.917

Source Authors' calculation

5 Results and Discussion

5.1 *TFP Growth Rate*

The result of the DEA-Malmquist Productivity Index is segregated into groups by time dimension and provincial dimension in Tables 4 and 5. TFPCH in year t indicates TFP changes between year t and year $t-1$. In general, provinces in key economic regions had unfavorable TFP growth rates (less than 1) during 2015–2021, indicating inefficiency in their GDP generation. The inefficiency situation worsened, following a continuous decline in subsequent years to 0.94 in 2021. Notably, the trends in efficiency change and technological progress displayed an inverse pattern throughout duration of the study. This phenomenon is likely associated with delayed impacts related to "spillovers" and "learning-by-doing" mentioned in our literature via FDI and trade channels. The gradual deceleration of TFP growth rate in subsequent years was influenced by a slowdown of innovation during 2019–2020 and efficiency in 2021. Regarding the regional dimension, all four areas experienced an improvement in efficiency change over the seven years, with the Mekong Delta area being the highest. Nevertheless, technological progress in those areas was below the efficient level, indicating a deterioration or low yield from technological tools.

5.2 *Drivers of TFP Growth*

5.2.1 Static Models

The Pooled OLS, fixed-effects (FE), and random effects (RE) estimation methods are applied to the empirical data, and the selection for appropriate estimations is then validated by Breusch and Pagan Lagrangian multiplier test (LM) and Hausman (Torres-Reyna, 2007) tests. The Modified Wald test identifies heteroskedasticity and provides recommendations for the use of robust option in the next estimations with the inclusion of the Covid pandemic dummy variable.

Table 5 Mean DEA-Malmquist index by province and region, 2015–2021

Province	TFPCH	Effch	Tech
Ha Noi	0.946	1.022	0.926
Vinh Phuc	0.912	1.013	0.909
Bac Ninh	0.915	0.982	0.936
Quang Ninh	1.055	1.093	0.971
Hai Duong	0.932	1.034	0.909
Hai Phong	0.953	1.041	0.926
Hung Yen	0.947	1.052	0.909
TTHue	0.946	1.052	0.909
Da Nang	0.957	1.037	1.054
Quang Nam	0.907	1.006	0.929
Quang Ngai	0.910	1.009	0.909
Binh Dinh	0.934	1.041	0.909
Binh Phuoc	0.964	1.073	0.909
Tay Ninh	0.932	1.037	0.909
Binh Duong	0.894	0.994	0.909
Dong Nai	0.909	1.011	0.909
BRVT	0.961	1.000	0.960
HCM	0.919	1.010	0.920
Long An	0.937	1.040	0.909
Tien Giang	0.921	1.025	0.909
An Giang	0.956	1.066	0.909
Kien Giang	0.941	1.050	0.909
Can Tho	0.998	1.111	0.909
Ca Mau	0.957	1.064	0.909
Regions			
North	0.951	1.034	0.926
Central	0.931	1.029	0.913
South	0.930	1.024	0.917
Mekong Delta	0.963	1.073	0.909
Means	0.942	1.036	0.917

Source Authors' calculation

Models 1–3 (Table 6) are baseline estimations with results highlighting the selection of fixed-effects models. P-values from both Hausman test and LM test indicate rejection of null hypotheses of pooled OLS and random effect applicability. Therefore, we employed the fixed-effects approach to control time-invariant unobserved characteristics across provinces reported in models 2, 4, and 5. In models 4 and 5, we observe positive impacts of "trade openness" and "patents" on the growth rate of TFP with incorporation of fixed-effects and robustness. Meanwhile, the productivity growth rate in key economic regions is found to be damaged by FDI flows when we include COVID-19 shock in the model. The damage is even magnified by the lagged effects of Covid. This is consistent with dependency theory, middle-path theory, and empirical literature on the negative relationship between FDI and economic growth in host countries where government intervention is necessary for sustainable development (Jensen, 2008; Lipsey, 2004; Sinani & Meyer, 2004; Taylor and Thrift, 2013). While the immediate effect of Covid pandemic is not significant in the model 4, its lagged effect is associated with a 0.029 decrease in productivity reported in the last model 5.

Recent reports and empirical studies highlighted contemporaneous resilience and lagged effects of macroeconomic factors as well as the COVID-19 pandemic (Layos and Peña, 2020; Hayakawa, et al., 2022; Dang, 2022). The introduction of lagged-dependent and independent variables as instruments in the subsequent GMM dynamic panel model below may shed further light on dynamic interactions and cumulative causation effects on TFP (Saini & Singhania, 2018).

Table 6 Results of static models

	(1)	(2)	(3)	(4)	(5)
TFPCH	POLS	FE	RE	FE	FE
lnFDI	− 0.0036	− 0.0199	− 0.0056	− 0.015*	− 0.0166*
	(0.0047)	(0.0195)	(0.0061)	(0.0081)	(0.0081)
Patent	0	0.0002	0	0.0002*	0.0002*
	(0)	(0.0002)	(0.0001)	(0.0001)	(0.0001)
Tradeopen	− 0.0051	0.0579***	− 0.0024	0.0687**	0.0765***
	(0.0039)	(0.0183)	(0.0052)	(0.0276)	(0.0252)
Indus	0.0007	0.0003	0.0006	− 0.0003	— 0.0002
	(0.0008)	(0.0009)	(0.0008)	(0.0011)	(0.0009)
Covid				− 0.0148	
				(0.0123)	
LagCovid					− 0.0291**
_cons	0.9174***	1.0347***	0.9394***	1.0261***	1.0229***
	(0.0968)	(0.2523)	(0.1092)	(0.1292)	(0.1315)
Observations	144	144	144	144	144
Hausman test		0.0096			
LM test			0.0474		
Wald test		0.000			
Robust	NO	NO	NO	YES	YES
Covid	NO	NO	NO	YES	YES

Notes Robust standard errors are in parentheses. ***$p < 0.01$, **$p < 0.05$, *$p < 0.1$

5.2.2 GMM Dynamic Panel Models

As mentioned previously, Sects. 1 and 2 provide a well-documented literature on the endogenous relationship between FDI, trade openness and relevant factors used in Eq. (1) . Endogeneity arising from the bidirectional causal relationship is addressed by Eq. (2), and results have been reported in different models of Table 7.

Introducing a lagged TFP growth rate variable (LagTFPCH) helps capture the effects of new information based on the model's history (Greene, 2008). Negative coefficients of LagTFPCH suggest either a volatility correction mechanism or a yearly decline in TFP growth. This aligns with the pattern of initial growth and later slowdown in GDP and TFPCH, as shown in Fig. 4 and discussed in Sect. 4.1. Azariadis and Stachurski (2005) suggest that poverty and low productivity persist due to various obstacles and a cycle of issues like corruption, depreciation, lack of capital, and difficulty in adopting new technology. Over time, this cycle perpetuates itself, leading to ongoing deterioration. However, the negative coefficients are relatively small, ranging from − 0.04 to − 0.1379, and not statistically significant when both present and lagged explanatory variables are included (models 3 and 6). This indicates that short-term positive factors, such as trade openness, play a crucial role in supporting productivity and moving toward stable efficiency.

Results of FDI, trade openness, and Covid align with results from static models. In the last three models, the Covid pandemic proves its significance of lagged impacts on immediate pain for TFP growth rate. This delayed effect can be attributed to the increasing severity of four consecutive waves of Covid in Vietnam, especially the intensive level of the last wave. The last wave resulted in the peak of outbreaks in 2021, leading to prolonged quarantine periods and subsequent economic downturns. These factors collectively slowed Vietnam's economic recovery and affected its export-driven revenues (Dang, 2022).

The trade openness level again affirms its importance in the TFP growth rate. The main effects of trade openness maintain its solid and positive significance compared to other factors among both contemporaneous and lagged models. Current and past growth of trade openness both lead to rises in TFP growth between the periods (in all models). This pertains to our literature about the effectiveness of the trade in Vietnam between 2020 and 2021, with a trade surplus of nearly 4 billion USD. Yet, trade openness and industrial production level are usually complementary (Le & Bui, 2022; Yanikkaya, 2003). In this study, we found that the trade openness level moderated by the growth rate of industrial production creates negative effects on overall productivity at a minimal level. Excessive reliance on imports of certain industries may reduce domestic production capacity and potentially harm the TFP growth rate if global supply chains are disrupted (in the case of COVID-19). We can also refer to the negative coefficient of the interaction term to the Pollution Haven hypotheses proposed by Copeland and Taylor (2004) that address the relationship between FDI, environmental regulations, trade, industry, and polluting activities. The negative result suggests that adverse FDI took advantage of lax environmental regulations to attract intensive or polluted industrial production and export–import practices over the last few years. This can be linked to our literature on Vietnam since

Table 7 Dynamic panel results of TFP's determinants (one-step difference GMM)

	(1)	(2)	(3)	(4)	(5)	(6)
TFPCH	Contemp.E	Lagged.E	Lagged.E	Contemp.E	Lagged.E	Lagged.E
LagTFPCH	– 0.088	– 0.348**	– 0.040	– 0.085	– 0.354**	– 0.137
	(0.096)	(0.150)	(0.137)	(0.097)	(0.143)	(0.177)
lnFDI	– 0.050***		– 0.048*	– 0.046*		– 0.042
	(0.017)		(0.026)	(0.026)		(0.043)
Patent	– 0.001***		– 0.002***	– 0.002***		– 0.001**
	(0.000)		(0.000)	(0.000)		(0.0008)
Tradeopen	0.116**		0.056	0.112**		0.161**
	(0.042)		(0.034)	(0.044)		(0.059)
Indus	0.004***	0.002	0.004**	0.003	0.002	0.003*
	(0.001)	(0.001)	(0.002)	(0.002)	(0.002)	(0.002)
Tradeopen*indus	– 0.0008***			– 0.0007**		
	(0.0002)			(0.0003)		
LaglnFDI		– 0.039	0.007		– 0.025	0.030
		(0.041)	(0.050)		(0.038)	(0.056)
Lagpatent		– 0.0006**	– 0.0001		– 0.0006***	– 0.0002
		(0.0002)	(0.0001)		(0.0002)	(0.000)
Lagtradeopen		0.117***	0.076***		0.112***	0.078
		(0.028)	(0.026)		(0.027)	(0.053)
Lagtradeopen*indus		-0.0007*	-0.0012*		– 0.000	– 0.001**
		(0.0003)	(0.0006)		(0.000)	(0.000)
Covid				– 0.005		– 0.007
				(0.018)		(0.020)
LagCovid					– 0.015*	– 0.046***
					(0.008)	(0.010)
Obs	96	96	96	96	96	96
Groups	24	24	24	24	24	24
Covid Effect	NO	NO	NO	YES	YES	YES

(continued)

Table 7 (continued)

	(1)	(2)	(3)	(4)	(5)	(6)
AR(2)	0.761	0.399	0.368	0.778	0.356	0.673
Hansen test	0.428	0.566	0.852	0.357	0.315	0.693

Robust standard errors are reported in parentheses "()". The values reported for the Hansen test are the *p*-values for the null hypothesis of instrument validity. The values reported for AR(2) are the *p*-values for second-order auto correlated disturbances in the first-differenced equations.
***$p < 0.01$, **$p < 0.05$, *$p < 0.1$

FDI accounted for 74.3 and 65% of shares of export and import activities during 2022. Indeed, manufactured products account for nearly 88% of total exports and the focus on export quantity rather than quality persists. Nevertheless, it is recommended to use more supplemental data, such as information on environmental policies, the structure of industries, living standards, pollution levels, and the types of products being imported or exported to validate our hypothesis.

Interestingly, not only FDI but also patents do not generate positive effects for TFP growth rate in models. Across six models, only contemporaneous effects of FDI are significant while the lagged effect does not create meaningful inference for the current productivity growth rate. In detail, short-run increases of FDI results in a drop in TFP growth rate during 2015–2021 (models 1, 3, and 4). Our literature suggests that the negative impact of FDI on provincial efficiency is due to conflicts between foreign investors and host countries over mutual returns, intellectual property rights versus technology transfers, and compatibility of technologies with local capacities such as trained labor and infrastructure. Additionally, interest groups often prioritize their own benefits over societal gains. In our static model, patents show positive effects, but in the GMM dynamic model, they become negative. This may be because FDI, driven by pollution-haven motives, affects innovation in Vietnam. The dominance of foreign investments in innovative activities increases competition for domestic firms. According to the Central Institute for Economic Management of Vietnam (2022), foreign applicants for intellectual property rights are, on average, ten times higher than domestic applicants.

Our dynamic panel analysis shows that past negative effects on TFP growth are modestly persistent, while "trade openness" significantly boosts productivity. The results show that FDI inflows and their negative spillovers harm innovation in key economic regions, especially during and after the COVID-19 pandemic. Given Vietnam's exposure to a high level of trade and foreign investments, the unforeseen adversity of trade openness moderated by industrial production growth should be considered for further investigation.

6 Conclusion and Policy Recommendations

In conclusion, the research examines the effects of Trade and FDI on productivity growth across 24 Vietnamese provinces in the four Key Economic Zones from 2015 to 2021. By utilizing the DEA-Malmquist Productivity Index and GMM dynamic panel model, our study provides a comprehensive evaluation of the TFP growth situation in Vietnam and jointly investigates the impacts of international trade and FDI on productivity.

The findings of this study suggest a self-reinforcing mechanism where barriers, corruption, limited capital, and technology challenges keep productivity low. This mechanism makes it difficult for regions to become efficient. However, trade openness helps mitigate this inefficiency. However, trade openness helps mitigate this inefficiency. Additionally, our evidence indicates that drawbacks induced by FDI on TFP can originate from substantial foreign capital invested in low-value-added sectors. It may also arise from conflicts between foreign contributors and low-value-added countries related to benefits. These adverse effects of FDI further spilled over outcomes of innovation activities, such as patents, between domestic and foreign firms. On the other hand, international trade emerges as a significant driver of TFP growth in Vietnam, irrespective of the challenges arising from the COVID-19 period.

This empirical research shows that international trade and FDI significantly impact TFP growth in Vietnam. Therefore, Vietnam needs a major strategic shift in its trade and FDI policies to boost TFP growth and adapt to the changing landscape.

In terms of international trade policy, Vietnam needs to continue promoting international trade, with particular emphasis on efficiently exploiting opportunities provided by FTAs, especially the new-generation ones. This strategic pursuit would enable Vietnam to access larger and potentially lucrative markets for trade and investment, thereby contributing to the convergence of efficiency and technological progress toward international standards (Anh, 2017). In addition, Vietnam should prioritize diversifying export markets and strengthening supply chain resilience. Adopting multiple input sources and fostering local production capabilities can avoid dependence on imports and reduce vulnerability derived from supply chain disruptions.

The negative impact of Vietnam's trade openness on TFP in manufacturing and potentially hampering TFP growth is attributed to structure shifts when reallocating resources among industries and sustainable practices among industries. Vietnam should implement retraining programs, job placement services, and income support to facilitate the transition of affected workers to new employment opportunities. Green certification and tax breaks can also encourage industrial businesses to adopt resource-efficient technologies and eco-friendly practices in trades or production processes.

Regarding FDI policy, the focus should not only be on attracting new investments and job creation but also on encouraging existing foreign enterprises to transfer technologies, expand their operations, and emphasize activities with higher value-added (Javorcik, 2004). Vietnam also needs to actively encourage FDI inflows in high-tech industries such as electronics, information technology, biotechnology, and advanced manufacturing. This can be achieved by providing tax incentives, grants, and R&D funding to facilitate technology transfer, sustainable investments and promote knowledge spillovers.

Moreover, Vietnam needs to enhance the absorptive capacity and innovation capabilities of businesses, particularly those in promising and strategic sectors such as processing and manufacturing industries, and information technology (Nguyen, 2021). At the macro level, it is essential to effectively implement national and sector-specific strategies and plans for human resource development. At the micro level, solutions should focus on improving the quality of education and training, particularly vocational training, to produce skilled and competent workers who can meet the evolving demands of businesses and economic entities (Loi & Thuy, 2022).

Apart from that, it is crucial to enhance linkages between domestic and foreign-invested enterprises in terms of R&D, knowledge exchange, and technology transfer. Additionally, strengthening the coordination mechanism of public–private partnerships (PPPs) in investment for science and technology is essential to leverage advantages in private sector. Furthermore, Vietnam should ensure effective enforcement of intellectual property rights to incentivize foreign investors to share their advanced technologies and knowledge without concerns regarding intellectual property violation.

We recommend further measurements and calculation methods for TFP to incorporate important yet challenging-to-measure factors, such as market power, labor quality (skilled labor), managerial capabilities, entrepreneurial spirit, and intangible assets.

References

Aitken, B., & Harrison, A. (1999). Do domestic firms benefit from direct foreign investment? Evidence from Venezuela. *American Economic Review, 89*(3), 605–618.

Allison, P. D. (2009). *Fixed effects regression models*. SAGE Publications.

Anderson, T. W., & Hsiao, C. (1981). Estimation of dynamic models with error components. *Journal of the American Statistical Association, 76*(375), 598–606.

Anh, D. (2017). *TFP is the bottleneck of Vietnam's economy*. Economy & Forecast Review. Retrieved from https://kinhtevadubao.vn/tfp-chinh-la-diem-nghen-cua-nen-kinh-te-viet-nam-12879.html

Anwar, S., & Lan, N. (2011). Foreign direct investment and trade: The case of Vietnam. *Research in International Business and Finance, 25*(1), 39–52. https://doi.org/10.1016/j.ribaf.2010.05.004

Anwar, S., & Nguyen, L. P. (2013). Is foreign direct investment productive? A case study of the regions of Vietnam. *Journal of Business Research, 67*(7), 1376–1387. https://doi.org/10.1016/j.jbusres.2013.08.015

Arellano, M., & Bond, S. (1991). Some tests of specification for panel data: Monte Carlo evidence and an application to employment equations. *The Review of Economic Studies, 58*(2), 277–297.

Azariadis, C., & Stachurski, J. (2005). Chapter 5 poverty traps. *Handbook of Economic Growth* (pp. 295–384). https://doi.org/10.1016/s1574-0684(05)01005-1

Bach, T. N. (2018). Trade-related R&D spillovers in Vietnamese manufacturing. *International Economic Journal, 32*(3), 438–453. https://doi.org/10.1080/10168737.2018.1485046

Bhatt, P. R. (2013). Causal relationship between exports, FDI and income: The case of Vietnam. *Applied Econometrics and International Development, 13*(1), 161–178.

Central Institute for Economic Management of Vietnam. (2022). Economic reform for effective intellectual property protection in the context of economic integration and digital transformation in Vietnam. In *Vietnam Journal of Science, Technology and Engineering*. Retrieved September 17, 2023, from https://vjst.vn/vn/tin-tuc/6393/thuc-trang-hoat-dong-xac-lap-quyen-so-huu-tri-tue-o-viet-nam.aspx

Charnes, A., Cooper, W., & Rhodes, E. (1978). Measuring the efficiency of decision-making units. *European Journal of Operational Research, 2*(6), 429–444. https://doi.org/10.1016/0377-2217(78)90138-8

Choi, J., Hinojales, M., Hong, H., & Vichyanond, J. (2021). *Working paper WP/21-02: The role of Vietnam's FDI inflow in global value chains participation and economic growth*. ASEAN+3 Macroeconomic Research Office.

Copeland, B. R., & Taylor, M. S. (2004, March). Trade, growth, and the environment. *Journal of Economic Literature, 42*(1), 7–71. https://doi.org/10.1257/.42.1.7

Dang, H. (2022). *Kinh tế Việt Nam và triển vọng trong bối cảnh đại dịch*. Communist Party of Vietnam Online Newspaper. Retrieved September 16, 2023, from https://dangcongsan.vn/kinh-te/kinh-te-viet-nam-va-trien-vong-trong-boi-canh-dai-dich-602523.html

Duong, M., Holmes, M. J., & Strutt, A. (2021). The impact of free trade agreements on FDI inflows: The case of Vietnam. *Journal of the Asia Pacific Economy, 26*(3), 483–505. https://doi.org/10.1080/13547860.2020.1765717

European Central Bank. (2017). Does trade play a role in helping to explain productivity growth? *Economic Bulletin*, 7.

Färe, R., Grosskopf, S., Lindgren, B., & Roos, P. (1992). Productivity changes in Swedish pharmacies 1980–1989: A non-parametric Malmquist approach. *Journal of Productivity Analysis, 3*(1–2), 85–101.

Färe, R., Grosskopf, S., Norris, M., & Zhang, Z. (1994). Productivity growth, technical progress, and efficiency change in industrialized countries. *The American Economic Review, 84*(1), 66–83. http://www.jstor.org/stable/2117971

Feenstra, R. C., Inklaar, R., & Timmer, M. P. (2015). The next generation of the Penn world table. *American Economic Review, 105*(10), 3150–3182. https://doi.org/10.1257/aer.20130954

Gammoudi, M., Cherif, M., & Asongu, S. (2016). FDI and growth in the MENA countries: Are the GCC countries different? *African Governance and Development Institute* No. WP/16/015, Yaoundé

General Statistics Office of Vietnam (GSO). (2020). *Socio-economic report in quarter IV and year 2020*. Archive on 9 September 2023. Available at https://www.gso.gov.vn/du-lieu-va-so-lieu-thong-ke/2020/12/baocao-tinh-hinh-kinh-te-xa-hoi-quy-iv-va-nam-2020/

Greene, W. H. (2008). *Econometric analysis*. Prentice Hall.

Grossman, G., & Helpman, E. (1991). *Innovation and growth in the global economy*. MIT Press.

Ha, T. T. (2017). *The impact of foreign direct investment (FDI) and exports on the growth of total factor productivity (TFPG) at the provincial level (Master's thesis)*. University of Economics Ho Chi Minh City.

Hair, J. F., Hult, G. T. M., Ringle, C. M., Sarstedt, M., Danks, N. P., & Ray, S. (2021). Evaluation of formative measurement models. In *Partial least squares structural equation modeling (PLS-SEM) using R. classroom companion: Business*. Springer.

Hansen, L. P. (1982). Large sample properties of generalized method of moments estimators. *Econometrica, 50*(4), 1029–1054.

Hausman, J. A., & Taylor, W. E. (1981). Panel data and unobservable individual effects. *Econometrica, 49*(6), 1377–1398. https://doi.org/10.2307/1911406

Hayakawa, K., Lee, H. H., & Park, C. Y. (2022). The effect of COVID-19 on foreign direct investment. *ADB Working Paper Series*. https://doi.org/10.22617/wps220092-2

Huang, C. H., & Yang, C. H. (2016). Ownership, trade, and productivity in Vietnam's manufacturing firms. *Asia-Pacific Journal of Accounting and Economics, 23*(3), 327–342. https://doi.org/10.1080/16081625.2016.1188449

Huynh, H. T. N., Nguyen, P. V., Trieu, H. D. X., & Tran, K. T. (2019). Productivity spillover from FDI to domestic firms across six regions in Vietnam. *Emerging Markets Finance and Trade, 57*(1), 59–75.

Huynh, L. T. D., Hoang, H. T., & Tran, H. N. (2021). Does FDI enhance provincial productivity? A panel data analysis in Vietnam. *Journal of the Asia Pacific Economy, 28*(3), 1174–1195. https://doi.org/10.1080/13547860.2021.1967023

Javorcik, B. S. (2004). Does foreign direct investment increase the productivity of domestic firms? In search of spillovers through backward linkages. *American Economic Review, 94*(3), 605–627. https://doi.org/10.1257/0002828041464605

Jensen, N. M. (2008). *Nation-states and the multinational corporation: A political economy of foreign direct investment.* Princeton University Press.

Krugman, P. (1981). Intra-industry specialization and the gains from trade. *Journal of Political Economy, 89*, 959–973.

Layos, J. M., & Peña, P. J. (2020). *Can innovation save us? Understanding the role of innovation in mitigating the covid-19 pandemic in ASEAN-5 economies.* MPRA Paper 100152, University Library of Munich.

Le, A. (2009). *FDI-growth Nexus in Vietnam.* Nagoya University.

Le, H., & Bui L. (2022). The impacts of trade openness on industrial performance at regional and provincial level in Vietnam. *Journal of Economic Development*, *47*(1), 85–107 (The Economic Research Institute, Chung-Ang University).

Le, T. T. (2015). Productivity spillovers from foreign direct investment in Vietnam. *Review of Business and Economics Studies, 3*(2), 52–57.

Lipsey, R. E. (2004). Home-and host-country effects of foreign direct investment. In *Challenges to globalization: Analyzing the economics* (pp. 333–382). University of Chicago Press.

Loi, T., & Thuy, H. (2022). The role and impact of total factor productivity on Vietnam's economic growth. *Journal of Industry and Trade,* 4.

Malmquist, S. (1953). Index numbers and indifference surfaces. *Trabajos De Estadística, 4*(2), 209–242.

Ministry of Planning and Investment (MPI). (2023). *Status of foreign investment attraction in Vietnam (Yearly reports).* Website of Foreign Investment. Retrieved from https://fia.mpi.gov.vn/

National Office of Intellectual Property (IP Vietnam). (2023). *IP annual reports.* Ministry of Science and Technology. Retrieved from https://ipvietnam.gov.vn/en_US/web/english/annual-report

Nguyen, B., & Jonathan, H. (2002). Trade liberalization and foreign direct investment in Vietnam. *ASEAN Economic Bulletin, 19*(3), 302–318. https://doi.org/10.1355/AE19-3E

Nguyen, D., Anh, T., & Phuong, C. (2012). *On the linkage between FDI and trade: Evidence from Vietnam.* SECO/WTI Academic Cooperation Project Working Paper Series 2012/05.

Nguyen, P. V., Tran, K. T., Le, N. T. T., & Trieu, H. D. X. (2020). Examining FDI spillover effects on productivity growth: Firm-level evidence from Vietnam. *Journal of Economic Development, 45*(1), 97–121.

Nguyen, T. (2021). What to do to improve labor productivity and contribute TFP to economic growth? *Review of Finance.* Retrieved from https://tapchitaichinh.vn/lam-gi-de-nang-cao-nang-suat-lao-dong-va-dong-gop-tfp-doi-voi-tang-truong-kinh-te.html

Pham, H. (2012). Temporal causality and the dynamics of foreign direct investment and trade in Vietnam. *The Journal of International Trade and Economic Development, 21*(1), 83–113. https://doi.org/10.1080/09638190903365922

Phuong, T. (2022). *International economic integration: Opportunities and challenges for Vietnamese enterprises in implementing new generation free trade agreements.* Communist Review. Retrieved from https://www.tapchicongsan.org.vn/web/guest/quoc-phong-an-ninh-oi-ngoai1/-/2018/826698/hoi-nhap-kinh-te-quoc-te--co-hoi-va-thach-thuc-doi-voi-cac-doanh-nghiep-viet-nam-trong-trien-khai-cac-hiep-dinh-thuong-mai-tu-do-the-he-moi.aspx

Roodman, D. (2009, March). How to do Xtabond2: An introduction to difference and system GMM in Stata. *The Stata Journal: Promoting Communications on Statistics and Stata, 9*(1), 86–136. https://doi.org/10.1177/1536867x0900900106

Saini, N., & Singhania, M. (2018). Determinants of FDI in developed and developing countries: A quantitative analysis using GMM. *Journal of Economic Studies, 45*(2), 348–382. https://doi.org/10.1108/jes-07-2016-0138

Sinani, E., & Meyer, K. E. (2004). Spillovers of technology transfer from FDI: The case of Estonia. *Journal of Comparative Economics, 32*(3), 445–466. https://doi.org/10.1016/j.jce.2004.03.002

Sun, P., & Heshmati, A. (2010). International trade and its effects on economic growth in China. *SSRN Electronic Journal*. https://doi.org/10.2139/ssrn.1667775

Taylor, M., & Thrift, N. (2013). *The geography of multinationals (RLE international business): Studies in the spatial development and economic consequences of multinational corporations*. Routledge.

Toone, J. E. (2013). *Mirage in the Gulf? Examining the upsurge in FDI in the GCC and its legal and economic implications for the MENA region. SSRN Scholarly Paper No. ID 2150603*. Social Science Research Network.

Torres-Reyna, O. (2007). *Panel data analysis fixed and random effects using Stata (v. 4.2)* (Vol. 112, p. 49). Data & Statistical Services, Princeton University.

Vietnam Customs Statistics. (2023). *Preliminary assessment of Vietnam international merchandise trade performance*. General Department of Vietnam Customs. Retrieved from https://www.customs.gov.vn/

Yanikkaya, H. (2003). Trade openness and economic growth: A cross-country empirical investigation. *Journal of Development Economics, 72*(1), 57–89. https://doi.org/10.1016/s0304-3878(03)00068-3

Nguyen Ngoc Hai Anh is a master student at the University of Economics of Ho Chi Minh City and the International Institute of Social Studies, Erasmus University Rotterdam. She received a bachelor's degree in international relations from the Diplomatic Academy of Vietnam. Her major research interests include international relations, economic politics, and development economics.

Long Hoang Vo is a master student at Vietnam—The Netherlands Programme of the University of Economics of Ho Chi Minh City. He received a bachelor's degree in business administration at Eastern International University. His primary research interest is in macroeconomics, cryptocurrency, and innovation.

SPRINGER NATURE

GPSR Compliance

The European Union's (EU) General Product Safety Regulation (GPSR) is a set of rules that requires consumer products to be safe and our obligations to ensure this.

If you have any concerns about our products, you can contact us on ProductSafety@springernature.com

In case Publisher is established outside the EU, the EU authorized representative is:

Springer Nature Customer Service Center GmbH
Europaplatz 3
69115 Heidelberg, Germany

The manufacturer's authorised representative in the EU is Springer
Nature Customer Service Centre GmbH, Europaplatz 3, 69115 Heidelberg,
Germany. If you have any concerns regarding our products, please
contact ProductSafety@springernature.com

Printed and bound by CPI Group (UK) Ltd, Croydon, CR0 4YY
01/10/2026
02225857-0006